Mastering Computer V
with TensorFlow 2.x

Build advanced computer vision applications using machine learning and deep learning techniques

Krishnendu Kar

BIRMINGHAM - MUMBAI

Mastering Computer Vision with TensorFlow 2.x

Commissioning Editor: Mrinmayee Kawalkar
Acquisition Editor: Nelson Morris
Content Development Editor: Nazia Shaikh
Senior Editor: Ayaan Hoda
Technical Editor: Utkarsha S. Kadam
Copy Editor: Safis Editing
Project Coordinator: Aishwarya Mohan
Proofreader: Safis Editing
Indexer: Manju Arasan
Production Designer: Nilesh Mohite

First published: May 2020

Production reference: 1140520

Published by Packt Publishing Ltd.
Livery Place
35 Livery Street
Birmingham
B3 2PB, UK.

ISBN 978-1-83882-706-9

www.packt.com

Packt.com

Subscribe to our online digital library for full access to over 7,000 books and videos, as well as industry leading tools to help you plan your personal development and advance your career. For more information, please visit our website.

Why subscribe?

- Spend less time learning and more time coding with practical eBooks and Videos from over 4,000 industry professionals
- Improve your learning with Skill Plans built especially for you
- Get a free eBook or video every month
- Fully searchable for easy access to vital information
- Copy and paste, print, and bookmark content

Did you know that Packt offers eBook versions of every book published, with PDF and ePub files available? You can upgrade to the eBook version at www.packt.com and as a print book customer, you are entitled to a discount on the eBook copy. Get in touch with us at customercare@packtpub.com for more details.

At www.packt.com, you can also read a collection of free technical articles, sign up for a range of free newsletters, and receive exclusive discounts and offers on Packt books and eBooks.

Contributors

About the author

Krishnendu Kar is passionate about research on computer vision and solving AI problems to make our life simpler. His core expertise is deep learning - computer vision, IoT, and agile software development. Krish is also a passionate app developer and has a dash cam-based object and lane detection and turn by turn navigation and fitness app in the iOS app store - *Nity Map AI Camera & Run timer.*

> *I want to thank my parents, my wife, and kids for supporting me during the 80 hours a week journey for the last year to complete the book. Special thanks to all the Packt past and current members and to my God, for giving me the strength, and the technical reviewer for reviewing my book contents, making suggestions, and answering all my queries in a timely manner.*

About the reviewers

Meng-Chieh Ling has a Ph.D. degree in theoretical condensed matter physics from Karlsruhe Institute of Technology in Germany. He switched from physics to data science to pursue a successful career. After working for AGT International in Darmstadt for 2 years, he joined CHECK24 Fashion as a data scientist in Düsseldorf. His responsibilities include applying machine learning to improve the efficiency of data cleansing, automatic attribute tagging with deep learning, and developing image-based recommendation systems.

Amin Ahmadi Tazehkandi is an Iranian author, software engineer, and computer vision expert. He has worked at numerous software companies across the globe and has a long list of awards and achievements, including a countrywide hackathon win and an award-winning paper. Amin is an avid blogger and long-time contributor to the open source, cross-platform, and computer vision developer communities. He is the proud author of *Computer Vision with OpenCV 3 and Qt5*, and *Hands-On Algorithms for Computer Vision*.

Packt is searching for authors like you

If you're interested in becoming an author for Packt, please visit `authors.packtpub.com` and apply today. We have worked with thousands of developers and tech professionals, just like you, to help them share their insight with the global tech community. You can make a general application, apply for a specific hot topic that we are recruiting an author for, or submit your own idea.

Table of Contents

Section 2: Advanced Concepts of Computer Vision with TensorFlow

Section 3: Advanced Implementation of Computer Vision with TensorFlow

Preface

Computer vision is a technique by which machines gain human-level ability to visualize, process, and analyze images or videos. This book will focus on using TensorFlow to develop and train deep neural networks to solve advanced computer vision problems and deploy solutions on mobile and edge devices.

You will start with the key principles of computer vision and deep learning and learn about various models and architectures, along with their pros and cons. You will cover various architectures, such as VGG, ResNet, Inception, R-CNN, YOLO, and many more. You will use various visual search methods using transfer learning. The book will help you to learn about various advanced concepts of computer vision, including semantic segmentation, image inpainting, object tracking, video segmentation, and action recognition. You will explore how various machine learning and deep learning concepts can be applied in computer vision tasks such as edge detection and face recognition. Later in the book, you will focus on performance tuning to optimize performance, deploying dynamic models to improve processing power, and scaling to handle various computer vision challenges.

By the end of the book, you will have an in-depth understanding of computer vision and will know how to develop models to automate tasks.

Who this book is for

This book is for computer vision professionals, image processing professionals, machine learning engineers, and AI developers who have some knowledge of machine learning and deep learning and want to build expert-level computer vision applications. Familiarity with Python programming and TensorFlow will be required for this book.

What this book covers

`Chapter 1`, *Computer Vision and TensorFlow Fundamentals*, discusses the foundational concepts of computer vision and TensorFlow to prepare you for the later, more advanced chapters of this book. We will look at how to perform image hashing and filtering. Then, we will learn about various methods of feature extraction and image retrieval. Moving on, we will learn about contour-based object detection, histogram of oriented gradients and various feature matching methods. Then, we will look at an overview of the high-level TensorFlow software and its different components and subsystems. The chapter provides many hands-on coding exercises for object detection, image filtering and feature matching.

`Chapter 2`, *Content Recognition Using Local Binary Patterns*, discusses local binary feature descriptor and the histogram for the classification of textured and non-textured images. You will learn to tune **local binary pattern (LBP)** parameters and calculate histogram difference between LBPs to match identical pattern between images. The chapter provides two coding exercises – one for matching flooring patterns and the other for matching face color with foundation color.

`Chapter 3`, *Facial Detection Using OpenCV and CNNs*, starts with Viola-Jones face- and key-feature detection and move on to the advanced concept of the neural-network-based facial key points detection and facial expressions recognition. The chapter will end by looking at the advanced concept of 3D face detection. The chapter provides two coding exercise one for OpenCV based face detection in webcam and the other one is a CNN based end to end pipeline for facial key point detection. The end to end neural network pipeline consists of facial image collection by cropping face images from webcam, annotating key points in face image, data ingestion into a CNN, building a CNN model, training and finally evaluating the trained model of key points against face images.

`Chapter 4`, *Deep Learning on Images*, delves into how edge detection is used to create convolution operations over volume and how different convolution parameters such as filter size, dimensions, and operation type affect the convolution volume. This chapter will give you a very detailed overview of how a neural network sees an image and how it uses that visualization to classify images. The chapter provides a TensorFlow Keras based coding exercise to construct a neural network and visualize an image as it goes through its different layers. You will then compare the network model's accuracy and visualization to an advanced network such as VGG 16 or Inception.

`Chapter 5`, *Neural Network Architecture and Models*, explores different neural network architectures and models. This will give you an understanding of how the concepts learned in the first and fourth chapters are applied in various scenarios by changing the parameters for the convolution, pooling, activation, fully connected, and softmax layers. Hopefully, with these exercises, you will develop an understanding of a range of neural network models, which will give you a solid foundation as a computer vision engineer.

`Chapter 6`, *Visual Search Using Transfer Learning*, is where you are going to use TensorFlow to input data into models and develop visual search methods for real-life situations. You will learn how to input images and their categories into the TensorFlow model using the Keras data generator and TensorFlow **tf.data** API and then cut a portion of pretrained model and add your own model content at the end to develop your own classifier. The idea behind these exercises is to learn how to code in TensorFlow for the neural network models you learned about in the fourth and fifth chapters.

`Chapter 7`, *Object Detection Using YOLO*, introducing two single-stage, fast object detection methods—**You Only Look Once** (**YOLO**) and RetinaNet. In this chapter, you will learn about different YOLO models, finding out how to change their configuration parameters and make inferences with them. You will also learn how to process your own images to train a custom **YOLO v3** model using **Darknet**.

`Chapter 8`, *Semantic Segmentation and Neural Style Transfer*, discusses how deep neural network is used to segment images into spatial regions, thereby producing artificial images and transferring styles from one image to another. We will perform hands on exercise for semantic segmentation using TensorFlow **DeepLab** and write TensorFlow codes for neural style transfer in Google Colab. We will also generate artificial images using **DCGAN** and perform image inpainting using OpenCV.

`Chapter 9`, *Action Recognition Using Multitask Deep Learning*, explains how to develop multitask neural network models for the recognition of actions, such as the movement of a hand, mouth, head, or leg, to detect the type of action using a vision-based system. This will then be supplemented with a deep neural network model using cell phone accelerometer data to validate the action.

`Chapter 10`, *Object Detection Using R-CNN, SSD, and R-FCN*, marks the beginning of an **end-to-end** (**E2E**) object detection framework by developing a solid foundation of data ingestion and training pipeline followed by model development. Here, you will gain a deep insight into the various object detection models, such as **R-CNN**, **single-shot detector** (**SSD**), **region-based fully convolutional networks** (**R-FCNs**), and **Mask R-CNN**, and perform hands-on exercises using Google Cloud and Google Colab notebooks. We will also carry out a detailed exercise on how to train your own custom image to develop an object detection model using a TensorFlow object detection API. We will end the chapter with a deep overview of various object tracking methods and a hands-on exercise using Google Colab notebooks.

`Chapter 11`, *Deep Learning on Edge Devices with CPU/GPU Optimization*, discusses how to take the generated model and deploy it on edge devices and production systems. This will result in a complete end-to-end TensorFlow object detection model implementation. In particular, TensorFlow models have been developed, converted, and optimized using the TensorFlow Lite and **Intel Open Visual Inference and Neural Network Optimization** (**VINO**) architectures and deployed to Raspberry Pi, Android, and iPhone. Although this chapter focuses mainly on object detection on Raspberry Pi, Android, and iPhone, the approach discussed can be extended to image classification, style transfer, and action recognition for any edge devices under consideration.

`Chapter 12`, *Cloud Computing Platform for Computer Vision,* discusses how to package your application for training and deployment in **Google Cloud Platform** (GCP), **Amazon Web Services** (AWS), and the **Microsoft Azure** cloud platform. You will learn how to prepare your data, upload to cloud data storage, and begin to monitor the training. You will also learn how to send an image or an image vector to the cloud platform for analysis and get a JSON response back. This chapter discusses a single application as well as running distributed TensorFlow on the compute engine. After training is complete, this chapter will discuss how to evaluate your model and integrate it into your application to operate at scale.

To get the most out of this book

If you are a beginner in computer vision and TensorFlow and you're trying to master the subject, it is better to go through the book's chapters in sequence rather than jumping around. The book slowly builds on the concepts of computer vision and neural networks and then ends with a code sample. Be sure to get a good grasp of the concepts and architecture presented and then apply the code sample.

We could not upload our image data to GitHub due to size limitations. You can either use images from your own camera or download image datasets from Kaggle:

- Food images (for the burger-and-fries sample): Take photos using your cell phone camera.
- Kaggle furniture detector: `https://www.kaggle.com/akkithetechie/furniture-detector`

If you do not understand a concept at first, revisit it and also read any cited papers.

Most of the code is written in Jupyter Notebook environments, so make sure that you have downloaded Anaconda. You also need to download TensorFlow 2.0 – follow the instructions in `Chapter 1`, *Computer Vision and TensorFlow Fundamentals,* for that.

Much of the object detection training is done using Google Colab – `Chapter 10`, *Object Detection Using R-CNN, SSD and R-FCN,* and `Chapter 11`, *Deep Learning on Edge with CPU/GPU Optimization,* provide explanations of how to use Google Colab.

If you want to deploy your computer vision code to edge devices and you're thinking about what to purchase, visit `Chapter 11`, *Deep Learning on Edge Devices with CPU/GPU Optimization,* for a detailed analysis of various devices.

The book relies heavily on terminal usage – make sure you have developed a basic understanding of that before reading anything from `Chapter 7`, *Object Detection Using YOLO*, onward.

`Chapter 12`, *Cloud Computing Platform for Computer Vision*, deals with cloud computing, so you must have an Amazon Web Services, Azure, or Google Cloud Platform account for this. Cloud computing can get expensive if you are not keeping track of your hours. Many providers give you free access to services for some time, but after that, charges can go up if your project is still open, even if you are not training. Remember to shut down your project before you end your account to stop accruing charges. If you have technical questions on cloud computing and are stuck, then you can read the documentation of the relevant cloud computing platform. Also, you can open a technical work ticket for a fee; typically, they are addressed within 1-2 business days.

The best way to get the most out of this book is to read the theory, get an understanding of why a model is developed the way it is, try the sample exercises, and then update the code to suit your needs.

If you have any questions about any section of the book and get stuck, you can always contact me on LinkedIn (`https://www.linkedin.com/in/krish-kar-554739b2/ext`).

Download the example code files

You can download the example code files for this book from your account at `www.packt.com`. If you purchased this book elsewhere, you can visit `www.packt.com/support` and register to have the files emailed directly to you.

You can download the code files by following these steps:

1. Log in or register at `www.packt.com`.
2. Select the **SUPPORT** tab.
3. Click on **Code Downloads & Errata**.
4. Enter the name of the book in the **Search** box and follow the onscreen instructions.

Once the file is downloaded, please make sure that you unzip or extract the folder using the latest version of:

- WinRAR/7-Zip for Windows
- Zipeg/iZip/UnRarX for Mac
- 7-Zip/PeaZip for Linux

The code bundle for the book is also hosted on GitHub at `https://github.com/PacktPublishing/Mastering-Computer-Vision-with-TensorFlow-2.0`. In case there's an update to the code, it will be updated on the existing GitHub repository.

We also have other code bundles from our rich catalog of books and videos available at `https://github.com/PacktPublishing/`. Check them out!

Download the color images

We also provide a PDF file that has color images of the screenshots/diagrams used in this book. You can download it here: `https://static.packt-cdn.com/downloads/9781838827069_ColorImages.pdf`.

Conventions used

There are a number of text conventions used throughout this book.

`CodeInText`: Indicates code words in text, database table names, folder names, filenames, file extensions, pathnames, dummy URLs, user input, and Twitter handles. Here is an example: "Each image that is read is converted to grayscale using the `OpenCV BGR2GRAY` command."

A block of code is set as follows:

```
faceresize = cv2.resize(detected_face, (img_size,img_size))
        img_name =
"dataset/opencv_frame_{}.jpg".format(img_counter)
        cv2.imwrite(img_name, faceresize)
```

Bold: Indicates a new term, an important word, or words that you see onscreen. For example, words in menus or dialog boxes appear in the text like this. Here is an example: "The **convolutional neural network** (**CNN**) is the most widely used tool in computer vision for classifying and detecting objects."

Warnings or important notes appear like this.

Tips and tricks appear like this.

Get in touch

Feedback from our readers is always welcome.

General feedback: If you have questions about any aspect of this book, mention the book title in the subject of your message and email us at `customercare@packtpub.com`.

Errata: Although we have taken every care to ensure the accuracy of our content, mistakes do happen. If you have found a mistake in this book, we would be grateful if you would report this to us. Please visit `www.packt.com/submit-errata`, selecting your book, clicking on the Errata Submission Form link, and entering the details.

Piracy: If you come across any illegal copies of our works in any form on the Internet, we would be grateful if you would provide us with the location address or website name. Please contact us at `copyright@packt.com` with a link to the material.

If you are interested in becoming an author: If there is a topic that you have expertise in and you are interested in either writing or contributing to a book, please visit `authors.packtpub.com`.

Reviews

Please leave a review. Once you have read and used this book, why not leave a review on the site that you purchased it from? Potential readers can then see and use your unbiased opinion to make purchase decisions, we at Packt can understand what you think about our products, and our authors can see your feedback on their book. Thank you!

For more information about Packt, please visit `packt.com`.

1

Section 1: Introduction to Computer Vision and Neural Networks

In this section, you will develop your understanding of the theory as well as learn hands-on techniques about the application of a convolutional neural network for image processing. You will learn key concepts such as image filtering, feature maps, edge detection, the convolutional operation, activation functions, and the use of fully connected and softmax layers in relation to image classification and object detection. The chapters provide many hands-on examples of an end-to-end computer vision pipeline using TensorFlow, Keras, and OpenCV. The most important learning that you will take from these chapters is to develop an understanding and intuition behind different convolutional operations – how images are transformed through different layers of convolutional neural networks.

By the end of this section, you will be able to do the following:

- Understand how image filters transform an image (chapter 1)
- Apply various types of image filters for edge detection (chapter 1)
- Detect simple objects using OpenCV contour detection and **Histogram of Oriented Gradients** (**HOG**) (Chapter 1)
- Find the similarity between objects using **Scale-invariant feature transform** (**SIFT**), **Local Binary Patterns** (**LBP**) pattern matching, and color matching (chapters 1 and 2)
- Face detection using the OpenCV cascade detector (chapter 3)
- Input big data into a neural network from a CSV file list and parse the data to recognize columns, which can then be fed to the neural network as x and y values (chapter 3)
- Facial keypoint and facial expression recognition (chapter 3)
- Develop an annotation file for facial keypoints (chapter 3)

- Input big data into a neural network from files using the Keras data generator method (chapter 4)
- Construct your own neural network and optimize its parameters to improve accuracy (chapter 4)
- Write code to transform an image through different layers of the convolutional neural network (chapter 4)

This section comprises the following chapters:

- `Chapter 1`, *Computer Vision and TensorFlow Fundamentals*
- `Chapter 2`, *Content Recognition Using Local Binary Pattern*
- `Chapter 3`, *Facial Detection Using OpenCV and CNN*
- `Chapter 4`, *Deep Learning on Images*

1
Computer Vision and TensorFlow Fundamentals

Computer vision is rapidly expanding in many different applications as traditional techniques, such as image thresholding, filtering, and edge detection, have been augmented by deep learning methods. TensorFlow is a widely used, powerful machine learning tool created by Google. It has user configurable APIs available to train and build complex neural network model in your local PC or in the cloud and optimize and deploy at scale in edge devices.

In this chapter, you will gain an understanding of advanced computer vision concepts using TensorFlow. This chapter discusses the foundational concepts of computer vision and TensorFlow to prepare you for the later, more advanced chapters of this book. We will look at how to perform image hashing and filtering. Then, we will learn about various methods of feature extraction and image retrieval. Moving on, we will learn about visual search in applications, its methods, and the challenges we might face. Then, we will look at an overview of the high-level TensorFlow software and its different components and subsystems.

The topics we will be covering in this chapter are as follows:

- Detecting edges using image hashing and filtering
- Extracting features from an image
- Object detection using Contours and the HOG detector
- An overview of TensorFlow, its ecosystem, and installation

Technical requirements

If you have not done so already, install Anaconda from `https://www.anaconda.com`. Anaconda is a package manager for Python. You also need to install OpenCV for all of the computer vision work you will be carrying out, using `pip install opencv-python`. OpenCV is a library of built-in programming functions for computer vision work.

Detecting edges using image hashing and filtering

Image hashing is a method used to find similarity between images. Hashing involves modifying an input image to a fixed size of binary vector through transformation. There are different algorithms for image hashing using different transformations:

- **Perpetual hash (phash)**: A cosine transformation
- **Difference hash (dhash)**: The difference between adjacent pixels

After a hash transformation, images can be compared quickly with the **Hamming distance**. The Python code for applying a hash transformation is shown in the following code. A hamming distance of `0` shows an identical image (duplicate), whereas a larger hamming distance shows that the images are different from each other. The following snippet imports Python packages, such as `PIL`, `imagehash`, and `distance`. `imagehash` is a Python package that supports various types of hashing algorithms. `PIL` is a Python imaging library, and `distance` is a Python package that calculates the hamming distance between two hashed images:

```
from PIL import Image
import imagehash
import distance
import scipy.spatial
hash1 = imagehash.phash(Image.open(.../car1.png))
hash2 = imagehash.phash(Image.open(.../car2.png))
print hamming_distance(hash1,hash2)
```

Image filtering is a fundamental computer vision operation that modifies the input image by applying a kernel or filter to every pixel of the input image. The following are the steps involved in image filtering, starting from light entering a camera to the final transformed image:

1. Using a Bayer filter for color pattern formation
2. Creating an image vector
3. Transforming the image
4. Linear filtering—convolution with kernels
5. Mixing Gaussian and Laplacian filters
6. Detecting edges in the image

Using a Bayer filter for color pattern formation

A Bayer filter transforms a raw image into a natural, color-processed image by applying a demosaic algorithm. The image sensor consists of photodiodes, which produce electrically charged photons proportional to the brightness of the light. The photodiodes are grayscale in nature. Bayer filters are used to convert the grayscale image to color. The color image from the Bayer filter goes through an **Image Signal Processing** (**ISP**) which involves several weeks of manual adjustment of various parameters to produce desired image quality for human vision. Several research work are currently ongoing to convert the manual ISP to a CNN based processing to produce an image and then merge the CNN with image classification or object detection model to produce one coherent neural network pipeline that takes Bayer color image and detects object with bounding boxes. Details of such work can be found in the 2019 paper by Sivalogeswaran Ratnasingam titled *Deep Camera: A Fully Convolutional Neural Network for Image Signal Processing*. The link for the paper is shown here: `http://openaccess.thecvf.com/content_ICCVW_2019/papers/LCI/Ratnasingam_Deep_Camera_A_Fully_Convolutional_Neural_Network_for_Image_Signal_ICCVW_2019_paper.pdf`.

Here is an example of a Bayer filter:

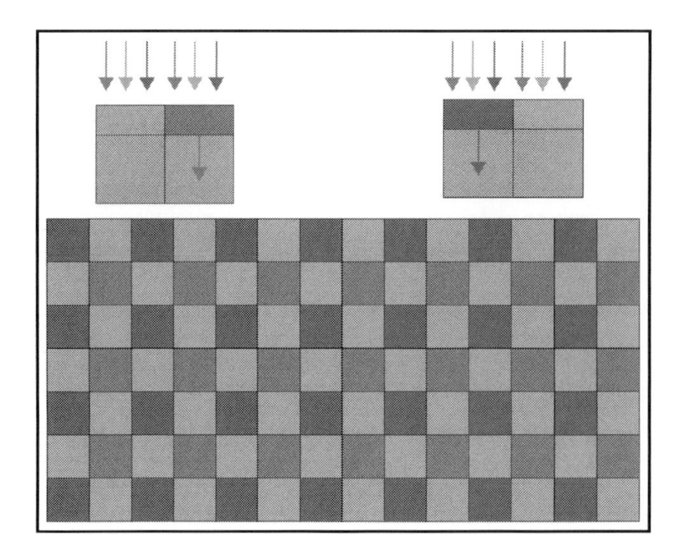

In the preceding diagram, we can observe the following:

- The Bayer filter consists of **Red** (**R**), **Green** (**G**), and **Blue** (**B**) channels in a predefined pattern, such that there is twice the number of G channels compared to B and R.
- The G, R, and B channels are alternately distributed. Most channel combinations are RGGB, GRGB, or RGBG.
- Each channel will only let a specific color to pass through, the combination of colors from different channels produce a pattern as shown in the preceding image.

Creating an image vector

Color images are a combination of R, G, and B. Colors can be represented as an intensity value, ranging from `0` to `255`. So, each image can be represented as a three-dimensional cube, with the x and y axis representing the width and height and the z axis representing three color channels (R, G, B) representing the intensity of each color. OpenCV is a library with built-in programming functions written for Python and C++ for image processing and object detection.

We will start by writing the following Python code to import an image, and then we will see how the image can be broken down into a NumPy array of vectors with RGB. We will then convert the image to grayscale and see how the image looks when we extract only one component of color from the image:

```
import numpy as np
import cv2
import matplotlib.pyplot as plt
%matplotlib inline
import matplotlib.pyplot as plt
from PIL import Image
image = Image.open('../car.jpeg'). # enter image path in ..
plt.imshow(image)
image_arr = np.asarray(image)  # convert image to numpy array
image_arr.shape
```

The preceding code will return the following output:

```
Output:
(296, 465, 4)
gray = cv2.cvtColor(image_arr, cv2.COLOR_BGR2GRAY)
plt.imshow(gray, cmap='gray')
```

The following figure shows the colored image and the corresponding grayscale image based on the preceding transformation:

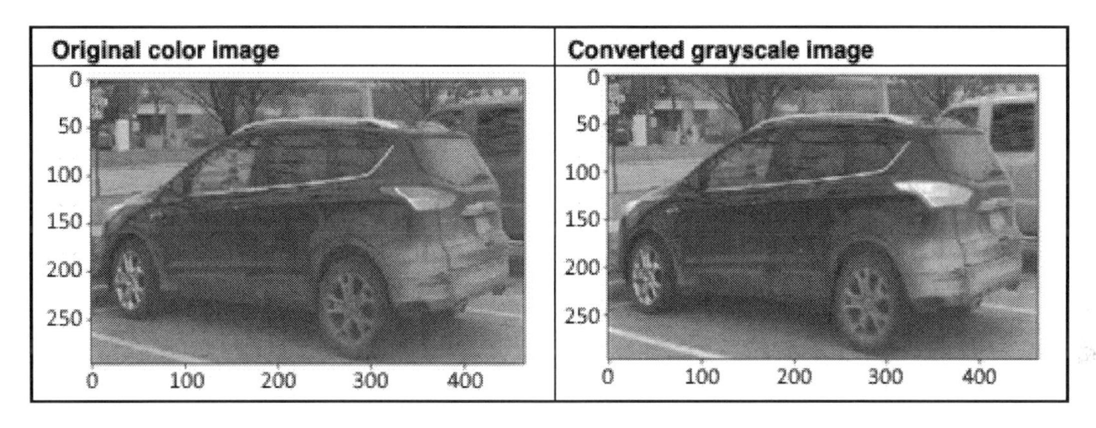

The following is the Python code that we will use to turn the image into R, G, and B color components:

```
plt.imshow(image_arr[:,:,0]) # red channel
plt.imshow(image_arr[:,:,1]) # green channel
plt.imshow(image_arr[:,:,2]) # blue channel
```

The following figure shows the transformed image of the car after extracting only one channel (either R, G, or B):

Red channel only
Green channel only
Blue channel only

The preceding figure can be represented as a 3D volume with the following axes:

- The x axis, representing the width.
- The y axis, representing the height.
- Each color channel represents the depth of the image.

Let's take a look at the following figure. It shows the **R**, **G**, and **B** pixel values for the image of the car at different x and y coordinates as a 3D volume; a higher value indicates a brighter image:

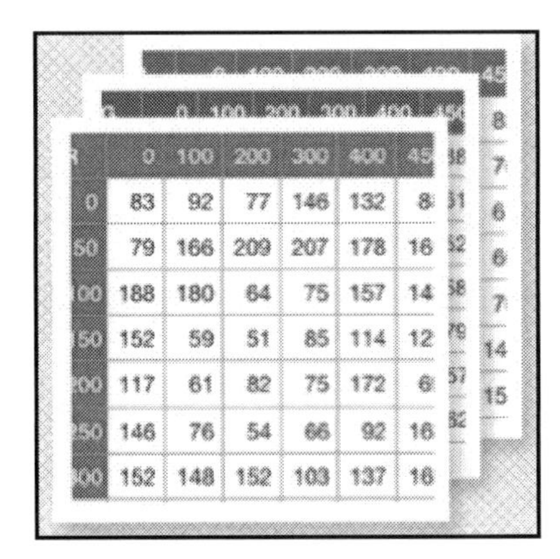

R	0	100	200	300	400	45
0	83	92	77	146	132	8
50	79	166	209	207	178	16
00	188	180	64	75	157	14
50	152	59	51	85	114	12
00	117	61	82	75	172	6
50	146	76	54	66	92	16
00	152	148	152	103	137	16

Transforming an image

Image transformation involves the translation, rotation, magnification, or shear of an image. If (x,y) is the coordinate of the pixel of an image, then the transformed image coordinate (u,v) of the new pixel can be represented as follows:

$$\begin{bmatrix} u \\ v \\ 1 \end{bmatrix} = \begin{bmatrix} c_{11} & c_{12} & c_{13} \\ c_{21} & c_{22} & c_{23} \\ 0 & 0 & 1 \end{bmatrix} \begin{bmatrix} x \\ y \\ 1 \end{bmatrix}$$

- **Translation**: Some examples of translation constant values are `c11` = 1, `c12` = 0, and `c13` = 10; `c21` = 0, `c22` = 1, and `c23` = 10. The resulting equation becomes `u` = `x` + 10 and `v` = `y` + 10:

$$\begin{bmatrix} u \\ v \\ 1 \end{bmatrix} = \begin{bmatrix} 0 & 0 & 10 \\ 0 & 1 & 10 \\ 0 & 0 & 1 \end{bmatrix} \begin{bmatrix} x \\ y \\ 1 \end{bmatrix}$$

- **Rotation**: Some examples of rotation constant values are `c11` = 1, `c12` =0.5, and `c13` = 0; `c21` = -0.5, `c22` = 1, and `c23` = 0.

The resulting equation becomes `u` = `x` + 0.5 `y` and `v` = -0.5 `x` + `y`:

$$\begin{bmatrix} u \\ v \\ 1 \end{bmatrix} = \begin{bmatrix} 1 & 0.5 & 0 \\ -0.5 & 1 & 0 \\ 0 & 0 & 1 \end{bmatrix} \begin{bmatrix} x \\ y \\ 1 \end{bmatrix}$$

- **Rotation + Translation**: Some examples of rotation and translation combined constant values are `c11` = 1, `c12` =0.5, and `c13` = 10; `c21` = -0.5, `c22` = 1, and `c23` = 10. The resulting equation becomes `u` = `x` + 0.5 `y` + 10 and `v` = -0.5 `x` + `y` +10:

$$\begin{bmatrix} u \\ v \\ 1 \end{bmatrix} = \begin{bmatrix} 1 & 0.5 & 10 \\ -0.5 & 1 & 10 \\ 0 & 0 & 1 \end{bmatrix} \begin{bmatrix} x \\ y \\ 1 \end{bmatrix}$$

- **Shear**: Some examples of shear constant values are `c11` = 10, `c12` =0, and `c13` = 0; `c21` = 0, `c22` = 10, and `c23` = 0. The resulting equation becomes `u` = 10 `x` and `v` = 10 `y`:

$$\begin{bmatrix} u \\ v \\ 1 \end{bmatrix} = \begin{bmatrix} 10 & 0 & 0 \\ 0 & 10 & 0 \\ 0 & 0 & 1 \end{bmatrix} \begin{bmatrix} x \\ y \\ 1 \end{bmatrix}$$

Image transformation is particularly helpful in computer vision for getting different images from the same image. This helps the computer develop a neural network model that is robust to translation, rotation, and shear. For example, if we only input an image of the front of a car in the **convoluted neural network** (**CNN**) during the training phase, the model will not be able to detect the image of a car rotated by 90 degrees during the test phase.

Next, we will discuss the mechanics of the convolution operation and how filters are applied to transform an image.

Linear filtering—convolution with kernels

Convolution in computer vision is a linear algebra operation of two arrays (one of them is an image and the other one is a small array) to produce a filtered image array whose shape is different than the original image array. Convolution is cumulative and associative. It can be represented mathematically as follows:

$$G(x,y) = U * F(x,y) = \sum_{i=-n}^{n} \sum_{j=-m}^{m} U(n,m) F(x-i, y-j)$$

The preceding formula is explained as follows:

- `F(x,y)` is the original image.
- `G(x,y)` is the filtered image.
- `U` is the image kernel.

Depending on the kernel type, `U`, the output image will be different. The Python code for the conversion is as follows:

```
import numpy as np
import cv2
import matplotlib.pyplot as plt
%matplotlib inline
import matplotlib.pyplot as plt
from PIL import Image
image = Image.open('.../carshort.png')
plt.imshow(image)
image_arr = np.asarray(image)  # convert image to numpy array
image_arr.shape
gray = cv2.cvtColor(image_arr, cv2.COLOR_BGR2GRAY)
plt.imshow(gray, cmap='gray')
kernel = np.array([[-1,-1,-1],
```

```
                    [2,2,2],
                    [-1,-1,-1]])
blurimg = cv2.filter2D(gray,-1,kernel)
plt.imshow(blurimg, cmap='gray')
```

The image output for the preceding code is as follows:

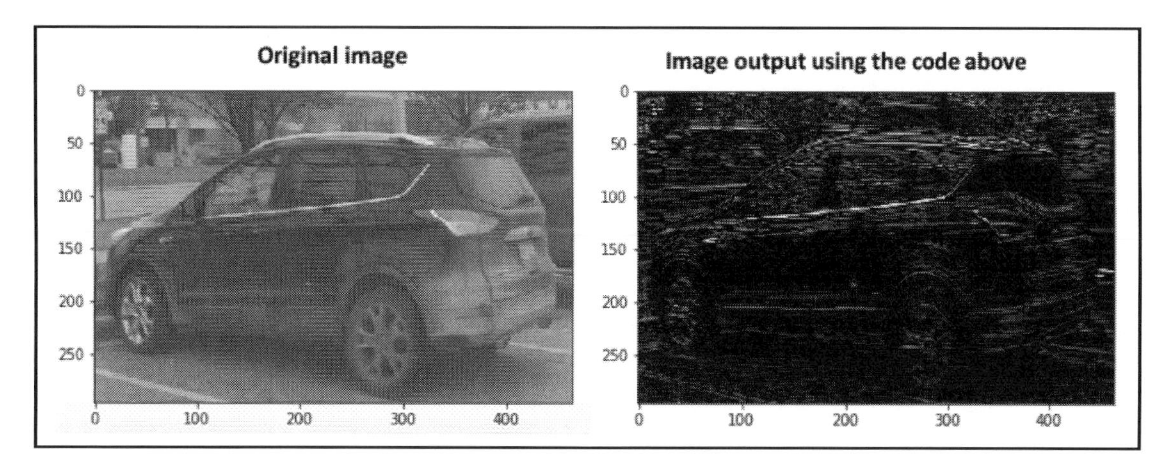

To the left is the input image and to the right is the image obtained by applying a horizontal kernel to the image. A horizontal kernel detects only the horizontal edges, which can be seen by the white streaks of horizontal lines. Details about the horizontal kernel can be seen in the *Image gradient* section.

The preceding code imports the necessary Python libraries for machine learning and computer vision work, such as NumPy to process an array, cv2 for openCV computer vision work, PIL to process images in the Python code, and Matplotlib to plot results. It then imports the image using PIL and converts it to grayscale using the OpenCV `BGr2GRAY` scale function. It creates a kernel for edge filtering using a NumPy array, blurs the image using the kernel, and then displays it using the `imshow()` function.

The filtering operation is broken down into three distinct classes:

- Image smoothing
- Image gradient
- Image sharpening

Image smoothing

In image smoothing, the high-frequency noise from an image is removed by applying low-pass filters, such as the following:

- A mean filter
- A median filter
- A Gaussian filter

This blurs the image and is performed by applying a pixel whose end values do not change sign and do not differ in value appreciably.

Image filtering is typically done by sliding a box filter over an image. A box filter is represented by an $n \times m$ kernel divided by (*n***m*), where *n* is the number of rows and *m* is the number of columns. For a 3 x 3 kernel this looks as follows:

$$\frac{1}{9}\begin{bmatrix} 1 & 1 & 1 \\ 1 & 1 & 1 \\ 1 & 1 & 1 \end{bmatrix}$$

Let's say this kernel is applied to the RGB image described previously. For reference, the 3 x 3 image value is shown here:

$$\begin{vmatrix} 83 & 92 & 77 \\ 79 & 166 & 209 \\ 188 & 180 & 64 \end{vmatrix}$$

The mean filter

The mean filter filters the image with an average value after the convolution operation of the box kernel is carried out with the image. The resulting array after matrix multiplication will be as follows:

$$\begin{vmatrix} 28 & 28 & 28 \\ 50.4 & 50.4 & 50.4 \\ 48 & 48 & 48 \end{vmatrix}$$

The mean value is `42` and replaces the center intensity value of `166` in the image, as you can see in the following array. The remaining values of the image will be converted in a similar manner:

$$\begin{vmatrix} 83 & 92 & 77 \\ 79 & 42 & 209 \\ 188 & 1\text{[illegible]} & 64 \end{vmatrix}$$

The median filter

The median filter filters the image value with the median value after the convolution operation of the box kernel is carried out on the image. The resulting array after matrix multiplication will be as follows:

$$\begin{vmatrix} 28 & 28 & 28 \\ 50.4 & 50.4 & 50.4 \\ 48 & 48 & 48 \end{vmatrix}$$

The median value is `48` and replaces the center intensity value of `166` in the image, as shown in the following array. The remaining values of the image will be converted in a similar manner:

$$\begin{vmatrix} 83 & 92 & 77 \\ 79 & 48 & 209 \\ 188 & 180 & 64 \end{vmatrix}$$

The Gaussian filter

The Gaussian kernel is represented by the following equation:

$$U(i, j) = \frac{1}{2\pi\sigma^2} exp\left(-\frac{(i-(k+1)^2 + (j-(k+1)^2}{2\sigma^2}\right)$$

σ is the standard deviation of the distribution and `k` is the kernel size.

For the standard deviation (σ) of `1`, and the 3 x 3 kernel (`k=3`), the Gaussian kernel looks as follows:

$$\frac{1}{2 * pi}\begin{bmatrix} 0.3678 & 0.6065 & 0.3678 \\ 0.6065 & 1 & 0.6065 \\ 0.3678 & 0.6065 & 0.3678 \end{bmatrix}$$

In this example, when the Gaussian kernel is applied, the image is transformed as follows:

$$\begin{vmatrix} 18 & 30 & 18 \\ 33 & 54 & 33 \\ 32 & 53 & 32 \end{vmatrix}$$

So, in this case, the center intensity value is `54`. Compare this value with the median and mean filter values.

Image filtering with OpenCV

The image filtering concepts described previously can be better understood by applying a filter to a real image. OpenCV provides a method to do that. The OpenCV code we will use can be found at `https://github.com/PacktPublishing/Mastering-Computer-Vision-with-TensorFlow-2.0/blob/master/Chapter01/Chapter1_imagefiltering.ipynb`.

The important code is listed in the following snippet. After importing the image, we can add noise. Without noise, the image filtering effect can not be visualized very well. After that, we need to save the image. This is not necessary for the mean and Gaussian filter, but if we don't save the image with the median filter and import it back again, Python displays an error.

Note that we use `plt.imsave` to save the image, rather than OpenCV. A direct save using `imwrite` will result in a black image as the image needs to be normalized to a 255 scale before saving. `plt.imsave` does not have that restriction.

After this, we use `blur`, `medianBlur`, and `GaussianBlur` to convert the image using the mean, median, and Gaussian filters:

```
img = cv2.imread('car.jpeg')
imgnoise = random_noise(img, mode='s&p',amount=0.3)
plt.imsave("car2.jpg", imgnoise)
imgnew = cv2.imread('car2.jpg')
meanimg = cv2.blur(imgnew,(3,3))
medianimg = cv2.medianBlur(imgnew,3)
gaussianimg = cv2.GaussianBlur(imgnew,(3,3),0)
```

The following figure shows the resulting image plotted using `matplotlib pyplot`:

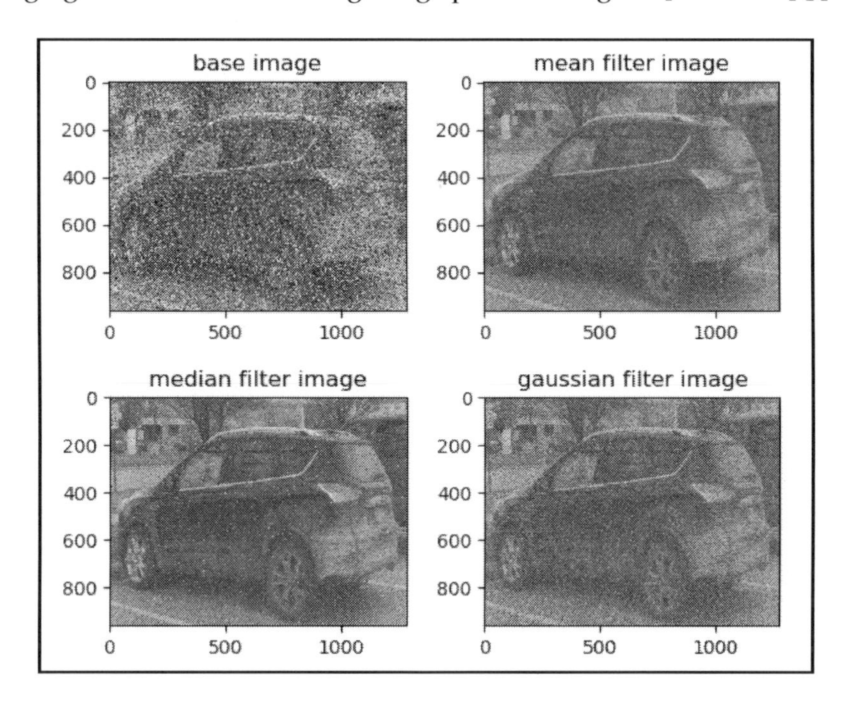

Note that in each of the three cases, the filter removes the noise from the image. In this example, it appears the median filter is the most effective of the three methods in removing the noise from the image.

Image gradient

The image gradient calculates the change in pixel intensity in a given direction. The change in pixel intensity is obtained by performing a convolution operation on an image with a kernel, as shown here:

$$\nabla f = \frac{\partial f(x,y)}{\partial x \partial y} = \frac{\partial f(x,y)}{\partial x} + \frac{\partial f(x,y)}{\partial y}$$

The kernel is chosen such that the two extreme rows or columns have opposite signs (positive and negative) so it produces a difference operator when multiplying and summing across the image pixel. Let's take a look at the following example:

- **The horizontal kernel**:

$$\begin{bmatrix} -1 & -1 & -1 \\ 2 & 2 & 2 \\ 1 & -1 & -1 \end{bmatrix}$$

- **The vertical kernel**:

$$\begin{bmatrix} -1 & 2 & -1 \\ -1 & 2 & -1 \\ -1 & 2 & -1 \end{bmatrix}$$

The image gradient described here is a fundamental concept for computer vision:

- The image gradient can be calculated in both the x and y directions.
- By using the image gradient, edges and corners are determined.
- The edges and corners pack a lot of information about the shape or feature of an image.
- So, the image gradient is a mechanism that converts lower-order pixel information to higher-order image features, which is used by convolution operation for image classification.

Image sharpening

In image sharpening, the low-frequency noise from an image is removed by applying a high-pass filter (difference operator), which results in the line structure and edges becoming more visible. Image sharpening is also known as a **Laplace operation**, which is represented by the second derivative, shown here:

$$\nabla^2 f = \frac{\partial^2 f(x,y)}{\partial x^2} + \frac{\partial^2 f(x,y)}{\partial y^2}$$

Because of the difference operator, the four adjacent cells relative to the midpoint of the kernel always have opposite signs. So, if the midpoint of the kernel is positive, the four adjacent cells are negative, and vice versa. Let's take a look at the following example:

$$\begin{bmatrix} 0 & -1 & 0 \\ -1 & 4 & -1 \\ 0 & -1 & 0 \end{bmatrix} \begin{bmatrix} 0 & 1 & 0 \\ 1 & -4 & 1 \\ 0 & 1 & 0 \end{bmatrix}$$

Note that the advantage of the second-order derivative over the first-order derivative is that the second-order derivative will always go through zero crossings. So, the edges can be determined by looking at the zero-crossing point (`0` value) rather than the magnitude of the gradients (which can change from image to image and within a given image) for the first-order gradient.

Mixing the Gaussian and Laplacian operations

So far, you have learned that the Gaussian operation blurs the image and the Laplacian operation sharpens the image. But why do we need each operation, and in what situation is each operation used?

An image consists of characteristics, features, and other non-feature objects. Image recognition is all about extracting features from an image and eliminating the non-feature objects. We recognize an image as a particular object, such as a car, because its features are more prominent compared to its non-features. Gaussian filtering is the method of suppressing the non-features from the features, which blurs the image.

Applying it multiple times blurs the image more and suppresses both the features and the non-features. But since the features are stronger, they can be extracted by applying Laplacian gradients. This is the reason why we convolve two or more times with a Gaussian kernel of sigma and then apply the Laplacian operation to distinctly show the features. This is a common technique used in most convolution operations for object detection.

The following figure shows the input 3 x 3 image section, the kernel value, the output value after the convolution operation, and the resulting image:

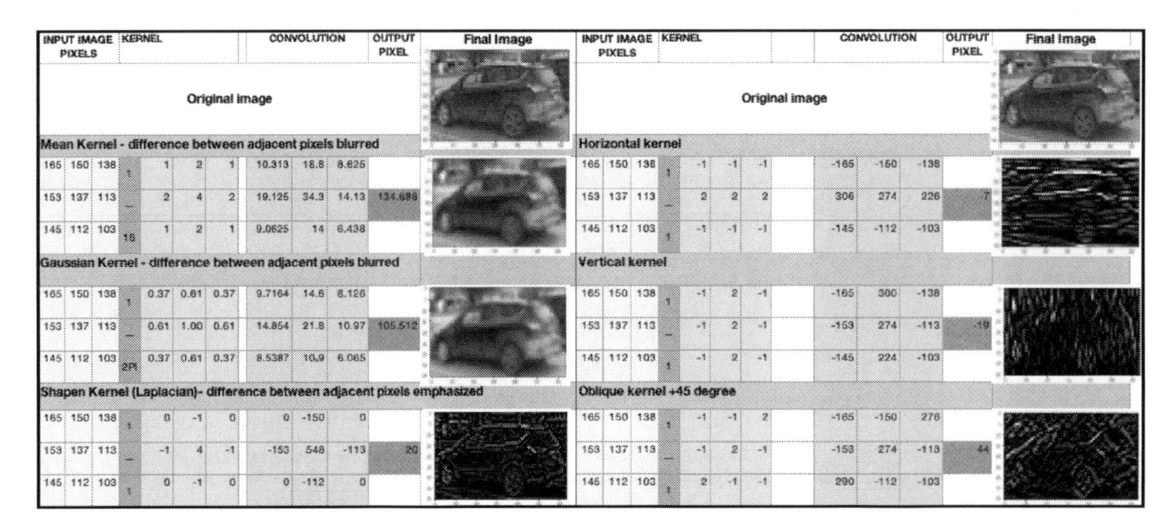

The preceding figure shows various Gaussian and oblique kernels and how a 3 x 3 section of the image is transformed by applying the kernel. The following figure is a continuation of the preceding one:

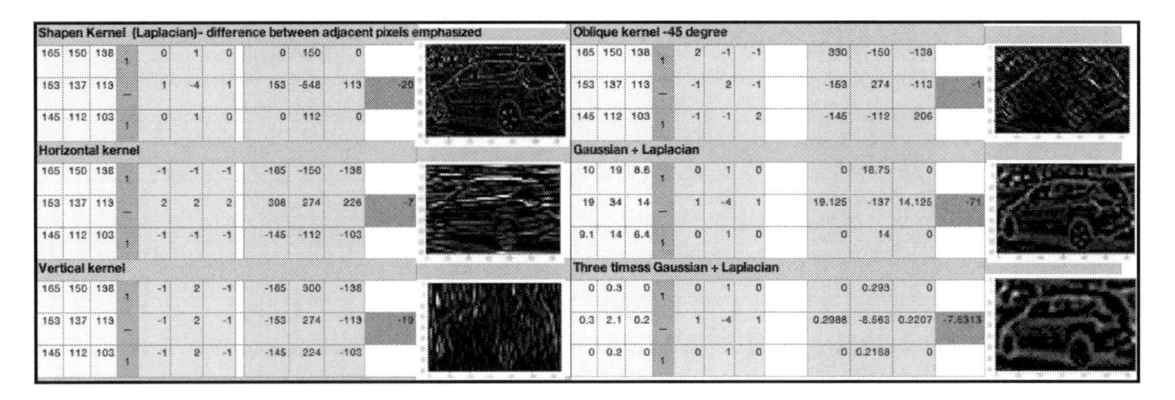

The preceding representation clearly shows how the image becomes more blurred or sharp based on the type of convolution operation. This comprehension of the convolution operation is fundamental as we learn more about using the CNN to optimize kernel selection in various stages of the CNN.

Detecting edges in an image

Edge detection is the most fundamental way of processing in computer vision to find features in an image based on the change in brightness and image intensity. A change in brightness results from discontinuity in depth, orientation, illumination, or corners. The edge detection method can be based on the first or second order:

$$\nabla^2 f = \frac{\partial^2 f(x,y)}{\partial x^2} + \frac{\partial^2 f(x,y)}{\partial y^2} = 0$$

The following graph illustrates the edge detection mechanism graphically:

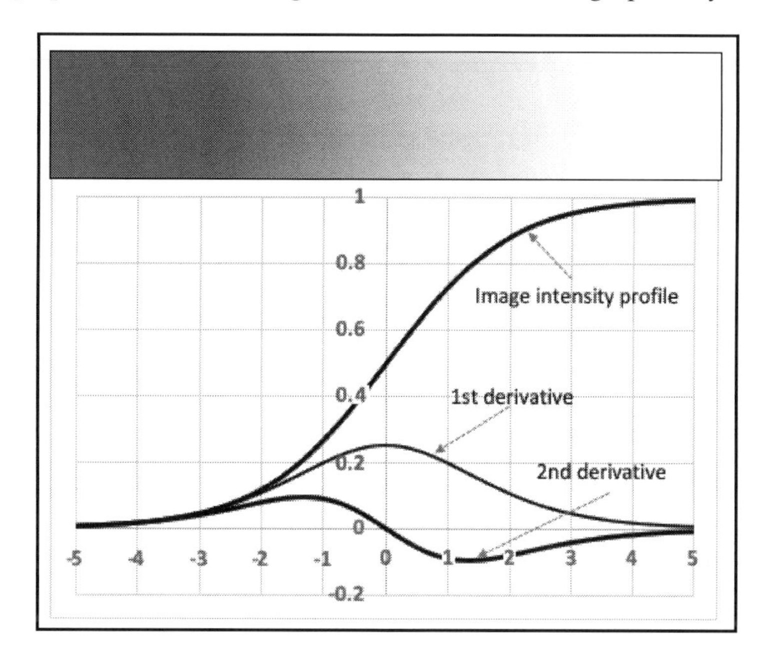

Here, you can see that the intensity of the image changes from dark to bright around the midway point, so the edge of the image is at the middle point. The first derivative (the intensity gradient) goes up and then down at the midway point, so the edge detection can be calculated by looking at the maximum value of the first derivative. However, the problem with the first derivative method is, depending on the input function, the maximum value can change, so the threshold value of the maximum value cannot be predetermined. However, the second derivative, as shown, always goes through zero points at the edges.

Sobel and **Canny** are the first-order edge detection methods, while the second-order method is a Laplacian edge detector.

The Sobel edge detector

The Sobel operator detects edges by calculating the gradient (`Sobelx` and `Sobely` in the following code) of the image intensity function. The gradient is calculated by applying a kernel to the image. In the following code, the kernel size (`ksize`) is `5`. After this, the **Sobel gradient (SobelG)** is calculated by taking the ratio of the gradients (`sobely/sobelx`):

```
Sobelx=cv2.Sobel(gray,cv2.CV_64F,1,0,ksize=5)
Sobely=cv2.Sobel(gray,cv2.CV_64F,0,1,ksize=5)
mag,direction = cv2.cartToPolar(sobelx,sobely,angleInDegrees =True)
sobelG = np.hypot(sobelx,sobely)
```

The Canny edge detector

The Canny edge detector uses a two-dimensional Gaussian filter to remove the noise, then applies Sobel edge detection with non-maximum suppression to pick out the maximum ratio value between the *x* and *y* gradients at any pixel point and, finally, applies edge thresholding to detect whether or not there is an edge. The following code shows Canny edge detection on a grayscale image. The `min` and `max` values are the thresholding values that compare the image gradient to determine the edges:

```
Canny = cv2.Canny(gray,minVal=100,maxVal=200)
```

The following figure shows the image of the car after applying `Sobel-x`, `Sobel-y`, and the Canny edge detector:

As we can see, Canny performs much better than Sobel in detecting the car. This is because Canny uses a two-dimensional Gaussian filter to remove the noise, then applies Sobel edge detection with non-maximum suppression to pick out the maximum ratio value between the *x* and *y* gradients at any pixel point and, finally, applies edge thresholding to detect whether or not there is an edge.

Extracting features from an image

Once we know how to detect edges, the next task is to detect features. Many edges combine to form features. Feature extraction is the process of recognizing visual patterns in an image and extracting any discriminating local features that match with the image of an unknown object. Before performing feature extraction, it is important to understand the image histogram. An image histogram is the distribution of the color intensity of the image.

An image feature matches with the test image if the histograms are similar. The following is the Python code used to create an image histogram of the car:

```
import numpy as np
import cv2
import matplotlib.pyplot as plt
%matplotlib inline
import matplotlib.pyplot as plt
from PIL import Image
image = Image.open('../car.png')
plt.imshow(image)
image_arr = np.asarray(image) # convert image to numpy array
image_arr.shape
color = ('blue', 'green', 'red')
for i,histcolor in enumerate(color):
 carhistogram = cv2.calcHist([image_arr],[i],None,[256],[0,256])
 plt.plot(carhistogram,color=histcolor)
 plt.xlim([0,256])
```

The preceding Python code first imports the necessary Python libraries, such as cv2 (OpenCV), NumPy (for array calculation), PIL (to import an image), and Matplotlib (to plot graphs). After that, it converts the image into an array and loops through each color and plots the histogram for each color (R, G, and B).

The following graph shows the histogram output of the car image. The *x* axis represents the color intensity value from `0` (black) to `256` (white) and the *y* axis represents the frequency of occurrence:

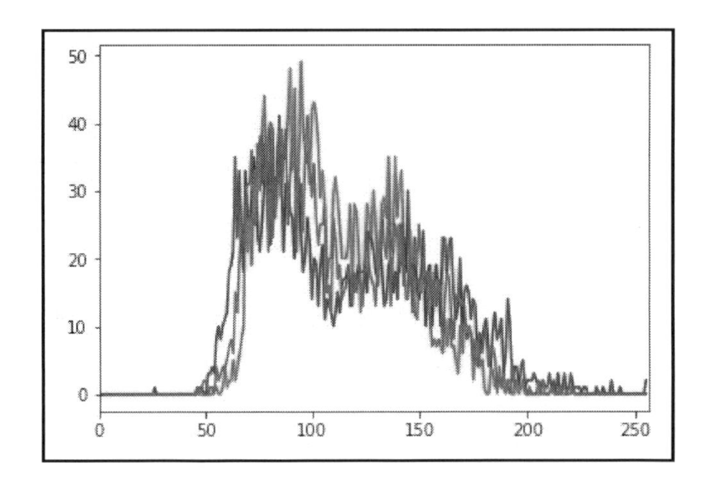

The histogram shows that the peak color intensity of R, G, and B is at around `100`, with a second peak at around `150`. This means that the average color of the car is gray. A frequency of `0` at an intensity value of `200` (seen on the far-right side of the image) shows that the car is definitely not white. Similarly, a frequency of `0` at an intensity value of `50` shows that the image is not completely black.

Image matching using OpenCV

Image matching is a technique that matches two different images to find common features. Image matching techniques have many practical applications, such as matching fingerprints, matching your carpet color with your floor or wall color, matching photographs to find two images of the same person, or comparing manufacturing defects to group them into similar categories for faster analysis. This section provides a high-level overview of the image matching techniques available in OpenCV. Two commonly used methods are described here: **BruteForce** (**BFMatcher**) and **Fast Library for Approximate Nearest Neighbors** (**FLANN**). Later on in this book, we will also discuss other types of matching techniques, such as histogram matching and local binary pattern in `Chapter 2`, *Content Recognition Using Local Binary Pattern*, and visual search in `Chapter 6`, *Visual Search Using Transfer Learning*.

In BFMatcher, the hamming distance between the test image and every section of the target image is compared for the best possible match. FLANN, on the other hand, is faster but will only find the approximate nearest neighbors—so, it finds good matches, but not necessarily the best possible one. The **KNN** tool assumes that similar things are flocked next to each other. It finds the first approximate nearest neighbors based on the distance between the target and the source. The Python code for image matching can be found at `https://github.com/PacktPublishing/Mastering-Computer-Vision-with-TensorFlow-2.0/blob/master/Chapter01/Chapter1_SIFT.ipynb`.

Note in the following figure that BFMatcher finds a more similar image. This figure is the output returned by the preceding code (`preface_SIFT.ipynb`). Let's have a look:

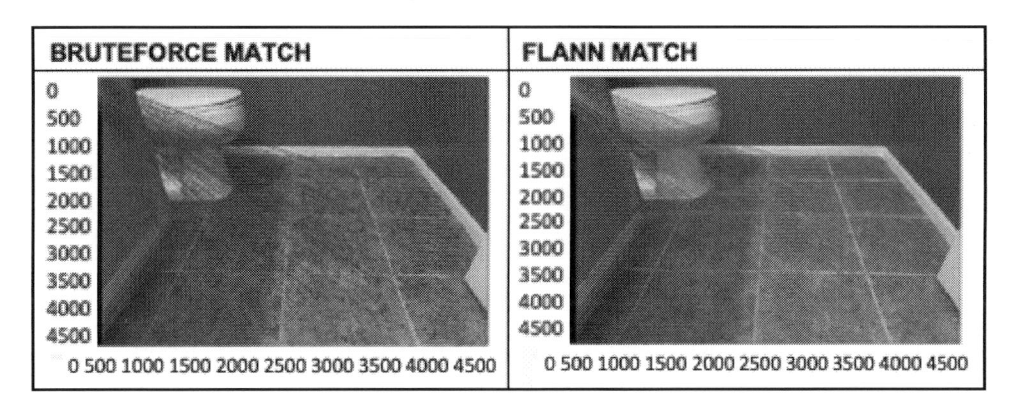

The preceding figure shows how we can apply BFMatcher and FLANN's KNN matcher to match a single tile to the whole bathroom floor. It is clear that BFMatcher (the blue lines) finds more tile points compared to the FLANN matcher (the red lines).

The image matching technique described preceding can also be used to find relative distance between two points - one point can be a reference point such as your car from where the image is taken and the other one can be another car in the road. Such distance is then used to develop a collision avoidance system.

Object detection using Contours and the HOG detector

Contours are closed regions within an image that has a similar shape. In this section, we will use Contours to classify and detect simple objects within an image. The image we will use consists of apples and oranges and we will use the Contour and the Canny edge detection method to detect the object and write the image class name on the bounding box. The code for this section can be found at `https://github.com/PacktPublishing/Mastering-Computer-Vision-with-TensorFlow-2.0/blob/master/Chapter01/Chapter1_contours_opencv_object_detection_HOG.ipynb`.

The methodology is described in the following subsections.

Contour detection

We first need to import the image and then use the Canny edge detector to find the edges in the image. This works very well as the shape of our object is a circle with a rounded edge. The following is the detailed code required:

```
threshold =100
canny_output = cv2.Canny(img, threshold, threshold * 2)
contours, hierarchy = cv2.findContours(canny_output, cv2.RETR_EXTERNAL,
cv2.CHAIN_APPROX_SIMPLE)
```

As the preceding code shows, after Canny edge detection, we applied the OpenCV `findContours()` method. This method has three arguments:

- The image, which in our case is a Canny edge detector output.
- The retrieval method, which has many options. The one we are using is an external method as we are interested in drawing a bounding box around the object.
- The contour approximation method.

Detecting a bounding box

This method essentially consists of understanding the characteristics of an image and its various classes and developing methods to classify the image class.

Note that the OpenCV method does not involve any training. For every contour, we define a bounding box using the OpenCV `boundingRect` property.

We will be using two important characteristics to select the bounding box:

- **The size of the region of interest**: We will eliminate all contours with a size that is less than `20`.

Note that `20` is not a universal number, it just works for this image. For a larger image, the value can be larger.

- **The color of the region of interest**: Within each bounding box, we need to define the region of interest from `25%` to `75%` of the width to ensure that we do not consider the empty region of rectangles outside the circle. This is important to minimize variation. Next, we define the mean color by using `CV2.mean`.

We will determine the color's mean and max thresholds by looking at the three images of oranges that encircle it. The following code uses OpenCV's built-in method to draw the bounding box using `cv2.boundingRect`. It then draws a **region of interest (ROI)** based on the width and height selection and finds the mean color within the region:

```
count=0
font = cv2.FONT_HERSHEY_SIMPLEX
for c in contours:
    x,y,w,h = cv2.boundingRect(c)
    if (w >20 and h >20):
        count = count+1
        ROI = img[y+int(h/4):y+int(3*h/4), x+int(h/4):x+int(3*h/4)]
        ROI_meancolor = cv2.mean(ROI)
        print(count,ROI_meancolor)
        if (ROI_meancolor[0] > 30 and ROI_meancolor[0] < 40 and
ROI_meancolor[1] > 70 and ROI_meancolor[1] < 105
            and ROI_meancolor[2] > 150 and ROI_meancolor[2] < 200):
                cv2.putText(img, 'orange', (x-2, y-2), font, 0.8,
(255,255,255), 2, cv2.LINE_AA)
                cv2.rectangle(img,(x,y),(x+w,y+h),(255,255,255),3)
```

```
                    cv2.imshow('Contours', img)
            else:
                    cv2.putText(img, 'apple', (x-2, y-2), font, 0.8, (0,0,255),
    2, cv2.LINE_AA)
                    cv2.rectangle(img,(x,y),(x+w,y+h),(0,0,255),3)
                    cv2.imshow('Contours', img)
```

In the preceding code, pay attention to the two `if` statements—size-based (`w,h`) and color-based (`ROI_meancolor[0,1,2]`):

- The size-based statement eliminates all contours of less than `20`.
- `ROI_meancolor [0,1,2]` indicates the RGB value of the mean color.

Here, the third, fourth, and eighth lines represent the orange and the `if` statement constrains the color to look between `30` and `40` for the `B` component, `70` and `105` for the `G` component, and `150` and `200` for the `R` component.

The output is as follows. In our example, `3`, `4`, and `8` are oranges:

```
1 (52.949200000000005, 66.38640000000001, 136.2072, 0.0)
2 (43.677693761814744, 50.94659735349717, 128.70510396975425, 0.0)
3 (34.418282548476455, 93.26246537396122, 183.0893351800554, 0.0)
4 (32.792241946088104, 78.3931623931624, 158.78238001314926, 0.0)
5 (51.00493827160494, 55.09925925925926, 124.42765432098766, 0.0)
6 (66.8863771564545, 74.85960737656157, 165.39678762641284, 0.0)
7 (67.8125, 87.031875, 165.140625, 0.0)
8 (36.25, 100.72916666666666, 188.67746913580245, 0.0)
```

Note that OpenCV processes images as `BGR` not `RGB`.

The HOG detector

The **Histogram of Oriented Gradients** (**HOG**) is a useful feature that can be used to determine the localized image intensity of an image. This technique can be used to find objects within an image. The localized image gradient information can be used to find similar images. In this example, we will use **scikit-image** to import the HOG and use it to plot the HOG of our image. You may have to install scikit-image, if it's not already installed, using `pip install scikit-image`:

```
from skimage.feature import hog
from skimage import data, exposure
```

```
fruit, hog_image = hog(img, orientations=8, pixels_per_cell=(16, 16),
cells_per_block=(1, 1), visualize=True, multichannel=True)
hog_image_rescaled = exposure.rescale_intensity(hog_image, in_range=(0,
10))
cv2.imshow('HOG_image', hog_image_rescaled)
```

The result of the preceding code on our sample image is illustrated in the following figure:

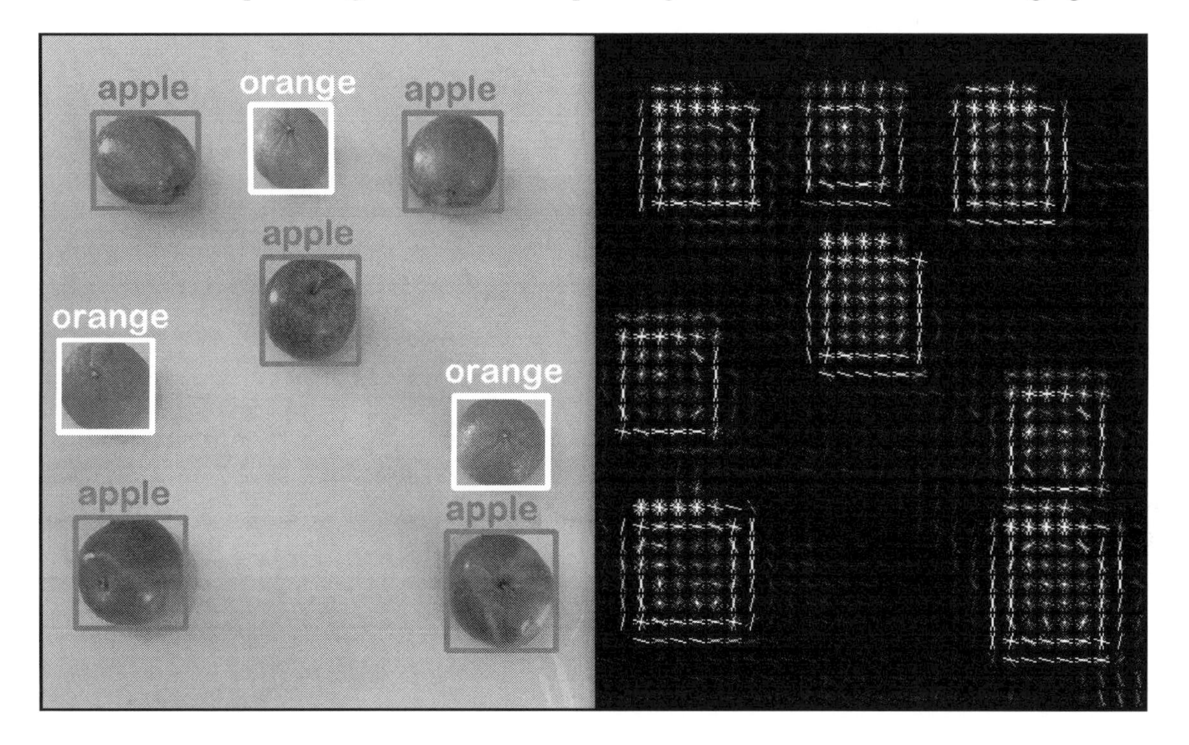

In the preceding figure, we can observe the following:

- The left side shows a bounding box, whereas the right side shows the HOG gradients for each object in the image.
- Note that each of the apples and oranges is correctly detected, with a bounding box encircling the fruit without any overlap.
- The HOG descriptors show a rectangular bounding box with gradients showing the circular patterns.
- The gradients between the oranges and apples show a similar pattern, with the only distinction being the size.

Limitations of the contour detection method

The example shown in the previous subsection looks very good in terms of object detection. We did not have to do any training and, with a little adjustment of a few parameters, we were able to detect the oranges and apples correctly. However, we will add the following variations and see if our detector is still able to detect the objects correctly:

- We will add objects other than apples and oranges.
- We will add another object with a similar shape to apples and oranges.
- We will change the light intensity and reflection.

If we execute the same code from the previous subsection, it will detect every object as if it is an apple. This is because the width and height parameters selected were too broad and included all objects as well as the RGB values, which appear differently in this image than before. In order to detect the objects correctly, we will introduce the following changes to the `if` statements for the size and color, as in the following code:

```
  if (w >60 and w < 100 and h >60 and h <120):
  if (ROI_meancolor[0] > 10 and ROI_meancolor[0] < 40 and ROI_meancolor[1]
> 65 and ROI_meancolor[1] < 105
```

Note that the preceding changes place constraints on the `if` statement that were not there before.

The RGB colors are as follows:

```
1 (29.87429111531191, 92.01890359168242, 182.84026465028356, 0.0) 82 93
2 (34.00568181818182, 49.73605371900827, 115.44163223140497, 0.0) 72 89
3 (39.162326388888886, 62.77256944444444, 148.98133680555554, 0.0) 88 96
4 (32.284938271604936, 53.324444444444445, 141.16493827160494, 0.0) 89 90
5 (12.990362811791384, 67.3078231292517, 142.0997732426304, 0.0) 84 84
6 (38.15, 56.9972, 119.3528, 0.0) 82 100
7 (47.102716049382714, 80.29333333333334, 166.3264197530864, 0.0) 86 90
8 (45.76502082093992, 68.75133848899465, 160.64901844140394, 0.0) 78 82
9 (23.54432132963989, 98.59972299168975, 191.97368421052633, 0.0) 67 76
```

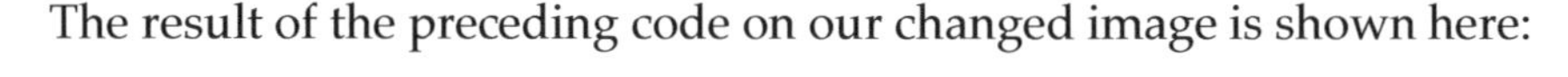

The result of the preceding code on our changed image is shown here:

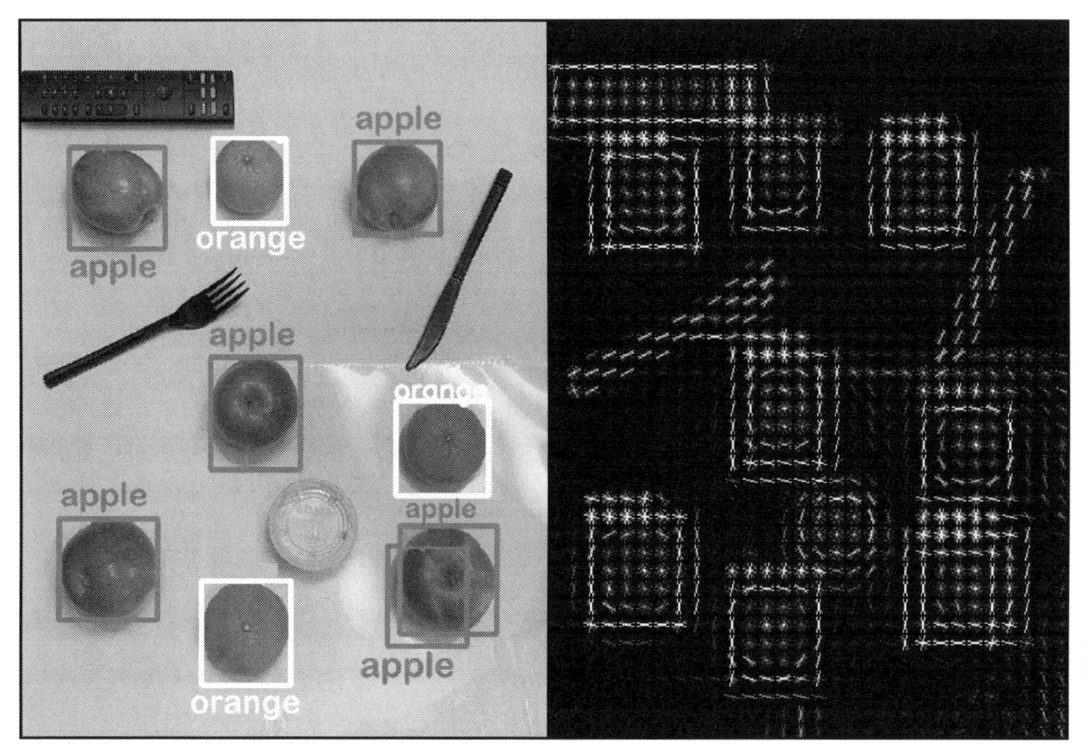

A remote control, fork, knife, and a plastic portion cup can be seen in the preceding figure. Note how the HOG features for the apples, oranges, and plastic cup are similar, which is as expected as each of these is circular in shape:

- The plastic cup does not have a bounding box around it as it was not detected.
- The fork and knife have a very different angular HOG shape compared to the apples and oranges.
- The remote control has a rectangular HOG shape.

This simple example suggests that this method of object detection will not work for larger image datasets and we will need to adjust parameters to take into account various lighting, shape, size, and orientation conditions. This is why we will be discussing the CNN throughout the rest of this book. Once we use this method to train the image on different conditions, it will detect objects correctly on the new set of conditions, regardless of the shape of the object. However, despite the limitations of the preceding method, we learned how to use the color and size to separate one image from another.

`ROI_meancolor` is a powerful method for detecting an object's average color within a bounding box. You can use it, for example, to differentiate players from one team from another based on their jersey color within a bounding box, a green apple from a red apple, or any type of color-based separation method.

An overview of TensorFlow, its ecosystem, and installation

In the previous sections, we covered the basics of computer vision techniques, such as image conversion, image filtering, convolution using a kernel, edge detection, histograms, and feature matching. This understanding and its various applications should develop a solid foundation for the advanced concept of deep learning, which will be introduced later on in this book.

Deep learning in computer vision is the cumulative learning of many different image features (such as edges, colors, boundaries, shapes, and so on) through a convolution operation of many intermediate (hidden) layers to gain a complete understanding of the image type. Deep learning augments computer vision techniques because it stacks many layers of calculations about how neurons behave. This is done by combining various inputs to produce outputs based on mathematical functions and computer vision methods, such as edge detection.

TensorFlow is an **End to End** (**E2E**) machine learning platform, where images and data are transformed into tensors to be processed by the neural network. For example, an image with a size of `224 x 224` can be represented as a tensor of rank `4` as `128, 224, 224, 3`, where `128` is the batch size of the neural network, `224` is the height and width, and `3` is the color channel (R, G, and B).

If your code is based on TensorFlow 1.0, then converting it to version 2.0 can be one of the biggest challenges. Follow the instructions found at `https://www.tensorflow.org/guide/migrate` to convert to version 2.0. Most of the time, problems in conversion happen in a low-level API when you execute the Python code in TensorFlow using the terminal.

Keras is the high-level API for TensorFlow. The following three lines of code are the starting point for installing Keras:

```
from __future__ import absolute_import, division, print_function,
unicode_literals
import tensorflow as tf
from tensorflow import keras
```

If you don't use the last line, then you may have to use the `from tensorflow.keras` import for all of your functions.

TensorFlow uses `tf.data` to build a complex input pipeline from simple code, which simplifies and speeds up the data input process. You will learn about this in `Chapter 6`, *Visual Search Using Transfer Learning*.

In Keras, layers of the model are stacked together in what is known as a **sequential**. This is introduced by `model=tf.keras.Sequential()`, and every layer is added by using the `model.add` statement. First, we need to compile the model using `model.compile` and then we can begin training using the `model.train` function.

TensorFlow models are saved as checkpoints and saved models. Checkpoints capture the value of parameters, filters, and weights used by the model. The checkpoint is associated with source code. The saved model, on the other hand, can be deployed to a production setting and does not need source code.

TensorFlow offers distributed training against multiple GPUs. The TensorFlow model output can be visualized using a Keras API or a TensorFlow graph.

TensorFlow versus PyTorch

PyTorch is another deep learning library similar to TensorFlow. It is based on Torch and has been developed by Facebook. While TensorFlow creates a static graph, PyTorch creates a dynamic graph. In TensorFlow, the entire computational graph has to be defined first and then the model is run whereas, in PyTorch, the graph can be defined parallel to model building.

TensorFlow Installation

To install TensorFlow 2.0 on your PC, type the following command in your Terminal. Make sure you hit *Enter* after each command:

```
pip install --upgrade pip
pip install tensorflow
```

The preceding command will download and extract the following packages in Terminal in addition to TensorFlow:

- Keras (a high-level neural network API written in Python that is capable of running over the top of TensorFlow)
- `protobuf` (a serializing protocol for structured data)
- TensorBoard (TensorFlow's data visualization tool)
- PyGPU (a Python feature used for image processing a GPU calculation for performance increase)
- `cctools` (the native IDE for Android)
- `c-ares` (the library function)
- `clang` (the compiler frontend for C, C++, Objective-C, OpenCL, and OpenCV)
- `llvm` (the compiler architecture used to produce frontend and backend binary code)
- `theano` (the Python library used to manage multi-dimensional arrays)
- `grpcio` (the `gRPC` package for Python used to implement a remote procedure call)
- `libgpuarray` (a common n-dimensional GPU array that can be used by all packages in Python)
- `termcolor` (a color formatting output in Python)
- `absl` (a collection of Python library code used to build Python applications)
- `mock` (substitutes a real object with the virtual environment to aid testing)
- `gast` (a library used to process Python abstract syntax)

During installation, press *y* for **yes** when asked:

```
Downloading and Extracting Packages
Preparing transaction: done
Verifying transaction: done
Executing transaction: done
```

If everything is installed correctly, you will see the preceding messages.

After installation, check the TensorFlow version by entering either of the following commands based on whether your PC has just a CPU or both a CPU and a GPU. Note that for all computer vision work, a GPU is preferred to speed up the calculation of images. Use `pip3` for Python 3.6 or higher and `pip` for Python 2.7:

```
pip3 show tensorflow
pip3 show tensorflow-gpu
pip show tensorflow
```

The output should show the following:

```
Name: tensorflow
Version: 2.0.0rc0
Summary: TensorFlow is an open source machine learning framework for
everyone.
Home-page: https://www.tensorflow.org/
Author: Google Inc.
Author-email: packages@tensorflow.org
License: Apache 2.0
Location: /home/.../anaconda3/lib/python3.7/site-packages
Requires: gast, google-pasta, tf-estimator-nightly, wrapt, tb-nightly,
protobuf, termcolor, opt-einsum, keras-applications, numpy, grpcio, keras-
preprocessing, astor, absl-py, wheel, six
Required-by: gcn
```

At times, you may notice that even after the installation of TensorFlow, the Anaconda environment doesn't recognize that TensorFlow is installed. In that case, it is best to uninstall TensorFlow using the following command in Terminal and then reinstall it:

```
python3 -m pip uninstall protobuf
python3 -m pip uninstall tensorflow-gpu
```

Summary

In this chapter, we learned how image filtering modifies the input image through a convolution operation to produce an output that detects a portion of a feature called an edge. This is fundamental to computer vision. As you will learn in the following chapters, subsequent application of image filtering will transform the edges to a higher-level pattern, such as features.

We also learned how to calculate an image histogram, perform image matching using SIFT, and use contour and the HOG detector to draw a bounding box. We learned how to use OpenCV's bounding box color and size method to segregate one class from another. The chapter concluded with an introduction to TensorFlow, which will provide a foundation for the remaining chapters of this book.

In the next chapter, we will learn about a different type of computer vision technique, called pattern recognition, and we will use it to classify the contents of an image with a pattern.

2
Content Recognition Using Local Binary Patterns

Local Binary Patterns (LBP) was first introduced in the International Pattern Recognition Conference in 1994 by Timo Ojala, Matti Pietik äinen, and David Harwood in the paper *Performance evaluation of texture measures with classification based on Kullback discrimination of distributions* (`https://ieeexplore.ieee.org/document/576366`).

In this chapter, you will learn how to create an LBP image type binary feature descriptor and the LBP histogram for the classification of textured and non-textured images. You will learn about the different methods you can use to calculate the differences between histograms in order to find a match between various images and how to tune LBP parameters to optimize its performance.

This chapter will cover the following topics:

- Processing images using LBP
- Applying LBP to texture recognition
- Matching face color with foundation color – LBP and its limitations
- Matching face color with foundation color– color matching technique

Processing images using LBP

LBP is a grayscale image thresholding operation that's used to classify images based on distinct patterns. The binary pattern is developed by comparing the neighborhood pixel value with that of the center pixel value and is used to construct histogram bins. In the following section, we will describe the LBP operation in detail.

Generating an LBP pattern

The principal steps for LBP pattern generation are as follows:

1. Convert RGB image A into grayscale image G.
2. For each pixel with intensity I_c (x,y) in image G, choose **P** neighboring points (p_0, p_1 .. p_{P-1}) with corresponding intensity (I_0, I_1 .. I_{P-1}) at radius **R**. The radius is defined in pixel units as the difference between two pixels. The pixel and the neighboring points represent a sliding window, W, of the image, G. For radius R = 1, P becomes 8, as shown here.

   The sliding window, W_0, is represented as an array with $W_0 = [I_c, I_0, I_1, I_{P-1}]$. Here, points 0 to P-1 represent the intensity of P points around the center pixel, c:

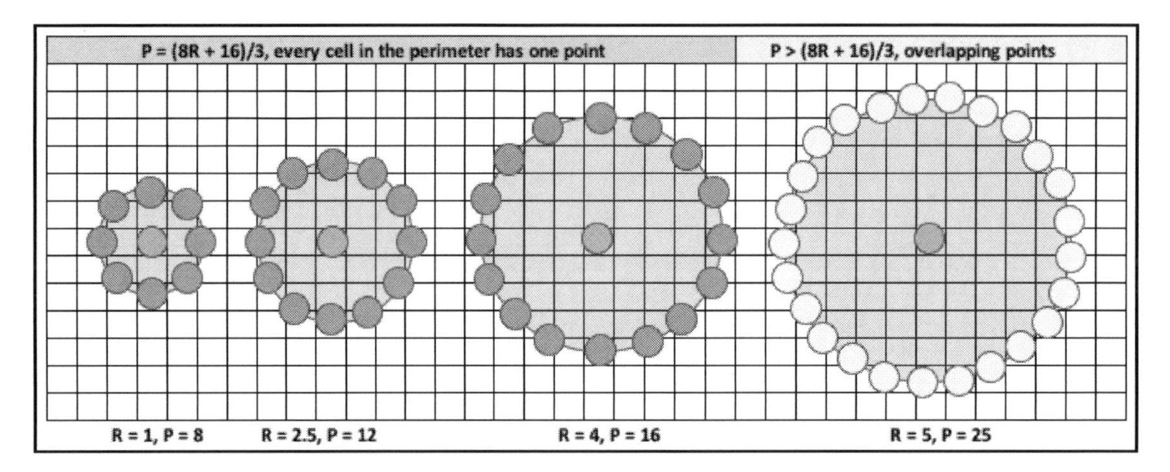

The relationship between radius R and the neighboring points, P, is determined so that every cell in the neighborhood has precisely one pixel. As shown by the first three circles in the preceding diagram, every cell in the perimeter has precisely one pixel, whereas the last cell has more than one pixel packed in the perimeter. From the first three circles, we can express that in order for every cell to have one pixel, the number of points, P, can be expressed as *(8R +16)/3*. The following diagram shows the linear relationship and the outlier shown by the fourth circle from the left, which has overlapping points in the neighboring cells:

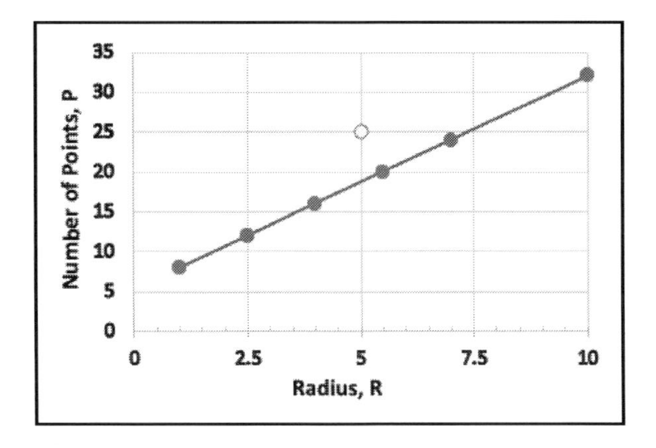

3. Calculate the intensity difference between the neighboring pixels and the center pixel and remove the first value, 0. The array can be represented as follows:

$$W_1 \sim [I_0\text{-}I_c, I_1\text{-}I_c, ..I_{P\text{-}1}\text{-}I_c]$$

4. Now, threshold the image. To do this, assign a value of 0 if the intensity difference is less than 0 and 1 if the intensity difference is greater than 0, as shown by the following equation:

$$f(x) = \begin{cases} 1, x >= 0 \\ 0, x < 0 \end{cases}$$

The difference array after applying the threshold function, *f*, is as follows:

$$W_2 = [f(I_0\text{-}I_c), f(I_1\text{-}I_c), ..f(I_{P\text{-}1}\text{-}I_c)$$

As an example, the array can be represented as follows when assuming the first difference is less than 0 and the second and last difference is greater than 0:

$$W_2 = [0, 1, ...1]$$

5. The difference array, W_2, is multiplied by binomial weight 2^P to translate the binary array, W_2, into LBP code representing decimal array $W_{3:}$

$$W_3 = LBP(P, R) = \sum_{p=0}^{P-1} f(I_p - I_c) \times 2^p$$

Note that the five steps described in this section will be referenced in the next few sections.

The following diagram shows the graphical representation of the LBP operation on a sliding window of a grayscale image:

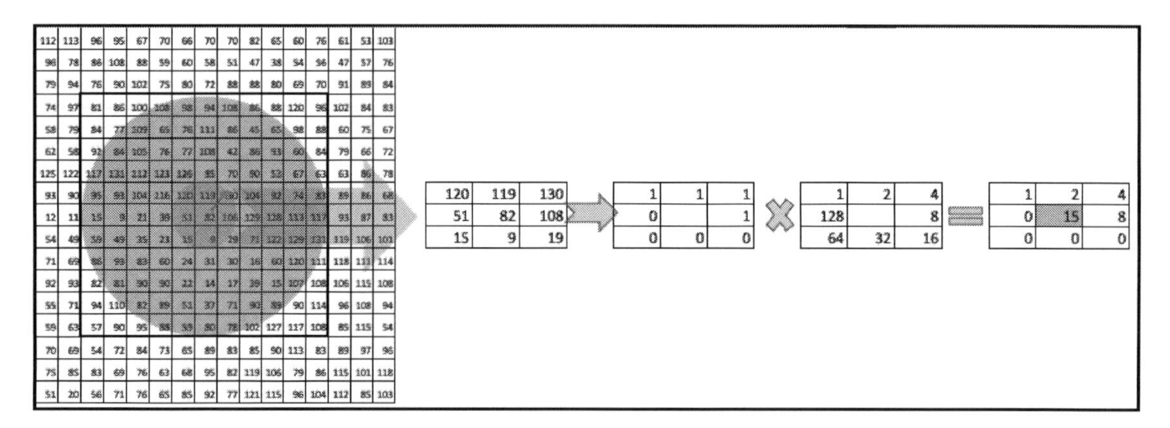

In the preceding diagram, we can see the following:

- The starting 3 x 3 kernel is just a section of the image.
- The next 3 x 3 is the binary representation.
- The top-left value is 1 since we're comparing 120 to 82.
- Going clockwise, the last value is 0 since we compared 51 to 82.
- The next 3 x 3 kernel is just a 2^n operation.
- The first value is 1 (2^0) and the last value going clockwise is 128 (2^7).

Understanding the LBP histogram

LBP array W_3 is represented in histogram form as follows:

$$W_4 = histogram(W_3, bins{=}P, range{=}W_3(min) \text{ to } W_3(max))$$

Steps 1 through *5* from the preceding section are repeated for both the trained image and test image to create an LBP histogram of images (W_{train}, W_{test}) each containing P bins, which are then compared using a histogram comparison method.

Histogram comparison methods

Different histogram comparison methods can be used to calculate the distance between histograms. These are as follows:

- **Intersection method:**

$$Distance = \frac{\sum_{p=0}^{P-1} min\left(W_{test} - W_{train}\right)}{\sum_{p=0}^{P-1} W_{train}}$$

In Python, this is expressed as follows:

```
minima = np.minimum(test_hist,train_hist)
intersection = np.true_divide(np.sum(minima),np.sum(train_hist))
```

- **Chi-Square method:**

$$Distance = \frac{1}{2} \sum_{p=0}^{P-1} \frac{\left(W_{test} - W_{train}\right)^2}{\left(W_{test} + W_{train}\right)}$$

- **Euclidean method:**

$$Distance = \sqrt{\sum_{p=0}^{P-1} \left(W_{test} - W_{train}\right)^2}$$

- **City Block method:**

$$Distance = \sum_{p=0}^{P-1} \left|W_{test} - W_{train}\right|$$

- **Bhattacharya method:**

$$Distance = -log \sum_{p=0}^{P-1} \sqrt{W_{test} W_{train}}$$

- **Wasserstein method:**

$$Distance = \left[\int_{p=0}^{P-1} \left(W_{test}^{-1} - W_{train}^{-1}\right)^2 dp\right]^{1/2}$$

- Given $Wtest = N(\mu test, \sigma test)$ and $Wtrain = N(\mu train, \sigma train)$, here, μ is the mean (1st moment) of the distribution, σ (2nd moment) is the standard deviation of the distribution, and ρ_{QQ} is the correlation of quantiles of two distributions, $Wtest$ and $Wtrain$, against each other.

$$Distance = \left[(\mu_{test} - \mu_{train})^2 + (\sigma_{test} - \sigma_{train})^2 + 2\sigma_{test}\sigma_{train} (1 - \rho_{QQ}) \right]^{1/2}$$

The preceding distance measures have the following characteristics:

- The absolute value of the distance is different for each method.
- The minimum distance between the test and training histogram values is similar for all methods except the Wasserstein method. The Wasserstein method calculates distance based on location (difference of mean), size (difference of standard deviation), and shape (correlation coefficient).

The following shows the original grayscale image and the corresponding LBP image for a given radius, **R=5**:

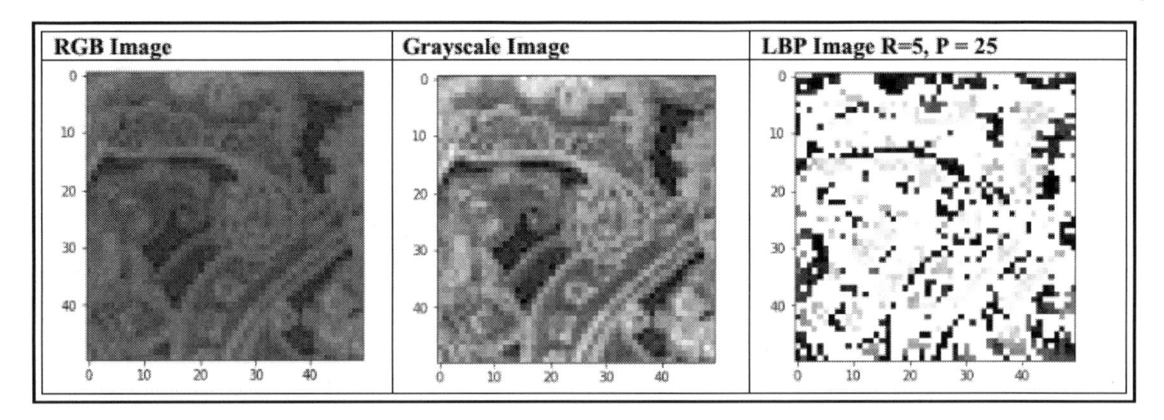

Next, we will evaluate the effect of change in radius regarding the image's sharpness. To do that, the Python code needs to be executed by changing the value of the radius from 1 to 10. The resultant effect on LBP image sharpness is shown in the following image.

The radius to a number of points has been obtained from the correlation *P = (8R+16)/3*. Notice that as the radius increases, the pattern in the image becomes more distinct. Around radius 5 and points 20-25, the pattern becomes clearer with the principal pattern of the main arch, along with the secondary pattern. At a very high radius, the secondary pattern becomes less distinct:

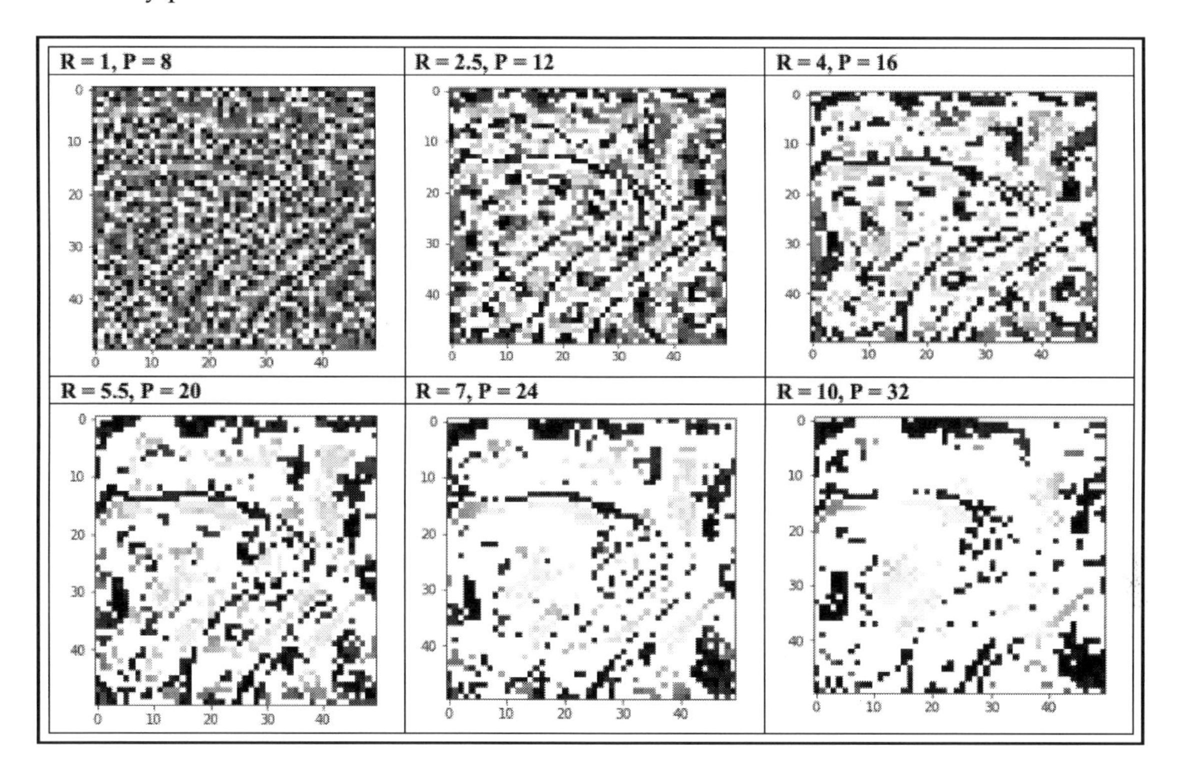

The following is also clear from the preceding images:

- Selecting **R** and **P** is important for pattern recognition.
- The initial value can be selected by *P = (8R +16)/3*, but for a given **R**, a value of **P** more than this does not mean adverse performance, as shown by **R=5, P=25** in the preceding example.
- The pattern that's been selected is clearly better than the **R=4**, **P=16** example and very similar to **R=5.5**, **P=20**.

Also, note that the example here just provides guidelines that are applicable to this image. For an image of a different size, apply the learning from this example of first selecting the initial value of **P** and then adjust **R** and **P** to get the desired pattern.

The computational cost of LBP

LBP is computationally less expensive compared to the traditional neural network method. The computational cost of LBP was presented by Li Liu, Paul Fieguth, Xiaogang Wang, Matti Pietik äinen, and Dewen Hu in their paper *Evaluation of LBP and Deep Texture Descriptors with A New Robustness Benchmark*. The details of the paper can be found in the here: `https://www.ee.cuhk.edu.hk/~xgwang/papers/liuFWPHeccv16.pdf`

The authors determined the computational cost in terms of average time spent on the feature extraction of 480 images that were 128 x 128 in size on a 2.9 GHz Intel Quad-Core CPU with 16 GB RAM. The time does not include training time. The study found that LBP feature extraction was very fast compared to AlexNet and VGG, which are considered moderate.

Applying LBP to texture recognition

Now that we know the basics of LBP, we will apply it to a texture recognition example. For this example, 11 trained images and 7 test images that are 50 x 50 in size have been developed into the following classes:

- **Trained image**
    - Pattern image (7)
    - Plain image (4)
- **Test image**
    - Pattern image (4)
    - Plain image (3)

Steps 1 through *5* from the *Generating an LBP pattern* section are applied, and then each test image's LBP histogram is compared with all of the trained images to find the best match. Although different histogram comparison methods have been used, for this analysis, the Chi-Square test is going to be used as the principal method for determining the match. The final summary output with correct matches is shown with a green line, whereas incorrect matches will be shown with a red line. The solid line is the first match with a minimum distance, while the dotted line is the next best match. If the distance between the histogram for the next best match is much further away than the minimum distance, then only one value (minimum distance) is shown, indicating that the system has pretty high confidence for this output.

The following image shows the matching process between the test and training grayscale images using LBP. The solid line represents the closest match, while the dotted line represents the second closest match. The third test image (from the left) has only one match, meaning the model is very confident about its prediction when an image is converted into grayscale. The second, third, and sixth training images (from the right) have no corresponding test image matches:

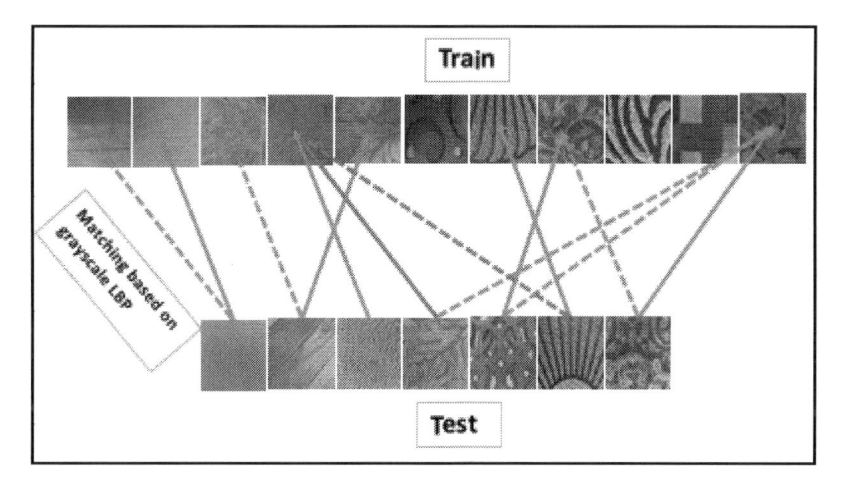

Here, we can see that, in general, LBP results in pretty good matches based on limited training data (11 samples), with only one error out of the seven test samples that were considered. To understand how the correlation was done in the preceding image, we need to draw the LBP histogram and compare the histogram between the training and test images. The following image analyzes each of the test images and compares their histograms with the histograms of the corresponding test images for the closest match.

`n_points = 25` implies 25 points in the LBP. The key advantage of using an LBP histogram is for the normalization of translation, thus making them rotation invariant. We will go through the analysis of each histogram one by one. The *x* axis of the histograms is 25, showing the number of points (25), while the *y* axis is the LBP histogram bins.

The two images shown in the following image both have patterns and appear to be similar:

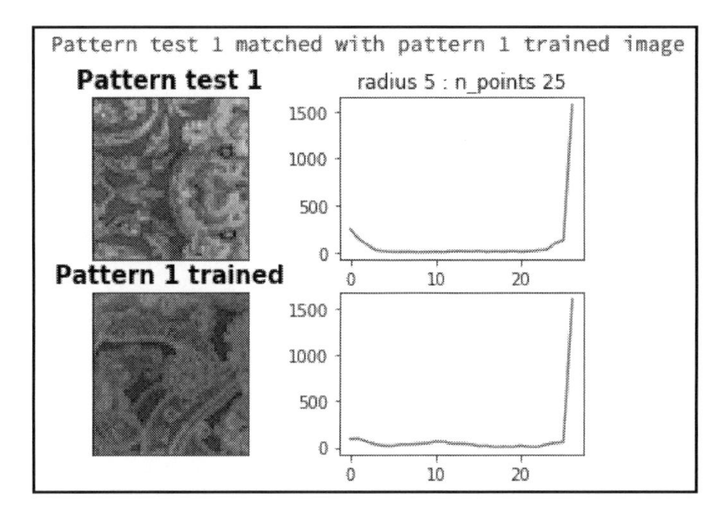

The histogram analysis of the preceding images shows a similar pattern, showing the correct match using LBP. The two images shown in the following image both have patterns and appear to be similar. Actually, they are the same image of a carpet taken from different orientations and different light shadings:

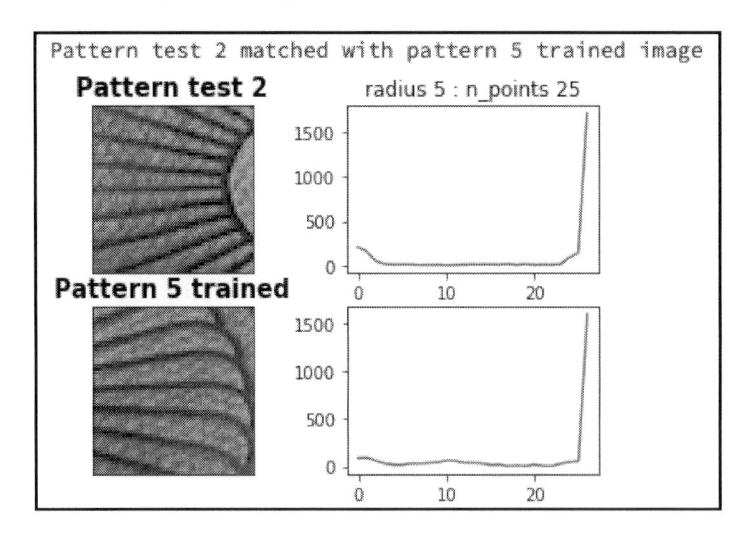

The histogram analysis of the preceding images shows a similar pattern, showing the correct match using LBP. The two images shown in the following image have patterns, but they are from different carpets:

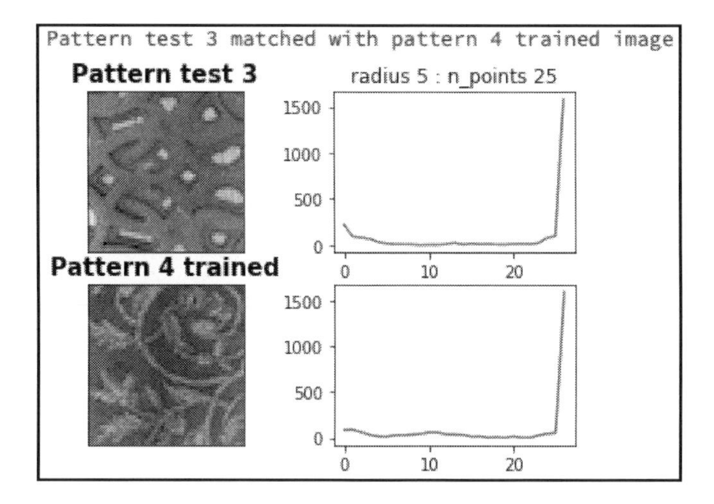

The histogram analysis of the preceding images shows a similar pattern. Their patterns appear similar, but the images are actually different. So, this is an example of a poor match.

The first image in the following image has a pattern (it is a weak pattern compared to what we have seen already) and the trained image has no pattern at all but appears to have a stain in the carpet:

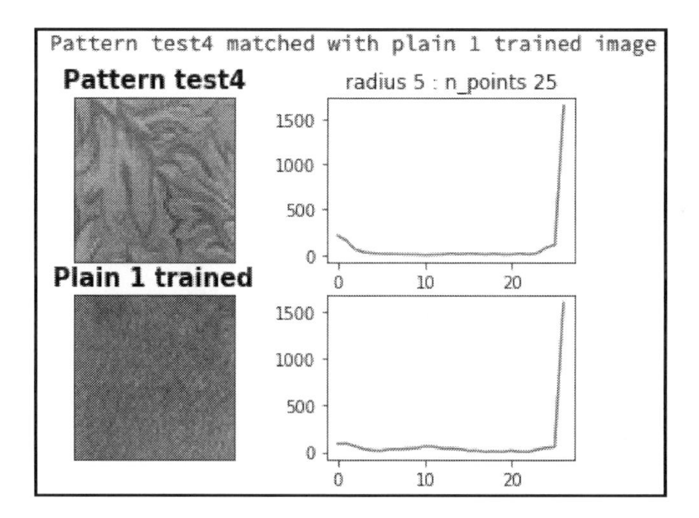

The histogram analysis of the preceding images shows a similar pattern. Their patterns appear similar, but the images are actually different. This is another example of a poor match. LBP appears to think the images are similar due to the stain on the red carpet.

The following image shows that the LBP matched a gray carpet with the same preceding red carpet:

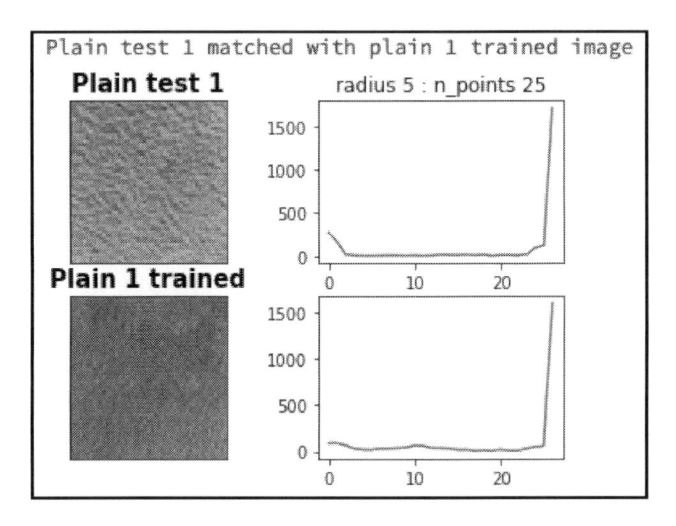

The LBP histogram shows a similar trend – this is justifiable as LBP is a grayscale image recognition technique.

The following image shows that the LBP matches a hardwood floor with a carpet:

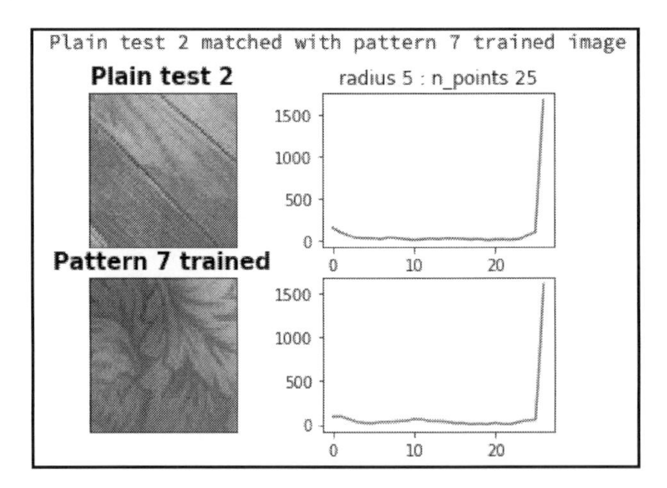

Note that the train image did not have a hardwood floor, so LBP found the carpet with a leaf shape as the next closest match to the wooden floor with the grain.

The last LBP image shows similar images with little to no pattern:

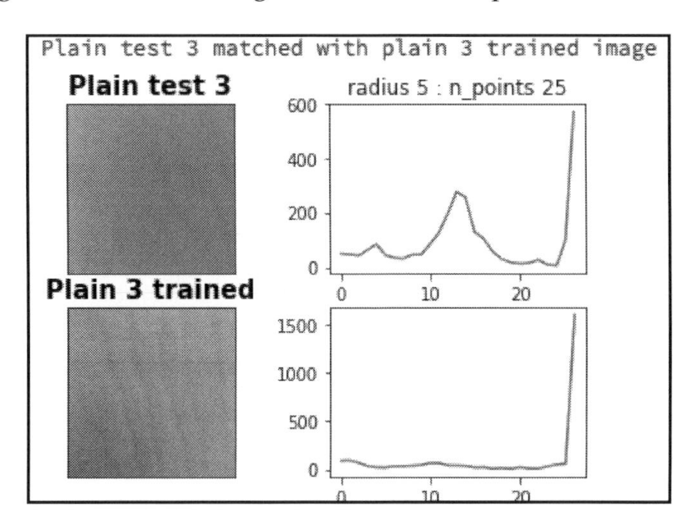

Here, the LBP prediction appears to be correct.

Compare the top histogram with the histogram at the bottom to visualize how the histograms compare between the test and trained images. The detailed Python code for this can be found at `https://github.com/PacktPublishing/Mastering-Computer-Vision-with-TensorFlow-2.0/blob/master/Chapter02/Chapter2_LBPmatching_texture.ipynb`.

Matching face color with foundation color – LBP and its limitations

Since we've had relatively good success using LBP in regards to texture recognition, let's try another example to understand the limitations of LBP. For this example, seven face colors from light to dark (test) will be matched with 10 foundation colors (train), which are images that are 50 x 50 in size.

Similar to the texture recognition examples, *Steps 1* through *5* from the *Generating an LBP pattern* section will be applied and then each face color image LBP histogram will be compared with all of the foundation color image LBP histograms to find the best match. Although different histogram comparison methods have been used, for this analysis, the Chi-Square test will be used as the principal method for determining the match. The final summary output can be seen in the following image:

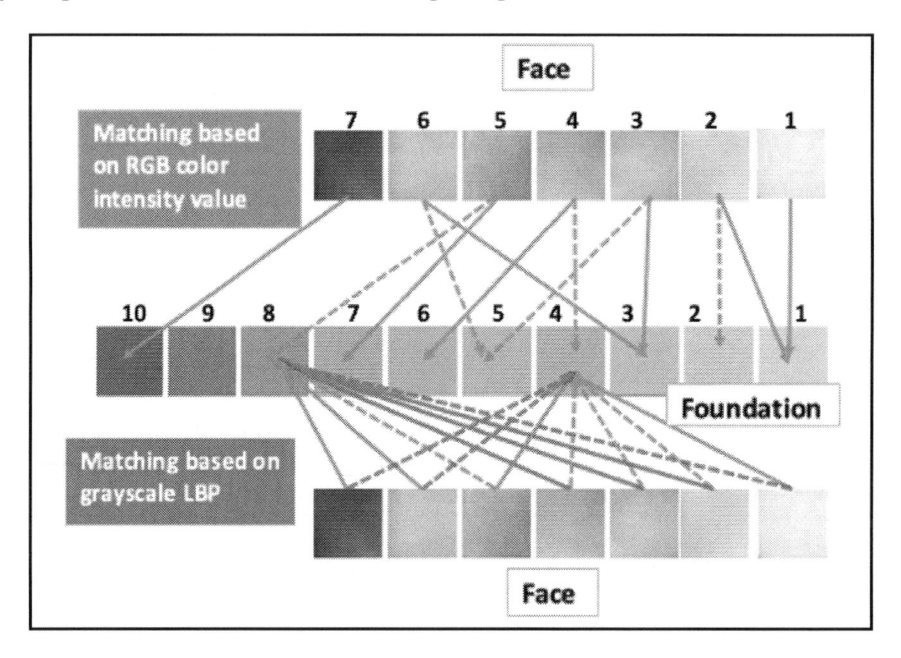

As we can see, the LBP provides poor results, with all the face colors resulting in either foundation color 4 or 8. To understand why this is the case, RGB, grayscale, and two levels of LBP image (one with R2.5, P12 and the other one with R5.5, P20) have been plotted. This is caused by two factors:

- RGB to grayscale conversion of face colors causes unnecessary brightness in the image, which is misleading during the comparison process.
- LBP conversion takes those patterns and generates arbitrary gray shades that can't be interpreted properly.

The following image shows two images – Face colors 1 and 7 – which represent fair and dark skin colors, as well as the result of the different steps of LBP. Each image is converted into grayscale, which shows both images have a bright spot in the middle that couldn't be seen from the original color image. Then, two LBP operations are applied to the image: one with a radius of 2.5 and the other with a radius of 5.5. Here, we can see there are considerable similarities after applying LBP, which was not expected from the original colored image. Let's have a look at the following image:

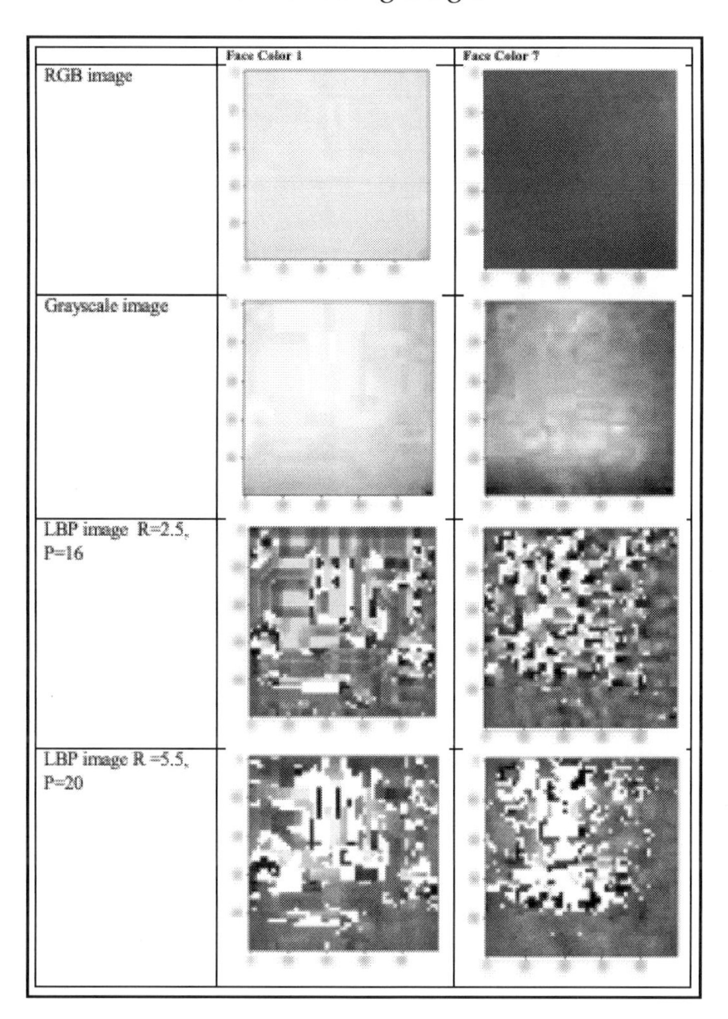

A possible fix for the first issue will be to apply Gaussian filtering, which we studied in `Chapter 1`, *Computer Vision and TensorFlow Fundamentals*,to suppress the pattern. The result of applying the Gaussian filter and then LBP can be seen in the following image:

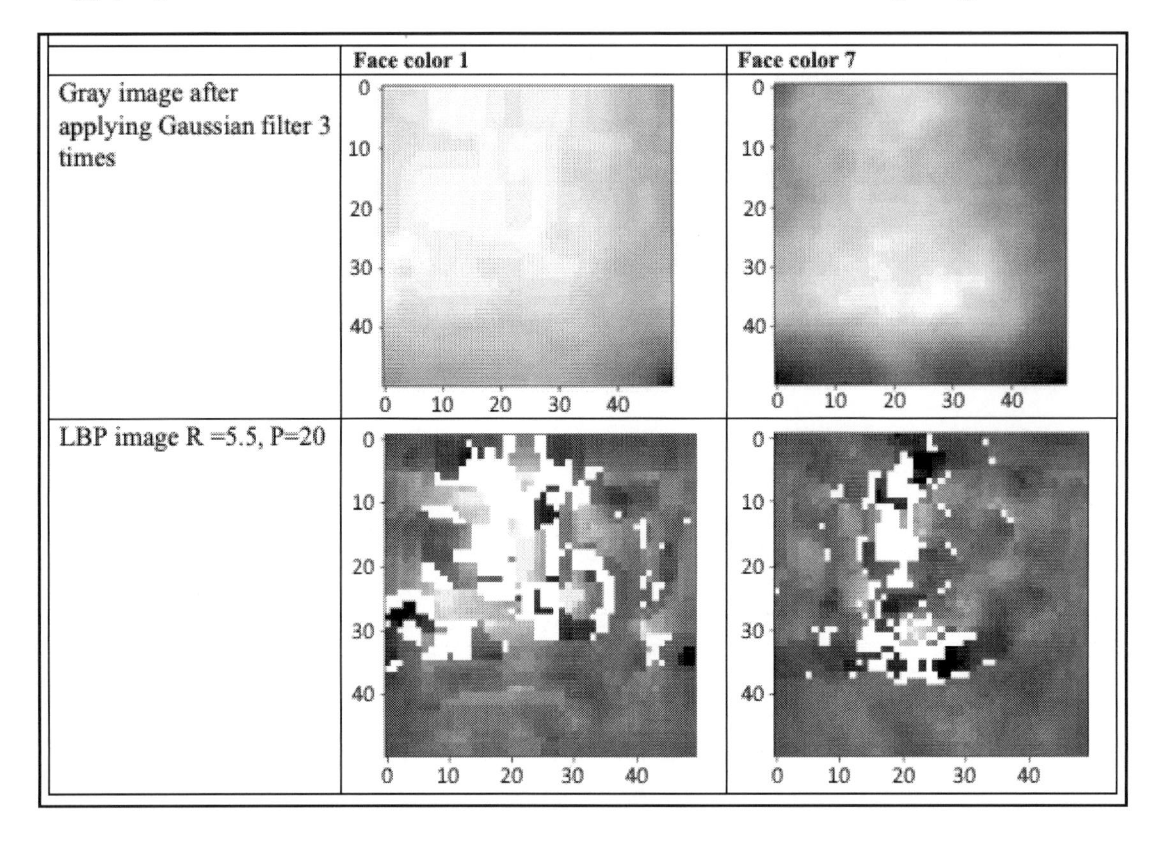

Even after applying the filter, the two shades of gray, from light and dark, can't be clearly distinguished. From this, we can conclude that LBP is not a good method for face color recognition.

Matching face color with foundation color – color matching technique

For this method, the RGB image is not converted into grayscale; instead, the color intensity value of each of the seven face colors and 10 foundation colors is determined using the following Python code (repeated for each case):

```
facecol1img = Image.open('/.../faceimage/facecol1.JPG')
facecol1arr = np.asarray(facecol1img)
(mfc1, sfc1) = cv2.meanStdDev(facecol1arr)
statfc1 = np.concatenate([mfc1, sfc1]).flatten()
print ("%s statfc1" %(statfc1))
```

The output has six elements. The first three are mean RGB values, while the next three are standard deviations of the RGB value.

The intensity difference between face and foundation color is calculated as follows:

$$\Delta I(face(i), found(j)) = 0.299 * (IfaceR - IfoundR) + 0.587 * (IfaceG - IfoundG) + 0.114 * (IfaceB - IfoundB)$$

Let's have a look at the following image, which represents the face and foundation color:

		Face color						
		1	2	3	4	5	6	7
Foundation color	1	18.4	1.9	19.6	32.2	48.3	18.1	135.8
	2	27.6	7.3	10.4	23.0	39.1	8.9	126.6
	3	36.5	16.3	1.5	14.1	30.2	0.1	117.7
	4	51.6	31.4	13.6	1.0	15.1	15.1	102.6
	5	46.3	26.0	8.3	4.3	20.5	9.8	107.9
	6	51.2	31.0	13.2	0.6	15.5	14.7	103.0
	7	58.3	38.1	20.3	7.7	8.4	21.9	95.9
	8	77.4	57.2	39.4	26.8	10.7	40.9	76.8
	9	95.6	75.4	57.6	45.0	28.9	59.2	58.6
	10	127.2	107.0	89.2	76.6	60.5	90.8	27.0

The value with the smallest difference in the matrix is the best match. We can see that for each face color, the matching (as shown by the most minimum value points lying across the diagonal) results in a reasonable value, indicating that the color matching technique should be the preferred method for face color-matching with foundation color.

Summary

In this chapter, we learned how to take an image pixel and threshold it with its neighboring pixels within a given radius and then perform a binary and integral operation to create an LBP pattern. The LBP pattern is a good example of unsupervised machine learning as we did not train the classifier with the output; instead, we learned how to adjust the parameters of LBP (radius and number of points) to arrive at the correct output. LBP was found to be a very powerful and simple tool for texture classification. However, when the image was non-textured, LBP did not return good results and we learned how to develop an RGB color matching model to match colored non-textured images such as face and foundation color. To create an LBP representation, the image has to be converted into grayscale.

In the next chapter, we will introduce the concept of the integral image by combining various edge detection methods to recognize faces, eyes, and ears. We will then introduce the convolution neural network and use it to determine facial key points and facial expressions.

3
Facial Detection Using OpenCV and CNN

Facial detection is an important part of computer vision and is an area that has seen significant growth in recent years. In this chapter, you will start with the simple concept of Viola-Jones face- and key-feature detection and move on to the advanced concept of the neural-network-based facial key points and facial expressions detection. The chapter will end by looking at the advanced concept of 3D face detection.

The chapter will cover the following topics:

- Applying Viola-Jones AdaBoost learning and the Haar cascade classifier for face recognition
- Predicting facial key points using deep neural network
- Predicting facial expressions using CNN
- Overview of 3D face detection

Applying Viola-Jones AdaBoost learning and the Haar cascade classifier for face recognition

In 2001, Paul Viola of Microsoft Research and Michael Jones of Mitsubishi Electric developed a revolutionary method of detecting faces in an image by developing a classifier called the **Haar cascade classifier** `https://www.face-rec.org/algorithms/Boosting-Ensemble/16981346.pdf`. The Haar cascade classifier is based on Haar features, which are the sum of the difference of pixel values in a rectangular region. The magnitude of the difference value is calibrated to indicate the characteristics of a given region in the face—for example, nose, eyes, and so on. The final detector has 38 cascade classifiers with 6,060 features consisting of about 4,916 face images and 9,500 non-face images. The total training time was several months, but the detection time was very fast.

First, the image is transformed from RGB to grayscale, then image filtering and segmentation are applied so that the classifier can quickly detect the object. In the following sections, we 'll learn how to construct the Haar cascade classifier.

Selecting Haar-like features

The Haar cascade classifier algorithm is based on the idea that the image of a human face has distinctive features of intensity in different regions of the face—for example, the eye region of a face is darker than the bottom of the eyelid and the nose region is brighter than the two facial regions next to it. A Haar-like feature is represented by black and white adjacent rectangles, as shown in the following image. In this image, there are several potential Haar-like features (two-rectangle, three-rectangle, and four-rectangle features):

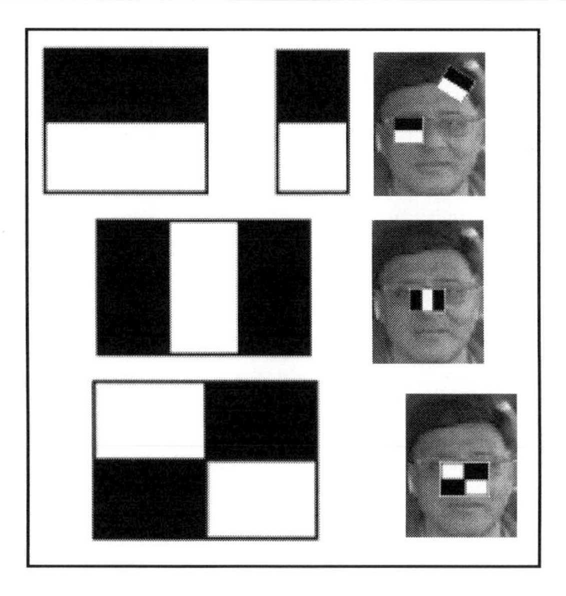

Note that the rectangle section is placed over the characteristic feature of the face. As the intensity of the eye region is darker than the face, the black region of the rectangle goes near the eye and the white region goes below the eye. Similarly, as the nose region is brighter than its surroundings, the white rectangle goes on the nose and the black rectangles rest on the two sides.

Creating an integral image

Integral images are used to calculate rectangular feature pixel values very quickly in one pass. To understand integral images better, let's look at the following breakdown of its calculation:

- The value of the Haar like feature can be calculated as the difference between sum of the pixel values in the white region and the sum of the pixel values in the black region.
- The sum of the pixel $I(x,y)$ can be represented by the value of all of the pixels to the left and above the current pixel location $i(x,y)$, including the current pixel value, and can be represented as follows:

$$I(x,y) = I(x-1,y) + I(x,y-1) - I(x-1,y-1) + i(x,y)$$

In the following image, *I(x,y)* is the final integral image value consisting of nine-pixel values (*62, 51, 51, 111, 90, 77, 90, 79,* and *73*). Summing all of these gives a value of 684:

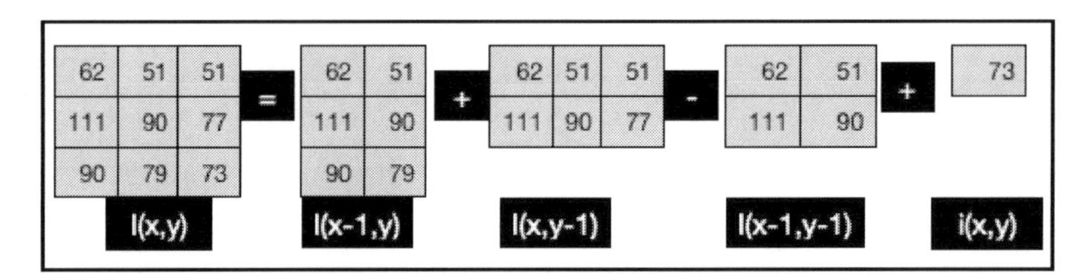

The following figure shows the pixel intensity of the eye region of the face and the corresponding integral image:

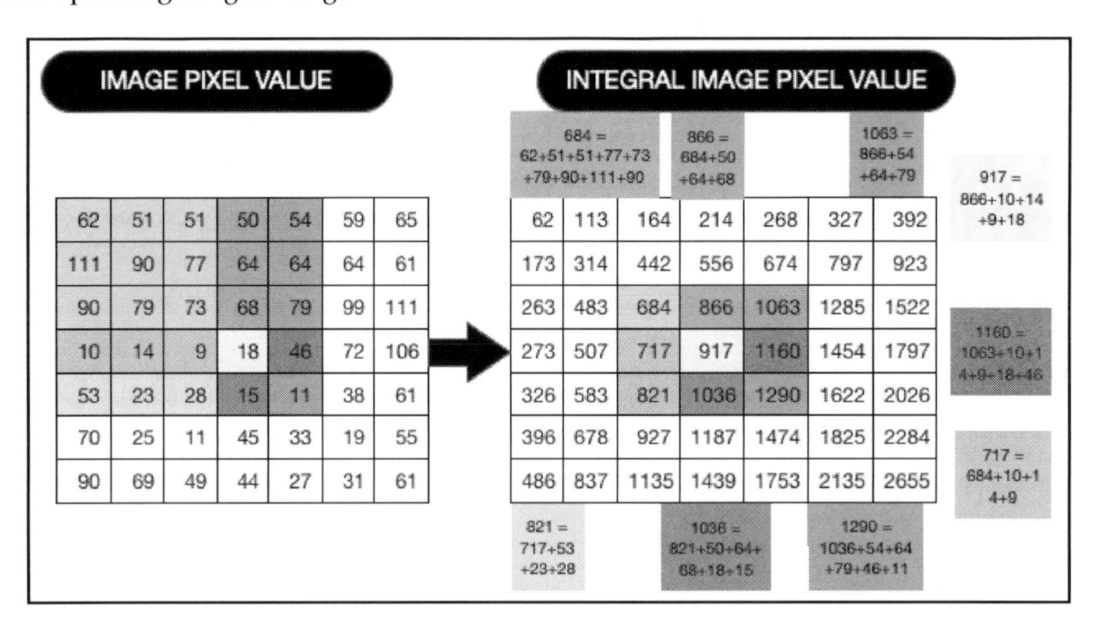

The preceding figure shows that the sum of the pixel intensity of the rectangular region is obtained by summing all pixel values that are above and to the left—for example, *917* is obtained by summing *866* (which is the sum of *73, 79, 90, 111,...68,* clockwise) and *10, 14, 9,* and *18*. Note that *917* can also be obtained by summing *717* and then adding to it the sum of *50, 64, 68,* and *18*.

The sum of the preceding pixel equation can be rewritten as follows:

$$i(x,y) = I(x,y) + I(x-1,y-1) - I(x-1,y) - I(x,y-1)$$

In the integral image, the area for any rectangular region in the image can be computed by summing the four arrays (as shown in the preceding equation) as opposed to six memory accesses for a sum of all individual pixels. The Haar classifier rectangular sum can be obtained from the preceding equation, as shown in the following equation:

$$\sum_{x=xa}^{xb}\sum_{y=ya}^{yb} i(x,y) = I(x_b, y_b) + I(x_a - 1, y_a - 1) - I(x_a - 1, y_b) - I(x_b, y_a - 1)$$

The preceding equation can be rearranged as follows:

$$=> \sum_{x=xa}^{xb}\sum_{y=ya}^{yb} i(x,y) = (I(x_b, y_b) \; - \; I(x_b, y_a - 1)) \; - (I(x_a - 1, y_b) - I(x_a - 1, y_a - 1))$$

The following figure shows the image pixel value converted to an integral image pixel value:

IMAGE PIXEL VALUE

62	51	51	50	54	59	65
111	90	77	64	64	64	61
90	79	73	68	79	99	111
10	14	9	18	46	72	106
53	23	28	15	11	38	61
70	25	11	45	33	19	55
90	69	49	44	27	31	61

SUM of Haar features = 77 +64 + 64 + 73 + 68 + 79 = 425

SUM of Haar features = 9 +18 + 46 + 28 + 15 + 11 = 127

INTEGRAL IMAGE PIXEL VALUE

62	113	164	214	268	327	392
173	314	442	556	674	797	923
263	483	684	866	1063	1285	1522
273	507	717	917	1160	1454	1797
326	583	821	1036	1290	1622	2026
396	678	927	1187	1474	1825	2284
486	837	1135	1439	1753	2135	2655

SUM of Haar features using integral image = (1063-268) - (483-113) = 425

SUM of Haar features using integral image = (1290-1063)-(583-483) = 127

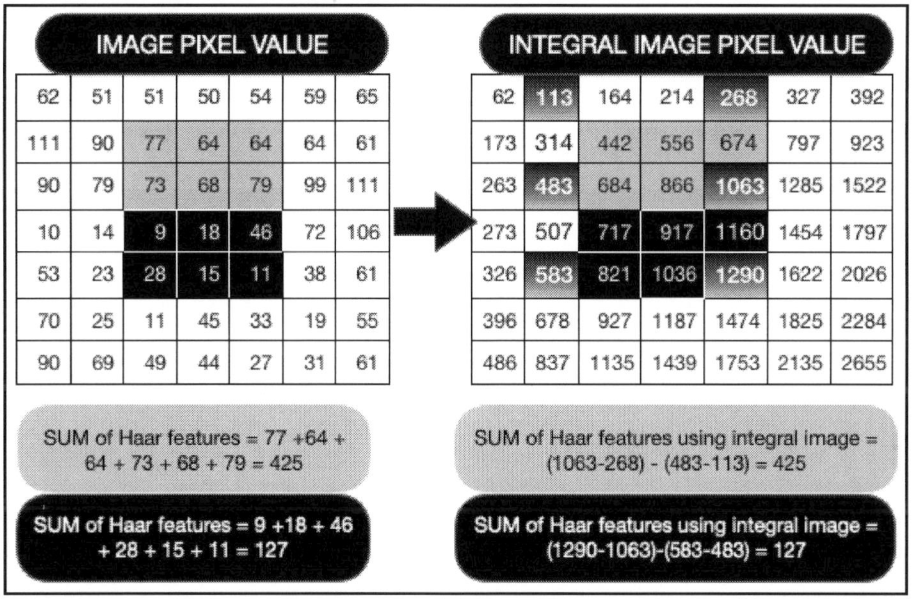

The integral image on the right is just the sum of the pixel value of the left—so 113 = 62 + 51, and so on. The black shaded area pixel value represents the black Haar rectangle as described previously. To calculate the intensity value in the light shaded area, we take the integral intensity value of, say, 1,063 and subtract 268 from it.

Running AdaBoost training

The image is divided into T windows where Haar-like features are applied and their value is calculated as described previously. AdaBoost builds a strong classifier from a large number of weak classifiers by iterating over a training set of T windows. At each iteration, the weights of the weak classifier are adjusted based on a number of positive samples (faces) and a number of negative samples (non-faces) to evaluate the number of misclassified items. Then, for the next iteration, the weights of the misclassified item are assigned a higher weight to increase the likelihood of these being detected. The final strong classifier $h(x)$ is a combination of weak classifiers weighted according to their error.

- **Weak classifier**: Each weak classifier takes a single feature, f. It has a polarity, p, and a threshold, θ:

$$h(x, f, p, \theta) = \begin{cases} 1, & pf(x) < p(\theta) \\ 0, & else \end{cases}$$

- **Strong classifier**: The final strong classifier, $h(x)$, has the lowest error, E_t, and is given by the following:

$$h(x) = \begin{cases} 1, & \sum_{t=1}^{T} \alpha_t h_t \geq \frac{1}{2} \sum_{t=1}^{T} \alpha_t \\ 0, & else \end{cases}$$

Here, $\alpha_t = \log(1/\beta_t)$ and $\beta_t = E_t / (1-E_t)$:

$$E_t = \frac{1}{T} \sum_{t=1}^{T} w_t \left| h(x) - y_t \right|$$

The weight (W_t) is initialized as follows:

$$W_t = \begin{cases} \frac{1}{2P}, y_t = 1 \\ \frac{1}{2N}, y_t = 0 \end{cases}$$

Here, P and N are the numbers of positive and negative samples respectively. The weight value is updated as follows:

$$W_{t+1,i} = W_{t,i} \cdot \beta_t^{1-E_i}$$

Each weak classifier computes one feature. Note that the weak classifier cannot do the classification by itself, but several of them combined can classify well.

Attentional cascade classifiers

Each of the strong classifiers previously described forms a cascade where each weak classifier represents one stage to quickly remove the negative subwindow and retain the positive subwindow. A positive response from the first classifier implies that the region of the face (for example, the eye region) has been detected and then the algorithm moves on to the next feature (for example, the nose region) to trigger the evaluation of a second classifier, and so on. A negative outcome at any point leads to the immediate rejection of the stage. The following image illustrates this point:

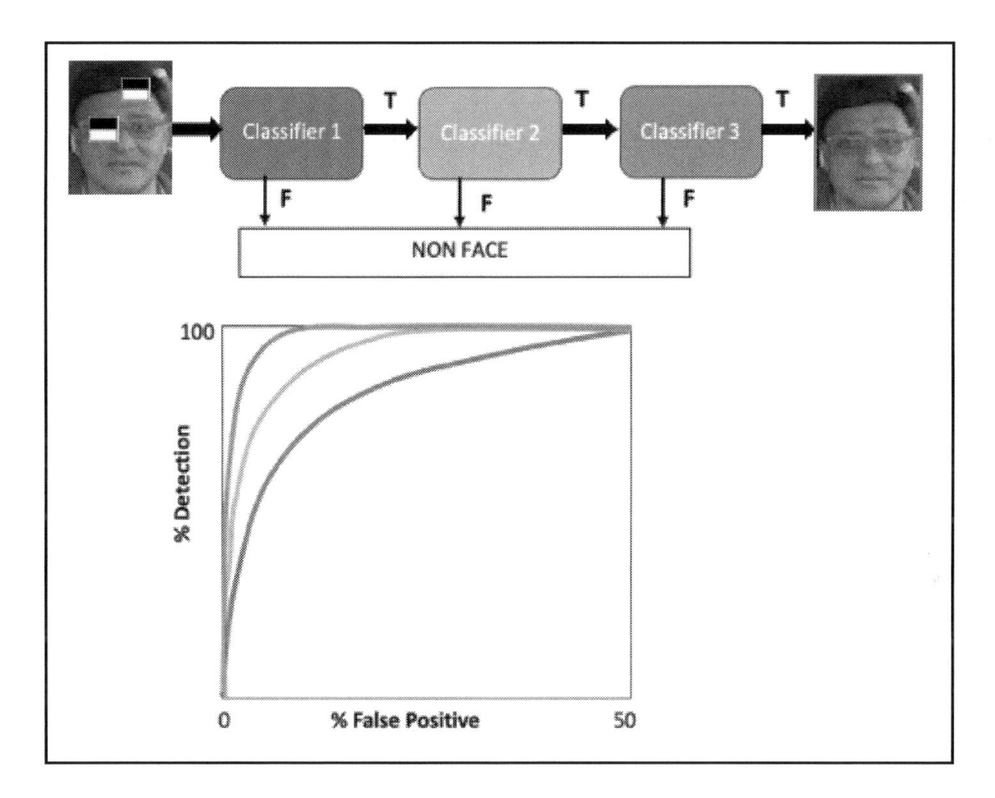

This image shows that the negative feature is eliminated right away. As the classification moves from left to right, its accuracy increases.

Training the cascade detector

The overall training system was developed to maximize the detection rate and minimize the false-positive rate. Viola and Jones achieved this by setting the target detection rate and false-positive rate for each stage of the cascade detector as follows:

- The number of features in each layer of the cascade detector is increased until the target detection rate and the false-positive targets are achieved for that layer.
- Another stage is added if the overall false-positive rate is not low enough.
- A rectangular feature is added to the current stage until its target rates have been met.
- The false-positive target from the current stage is used as a negative training set for the next stage.

The following image shows an OpenCV Python Haar cascade classifier for frontal faces and eyes to detect a face and eyes. Both left and right images show that it can detect the face correctly; however, in the first image, only the right eye is detected because of the glare in the left eye, whereas both eyes are detected in the second image. The Viola-Jones cascade detection method looks for an intensity gradient (where the eye region is darker than the region below) and in this case, it can't detect it in the right eye because of the glare in the right lens of the glasses:

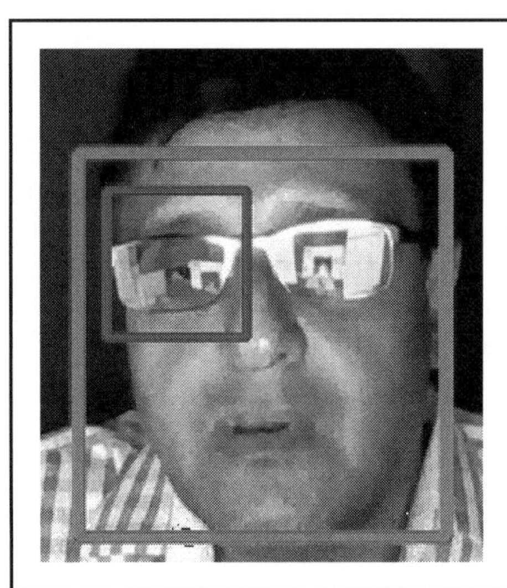

The OpenCV Python code for face and eye detection in a webcam video can be found at `https://github.com/PacktPublishing/Mastering-Computer-Vision-with-TensorFlow-2.0/blob/master/Chapter03/Chapter3_opencv_face%26eyedetection_video.ipynb`. Note that in order for the code to work, you need to specify the path where the Haar cascade detector is located in your folder.

So far, we have learned about the Haar cascade classifier and how to use built-in OpenCV code to apply the Haar cascade classifier for face and eye detection. The preceding concepts are based on detecting Haar-like features using an integral image. This method is well suited for face, eye, mouth, and nose detection; however, different facial expressions and textures of the skin can be used for mood (happy versus sad) or age determination, and so on. The Viola-Jones method is not well suited to handle these varieties of different facial expressions, and so we need to use the Viola-Jones method for face detection and then apply the neural network to determine facial key points within the face's bounding box. In the next section, we will learn this method in detail.

Predicting facial key points using a deep neural network

In this section, we will discuss the end-to-end pipeline for facial key-point detection. Facial key-point detection is a challenge for computer vision as it requires the system to detect the face and obtain meaningful key point data, plotting this data on the face and developing a neural network to predict the key-points on the face. This is a difficult problem compared to object detection or image classification, as it first requires facial detection within a bounding box and then key-point detection. Normal object detection just involves the detection of four points representing the four corners of the rectangular bounding box around the object, but key-point detection requires multiple points (more than 10) at various orientations. Extensive key-point detection data and a tutorial on its use can be found at `https://www.kaggle.com/c/facial-keypoints-detection`. The Kaggle key point detection challenge involves a CSV file containing links to 7,049 images (96 x 96), each containing 15 key-points.

We will not use Kaggle data in this section but will show you how to prepare your own data for key-point detection. Detailed information on the model can be found at `https://github.com/PacktPublishing/Mastering-Computer-Vision-with-TensorFlow-2.0/blob/master/Chapter03/Chapter3_face%20keypoint_detection.ipynb`.

Preparing the dataset for key-point detection

In this section, you will learn how to create your own data. This involves writing code and executing it so that the webcam in your PC lights up. Move your face to different positions and orientations and hit the spacebar and it will save an image of your face after cropping everything else out from the image. The key steps for this process are as follows:

1. First, we begin by specifying the path to the Haar cascade classifier. This should be located in your `OpenCV/haarcascades` directory. There will be many `.xml` files located there, so include the path for `frontalface_default.xml`:

```
face_cascade = cv2.CascadeClassifier('path
tohaarcascade_frontalface_default.xml')
```

2. Next, we will define the webcam operation using the `videoCapture(0)` statement. If you have an external camera plugged into your PC, you can use `videoCapture(1)`:

```
cam = cv2.VideoCapture(0)
```

3. The camera frame reads data using `cam.read()` and then within each frame, the face is detected using the Haar cascade detector defined in *Step 1*. A bounding box is drawn around the detected face with `(x,y,w,h)` parameters. Using the `cv2.imshow` parameter, only the detected face is shown on the screen:

```
while(True):
    ret, frame = cam.read()
    faces = face_cascade.detectMultiScale(frame, 1.3, 5)
    for (x,y,w,h) in faces:
        if w >130:
            detected_face = frame[int(y):int(y+h), int(x):int(x+w)]
            cv2.imshow("test", detected_face)
    if not ret:
        break
    k = cv2.waitKey(1)
```

4. Next, the image is resized to `img_size`, which is defined as `299`, and the resulting image is saved in your dataset directory. Note that we use image size of `299` for this exercise, but this can be changed. But if you do decide to change it, make sure that you change it in the annotation file creation as well as in the final model to avoid a mismatch between the annotation and images. Now create a folder called `dataset` in the directory where this Python code exists. Note that each time you hit the spacebar, the image file number will be auto-incremented:

```
faceresize = cv2.resize(detected_face, (img_size,img_size))
        img_name =
"dataset/opencv_frame_{}.jpg".format(img_counter)
        cv2.imwrite(img_name, faceresize)
```

Create about 100 or more images (for this test, I took a total of 57 images) for different people with different facial orientations. If you have more images, then the detection will be better. Note that the Kaggle face point detection uses 7,049 images. Take all the images and perform face key-point annotation using the VGG annotator, which you can get from `http://www.robots.ox.ac.uk/~vgg/software/via/`. You can use another annotation tool of your choice, but I find that this tool (which is free) is very helpful. It plots the bounding box, as well as irregular shape and draw points. For this exercise, I loaded all my images and used the point marker to draw 16 points in the image, as illustrated in the following image:

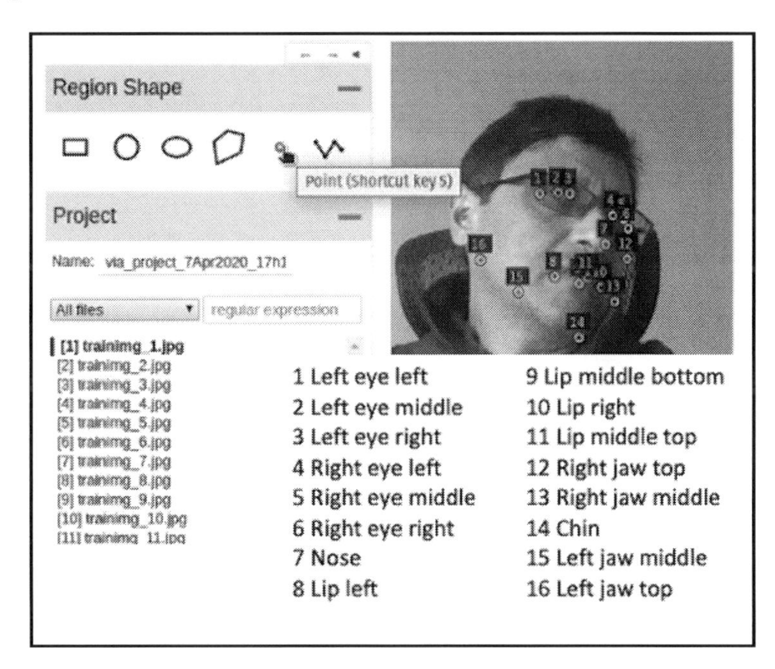

The 16 points in the preceding image represent the left eye (1–3), right eye (4–6), nose (7), lips (8–11), and outer face (12–16). Note that when we present the image key-points as an array form, they will be represented as 0–15 rather than 1–16. For better accuracy, you can just capture an image of the face rather than any of its surroundings.

Processing key-point data

The VGG annotator tool generates an output CSV file that needs to be preprocessed twice to generate the (x,y) coordinates for each of the 16 key points for each image. This is a very important concept for large data processing that you can use for other computer vision tasks for three main reasons:

- Our Python code will not search a directory for lots of image files directly but will search the input CSV for the data path.
- For each CSV file, there are 16 corresponding key-points that need to be processed.
- This is alternative to using a Keras `ImageDataGenerator` and `flow_from_directory` method to look through each file in a directory.

To clarify this content, this section is broken down into the following two subsections:

- Preprocessing before being input into the Keras–Python code
- Preprocessing within the Keras–Python code

Let's discuss each of these in detail.

Preprocessing before being input into the Keras–Python code

The VGG annotator tool generates an output CSV file that needs to be preprocessed in a format that is acceptable by our TensorFlow code. The output of the annotation is a CSV file that shows each key-point in a row format, with 16 rows per image; we need to preprocess this file so that we have one row per image. There are 33 columns indicating 32 key point values and `1` image value, shown as follows:

$(x0,y0), (x1,y1), (x2, y2), \ldots,(x15,y15)$, image file name

You can use a custom Python program to convert this, although it is not shown here. The GitHub page includes the processed CSV file for your reference at `https://github.com/PacktPublishing/Mastering-Computer-Vision-with-TensorFlow-2.0/blob/master/Chapter03/testimgface.csv`.

Preprocessing within the Keras–Python code

In this section, we will read the CSV file as *X* and *Y* data, where *X* is the image corresponding to each filename, and *Y* has 32 values for 16 key-points coordinate. We will then slice the *Y* data into 16 *Yx* and *Yy* coordinates for each of the key-points. The detailed steps are shown as follows:

1. Read the CSV file from the previous section using the standard Python command. Here, we use two CSVs, `trainimgface.csv`, and `testimgface.csv`, located in the `faceimagestrain` directory. You can use a different folder if you want:

```
train_path = 'faceimagestrain/trainimgface.csv'
test_path = 'faceimagestrain/testimgface.csv'
train_data = pd.read_csv(train_path)
test_data = pd.read_csv(test_path)
```

2. Next, we find the column corresponding to the image file in the CSV file. In the following code, the column name for the image file is `'image'`:

```
coltrn = train_data['image']
print (coltrn.shape[0])
```

3. Next, we initialize two image arrays `imgs` and `Y_train`. We read the `train_data` array to add a path to the image column and read the image file for each of the 50 image files defined by `coltrn.shape[0]` in a `for` loop and append it to the array for the images. Each image that is read is converted to grayscale using the `OpenCV BGR2GRAY` command. Within the same `for` loop, we also read each of the 32 columns using the `training.iloc[i,:]` command and append it to the array for `Y_train`:

```
imgs = []
training = train_data.drop('image',axis = 1)
Y_train = []
for i in range (coltrn.shape[0]):
    p = os.path.join(os.getcwd(),
'faceimagestrain/'+str(coltrn.iloc[i]))
    img = cv2.imread(p, 1)
    gray_img = cv2.cvtColor(img, cv2.COLOR_BGR2GRAY)
```

```
        imgs.append(gray_img)
           y = training.iloc[i,:]
        Y_train.append(y)
```

4. This finally converts the images as a NumPy array called `X_train` using the following code, which is required for the input to the Keras model:

```
X_train = np.asarray(imgs)
Y_train = np.array(Y_train,dtype = 'float')
print(X_train.shape, Y_train.shape)
```

5. The same process is repeated for the test data. Now we have both the training and test data ready. Before proceeding, we should visualize the key-points in the image to make sure they look OK. This is done using the following command:

```
x0=Y_trainx.iloc[0,:]
y0=Y_trainy.iloc[0,:]
plt.imshow(np.squeeze(X_train[0]),cmap='gray')
plt.scatter(x0, y0,color ='red')
plt.show()
```

In the preceding code, `np.squeeze` is used to remove the last dimension, so we have only the *x* and *y* values in the image. The `plt.scatter` plots the key-points on the top of the image. The output is shown in the following image:

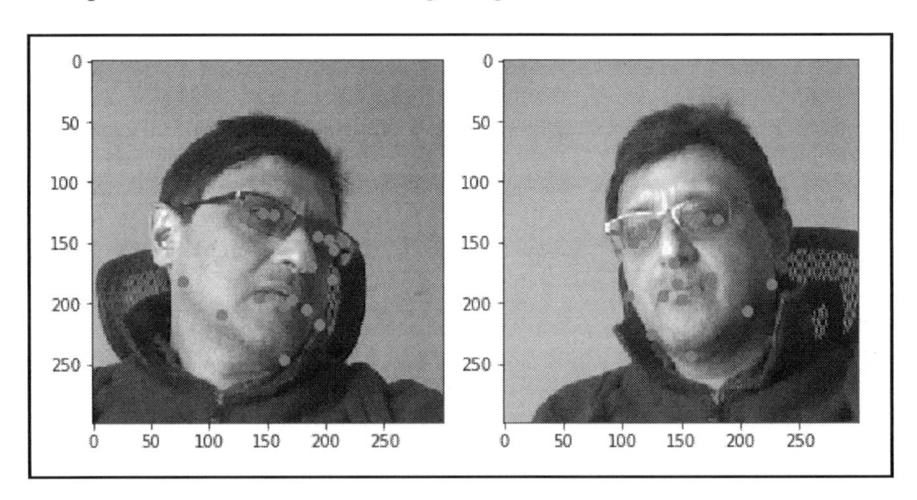

The preceding figure shows 16 key-points superimposed on the top of the image, indicating that the images and key-points are aligned. The left and right images indicate the train and test image. This visual check is critical to ensure that all the preprocessing steps do not result in incorrect face-to-key-points alignment.

Defining the model architecture

The model involves using a **convolutional neural network** (**CNN**) to process the facial image along with its 16 key-points. For details on CNNs, please refer to `Chapter 4`, *Deep Learning on Images*. The input to the CNN is train and test images, along with their key-points, and its output will be key-points corresponding to a new image. The CNN will learn to predict the key-points. Details of the model architecture are shown in the following image:

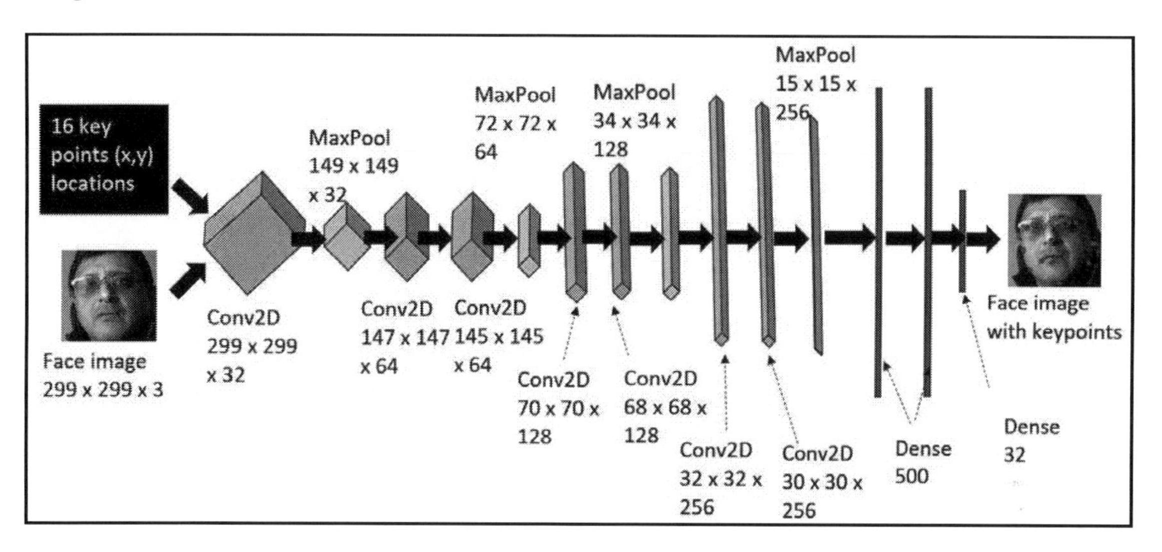

The code for the preceding model is as follows:

```
model = Sequential()
model.add(Conv2D(32, (3, 3), input_shape=(299,299,1), padding='same',
activation='relu'))
model.add(MaxPooling2D(pool_size=(2, 2)))
model.add(Conv2D(64, (3, 3), activation='relu'))
model.add(Conv2D(64, (3, 3), activation='relu'))
model.add(MaxPooling2D(pool_size=(2, 2)))
model.add(Dropout(0.2))
model.add(Conv2D(128, (3, 3), activation='relu'))
model.add(Conv2D(128, (3, 3), activation='relu'))
model.add(MaxPooling2D(pool_size=(2, 2)))
model.add(Dropout(0.2))
model.add(Conv2D(256, (3, 3), activation='relu'))
model.add(Conv2D(256, (3, 3), activation='relu'))
model.add(MaxPooling2D(pool_size=(2, 2)))
model.add(Dropout(0.2))
model.add(Flatten())
```

```
model.add(Dense(500, activation='relu'))
model.add(Dense(500, activation='relu'))
model.add(Dense(32))
```

The code takes an image and applies 32 convolution filters of size (3,3) followed by activation and the max-pooling layer. It repeats the same process multiple times with an increasing number of filters followed by a flatten and dense layer. The final dense layer has 32 elements representing each of the 16 *x* and *y* values of key points that we want to predict.

Training the model to make key point predictions

Now that we have defined the model, in this subsection we will compile the model, reshape its input, and begin the training by going through the following steps:

1. We will start by defining the model loss parameter as follows:

```
adam = Adam(lr=0.001)
model.compile(adam, loss='mean_squared_error',
metrics=['accuracy'])
```

2. Then the data is reshaped to be input to the Keras model. Reshaping the data is important as Keras expects data in 4D form—# of data (50), image width, image height, 1 (grayscale):

```
batchsize = 10
X_train= X_train.reshape(50,299,299,1)
X_test= X_test.reshape(7,299,299,1)
print(X_train.shape, Y_train.shape, X_test.shape, Y_test.shape)
```

The model *X* and *Y* parameters are explained as follows:

- `X_train (50, 299, 299, 1)` # of training data, image width, image height, grayscale for 1
- `Y_train (50, 32)` # of training data, # of key points—here, we have 16 key points for *x* and *y* values, making it 32
- `X_test (7, 299, 299, 1)` # of test data, image width, image height, greyscale for 1
- `Y_test (7, 32)` # of test data, # of key points—here, we have 16 key points for *x* and *y* values, making it 32

3. Training is initiated by the `model.fit` command, as follows:

```
history = model.fit(X_train, Y_train, validation_data=(X_test,
Y_test), epochs=20, batch_size=batchsize)
```

The output of the training steps is shown in the following figure:

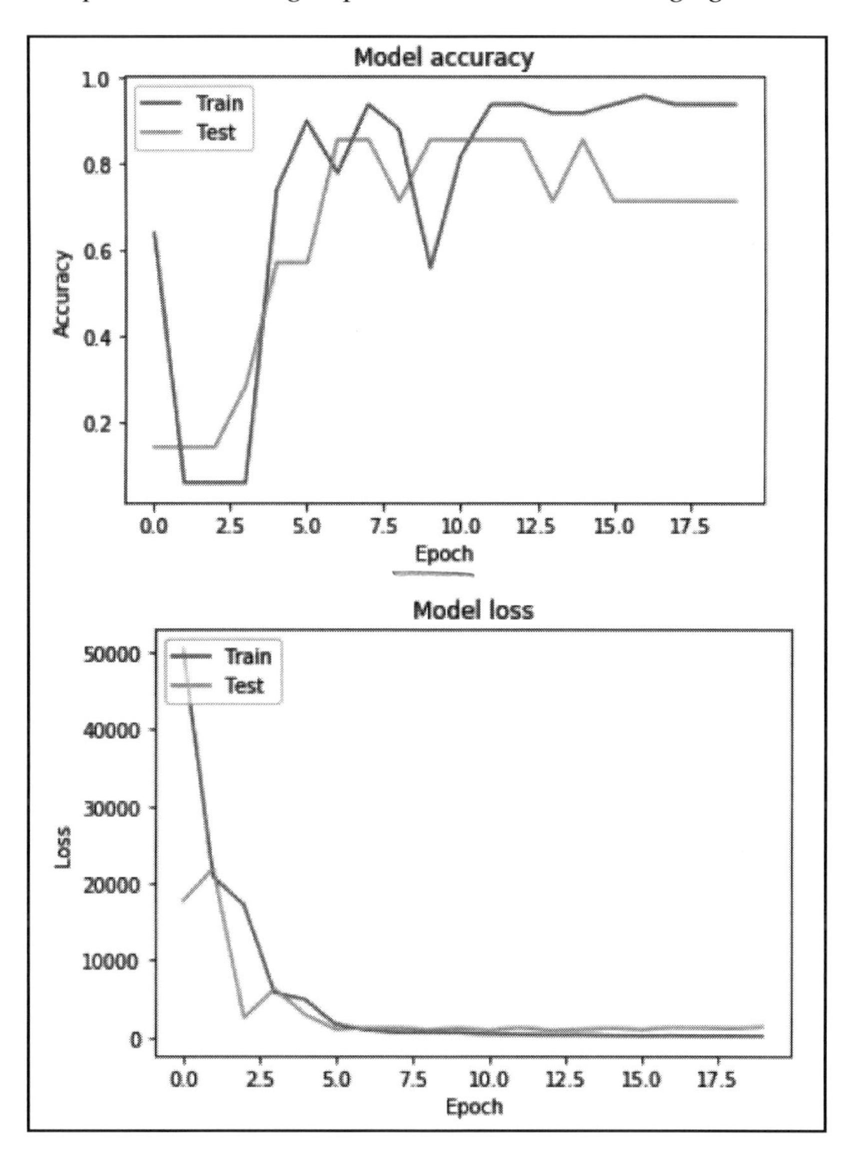

The model receives fairly good accuracy in about 10 epochs, but the loss term is about 7000. We need to collect more image data to bring the loss term to below 1:

1. We will predict the model output, `y_val`, against the test data, `X_test`, using `model.predict`. The test data, `X_test`, are images, but they are already preprocessed in an array form that the model can understand:

```
y_val = model.predict(X_test)
```

2. Note that `y_val` here has 32 points for each preprocessed image array input. Next, we break down the 32 points into *x* and *y* columns representing 16 key points:

```
yvalx = y_val[::1,::2]
yvaly = y_val[:, 1::2]
```

3. Finally, we plot the 16 key-points of our prediction on top of the image using the following code:

```
plt.imshow(np.squeeze(X_test[6]),cmap='gray')
plt.scatter(yvalx[6], yvaly[6], color = 'red')
plt.show()
```

Note that the model prediction will not be very good for 50 images; the idea here is to show you the process so that you can then build on top of this code by collecting more images. With the increasing number of images, the model accuracy will increase. Try to take images for different people and in different orientations. The technique described here can be extended to be used with body key-point detection, as described in `Chapter 9`, *Action Recognition Using Multitask Deep Learning*. Also, `Chapter 11`, *Deep Learning on Edge Devices with CPU/GPU Optimization*, has a section for OpenVINO on Raspberry Pi, where a Python code is provided to predict and display 35 facial key points based on OpenVINO toolkit pre-trained models.

Predicting facial expressions using a CNN

Facial expression recognition is a challenging problem because of the variations of faces, lighting, and expressions (mouth, the degree that the eyes are open, and so on) and also the need to develop an architecture and select parameters that can result in consistently high accuracy. This means that the challenge is to not only determine one facial expression correctly in one lighting condition for one person, but to correctly identify all facial expressions for all people with or without glasses, caps, and so on, and in all lighting conditions. The following CNN example categorizes emotion in seven different classifications: Angry, Disgusted, Afraid, Happy, Sad, Surprised, and Neutral. The steps involved in facial expression recognition are as follows:

1. Import functions—`Sequential`, `Conv2D`, `MaxPooling2D`, `AvgPooling2D`, `Dense`, `Activation`, `Dropout`, and `Flatten`.
2. Import `ImageDataGenerator`—it generates batches of tensor images with real-time augmentation (orientation).
3. Determine the batch size and epochs for the classification.
4. Dataset—train, test, and resize(48,48).
5. Establish the CNN architecture (shown in the following figure).
6. Use the `fit-generator()` function to train the model that is developed.
7. Evaluate the model.

The CNN architecture is shown in the following image:

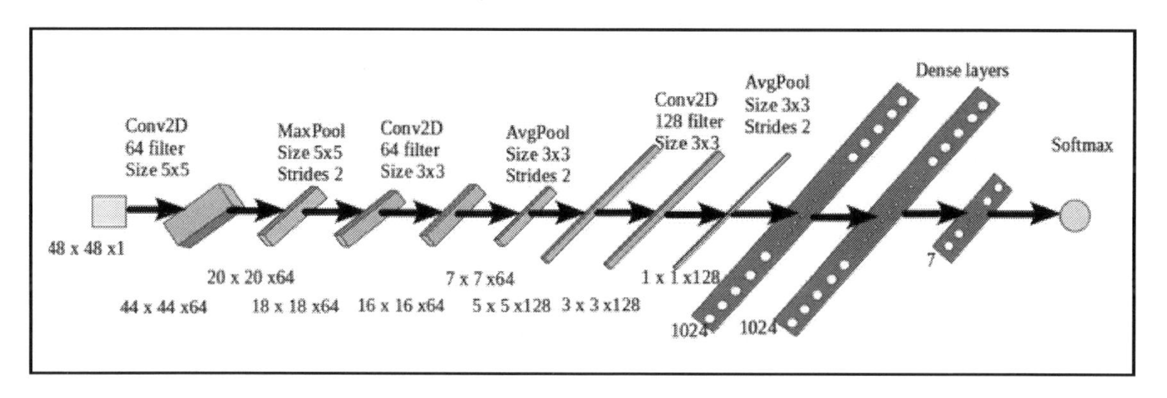

The results of the model are shown in the following image. In most cases, it is able to predict facial expressions correctly:

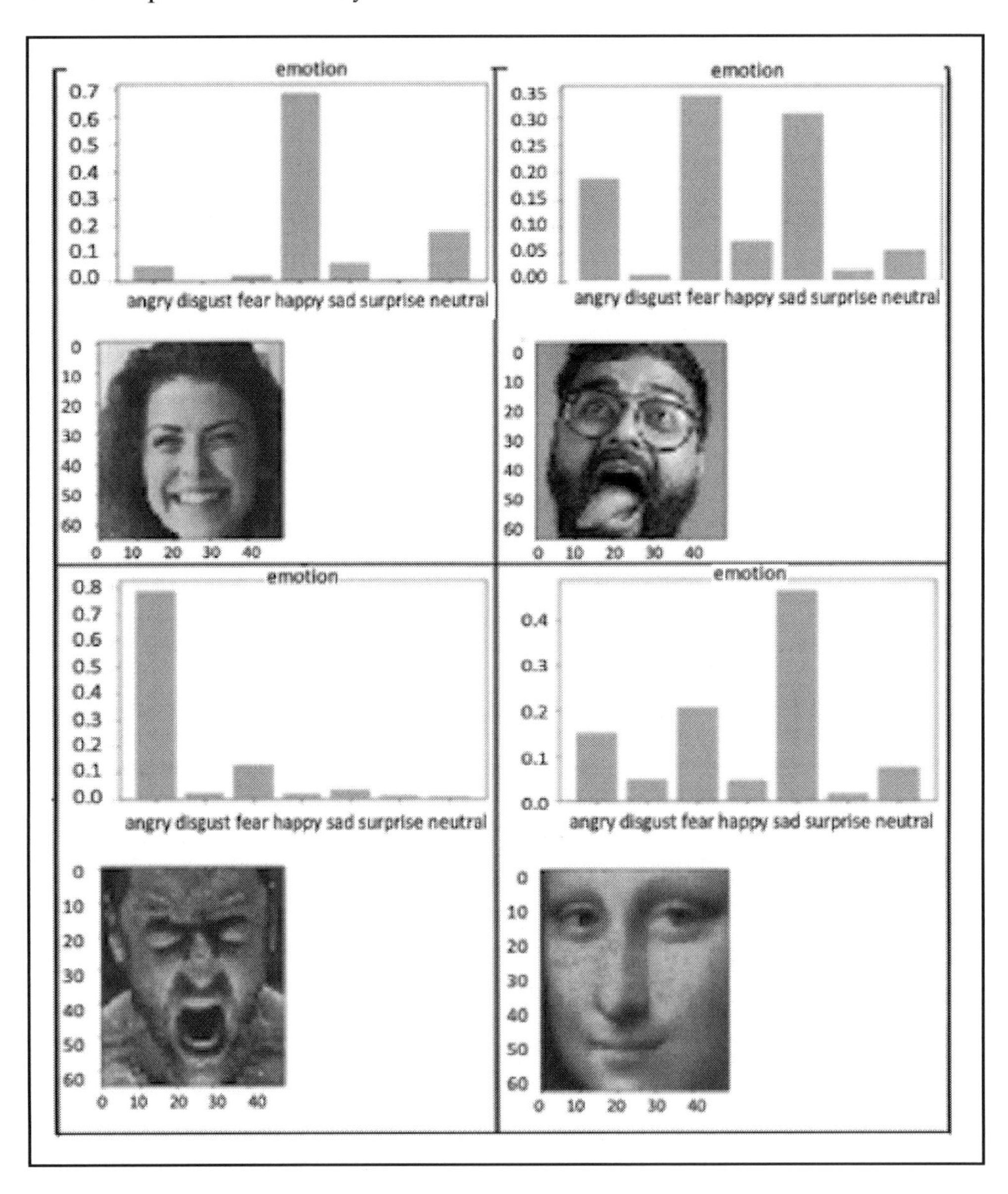

The strong emotions (smiley face or angry face) are very clearly detected. The CNN model is able to predict various emotions correctly, even subtle ones.

Overview of 3D face detection

3D face recognition involves measuring the geometry of rigid features in the face. It is typically obtained by generating 3D images using time of flight, a range camera, or getting multiple images from a 360-degree orientation of the object. A conventional 2D camera converts a 3D space into a 2D image, which is why depth sensing is one of the fundamental challenges of computer vision. Time-of-flight-based depth estimation is based on the time it takes for a light pulse to travel from a light source to the object and back to the camera. The light source and image acquisition are synchronized to get depth. Time-of-flight sensors are able to estimate full depth frames in real time. A major issue for the time of flight is the low spatial resolution. The 3D face recognition can be broken down into the following three segments:

- Overview of hardware design for 3D reconstruction
- Overview of 3D reconstruction and tracking
- Overview of parametric tracking

Overview of hardware design for 3D reconstruction

3D reconstruction involves cameras, sensors, lighting, and depth estimation. The sensors used in 3D reconstruction can be divided into three categories:

- **Multiview setups**: A calibrated dense stereo camera array with controlled illumination. From each stereo pair, the face geometry is reconstructed using triangulation and then aggregated while enforcing geometric consistency.
- **RGB camera**: Multiple RGB cameras are combined to calculate depth based on the time-of-flight approach.
- **RGBD camera**: RGBD camera captures both color and depth—some examples are Microsoft Kinect, Primesense Carmine, and Intel Realsense.

Overview of 3D reconstruction and tracking

The 3D face reconstruction involves estimating the coordinates of the 3D face from the corresponding 2D image by regressing the depth by constructing a CNN. The following image illustrates this graphically:

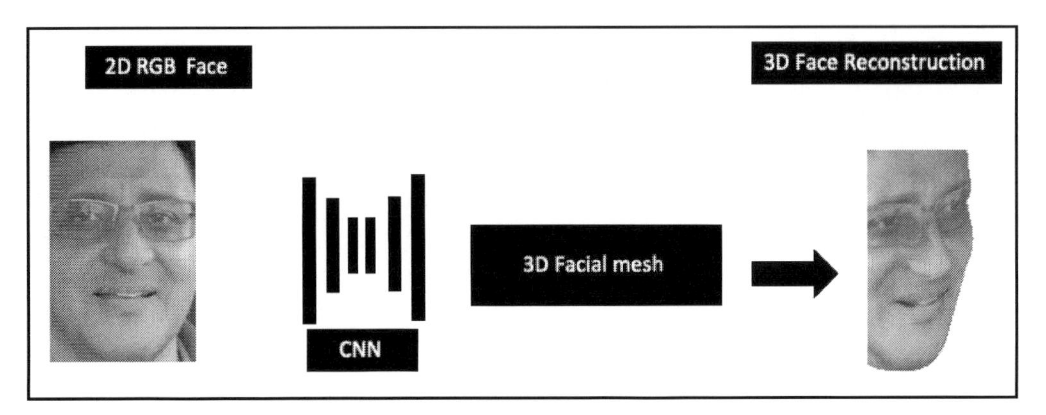

Some of the popular algorithms for real-time 3D surface mappings are described as follows:

- **Kinect Fusion**: Real-time 3D construction using a Kinect depth sensor. Kinect is a commodity sensor platform that incorporates a structured time-of-flight-based depth sensor at 30 Hz.
- **Dynamic Fusion**: Dynamic scene reconstruction system using volumetric TSDF (truncated signed distance fusion) technique using a single Kinect sensor. It takes a noisy depth map and reconstructs a real-time 3D moving scene by estimating a volumetric 6D motion field.
- **Fusion4D**: This uses multiple live RGBD cameras as input and processes multiple images using volumetric fusion along with nonrigid alignment using a dense correspondence field. The algorithm can handle large frame-to-frame motion and topology changes, such as a person removing a jacket or changing their facial orientation from left to right very quickly.
- **Motion2Fusion**: This methodology is a 360-degree performance capture system for real-time (100 frames per second) reconstruction. It is based on a nonrigid alignment strategy with learned 3D embeddings, a faster-matching strategy, machine learning for 3D correspondence estimation, and a backward/forward nonrigid alignment strategy for complex topology changes.

Overview of parametric tracking

The face tracking model uses the projected linear 3D model for a video camera input. It does the following:

- Tracks visual features from the previous frame to the current frames
- Aligns a 2D shape to track features
- Computes a 3D point cloud data from depth measurement
- Minimizes the loss function

Summary

Face recognition is a computer vision success story, despite the complications arising from various skin colors, orientations, facial expressions, hair colors, and lighting conditions. In this chapter, we learned the techniques for facial detection. For each of these techniques, you need to remember that facial detection requires a lot of trained images. Face detection is being widely used in many video surveillance applications, and standard APIs are available for both cloud-based and edge devices from Google, Amazon, Microsoft, and Intel, among others. We will learn about the cloud-based API in `Chapter 11`, *Deep Learning on Edge Devices with CPU/GPU Optimization*, and techniques for CNN in `Chapter 4`, *Deep Learning on Images*, and Chapter 5, *Neural Network Architecture and Models*. In this chapter, the CNN model for face detection and expression classification was briefly introduced.

In the next chapter, CNNs will be explained in detail. This will help you understand the building blocks of CNNs, why certain functional blocks are chosen, and the effects of each block in the final object detection metrics. After this, we will refer to the example in `Chapter 3`, *Facial Detection Using OpenCV and CNN*, to evaluate how the CNN parameter can be optimized for better facial detection.

4
Deep Learning on Images

The concept of edge detection was covered in `Chapter 1`, *Computer Vision and TensorFlow Fundamentals*. In this chapter, you will learn how edge detection is used to create convolution operations over volume and how different convolution parameters such as filter size, dimensions, and operation type (convolution versus pooling) affect the convolution volume (width versus depth). This chapter will give you a very detailed overview of how a neural network sees an image and how it uses that visualization to classify images. You will start by building your first neural network and then visualize an image as it goes through its different layers. You will then compare the network model's accuracy and visualization to an advanced network such as VGG 16 or Inception.

Note that this chapter and the next provides the foundational theory and concepts of neural networks and various models that are used in practice today. However, this concept is so broad that it is not possible to put everything you need to know in these two chapters. Therefore, for ease of reading, additional concepts will be introduced regarding the topic under discussion for each chapter, starting with `Chapter 6`, *Visual Search Using Transfer Learning*, to prevent you from having to refer to these chapters as you read this book.

In this chapter, we will cover the following topics:

- Understanding CNNs and their parameters
- Optimizing CNN parameters
- Visualizing the layers of a neural network

Understanding CNNs and their parameters

A **Convolutional Neural Network** (**CNN**) is a self-learning network that classifies images similar to how our human brain learns, by observing images of different classes. CNNs learn the content of an image by applying image filtering and by processing the methods of various filter size, quantity, and non-linear operations. These filters and operations are applied across many layers so that the spatial dimensions of each subsequent layer decrease and their depths increase during the image transformation process.

For each filtering application, the depth of the content that's learned increases. This starts with edge detection, followed by recognizing shapes, and then a collection of shapes called features, and so on. This is analogous to the human brain when it comes to how we comprehend information. For example, during a test on reading comprehension where we need to answer five questions about a passage, each question can be considered as a class that requires specific information from the passage that has to be answered:

1. First, we skim through the whole passage, meaning the spatial dimension is the complete passage and the depth (our comprehension of the passage) is low as we just skimmed through it.
2. Next, we skim the questions to understand the features of each class (questions) – that is, what to look for in the passage. In a CNN, this is equivalent to thinking about what convolution and pooling operations are to be used to extract the features.
3. Then, we read specific sections of the passage to find content similar to the class and deep dive into those sections – here, the spatial dimension is low but the depth is high. We repeat this process two to three times to answer all the questions. We continue increasing the depth of our understanding and become more focused on specific areas (shrink the dimension) until we have a good understanding. In a CNN, this is equivalent to gradually increasing the depth and shrinking the dimensions – the convolution operation changes the depth by changing the number of filters; pooling shrinks the dimensions.
4. To save time, we tend to skip paragraphs to find relevant passages that match the answer. In convolution, this is equivalent to the stride, which shrinks the dimension but does not change the depth.
5. The next process is matching the questions to the answers from the passage. We do this by mentally aligning the answers to the questions. Here, we aren't going any deeper – we're putting the questions and answers next to each other so we can match them up. In a CNN, this is equivalent to flattening and using a fully connected layer.

6. We may have excess information during this process – we drop it so that only information relevant to the questions in the passage is available to us. In a CNN, this is equivalent to dropout.
7. The last phase is actually performing the matching exercise to answer the questions. In a CNN, this is equivalent to the Softmax operation.

CNN's image filtering and processing method consists of doing a variety of things, all of which are carried out by using the following:

- Convolution (Conv2D)
- Convolution over volume – 3 x 3 filter
- Convolution over volume – 1 x 1 filter
- Pooling
- Padding
- Stride
- Activation
- Fully connected layer
- Regularization
- Dropout
- Internal covariance shift and batch normalization
- Softmax

The following diagram illustrates a CNN and its components:

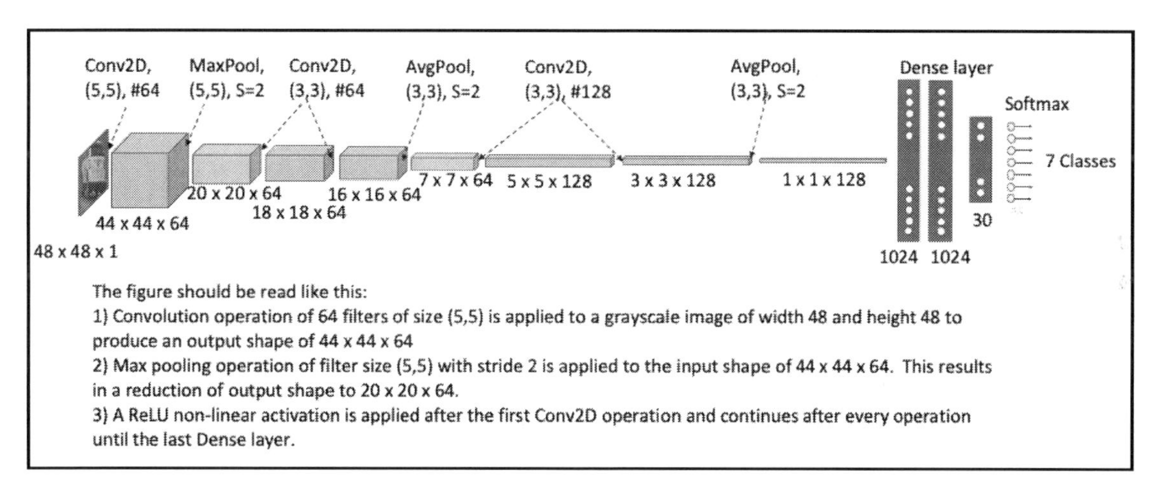

The figure should be read like this:
1) Convolution operation of 64 filters of size (5,5) is applied to a grayscale image of width 48 and height 48 to produce an output shape of 44 x 44 x 64
2) Max pooling operation of filter size (5,5) with stride 2 is applied to the input shape of 44 x 44 x 64. This results in a reduction of output shape to 20 x 20 x 64.
3) A ReLU non-linear activation is applied after the first Conv2D operation and continues after every operation until the last Dense layer.

Let's go over how each component functions.

Convolution

The convolution is the main building block of a CNN. It consists of multiplying a section of the image with a kernel (filter) to produce an output. The concept of convolution was briefly introduced in `Chapter 1`, *Computer Vision and TensorFlow Fundamentals*. Please refer to that chapter to understand the fundamental concepts. The convolution operation is performed by sliding the kernel over the input image. At every location, element-wise matrix multiplication is performed, followed by a cumulative sum over the multiplication range.

After every convolution operation, the CNN learns a little more about the image – it starts by learning the edge, then the shapes in the next convolution, followed by the features of the image. During the convolution operation, the filter size and the number of filters can change. Typically, the number of filters is increased after the spatial dimension of the feature map has been decreased through the convolution, pooling, and stride operations. The depth of the feature map increases when the filter increases in size. The following diagram explains Conv2D when we have two different kernel selections for edge detection:

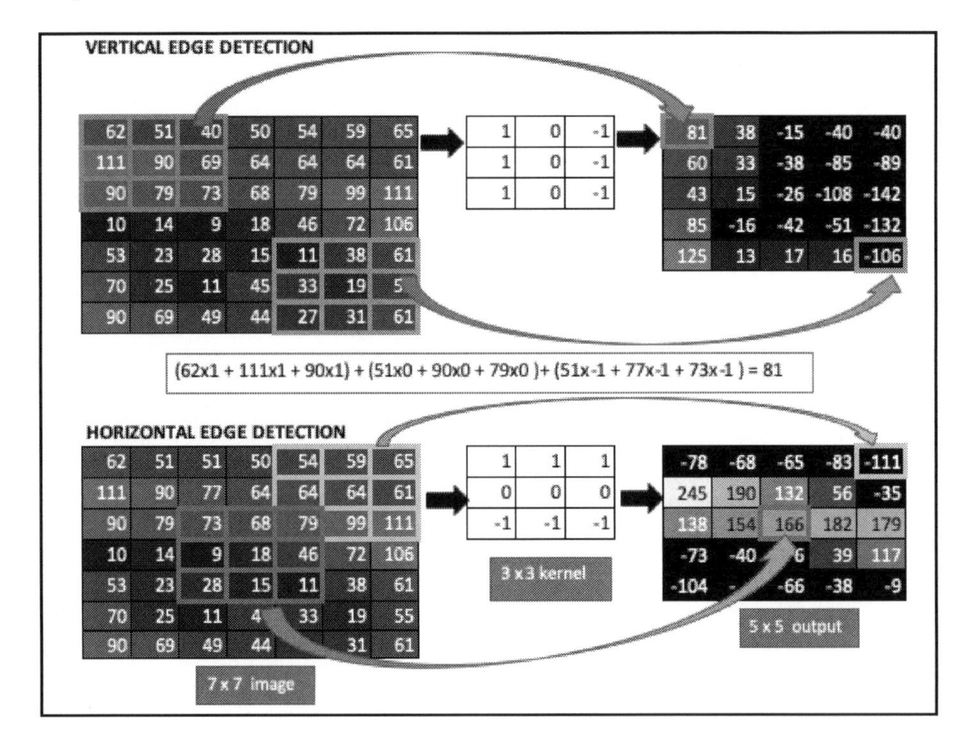

The preceding diagram shows the following important points:

- How the convolution operation is performed by sliding the 3 x 3 window over the input image.
- The element-wise matrix multiplication and the sum result, which are used to generate the feature map.
- Multiple feature maps being stacked as multiple convolution operations generate the final output.

Convolution over volume – 3 x 3 filter

In the preceding example, we applied a 3 x 3 convolution over a two-dimensional image (grayscale). In this section, we will learn how a three-dimensional image with three channels (**Red**, **Green**, and **Blue** (**RGB**)) is transformed by using a 3 x 3 edge filter using a convolution operation. The following diagram shows this transformation graphically:

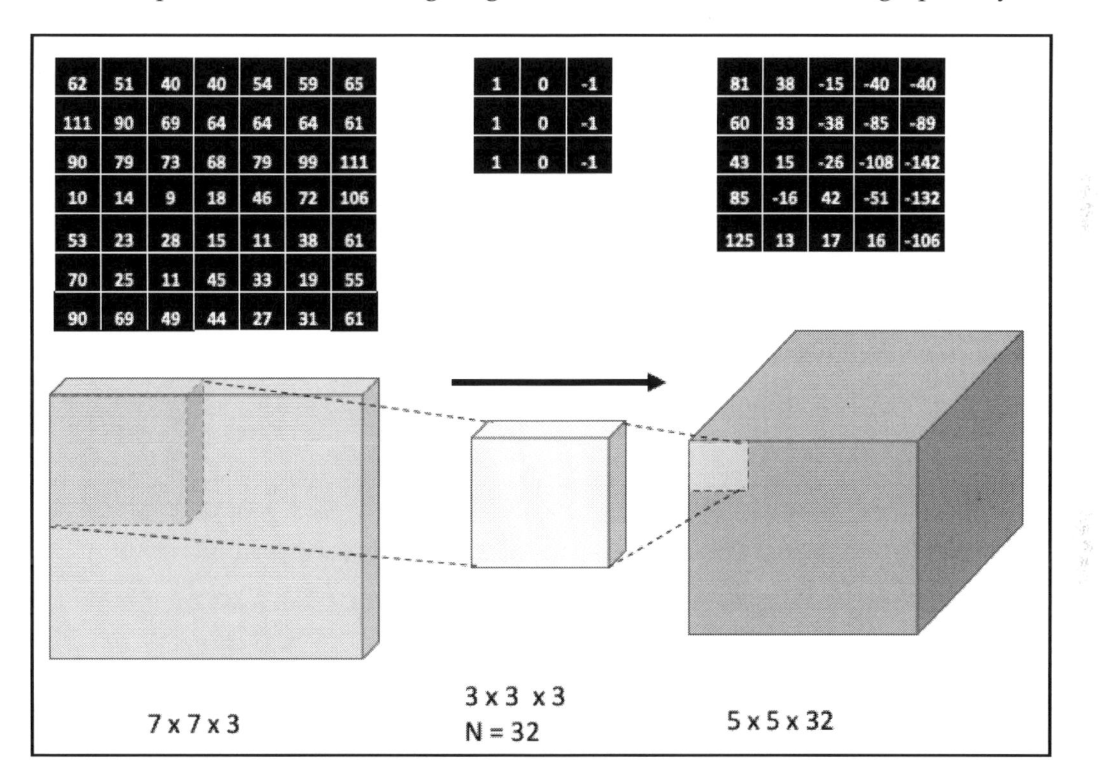

The preceding diagram shows how a section of a 7 x 7 image's graph can be transformed using a 3 x 3 filter (edge detector) in terms of width reduction and depth increase (from 3 to 32). Each of the 27 (3 x 3 x 3) cells in the kernel (f_i) is multiplied by the corresponding 27 cells of the input (A_i). Then, the values are added together, along with a **Rectified Linear Unit (ReLU)** activation function (b_i), to form a single element (Z), as shown in the following equation:

$$Z = \sum_{1}^{27}(A_i fi + b_i)$$

In general, in a convolution layer, there are many filters performing different types of edge detection. In the preceding example, we have 32 filters, which results in 32 different stacks, each consisting of 5 x 5 layers.

The 3 x 3 filter will be used extensively for neural network development for the remainder of this book. For example, you will see heavy use of this in the ResNet and Inception layers, which we'll discuss in `Chapter 5`, *Neural Network Architecture and Models*. 32 filters that are 3 x 3 in size can be expressed in TensorFlow as `.tf.keras.layers.Conv2D(32, (3,3))`. Later in this chapter, you will learn how this convolution can be used with other layers of a CNN.

Convolution over volume – 1 x 1 filter

In this section, we will learn the significance of a 1 x 1 convolution and its use cases. A 1 x 1 convolution filter is a straight multiple of the image, as shown in the following diagram:

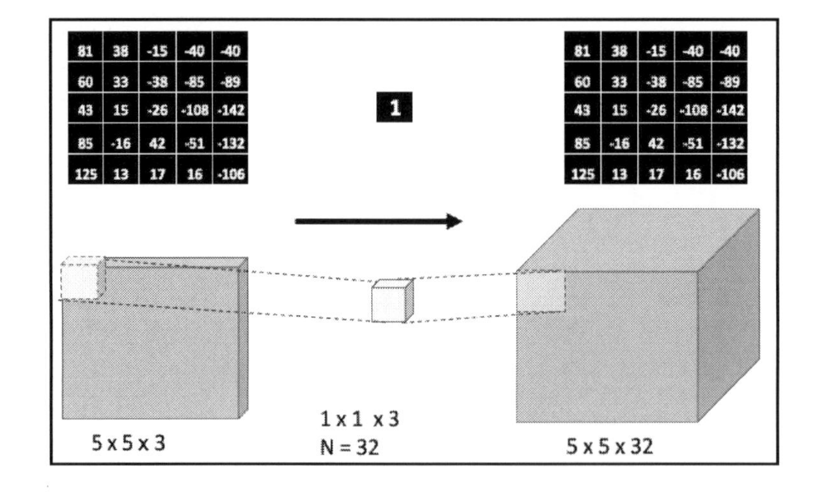

In the preceding diagram, the 1 x 1 convolution filter value of 1 is being used on a 5 x 5 image output from the previous section, but it can be any number in practice. Here, we can see that the use of a 1 x 1 filter conserves its height and width, whereas the depth increases to the filter channel's number. This is the fundamental advantage of a 1 x 1 filter. Each of the three (1 x 1 x 3) cells in the three-dimensional kernel (f_i) is multiplied by the corresponding three cells of the input (A_i). Then, the values are added together, along with the ReLU activation function (b_i), to form a single element (Z):

$$Z = \sum_{1}^{3}(A_i fi + b_i)$$

The preceding diagram shows that the 1 x 1 filter causes the depth to increase, whereas the same 1 x 1 filter can be used to make the value decrease, as shown in the following diagram:

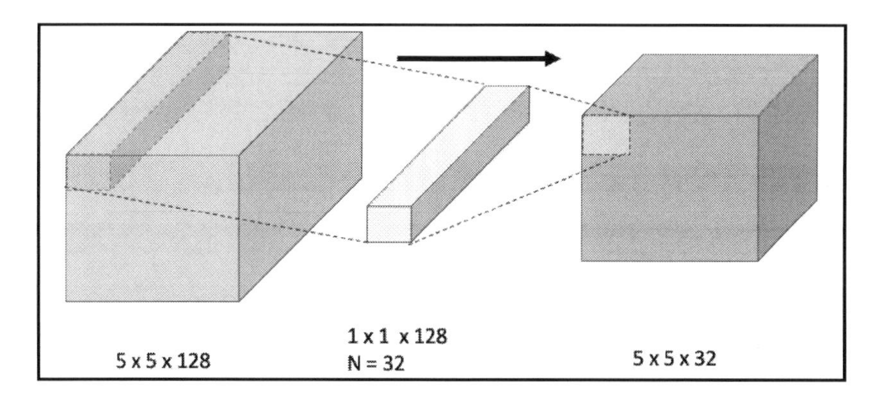

The preceding diagram shows how a 1 x 1 x 128 image filter reduces the depth of the convolution to 32 channels.

The 1 x 1 convolution performs an element-wise multiplication with the 5 x 5 input layer in all of the 128 channels – it sums it up in the depth dimension and a ReLU activation function is applied to create a single point in the 5 x 5 output representing the input depth of 128. Essentially, by using this mechanism (convolution + sum across the depth), it collapses the three-dimensional volume into a two-dimensional array with the same width and height. Then, it applies 32 filters to create a 5 x 5 x 32 output, as shown previously. This is a fundamental concept regarding CNNs, so take your time to ensure you understand this.

A 1 x 1 convolution will be used throughout this book. Later, you will learn that pooling reduces the width, whereas a 1 x 1 convolution preserves the width but can contract or expand the depth as needed. For example, you will see that a 1 x 1 convolution is used in the Network and the Inception layers (in `Chapter 5`, *Neural Network Architecture and Models*. A 32 filter with a 1 x 1 convolution in size can be expressed in TensorFlow as `.tf.keras.layers.Conv2D(32, (1,1))`.

Pooling

Pooling is the next operation after convolution. It is used to reduce the dimensionality and feature map size (width and height) without changing the depth. The number of parameters for polling is zero. The two most popular types of pooling are as follows:

- Max pooling
- Average pooling

In max pooling, we slide the window over the feature map and take the max value of the window, while with average pooling, we take the average value in the window. Together, the convolution and pooling layers perform the task of feature extraction. The following diagram shows the max and average pooling operations being used on a 7 x 7 image:

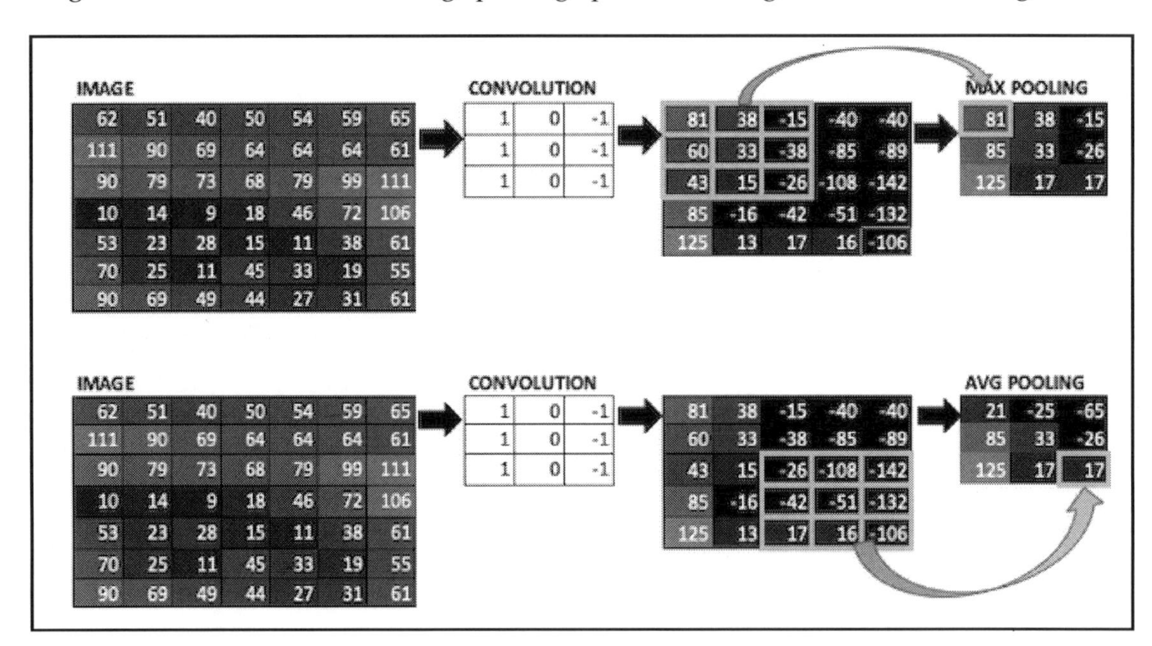

Note how a 3 x 3 window shrinks (shown by the green line) to a single value due to pooling, resulting in a 5 x 5 matrix dimension changing to a 3 x 3 matrix.

Padding

Padding is used to preserve the size of the feature map. With convolution, two issues can occur, and padding addresses both:

- The feature map's size shrinks with each convolution operation. For example, in the preceding diagram, a 7 x 7 feature map shrinks down to 5 x 5 due to convolution.
- Information at the edge is lost as the pixel on the edge is altered only once, whereas the pixel in the middle is altered many times by many convolution operations.

The following diagram shows a padding operation of size 1 being used on a 7 x 7 input image:

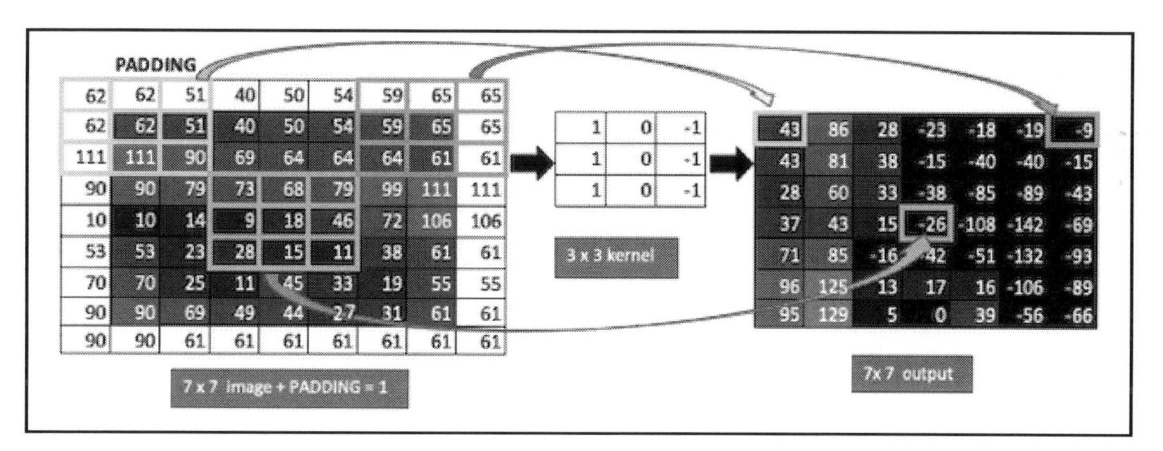

Note how padding conserves the dimension so that the output is the same size as the input.

Stride

Normally, in a convolution, we move the kernel by one step, apply a convolution to that step, and so on. The stride allows us to skip a step. Let's take a look:

- When stride = 1, we apply normal convolution without skipping.
- When stride = 2, we skip a step. This reduces the image size from 7 x 7 to 3 x 3 (see the following diagram):

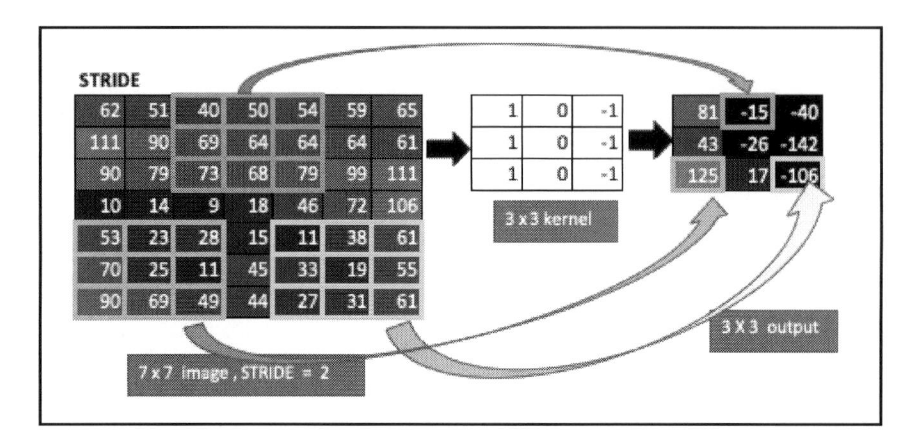

Here, each 3 x 3 window shows the results of skipping one step. The result of a stride is to shrink the dimension since we are skipping over potential *x*, *y* locations.

Activation

The activation layer adds nonlinearity to the neural network. This is critical as images and features within an image are highly non-linear problems, and most other functions within CNNs (Conv2D, pooling, fully connected layers, and so on) generate only linear transformations. The activation function generates the non-linearity while mapping input values to its ranges. Without the activation function, no matter how many layers are added, the final result will still be linear.

Many types of activation functions are used, but the most common ones are as follows:

- Sigmoid
- Tanh
- ReLU

The preceding activation functions can be seen in the following graph:

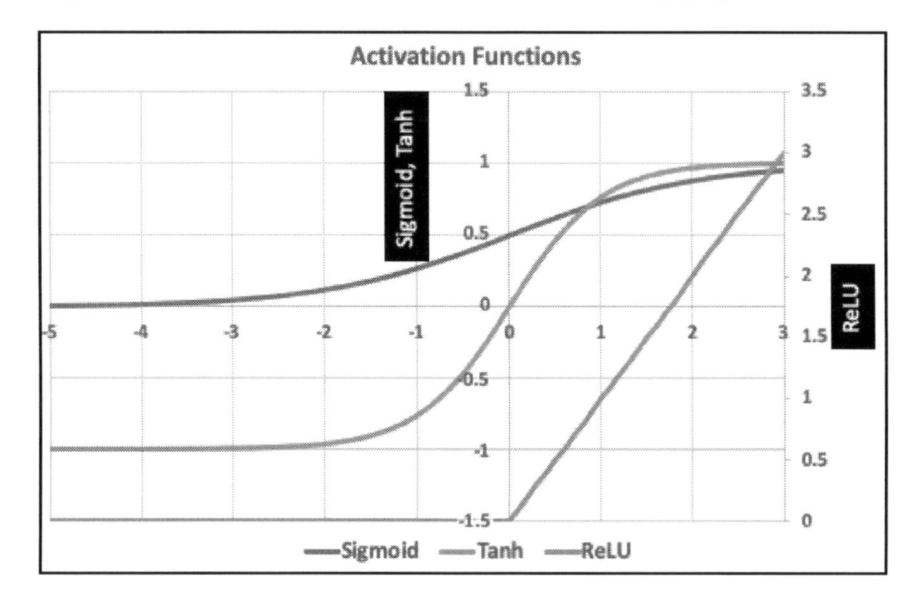

Each of the activation functions shows non-linear behavior, with **Sigmoid** and **Tanh** approaching a value of 3 when input is greater than 3, while **ReLU** continues to increase.

The following diagram shows the effect that different activation functions have on input size:

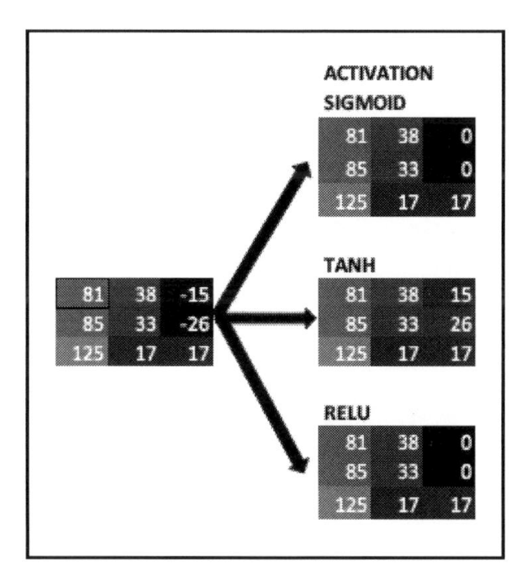

The ReLU activation function has the following advantages over the Tanh and Sigmoid activation functions:

- Sigmoid and Tanh have vanishing gradient problems (slow learners) compared to ReLU as they both approach 1 at input value greater than 3.
- The Sigmoid activation function only has positive values for input values less than 0.
- ReLU functions are effective for computation.

Fully connected layers

Fully connected layers, also known as dense layers, connect every connected neuron in the current layer to every connected neuron in the previous layer by applying weight and bias to them. The vector of the weights and biases is called a **filter**. This can be represented by the following equation:

$$\begin{bmatrix} w_{11} & w_{12} & w_{13} \\ w_{21} & w_{22} & w_{23} \end{bmatrix} \begin{bmatrix} x1 \\ x2 \\ x3 \end{bmatrix} + \begin{bmatrix} b1 \\ b2 \end{bmatrix} = \begin{bmatrix} y1 \\ y2 \end{bmatrix}$$

As explained in the *Convolution* section, the filter can take the form of an edge filter to detect edges. In a neural network, many neurons share the same filter. The weights and the filter allow the fully connected layer to act as a classifier.

Regularization

Regularization is a technique that's used to reduce overfitting. It does this by adding an additional term to the model error function (model output – trained value) to prevent the model weight parameters from taking extreme values during training. Three types of regularization are used in CNNs:

- **L1 regularization**: For each model weight, w, an additional parameter, $\lambda|w|$, is added to the model objective. This regularization makes the weight factor sparse (close to zero) during optimization.
- **L2 regularization**: For each model weight, w, an additional parameter, $1/2\lambda\, w^2$, is added to the model objective. This regularization makes the weight factor diffused during optimization. L2 regularizations can be expected to give superior performance over L1 regularizations.

- **Max norm constraints**: This type of regularization adds a maximum bound to the weights of the CNN so that $|w| < c$, where c can be 3 or 4. Max norm constraints prevent the neural network from overfitting even when the learning rates are high.

Dropout

Dropout is a special type of regularization and refers to ignoring neurons in the neural network. A fully connected layer with dropout = 0.2 means that only 80% of the fully connected neurons are connected to the next layer. The neurons are dropped at the current step but are active at the next step. Dropout prevents the network from being dependent on a small number of neurons, thus preventing overfitting. Dropout is applied to input neurons, but not the output neurons. The following diagram shows the neural network with and without dropout:

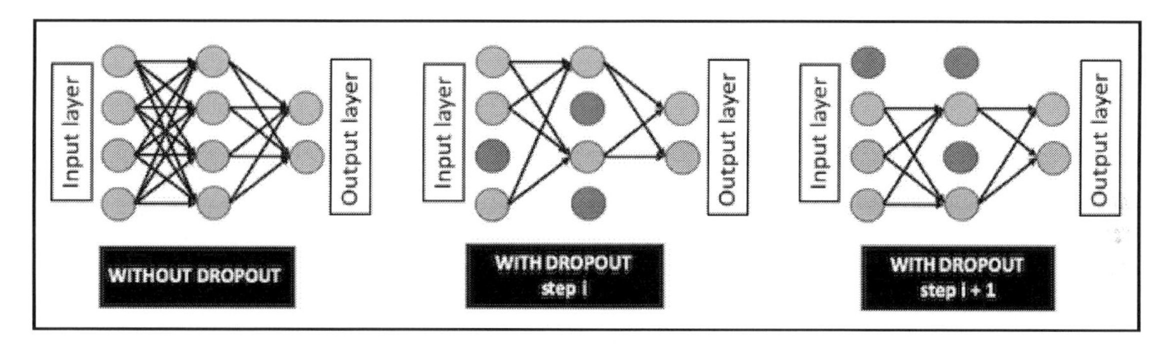

The following are the advantages of dropout:

- Dropout forces the neural network to learn more robust features.
- The training time for each epoch is less, but the number of iterations doubles.
- Dropout results in an accuracy boost – about 1 to 2%.

Internal covariance shift and batch normalization

During training, the distribution of each layer's input changes as the weight factor of the previous layer changes, which causes the training to slow down. This is because it requires a lower learning rate and weight factor selection. Sergey Ioffe and Christian Szegedy called this phenomenon **internal covariance shift** in their paper titled *Batch Normalization: Accelerating Deep Network Training by Reducing Internal Co-variance Shift*. For details, refer to: `https://arxiv.org/abs/1502.03167`.

Batch normalization addresses the issue of the covariance shift by subtracting the previous layer's batch mean from the current input and dividing it with batch standard deviation. This new input is then multiplied by the current weight factor and added by the bias term to form the output. The following diagram shows the intermediate output function of a neural network, with and without batch normalization:

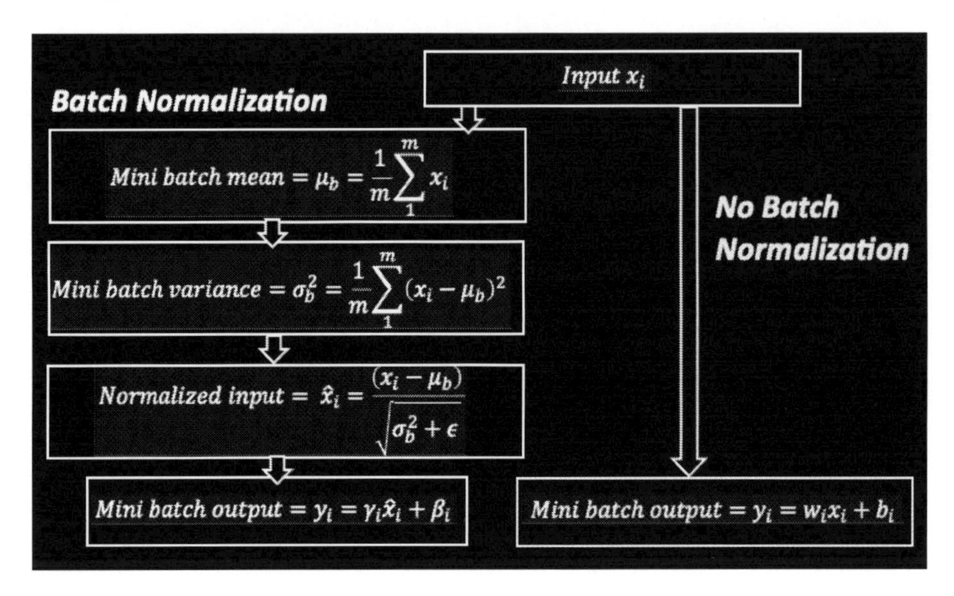

When batch normalization is applied, we calculate the mean (μ) and variance (σ) over the entire mini-batch of size m. Then, with that information, we calculate the normalized input. The output from the mini-batch is calculated as the scale (γ) multiplied by the normalized input, plus the offset (β). In TensorFlow, this can be expressed as follows. All the terms have been explained in the preceding diagram except for the variance epsilon, which is the ε term in normalized input calculation to avoid division by zero:

```
tf.nn.batch_normalization(x,mean,variance,offset,scale,variance_epsilon,nam
e=None)
```

The advantages of batch normalization have been elaborately explained by Shibani Santurkar, Dimitris Tsipras, Andrew Ilyas, and Aleksander Madry from MIT in their paper titled, *How Does Batch Normalization Help Optimization?*. The details of the paper can be found at `https://arxiv.org/abs/1805.11604`.

The authors of the paper found that batch normalization does not reduce the internal covariance shift. The speed of learning in batch normalization can be attributed to the smoothness of the input due to the use of normalized input rather than regular input data, which may have large variations due to kinks, sharp edges, and local minima or maxima. This makes the gradient descent algorithm more stable, thus allowing it to use larger steps for faster convergence. This ensures it doesn't run into any errors.

Softmax

Softmax is an activation function that is used in the final layer of a CNN. It is represented by the following equation, where *P* is the probability of each class and *n* is the total number of classes:

$$P_i = \frac{e^{y_i}}{\sum_{i=0}^{n} e^{y_i}}$$

The following table shows the probability for each of the seven classes when using the previously described Softmax function:

yi	exp(yi)	Probability = exp(yi)/Σexp(yi)
0.1	1.1	3%
1.5	4.5	12%
0.01	1.0	3%
2	7.4	20%
0.5	1.6	4%
3	20.1	54%
0.25	1.3	3%
SUM	**37.0**	**100%**

This is used to calculate the probability of the distribution for each class.

Optimizing CNN parameters

CNNs have many different parameters. Training a CNN model requires many input images and performing processing, which can be very time-consuming. If the parameters that are selected are not optimal, the whole process has to be repeated again. This is why it is important to understand the functions of each parameter and their interrelationship: so that their values can be optimized before running the CNN to minimize repeat runs. The parameters of a CNN are as follows:

- Image size = $(n \times n)$
- Filter = (f_h, f_w), f_h = filter applied to image height, f_w = filter applied to image width
- Number of filters = n_f
- Padding = p
- Stride = s
- Output size = $\{(n + 2p - f)/s + 1\} \times \{(n + 2p - f)/s + 1\}$
- Number of parameters = $(f_h \times f_w + 1) \times n_f$

The critical task is to select the aforementioned parameters (filter size (**f**), number of filters (**nf**), stride (**s**) in each layer, padding value (**p**), activation (**a**), and bias) for each layer of the CNN. The following table shows the feature maps for various CNN parameters:

Feature map operations	Feature map shape	Feature map size	# of parameters
Input image	(48,48,1)	2304	0
CONV1 (f=5, nf=64, s=1)	(44,44,64)	123904	1664
POOL1(f=5,s=2)	(20,20,64)	25600	0
CONV2 (f=3, nf=64, s=1)	(18,18,64)	20736	640
CONV3 (f=3, nf=64, s=1)	(16,16,64)	16384	640
POOL2(f=3,s=2)	(7,7,64)	3136	0
CONV4 (f=3, nf=128, s=1)	(5,5,128)	3200	1280
CONV5 (f=3, nf=128, s=1)	(3,3,128)	1152	1280
POOL3(f=3,s=2)	(1,1,128)	128	0
FC1 (1024)	(1024,1)	1024	131073
DROP(.2)	(820,1)	820	104961
FC1 (1024)	(1024,1)	1024	1048577
DROP(.2)	(820,1)	820	672401
Softmax	(7,1)	7	5741

Each parameter of the preceding table is described as follows:

- **Input image**: The first input layer is a grayscale image of size *(48 x 48)*, so the depth is *1*. The feature map size = *48 x 48 x 1 = 2,304*. It has no parameters.
- **First convolution layer**: The *CONV1* (*filter shape =5*5, stride=1*) layer's height, width = *(48-5+1) =44*, feature map size = *44 x 44 x 64 = 123904*, and number of parameters = *(5 x 5 + 1) x 64 = 1,664*.
- **First pooling layer (POOL1)**: The pooling layer has no parameters.
- **Remaining convolution and pooling layers**: The remaining calculation – *CONV2, CONV3, CONV4, CONV5, POOL2* – follows the same logic that the first convolution layer follows.
- **Fully connected (FC) layers**: For fully connected layers (*FC1, FC2*), the *number of parameters = [(current layer n * previous layer n) + 1] parameters = 128 * 1,024 + 1 = 131,073*.
- **Dropout (DROP)**: For the dropout, 20% of neurons are dropped. The remaining neurons is = *1,024 * 0.8 = 820*. The number of parameters for the second dropout = *820 x 820 + 1 = 672,401*.
- **The last layer of a CNN is always Softmax**: For Softmax, the number of parameters = *7 x 820 + 1 = 5,741*.

The neural network class shown in the first diagram for facial expression recognition in `Chapter 3`, *Facial Detection Using OpenCV and CNN* has seven classes and its accuracy is around 54%.

In the following sections, we will use TensorFlow output to optimize various parameters. We start with a baseline case and then try five iterations by adjusting the parameters described here. This exercise should give you a good understanding of the parameters of a CNN and how they affect the final model's output.

Baseline case

The baseline case is denoted by the following parameters of the neural network:

- **Number of instances**: 35,888
- **Instance length**: 2,304
- 28,709 train samples
- 3,589 test samples

The model iterations are as follows:

```
Epoch 1/5
 256/256 [======================] - 78s 306ms/step - loss: 1.8038 - acc:
0.2528
 Epoch 2/5
 256/256 [======================] - 78s 303ms/step - loss: 1.6188 - acc:
0.3561
 Epoch 3/5
 256/256 [======================] - 78s 305ms/step - loss: 1.4309 - acc:
0.4459
 Epoch 4/5
 256/256 [======================] - 78s 306ms/step - loss: 1.2889 - acc:
0.5046
 Epoch 5/5
 256/256 [======================] - 79s 308ms/step - loss: 1.1947 - acc:
0.5444
```

Next, we will optimize the CNN parameters to determine which parameters have the most significant influence when it comes to changing the accuracy. We will run this experiment in four iterations.

Iteration 1 – CNN parameter adjustment

Drop one Conv2D 64 and one Conv2D 128 so that the CNN has only one Conv2D 64 and one Conv2D 128 with this change:

```
Epoch 1/5
 256/256 [========================] - 63s 247ms/step - loss: 1.7497 - acc:
0.2805
 Epoch 2/5
 256/256 [========================] - 64s 248ms/step - loss: 1.5192 - acc:
0.4095
 Epoch 3/5
 256/256 [========================] - 65s 252ms/step - loss: 1.3553 -acc:
0.4832
 Epoch 4/5
 256/256 [========================] - 66s 260ms/step - loss: 1.2633 - acc:
0.5218
 Epoch 5/5
 256/256 [========================] - 65s 256ms/step - loss: 1.1919 - acc:
0.5483
```

Result: Dropping a Conv2D layer did not adversely affect the performance but did not make it better either.

Next, we are going to keep the change we made here, but we will convert average pooling into max pooling.

Iteration 2 – CNN parameter adjustment

Drop one Conv2D 64 and one Conv2D 128 so that the CNN has only one Conv2D 64 and one Conv2D 128 with this change. Also, convert average pooling into max pooling, as shown here:

```
Epoch 1/5
 256/256 [========================] - 63s 247ms/step - loss: 1.7471 - acc: 0.2804
 Epoch 2/5
 256/256 [========================] - 64s 252ms/step - loss: 1.4631 - acc: 0.4307
 Epoch 3/5
 256/256 [========================] - 66s 256ms/step - loss: 1.3042 - acc: 0.4990
 Epoch 4/5
 256/256 [========================] - 66s 257ms/step - loss: 1.2183 - acc: 0.5360
 Epoch 5/5
 256/256 [========================] - 67s 262ms/step - loss: 1.1407 - acc: 0.5691
```

Result: Again, this change has no significant effect on accuracy.

Next, we will significantly reduce the number of hidden layers. We will change the input layer and completely remove the second Conv2D and associated pooling. After the first Conv2D, we'll move directly to the third Conv2D.

Iteration 3 – CNN parameter adjustment

The second convolution layer was dropped completely; the input layer was changed from 5 x 5 to 3 x 3:

```
model.add(Conv2D(64, (3, 3), activation='relu', input_shape=(48,48,1)))
```

The third convolution layer remains unchanged. This layer is as follows:

```
model.add(Conv2D(128, (3, 3), activation='relu'))
model.add(AveragePooling2D(pool_size=(3,3), strides=(2, 2)))
```

There is no change in the dense layer. The output of this is as follows:

```
Epoch 1/5
 256/256 [==========================] - 410s 2s/step - loss: 1.6465 - acc:
0.3500
 Epoch 2/5
 256/256 [==========================] - 415s 2s/step - loss: 1.3435 - acc:
0.4851
 Epoch 3/5
 256/256 [==========================] - 412s 2s/step - loss: 1.0837 - acc:
0.5938
 Epoch 4/5
 256/256 [==========================] - 410s 2s/step - loss: 0.7870 - acc:
0.7142
 Epoch 5/5
 256/256 [==========================] - 409s 2s/step - loss: 0.4929 - acc:
0.8242
```

Result: The calculation time is very slow, but the accuracy is at its best, that is, 82%.

Iteration 4 – CNN parameter adjustment

In this iteration, all the parameters are the same as they were in the previous iteration, except for `strides = 2`, which is added after the first Conv2D.

Next, we keep everything the same but add a pooling layer after the first Conv2D:

```
model.add(Conv2D(64, (3, 3), activation='relu', input_shape=(48,48,1)))
model.add(AveragePooling2D(pool_size=(3,3), strides=(2, 2)))
model.add(Conv2D(128, (3, 3), activation='relu'))
model.add(AveragePooling2D(pool_size=(3,3), strides=(2, 2)))
```

In this iteration, no change is made to the dense layer. The calculation time is faster but the accuracy has dropped:

```
Epoch 1/5
 256/256 [=======================] - 99s 386ms/step - loss: 1.6855 - acc:
0.3240
 Epoch 2/5
 256/256 [=======================] - 100s 389ms/step - loss: 1.4532 - acc:
0.4366
 Epoch 3/5
 256/256 [=======================] - 102s 397ms/step - loss: 1.3100 - acc:
0.4958
 Epoch 4/5
 256/256 [======================] - 103s 402ms/step - loss: 1.1995 - acc:
```

```
0.5451
 Epoch 5/5
 256/256 [==============================] - 104s 407ms/step - loss: 1.0831 - acc:
0.5924
```

The result is similar to what we had in the baseline iterations, that is, 1 and 2.

From this experiment, we can conclude the following regarding CNN parameter optimization:

- Reducing the number of Conv2Ds and eliminating one pooling layer with *strides* =2 has the most significant effect as it increases the accuracy (by about 30%). However, this came at the expense of speed as the size of the CNN was not reduced.
- The pooling type (average pooling versus max pooling) has an insignificant effect on test accuracy.

The architecture of the CNN that resulted in the best accuracy is as follows:

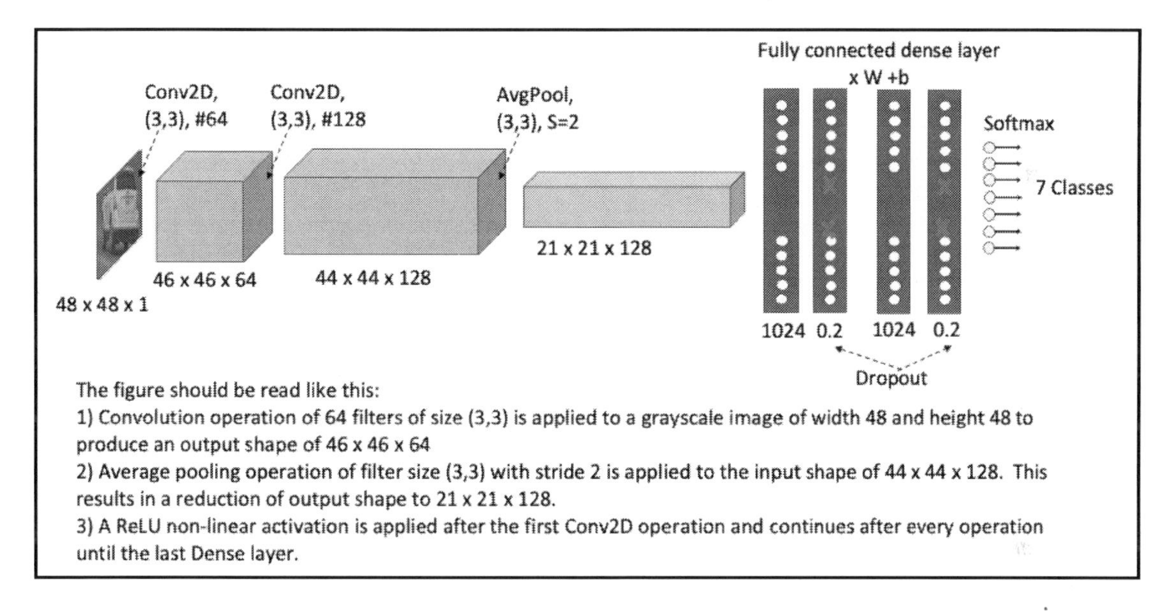

Note that this architecture is much simpler compared to the original one. In the next chapter, you will learn about some of the state-of-the-art convolution models and why they are used. Then, we will come back to this optimization problem and learn how to select the parameters more efficiently for even better optimization.

Visualizing the layers of a neural network

In this chapter, we've learned about how an image is transformed into edges and then into feature maps and that by doing this, the neural network is able to predict the classes by combining many of the feature maps. In the first few layers, the neural network visualizes lines and corners, whereas in the last few layers, the neural network recognizes complex patterns such as feature maps. This can be broken down into the following categories.

- Building a custom image classifier model and visualizing its layers
- Training an existing advanced image classifier model and visualizing its layers

Let's take a look at these categories.

Building a custom image classifier model and visualizing its layers

In this section, we will develop our own classifier network for furniture. This will consist of three classes: sofa, bed, and chair. The basic process is described as follows.

The detailed code for this example can be found on GitHub at: `https://github.com/PacktPublishing/Mastering-Computer-Vision-with-TensorFlow-2.0/blob/master/Chapter04/Chapter4_classification_visualization_custom_model%26VGG.ipynb`.

Note that in `Chapter 6`, *Visual Search Using Transfer Learning,* we will perform more advanced coding and provide a detailed explanation using the same three classes.

Neural network input and parameters

In this section, the model inputs various Keras libraries and TensorFlow. This can be seen in the following code. For now, take this with a pinch of salt; this will be explained in full in `Chapter 6`, *Visual Search Using Transfer Learning*:

```
from __future__ import absolute_import, division, print_function,
unicode_literals,
import tensorflow as tf,
from tensorflow.keras.applications import VGG16\n
from keras.applications.vgg16 import preprocess_input,
from keras import models
from tensorflow.keras.models import Sequential, Model
```

```
from tensorflow.keras.layers import Dense, Conv2D, Flatten, Dropout,
GlobalAveragePooling2D, MaxPooling2D
from tensorflow.keras.preprocessing.image import ImageDataGenerator\n",
from tensorflow.keras.optimizers import SGD, Adam
import os
import numpy as np
import matplotlib.pyplot as plt
```

Input image

In this section, we define the train and validation directory paths and use the `os.path.join` feature and the class name to define the directories within the train and validation directories. After that, we calculate the total number of images in each class directory using the `len` command:

```
train_dir = 'furniture_images/train'
train_bed_dir = os.path.join(train_dir, 'bed')
num_bed_train = len(os.listdir(train_bed_dir))
```

The total number of images in the train directories is obtained by summing the number of images in each class. The same method is applied for validation, which results in the output at the end being the total number of images in the train and validation directory. This information will be used by the neural network during training.

Defining the train and validation generators

The train and validation generators use a method called image data generation and flow. They use this on a directory to input batches of the image as a tensor. For details of this process, please refer to the Keras documentation at: `https://keras.io/preprocessing/image/`.

A typical example of this is as follows. As explained in the Keras documentation, the image data generator has many parameters, but we're only using a few of them here. The preprocessing input converts the image into a tensor. The input rotation range rotates the image by 90 degrees and flips it vertically for image augmentation. We can use what we learned about image transformation in `Chapter 1`, *Computer Vision and TensorFlow Fundamentals*, and make use of the `rotation` command. Image augmentation increases the training datasets, thus increasing the accuracy of the model without increasing how much test data we have:

```
train_datagen =
ImageDataGenerator(preprocessing_function=preprocess_input,rotation_range=9
0,horizontal_flip=True,vertical_flip=True)
```

Developing the model

Once the images have been prepared, we can start building the model. The Keras sequential model allows us to do just that. It is a list of model layers stacked on top of each other. Next, we build a sequential model by stacking convolution, activation, max pooling, dropout, and padding, as shown in the following code:

```
model = Sequential([Conv2D(96, 11, padding='valid',
activation='relu',input_shape=(img_height, img_width,3)),
MaxPooling2D(),Dropout(0.2),Conv2D(256, 5, padding='same',
activation='relu'),MaxPooling2D(),Conv2D(384, 3, padding='same',
activation='relu'),Conv2D(384, 3, padding='same', activation='relu'),
Conv2D(256, 3, padding='same', activation='relu'),MaxPooling2D(),
Dropout(0.2),Conv2D(1024, 3, padding='same', activation='relu'),
MaxPooling2D(),Dropout(0.2),Flatten(),Dense(4096, activation='relu'),
Dense(3)])
```

The basic idea of the model is similar to AlexNet, which will be introduced in `Chapter 5`, *Neural Network Architecture and Models*. The model has about 16 layers.

Compiling and training the model

Next, we compile the model and start training. The compile `option` specifies three parameters:

- **Optimizer**: The optimizers we can use are `adam`, `rmsprop`, `sgd`, `adadelta`, `adagrad`, `adamax`, and `nadam`. For a list of Keras optimizers, please refer to `https://keras.io/optimizers`:
    - `sgd` stands for Stochastic gradient descent. As the name suggests, it uses the gradient value for the optimizer.
    - `adam` stands for adaptive moment. It uses the gradient in the last step to adjust the gradient descent parameter. Adam works well and needs very little tuning. It will be used often throughout this book.
    - `adagrad` works well for sparse data and also needs very little tuning. For `adagrad`, a default learning rate is not required.

- **Loss function**: The most commonly used loss function for image processing is binary cross-entropy, categorical cross-entropy, mean squared error, or `sparse_categorical` cross-entropy. A binary cross-entropy is used when the classification task is binary, such as processing cat and dog images or stop sign versus no stop sign images. Categorical cross-entropy is used when we have more than two classes, such as a furniture shop with beds, chairs, and sofas. Sparse categorical cross-entropy is similar to categorical cross-entropy, except the class is replaced by its index – for example, instead of passing bed, chair, and sofa as classes, we will pass 0, 1, and 2. If you get errors when specifying a class, you can fix this by using sparse categorical cross-entropy. There are many other loss functions available in Keras. For more details, please refer to `https://keras.io/losses/`.
- **Metrics**: The metrics are used to set the accuracy.

In the following code, we're using the `adam` optimizer. After the model has been compiled, we use the Keras `model.fit()` function to begin training. The `model.fit()` function takes the train generator as the input image vector that we defined previously. It also takes the number of epochs (iteration parameters), steps per epoch (number of batches per epoch), validation data, and validation steps. Note that each of these parameters will be described in detail in `Chapter 6`, *Visual Search Using Transfer Learning*:

```
model.compile(optimizer='adam',loss=tf.keras.losses.BinaryCrossentropy(from
_logits=True), metrics=['accuracy'])

history =
model.fit(train_generator,epochs=NUM_EPOCHS,steps_per_epoch=num_train_image
s // batchsize,validation_data=val_generator,
validation_steps=num_val_images // batchsize)
```

The training continues with 10 epochs. During training, the accuracy of the model increases with the number of epochs:

```
WARNING:tensorflow:sample_weight modes were coerced from
 ...
 to
 ['...']
 Train for 10 steps, validate for 1 steps
 Epoch 1/10
 10/10 [==============================] - 239s 24s/step - loss: 13.7108 -
accuracy: 0.6609 - val_loss: 0.6779 - val_accuracy: 0.6667
 Epoch 2/10
 10/10 [==============================] - 237s 24s/step - loss: 0.6559 -
accuracy: 0.6708 - val_loss: 0.5836 - val_accuracy: 0.6693
 Epoch 3/10
 10/10 [==============================] - 227s 23s/step - loss: 0.5620 -
```

```
accuracy: 0.7130 - val_loss: 0.5489 - val_accuracy: 0.7266
 Epoch 4/10
 10/10 [==============================] - 229s 23s/step - loss: 0.5243 -
accuracy: 0.7334 - val_loss: 0.5041 - val_accuracy: 0.7292
 Epoch 5/10
 10/10 [==============================] - 226s 23s/step - loss: 0.5212 -
accuracy: 0.7342 - val_loss: 0.4877 - val_accuracy: 0.7526
 Epoch 6/10
 10/10 [==============================] - 226s 23s/step - loss: 0.4897 -
accuracy: 0.7653 - val_loss: 0.4626 - val_accuracy: 0.7604
 Epoch 7/10
 10/10 [==============================] - 227s 23s/step - loss: 0.4720 -
accuracy: 0.7781 - val_loss: 0.4752 - val_accuracy: 0.7734
 Epoch 8/10
 10/10 [==============================] - 229s 23s/step - loss: 0.4744 -
accuracy: 0.7508 - val_loss: 0.4534 - val_accuracy: 0.7708
 Epoch 9/10
 10/10 [==============================] - 231s 23s/step - loss: 0.4429 -
accuracy: 0.7854 - val_loss: 0.4608 - val_accuracy: 0.7865
 Epoch 10/10
 10/10 [==============================] - 230s 23s/step - loss: 0.4410 -
accuracy: 0.7865 - val_loss: 0.4264 - val_accuracy: 0.8021
```

Inputting a test image and converting it into a tensor

So far, we've developed an image directory and prepared and trained the model. In this section, we'll convert the image into a tensor. We develop a tensor from an image by converting the image into an array and then use NumPy's `expand_dims()` function to expand the shape of the array. Subsequently, we preprocess the input to prepare the image so that it's in the format the model requires:

```
img_path = 'furniture_images/test/chair/testchair.jpg'
img = image.load_img(img_path, target_size=(150, 150))
img_tensor = image.img_to_array(img)
img_tensor = np.expand_dims(img_tensor, axis=0)
img_tensor = preprocess_input(img_tensor)
featuremap = model.predict(img_tensor)
```

Finally, we use the Keras `model.predict()` function to input the image tensor, which then converts the tensor into a feature map. Now you know how to calculate a feature map by passing the image tensor through a model like the one we just developed.

Visualizing the first layer of activation

To calculate activation, we calculate the model output from each layer. In this example, there are 16 layers, so we use `model.layers[:16]` to specify all 16 layers. The code we use to do this is as follows:

```
layer_outputs = [layer.output for layer in model.layers[:16]]
activation_modelfig = Model(inputs=model.input, outputs=layer_outputs)
activationsfig = activation_modelfig.predict(img_tensor)
```

To use activation, we use the Keras `Model` functional API, which calculates all the layers required for calculating `b` when given `a`:

```
model = Model(inputs=[a1, a2], outputs=[b1, b2, b3])
```

For our exercise, the input is the image tensor we calculated previously, while the output is the activation layer.

Next, we visualize the first layer using the following command, where `activationsfig[0]` implies the first layer. To plot it, we use `plt.matshow()`. Here, `95` is the penultimate activation filter for the first neural network layer:

```
first_layer_activation = activationsfig[0]
print(first_layer_activation.shape)
plt.matshow(first_layer_activation[0, :, :, 95], cmap='viridis')
```

Visualizing multiple layers of activation

Following what we did previously, we run a `for` loop and use the `plt.imshow` method to display the activation layers in the first, middle, and last filter values of a given neural network layer:

```
for i in range(0,12):
    current_layer_activation = activationsfig[i]
    ns = current_layer_activation.shape[-1]
    plt.imshow(current_layer_activation[0, :, :, 0], cmap='viridis')
    plt.imshow(current_layer_activation[0, :, :, int(ns/2)],
cmap='viridis')
    plt.imshow(current_layer_activation[0, :, :, ns-1], cmap='viridis')
```

The following diagram shows the resulting output value of the chair image:

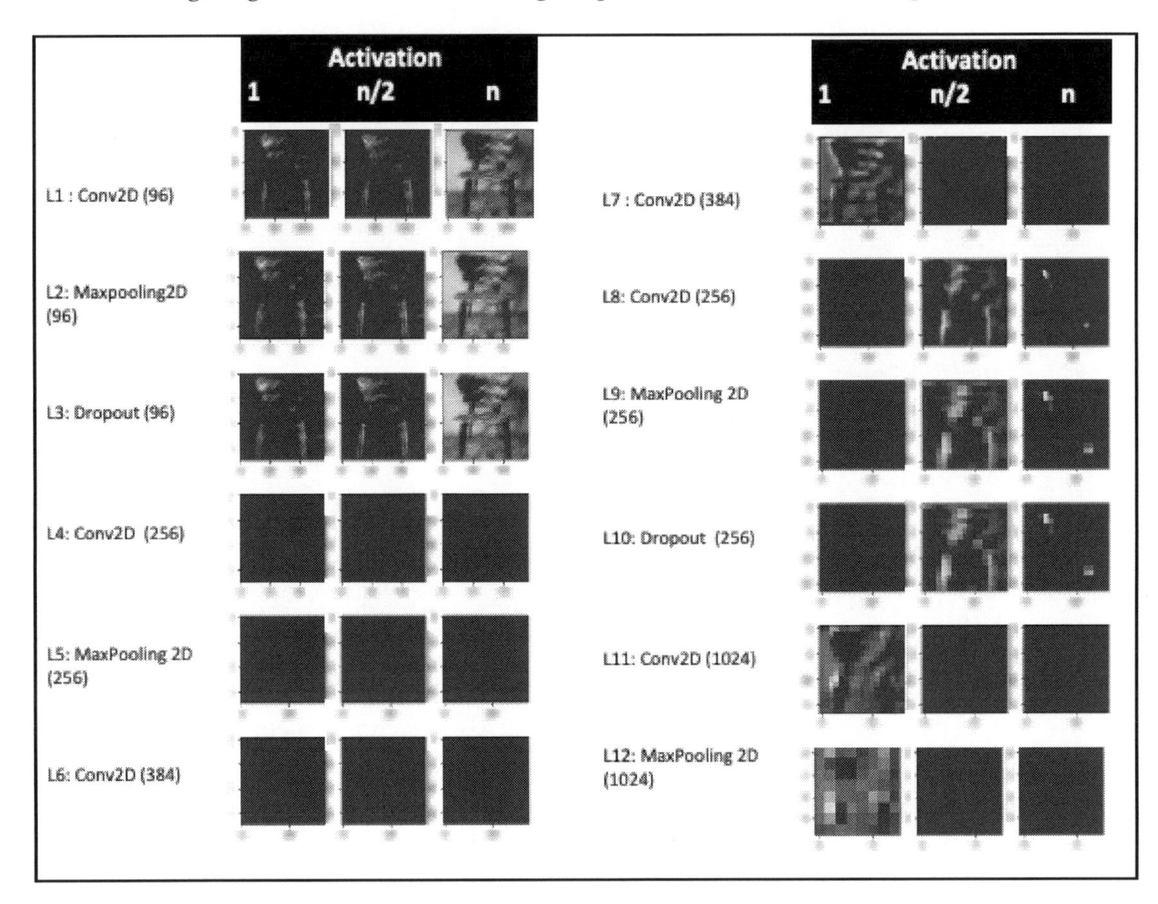

In the preceding diagram, the `n` represents the maximum number of filters for a given layer. The value of `n` can be different at different layers. For example, for the first layer, the value of `n` is `96`, whereas for the fourth layer, it is `256`. The following table shows the parameters, output shape, and filters at the different layers of our custom neural network:

```
Model: "sequential'
_________________________________________________________________
Layer (type)          Output Shape              Param #
=================================================================
conv2d (Conv2D)       (None, 140, 140, 96)      3494
_________________________________________________________________
max_pooling2d (MaxPooling2D) (None, 70, 70, 96)       0
_________________________________________________________________
dropout (Dropout)         (None, 70, 70, 96)      0
_________________________________________________________________
conv2d_1 (Conv2D)         (None, 70, 70, 256)     614656
_________________________________________________________________
max_pooling2d_1 (MaxPooling2 (None, 35, 35, 256)      0
_________________________________________________________________
conv2d_2 (Conv2D)         (None, 35, 35, 384)     885120
_________________________________________________________________
conv2d_3 (Conv2D)         (None, 35, 35, 384)     1327488
_________________________________________________________________
conv2d_4 (Conv2D)         (None, 35, 35, 256)     884992
_________________________________________________________________
max_pooling2d_2 (MaxPooling2 (None, 17, 17, 256)      0
_________________________________________________________________
dropout_1 (Dropout)       (None, 17, 17, 256)     0
_________________________________________________________________
conv2d_5 (Conv2D)         (None, 17, 17, 1024)     2360320
_________________________________________________________________
max_pooling2d_3 (MaxPooling2 (None, 8, 8, 1024)      0
_________________________________________________________________
dropout_2 (Dropout)       (None, 8, 8, 1024)      0
_________________________________________________________________
flatten (Flatten)         (None, 65536)  0
_________________________________________________________________
dense (Dense)             (None, 4096)    268439552
_________________________________________________________________
dense_1 (Dense)           (None, 3)       12291
=================================================================
Total params: 274,559,363
Trainable params: 274,559,363
Non-trainable params: 0
```

As you can see, each layer has many different activation filters, so for our visualization, we are looking at the visualization value at the first filter, the middle filter, and the last filter of a given layer.

The first initial layers represent a chair, but as we go deeper into the model's layers, the structure becomes increasingly abstract. This means the image looks less like a chair and more like something that represents the class. Also, you can see that some of the layers are not activating at all, indicating that the model's structure has become complex and not very efficient.

The big question that comes naturally is, how does the neural network process the seemingly abstract images from the last layer and extract a class from it? This is something a human is unable to do.

The answer lies in the fully connected layer. As shown in the preceding table, there are 16 layers, but the visualization code for *i* is in the range *(0,12)*, so we only visualize the first 12 layers. If you try to visualize more than that, you will receive errors. After the 12th layer, we flatten the layer and map each element of the layer – this is called a fully connected layer. This is essentially a mapping exercise. This neural network maps each of the elements of the fully connected layer to a specific class. This process is repeated for all the classes. Mapping the abstract layer to the class is a machine learning exercise. By doing this, the neural network is able to predict the class.

The following diagram shows the output value of the image of a bed:

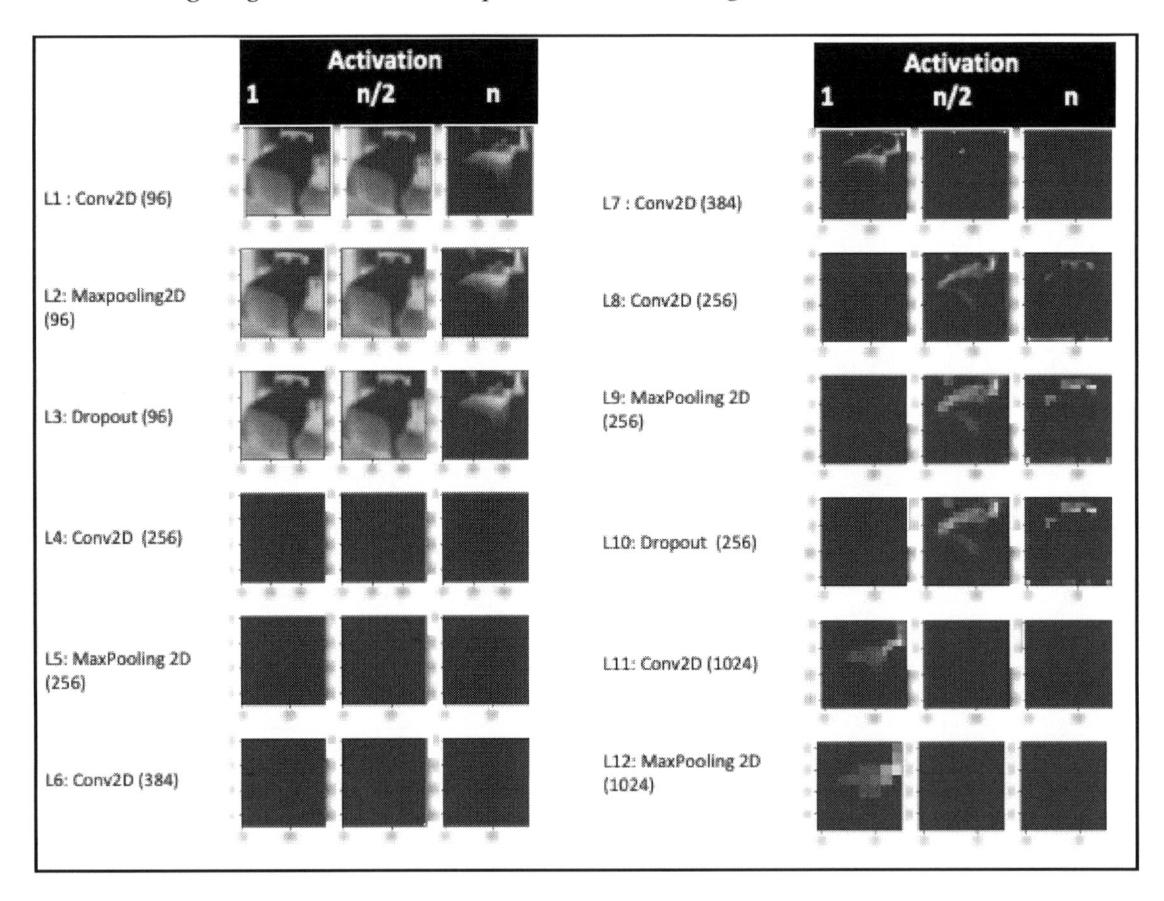

Just like the chair image, the initial activation started with an output similar to a bed, but as we go deep into the networks, we start seeing distinctive characteristics of the bed compared to the chair.

The following diagram shows the output value of the image of a sofa:

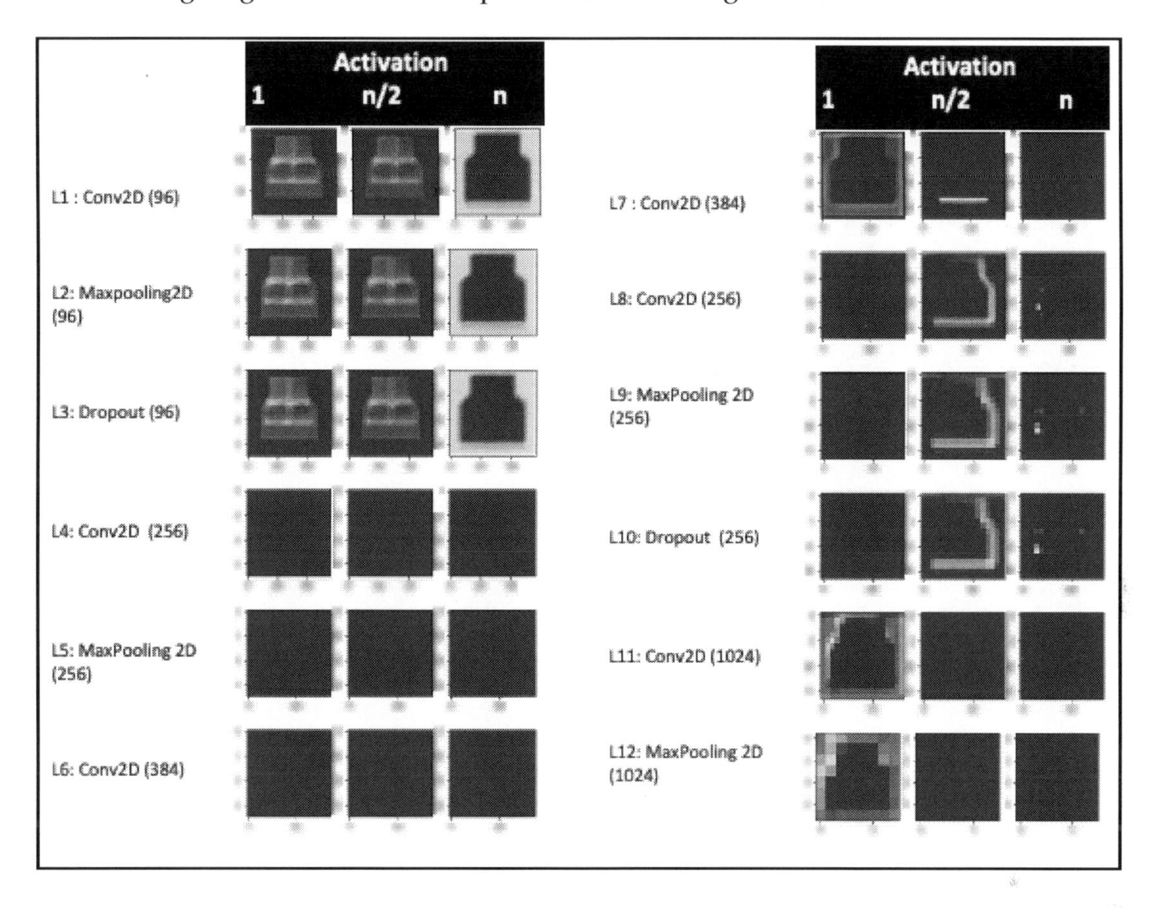

Just like the chair and bed examples, the preceding diagram starts with the top layers, which have distinct characteristics, whereas the last few layers show very abstract images that are specific to the class. Note that layers 4, 5, and 6 can easily be replaced as the layers are not activating at all.

Training an existing advanced image classifier model and visualizing its layers

We found that the model that we developed has about 16 layers and that its validation accuracy is about 80%. From this, we observed how the neural network sees the images at different layers. This brings up two questions:

- How does our custom neural network compare with the more advanced neural network?
- How does the advanced neural network see an image compared to our custom neural network? Do all neural networks see an image in a similar way or differently?

To answer these questions, we will train our classifier against two advanced networks, VGG16 and InceptionV3, and visualize a chair image at different layers of the network. `Chapter 5`, *Neural Network Architecture and Models*, provides a detailed explanation of the network, while `Chapter 6`, *Visual Search Using Transfer Learning*, provides a detailed explanation of the code. So, in this section, we'll just focus our attention on the visualization part. You may want to revisit the coding section after you've completed `Chapter 5`, *Neural Network Architecture and Models*, and `Chapter 6`, *Visual Search Using Transfer Learning*, so that you have a deep understanding of the code. The number of layers in VGG 16 is 26. You can find the code for this at `https://github.com/PacktPublishing/Mastering-Computer-Vision-with-TensorFlow-2.0/blob/master/Chapter04/Chapter4_classification_visualization_custom_model%26VGG.ipynb`.

Note that the preceding code runs both the custom network as well as the VGG 16 model. Don't run the cells marked as custom networks for this exercise to ensure that only the VGG16 model is executed. Keras has a simple API where the VGG16 or InceptionV3 models can be imported. The key thing to note here is that both VGG 16 and InceptionV3 are trained on an ImageNet dataset with 1,000 classes. However, in this case, we will be training this model with three classes so that we can just use the VGG 16 or Inception models. Keras will throw an error regarding incompatible shapes: `[128,1000]` versus `[128,3]`, where `128` is the batch size. To fix this, use `include_top = False` in the model definition, which removes the last fully connected layers and replaces them with our own layer with only three classes. Again, `Chapter 6`, *Visual Search Using Transfer Learning*, describes this in detail. The VGG 16 model results in a validation accuracy of around `0.89` after training for 135 steps and validating for 15 steps:

```
Epoch 1/10
 135/135 [==============================] - 146s 1s/step - loss: 1.8203 -
accuracy: 0.4493 - val_loss: 0.6495 - val_accuracy: 0.7000
 Epoch 2/10
 135/135 [==============================] - 151s 1s/step - loss: 1.2111 -
accuracy: 0.6140 - val_loss: 0.5174 - val_accuracy: 0.8067
 Epoch 3/10
 135/135 [==============================] - 151s 1s/step - loss: 0.9528 -
accuracy: 0.6893 - val_loss: 0.4765 - val_accuracy: 0.8267
 Epoch 4/10
 135/135 [==============================] - 152s 1s/step - loss: 0.8207 -
accuracy: 0.7139 - val_loss: 0.4881 - val_accuracy: 0.8133
 Epoch 5/10
 135/135 [==============================] - 152s 1s/step - loss: 0.8057 -
accuracy: 0.7355 - val_loss: 0.4780 - val_accuracy: 0.8267
 Epoch 6/10
 135/135 [==============================] - 152s 1s/step - loss: 0.7528 -
accuracy: 0.7571 - val_loss: 0.3842 - val_accuracy: 0.8333
 Epoch 7/10
 135/135 [==============================] - 152s 1s/step - loss: 0.6801 -
accuracy: 0.7705 - val_loss: 0.3370 - val_accuracy: 0.8667
 Epoch 8/10
 135/135 [==============================] - 151s 1s/step - loss: 0.6716 -
accuracy: 0.7906 - val_loss: 0.4276 - val_accuracy: 0.8800
 Epoch 9/10
 135/135 [==============================] - 152s 1s/step - loss: 0.5954 -
accuracy: 0.7973 - val_loss: 0.4608 - val_accuracy: 0.8533
 Epoch 10/10
 135/135 [==============================] - 152s 1s/step - loss: 0.4926 -
accuracy: 0.8152 - val_loss: 0.3550 - val_accuracy: 0.8933
```

The following diagram shows the neural network's visualization after using the VGG 16 model for the chair:

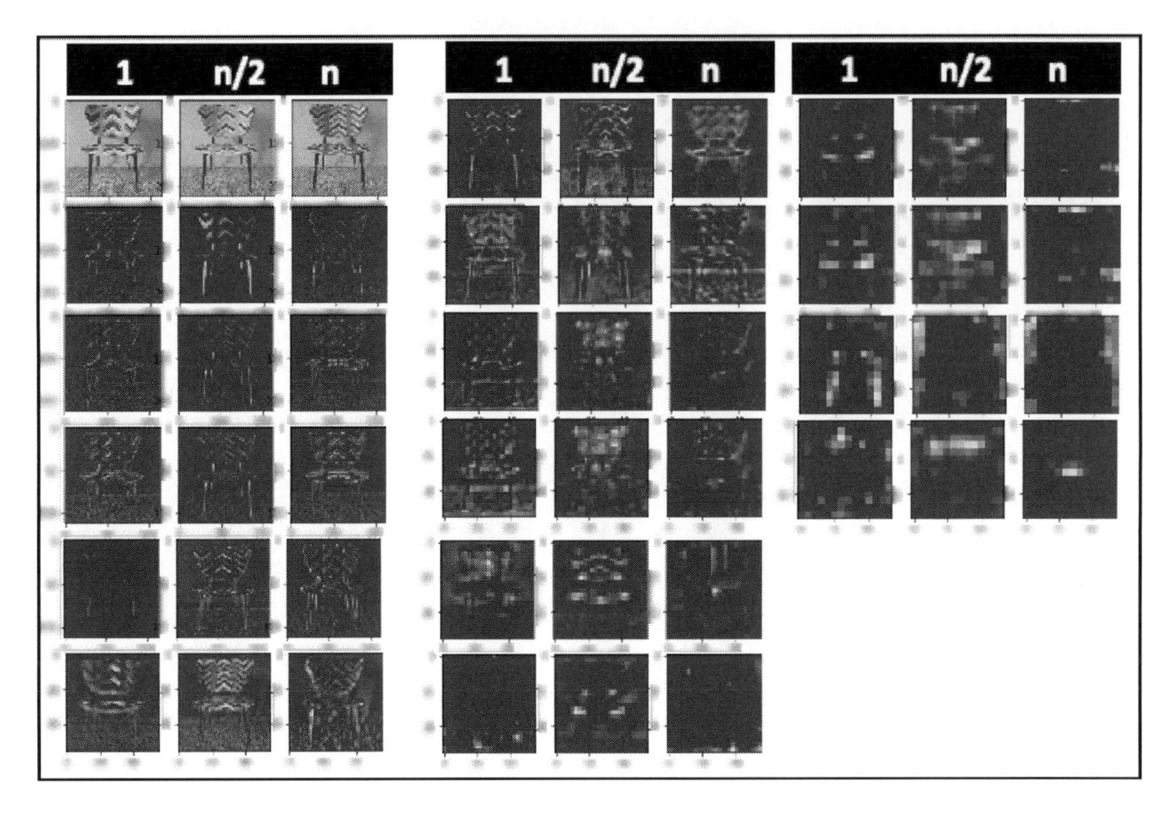

The preceding diagram shows how the VGG 16 model sees the chair in its first 16 layers. Note that compared to our custom model, the VGG 16 model is much more efficient as every layer is performing some type of activation of the image. The image characteristics at different layers are different but the general trend is the same – the image is transformed into a more abstract structure as we go deeper into the layers.

Next, we perform the same exercise with the Inception V3 model. The code for this is described in `Chapter 6`, *Visual Search Using Transfer Learning*. The following images shows how the Inception V3 model visualizes the chair image:

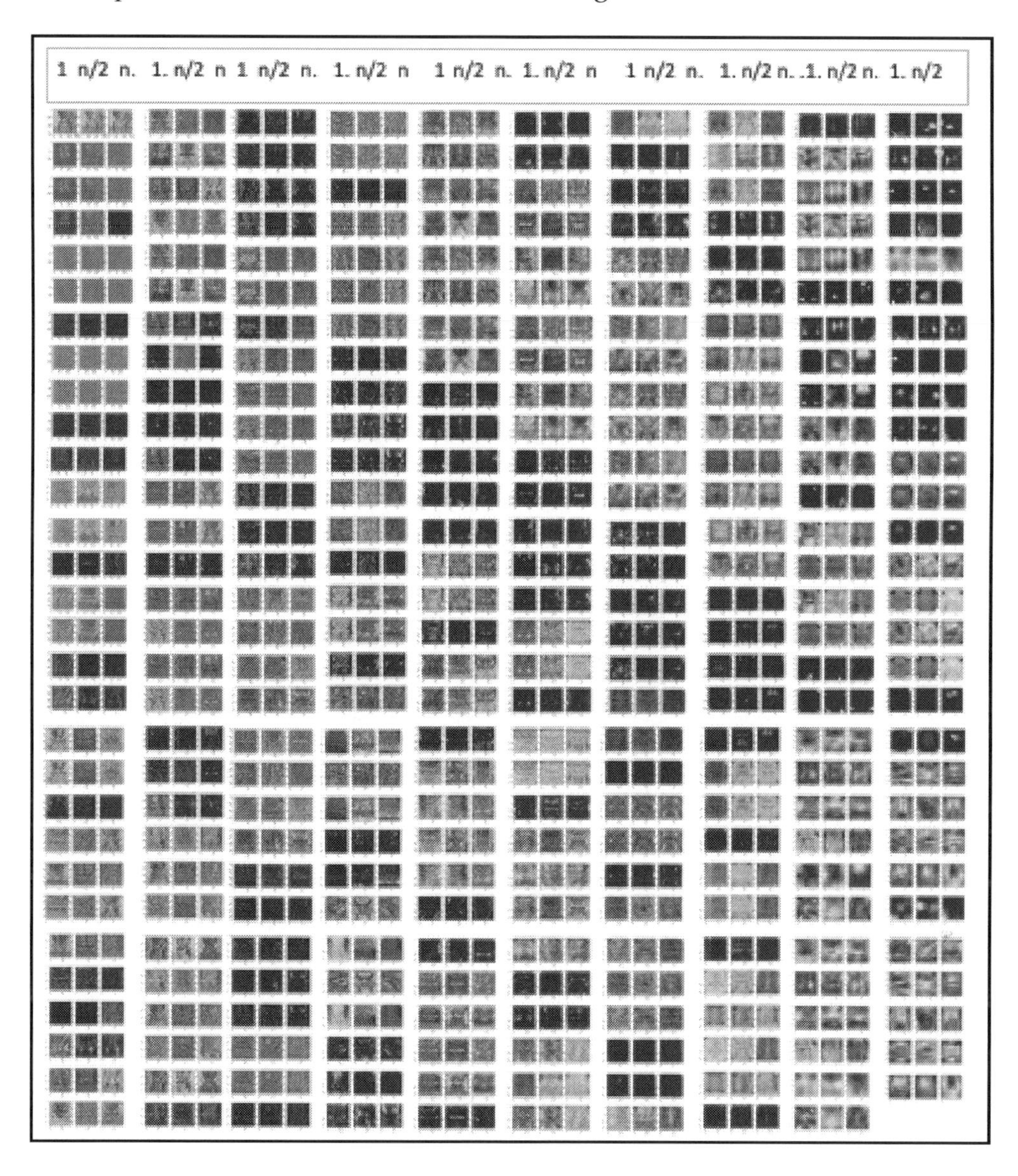

The validation accuracy for the Inception V3 model is about 99%. As you can see, there are a lot more layers in the Inception V3 model compared to VGG16. The preceding image is difficult to visualize. The following image shows the first, last, and some select in-between layers:

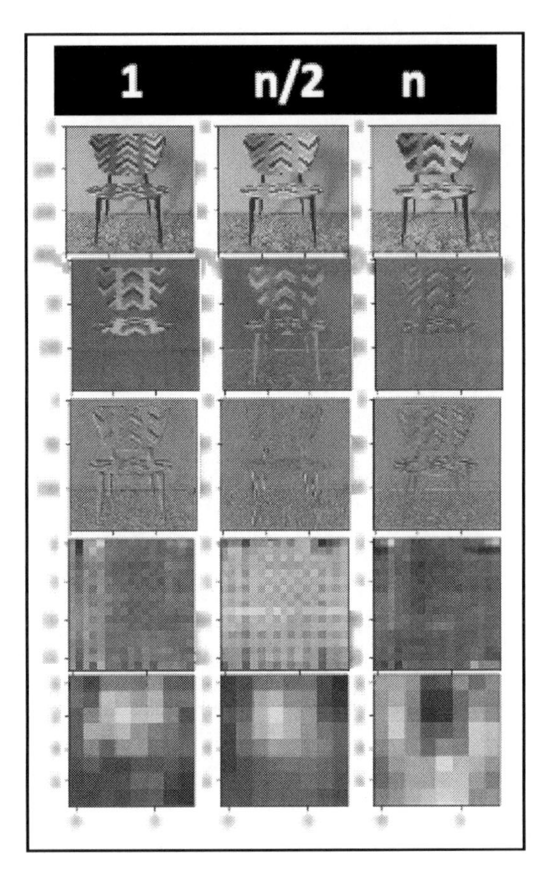

The preceding image clearly shows how the chair image loses its sharpness and becomes increasingly blurred as we go deeper into the neural network. The final image looks less like a chair. The neural network sees many similar chair images and interprets a chair from them.

In this section, we described how to view the intermediate activation layer during training to understand how feature maps are transformed across the neural network. However, if you want to understand how a neural network transforms features and hidden layers into output, refer to the TensorFlow Neural Network Playground at `https://bit.ly/2VNfkEn`.

Summary

CNNs are the de facto image classification models due to their ability to learn the distinctive features of each class by themselves, without deriving any relationship between input and output. In this chapter, we learned about the components of CNNs that are responsible for learning the image feature and then classifying it into predefined classes. We learned how convolution layers stack on top of each other to learn from simple shapes (such as edges) to create a complex shape (such as an eye) and how the dimensionality of the feature map changes due to the convolution and pooling layers. We also understood the functions of the nonlinear activation function, Softmax, and the fully connected layers. This chapter highlighted how to optimize different parameters to reduce overfitting issues.

We also constructed a neural network for classification purposes and used the model we developed to create an image tensor that's used by the neural network to develop an activation layer for visualization. The visualization method helps us understand how the feature maps are transformed within the neural network and how a neural network assigns a class from this transformed feature map using a fully connected layer. We also learned how to compare our custom neural network visualization with that of advanced networks such as VGG16 and Inception V3.

In the next chapter, you will learn about some of the most well-known neural network models in order to gain a deeper understanding of CNN parameter selection.

2
Section 2: Advanced Concepts of Computer Vision with TensorFlow

In this section, you will build on the knowledge learned in the last section to perform complex computer vision tasks such as visual search, object detection, and neural style transfer. You will solidify your understanding of neural networks and perform many hands-on coding exercises using TensorFlow.

By the end of this section, you will be able to do the following:

- Develop a fundamental understanding of various neural network models, including AlexNet, VGG, ResNet, Inception, **Region-specific CNN** (**RCNN**), **Generative adversarial networks** (**GANs**), reinforcement learning, and transfer learning (chapter 5)
- Learn techniques used by some of the famous models for image recognition and object detection (chapter 5)
- Input images and their categories into the TensorFlow model using the Keras data generator and `tf.data` (chapter 6)
- Develop a TensorFlow model using transfer learning for furniture images and use the model to perform a visual search on furniture images (chapter 6)
- Perform bounding box annotation on images to generate an `.xml` file and convert it into a `.txt` file format to input into a YOLO object detector (chapter 7)
- Develop an understanding of how YOLO and RetinaNet function, and learn how to detect objects using YOLO (chapter 7)

- Train a YOLO object detector and optimize its parameters to complete the training (chapter 7)
- Perform semantic segmentation using TensorFlow DeepLab and write TensorFlow code for neural style transfer in Google Colab (chapter 8)
- Generate artificial images using DCGAN and perform image inpainting using OpenCV (chapter 8)

This section comprises the following chapters:

- `Chapter 5`, *Neural Network Architecture and Models*
- `Chapter 6`, *Visual Search Using Transfer Learning*
- `Chapter 7`, *Object Detection Using YOLO*
- `Chapter 8`, *Semantic Segmentation and Neural Style Transfer*

5
Neural Network Architecture and Models

The **convolutional neural network** (**CNN**) is the most widely used tool in computer vision to classify and detect objects. A CNN maps an input image to an output class or a bounding box by stacking many different layers of linear and nonlinear functions. The linear functions consist of convolution, pooling, fully connected, and softmax layers, whereas the nonlinear layers are the activation functions. A neural network has many different parameters and weight factors that need to be optimized for a given problem set. Stochastic gradient descent and backpropagation are two ways of training the neural network.

In `Chapter 4`, *Deep Learning on Images*, you learned some basic coding skills to build and train a neural network and gained an understanding of the visual transformation of feature maps within different layers of a neural network. In this chapter, you will gain an in-depth understanding of the theory behind a neural network architectures and models and understand critical concepts such as neural network saturation with depth, vanishing gradient problem, overfitting due to large parameter sets and many others. This will help you create your own efficient model for your research purposes and follow the topics of the next few chapters where these theories are applied in code.

The topics covered in this chapter are as follows:

- Overview of AlexNet
- Overview of VGG16
- Overview of Inception
- Overview of ResNet
- Overview of R-CNN
- Overview of Fast R-CNN
- Overview of Faster R-CNN
- Overview of GANs

- Overview of GNNs
- Overview of Reinforcement Learning
- Overview of Transfer Learning

Overview of AlexNet

AlexNet was introduced in 2012 by Alex Krizhevsky, Ilya Sutskever, and Geoffrey E. Hinton in a paper titled *ImageNet Classification with Deep Convolutional Neural Networks*. The original paper can be found at `http://www.cs.utoronto.ca/~ilya/pubs/2012/imgnet.pdf`.

It was the first successful introduction of an optimized CNN model to solve computer vision problems regarding the classification of a large number of images (over 15 million) from many different categories (over 22,000). Before AlexNet, computer vision problems were mainly solved by traditional machine learning methods, which made incremental improvements by collecting larger datasets and improving the model and techniques to minimize overfitting.

CNN models classify error rates in terms of a top-five error rate, which is the percentage of instances where the true class of a given image is not amongst the top five prediction classes. AlexNet won the 2012 ILSVRC (ImageNet Large-Scale Visual Recognition Challenge) by having a top-five error rate of 15.3%, taking a significant lead over the second-best result, which scored top-five error rate of 26.2%. The AlexNet architecture is shown in the following diagram:

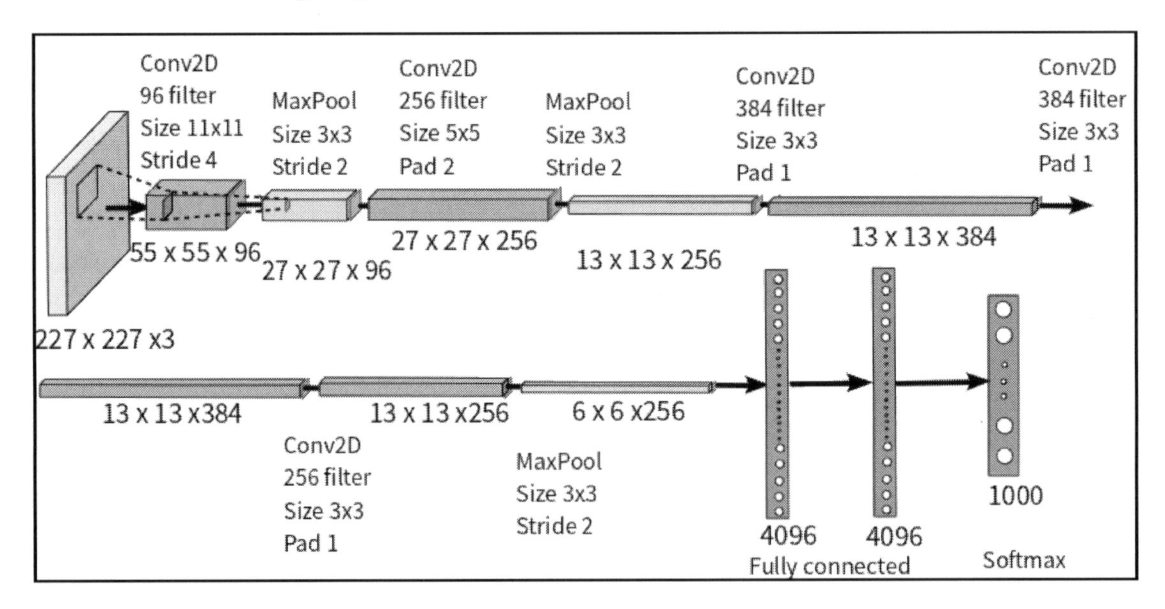

The basic idea of AlexNet is summarized as follows:

- It contains 8 learned layers—5 convolution layers and 3 fully connected layers.
- It uses large kernel filters—96 filters of size 11 x 11 in the first layer, 256 filters of size 5 x 5 in the second layer, 384 filters of size 3 x 3 in the third and fourth layers, and 256 filters of size 3 x 3 in the fifth layer.
- The ReLU activation layer is applied after every convolutional and fully connected layer. It trains much faster than Tanh.
- Dropout regularization is applied to the first and second fully connected layers.
- Overfitting is reduced by two data-augmentation techniques:
    - Creating random patches of 224 x 224 from a 256 x 256 image size and performing translation and horizontal reflections
    - Altering the intensities of the RGB channels in training images
- Training is done over two GPUs—90 epochs in 5 or 6 days to train on two Nvidia GeForce high-end GTX 580 GPUs.
- The 1,000 output from the softmax layer maps to each of the 1,000 ImageNet classes to predict the class output.

The following code imports all the functions that are necessary to run the TensorFlow backend. This model imports the `Sequential` model, which is a layer-by-layer model structure in Keras:

```
from __future__ import print_function
import keras
from keras.models import Sequential
from keras.layers import Dense, Dropout, Activation, Flatten
from keras.layers import Conv2D, MaxPooling2D, ZeroPadding2D
from keras.layers.normalization import BatchNormalization
from keras.regularizers import l2
```

The following code loads the CIFAR dataset.

The CIFAR dataset (`https://www.cs.toronto.edu/~kriz/cifar.html`) has 10 different classes with 6,000 images per class. The classes are airplane, automobile, bird, cat, deer, dog, frog, horse, ship, and truck. TensorFlow has built-in logic to import the CIFAR dataset.

The dataset consists of training and test images that will be used to develop the model (train) and to verify its results (test). Each dataset has two parameters, x and y, representing width (x) and height (y) of the image:

```
from keras.datasets import cifar10
(x_train, y_train), (x_test, y_test) = cifar10.load_data()
```

A neural network has many different parameters, that need to be optimized—these are also called model constants. For AlexNet, these are as follows:

- `batch_size` is `32` number of training examples on one forward or backward pass.
- `num_classes` is `2`.
- `epochs` is `100` number of times the training will repeat.
- `data_augmentation` is `True`.
- `num_predictions` is `20`.

Let's convert the input vector into a binary class matrix, as we have two classes in this example:

```
y_train = keras.utils.to_categorical(y_train, num_classes)
y_test = keras.utils.to_categorical(y_test, num_classes)
# Initialize model
model = Sequential()
```

The following table describes the TensorFlow code for different AlexNet model layers. In subsequent sections, other models will be introduced, but the basic idea of creating the model is similar:

Convolution and Pooling 1	**Convolution and Pooling 5**

`model.add(Conv2D(96, (11, 11),`
`input_shape=x_train.shape[1:],`
`padding='same',`
`kernel_regularizer=l2(l2_reg)))`
`model.add(BatchNormalization())`
`model.add(Activation('relu'))`
`model.add(MaxPooling2D(pool_size=(2,`
`2))`
	`model.add(ZeroPadding2D((1, 1)))`
	`model.add(Conv2D(1024, (3, 3),`
	`padding='same'))`
	`model.add(BatchNormalization())`
	`model.add(Activation('relu'))`
	`model.add(MaxPooling2D(pool_size=(2,`
	`2)))`

Convolution and Pooling 2	**Fully Connected 1**

`model.add(Conv2D(256, (5, 5),`
`padding='same'))`
`model.add(BatchNormalization())`
`model.add(Activation('relu'))`
`model.add(MaxPooling2D(pool_size=(2,`
`2)))`
	`model.add(Flatten())`
	`model.add(Dense(3072))`
	`model.add(BatchNormalization())`
	`model.add(Activation('relu'))`
	`model.add(Dropout(0.5))`

Convolution and Pooling 3	**Fully Connected 2**

model.add(ZeroPadding2D((1, 1))) model.add(Conv2D(512, (3, 3), padding='same')) model.add(BatchNormalization()) model.add(Activation('relu')) model.add(MaxPooling2D(pool_size=(2, 2)))	model.add(Dense(4096)) model.add(BatchNormalization()) model.add(Activation('relu')) model.add(Dropout(0.5))
Convolution and Pooling 4	**Fully Connected 3**
model.add(ZeroPadding2D((1, 1))) model.add(Conv2D(1024, (3, 3), padding='same')) model.add(BatchNormalization()) model.add(Activation('relu'))	model.add(Dense(num_classes)) model.add(BatchNormalization()) model.add(Activation('softmax'))

The key model configuration parameters are described in the following list. This should give you a high-level overview of the parameters that need to be optimized to train a neural network model:

- **Model compilation**: Once the model is developed, the next step is to compile the model using TensorFlow. For model compilation, we need to define two parameters:
    - **Loss function**: A loss function determines how close the model value is to the actual results. Categorical cross-entropy is the most common loss function—it determines the loss using a logarithmic scale with an output value between 0 to 1, wherein a small output signifies a small difference and a large output signifies a large difference. Another loss function that can also be used is the RMS (root mean square) loss function.
    - **Optimizer**: An optimizer fine-tunes the parameters of the model to minimize the loss function. The Adadelta optimizer fine-tunes the learning rate based on a moving window of past gradients. Other optimizers that are commonly used are the Adam optimizer and RMSprop optimizer.

The following code shows how to use an optimizer during model compilation in Keras:

```
model.compile(loss = 'categorical_crossentropy',
              optimizer = keras.optimizers.Adadelta(),
              metrics = ['accuracy'])
```

Once the model is constructed, the model must be compiled by the preceding method before it can be used for prediction (`model.predict()`).

Note that in this section we studied AlexNet, which won the ILSVRC competition in 2012. In 2013, an updated version of AlexNet, called ZFNet, was developed, which used 8 layers like AlexNet, but used 7 x 7 filters instead of 11 x 11 filters. As we go through the next sections, we will find that using the smaller filter size improves model accuracy as input image pixel information is preserved.

Overview of VGG16

After the success of AlexNet in 2012, more and more researchers worked on improving the CNN architecture of AlexNet to improve accuracy. The focus shifted to smaller window size, smaller filters, and smaller strides. VGG16 was introduced in 2014 by Karen Simonyan and Andrew Zisserman in the paper titled *Very Deep Convolutional Networks for Large-Scale Image Recognition*. The paper can be read at `https://arxiv.org/abs/1409.1556`.

The model achieved a 92.7% top-five test accuracy in ImageNet in ILSVRC-2014.

The VGG16 architecture is shown in the following image:

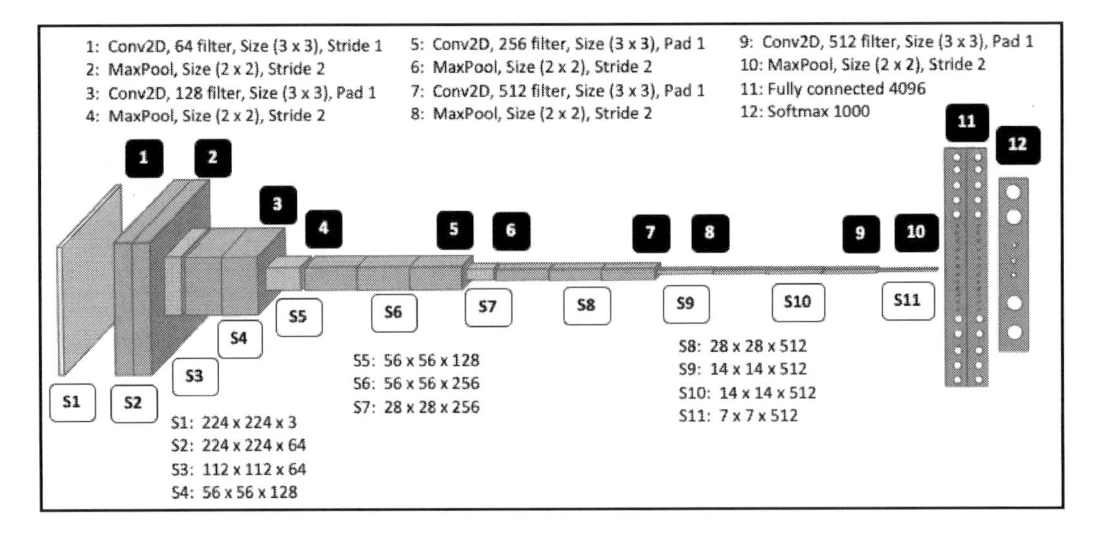

The basic idea of VGG16 is summarized as follows:

- The maximum filter size is 3 x 3 and the minimum size is 1 x 1. This means that a smaller filter size with a larger quantity is used, compared to a larger filter size and smaller quantity for AlexNet; this results in fewer parameters compared to AlexNet.
- Convolution stride is 1 and padding is 1 for a 3 x 3 convolutional layer. Max pooling is performed over a 2 x 2 window with a stride of 2.
- Three nonlinear ReLU functions are used instead of a single one in each layer, which makes the decision function more discriminative by reducing the vanishing gradient problem and enabling the network to learn deeply. Learning deeply here means learning complex shapes, such as edges, features, boundaries, and so on.
- The total number of parameters is 138 million.

Overview of Inception

Before the introduction of the inception layer, most CNN architectures had a standard configuration—stacked (in series) convolution, normalization, max pooling, and activation layers followed by a fully connected and softmax layer. This architecture led to an increasing depth of the neural network, which suffered from two major drawbacks:

- Overfitting
- Increased computation time

The inception model solved both issues by moving from dense network to sparse matrices and clustering them to form dense submatrices.

The inception model is also known as GoogLeNet. It was introduced by Christian Szegedy, Wei Liu, Yangqing Jia, Pierre Sermanet, Scott Reed, Dragmir Anguelov, Dumitru Erhan, Vincent Vanhoucke, and Andrew Rabinovich in a paper titled *Going Deeper with Convolutions*. The name of Inception came from the paper *Network in Network* by Min Lin, Qiang Chen, and Shuicheng Yan and the famous internet meme *We need to go deeper*. The links to the *Inception* paper and the *Network in Network* paper are given here:

- **Inception**: `https://arxiv.org/abs/1409.4842`
- **Network in Network**: `https://arxiv.org/abs/1312.4400`

In the paper *Network In Network*, instead of using a conventional linear filter over the input image, the authors constructed a micro neural network and slid that over the input image in a similar manner to a CNN. A deep neural network is constructed by stacking several of these layers together. The micro neural network (also known as a **multilayer perceptron**) consists of multiple fully connected layers with an activation function, as shown in the following figure:

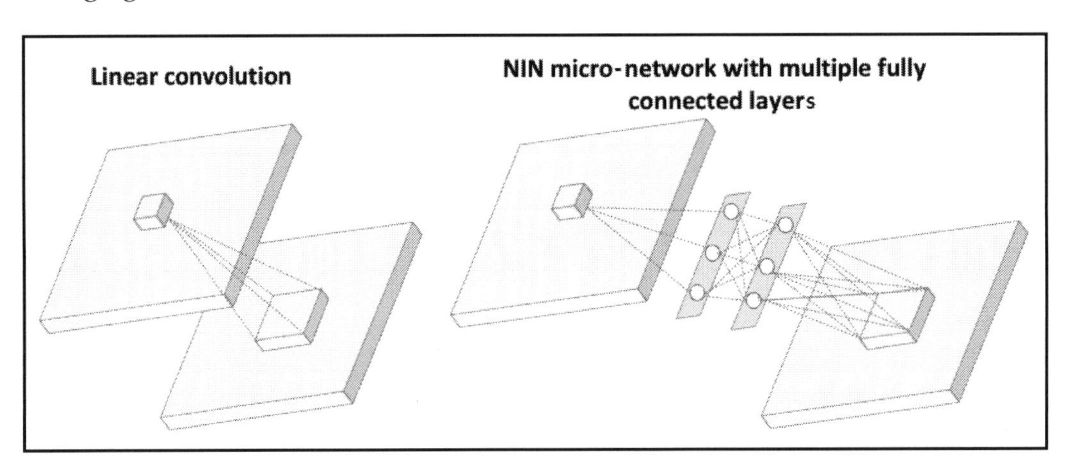

The figure on the left shows the linear filter in a conventional CNN connecting the input image to the next layer. The figure on the right shows the micro-network, consisting of multiple fully connected layers followed by an activation function connecting the input image to the next layer. The inception layer here is a logical culmination of NIN, described as follows:

- The main idea of the inception architecture is based on finding out how an optimal local sparse (multiple 1 x 1 in parallel) structure in a CNN can be supplemented with readily available dense components (3 x 3 and 5 x 5). The authors of the inception paper found the answer by utilizing 1 x 1 convolution in parallel with 3 x 3, 5 x 5 convolution and a pooling layer. An additional 1 x 1 convolution followed by ReLU can be thought of as equivalent to the NIN micro-network. The 1 x 1 convolution serves as a dimension-reduction mechanism, and also helps to increase the width of the network (by stacking them side by side), along with its depth. The deployment of multiple convolutions with multiple filters and pooling layers simultaneously in parallel within the same layer (the inception layer) results in the layer being a sparse layer with an increase in width. The 1 x 1 convolution suffers from less overfitting because of a smaller kernel size.
- The intention is to let the neural network learn the best weights when training the network and automatically select the more useful features.

- To further reduce the dimensions, the 1 x 1 convolution is used before the 3 x 3 and 5 x 5 convolution, as shown in the following diagram:

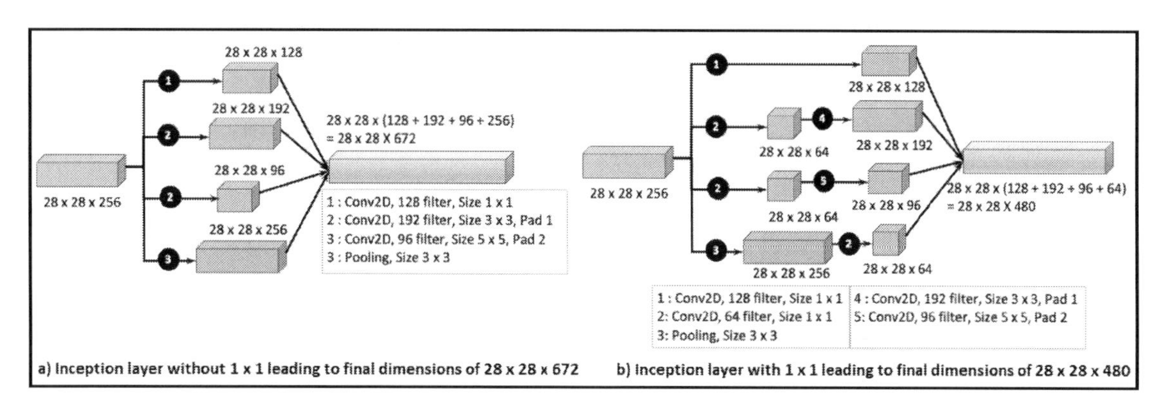

a) Inception layer without 1 x 1 leading to final dimensions of 28 x 28 x 672 b) Inception layer with 1 x 1 leading to final dimensions of 28 x 28 x 480

The preceding diagram shows that the utilization of the 1 x 1 layer before the 3 x 3 and 5 x 5 layers results in about a 30% dimensional reduction, from 672 (left image (a)) to 480 (right image (b)). The following figure shows the full inception network. The complete inception layer described in the middle section of the following figure is so large that it will not fit in one page, so it has been compressed. Do not try to read every element of the diagram here, but instead get the overall idea of the repeating content. The critical repeating module of the inception layer has been magnified, as shown in the top and bottom sections of the following image:

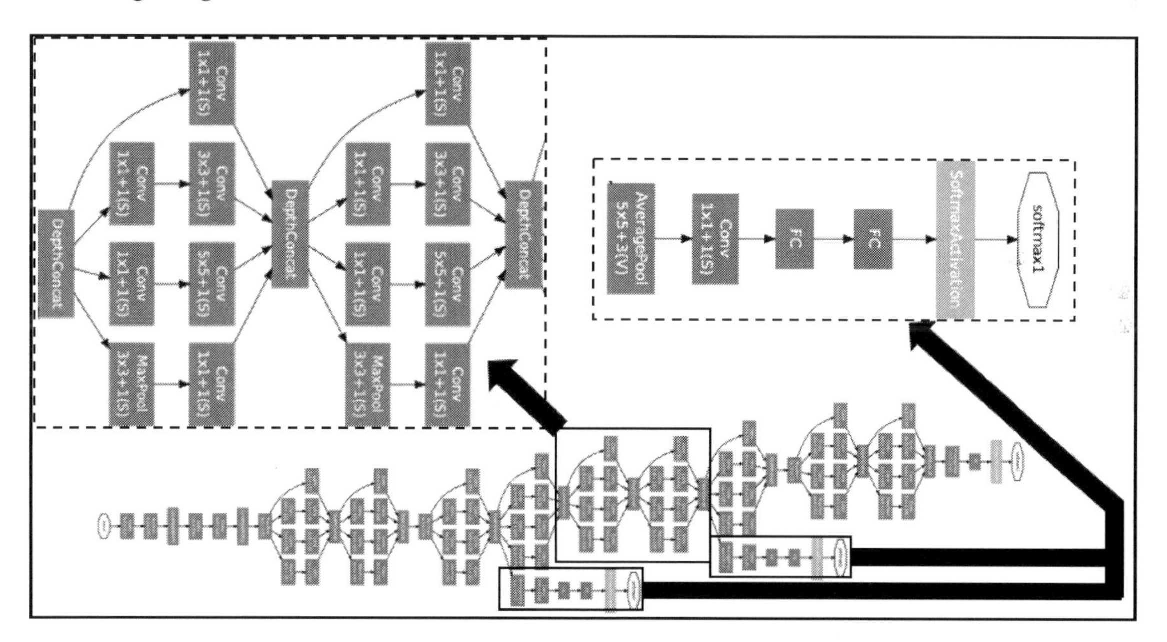

The network consists of the following sections:

- 1 x 1 convolution with 128 filters for dimension reduction and rectified linear activation
- A fully connected layer with 1,024 units and ReLU activation
- A dropout layer with a 70% ratio of dropped outputs
- A linear layer with softmax loss as the classifier (predicting the same 1,000 classes as the main classifier, but removed at inference time)

The following diagram illustrates the CNN filters and their corresponding connections in the inception network:

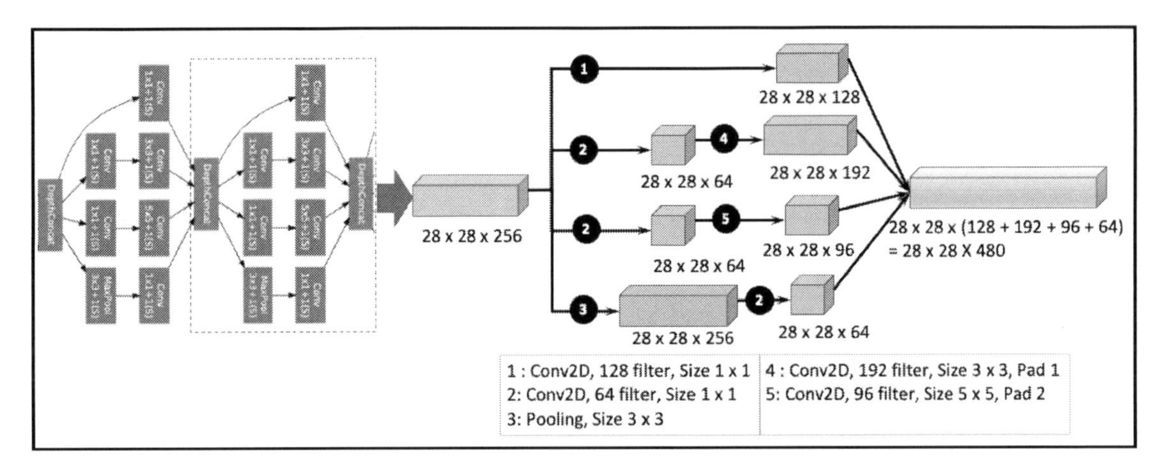

In the preceding diagram, the deep connection layer can either be connected with the max pool layer or it can connect directly to the 1 x 1 convolution layer. Either way, the calculation afterward follows the same pattern as that illustrated in the preceding figure.

GoogLeNet detection

The inception network (also known as **GoogLeNet**) improved upon the two-stage layer (region proposal based on color, texture, size, and shape, and then CNN for classification) proposal for **recurrent convolutional neural networks (R-CNN)**.

First, it replaced AlexNet with an improved inception for CNN. Next, the region proposal step is improved by combining the selective search (in R-CNN) approach with multi-box predictions for higher object bounding box recall. The region proposal is reduced by about 60% (from 2,000 to 1,200) while increasing the coverage from 92% to 93%, resulting in a 1% improvement of the mean average precision for the single model case. Overall, the accuracy improved from 40% to 43.9%.

Overview of ResNet

ResNet, introduced by Kaiminh He, Xiangyu Zhang, Shaoquing Ren, and Jian Sun in the paper titled *Deep Residual Learning for Image Recognition,* was developed to address the accuracy degradation problem of deep neural networks with an increase in depth. This degradation is not caused by overfitting, but results from the fact that after some critical depth, the output looses the information of the input, so the correlation between the input and output starts diverging resulting in an increase in inaccuracy. The paper can be found at `https://arxiv.org/abs/1512.03385`.

ResNet-34 achieved a top-five validation error of 5.71%, better than BN-inception and VGG. ResNet-152 achieves a top-five validation error of 4.49%. An ensemble of six models with different depths achieved a top-five validation error of 3.57%, and won first place in ILSVRC-2015. ILSVRC stands for the ImageNet Large-Scale Visual Recognition Competition; it evaluated object detection and image classification algorithms from 2010 to 2017.

The key features of ResNet are described as follows:

- The degradation problem is addressed by introducing a deep residual-learning framework.
- The framework introduces the concept of a shortcut or skips connection, which skips one or more layers.
- The underlying mapping between the input and the next layer is $H(x)$.
- The nonlinear layer is $F(x) = H(x) - x$, which can be reframed as $H(x) = F(x)+x$, where x is the identity mapping.

- The shortcut connections simply perform identity mapping, and their outputs are added to the outputs of the stacked layers (see the following diagram):

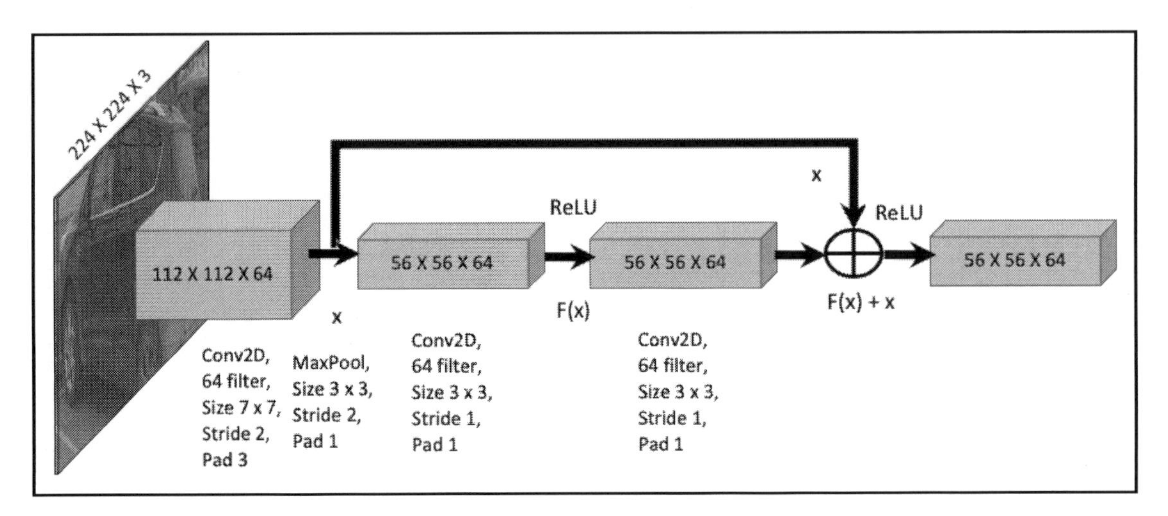

The preceding figure has the following features:

- The operation **F(x) + x** is performed by a shortcut connection and the addition of elements.
- Identity shortcut connections add neither an extra parameter nor computational complexity.

The complete ResNet model is shown in the following diagram:

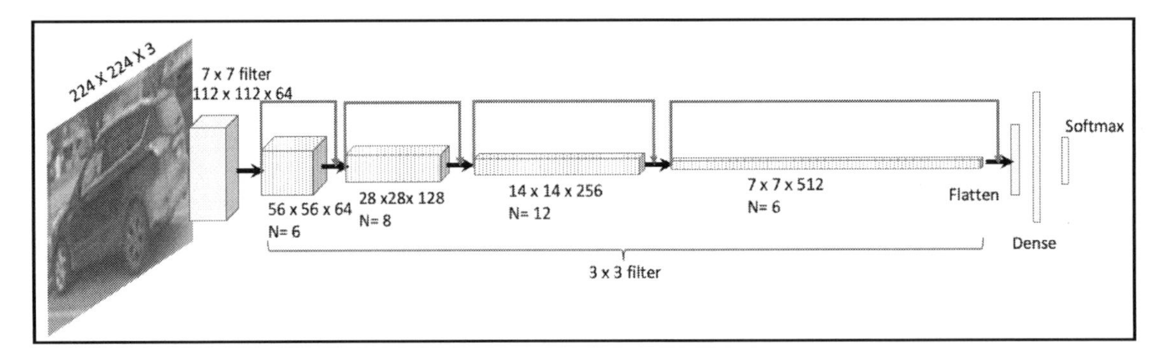

The ResNet model shown here has fewer filters and lower complexity than **visual geometry group(VGG)** networks. Dropout is not used. A comparison of performance between various neural network models is shown in the following screenshot:

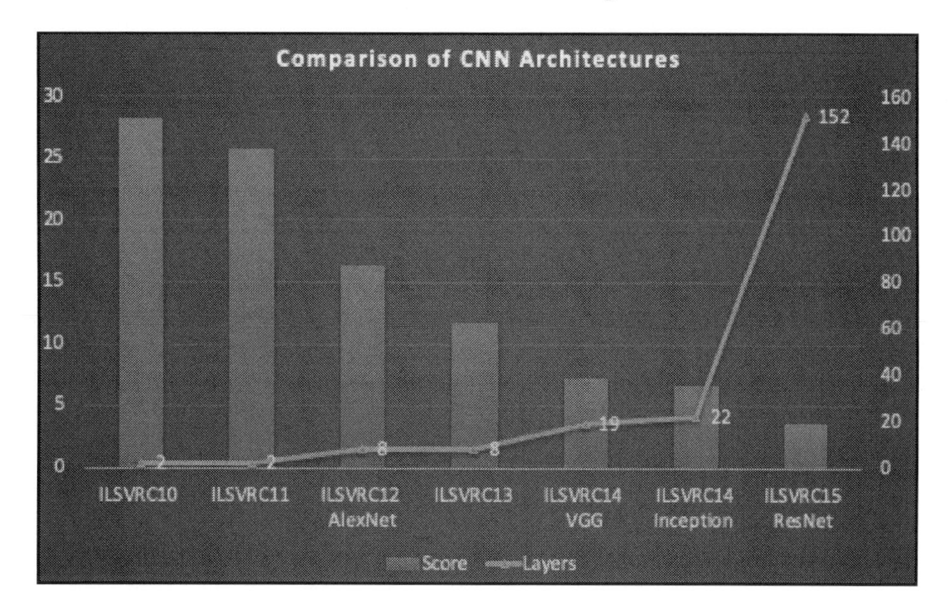

The preceding graph shows the following:

- The score and number of layers for various CNN architectures for the **ImageNet Large Scale Visual Recognition Challenge** (**ILSVRC**).
- The lower the score is, the better the performance.
- AlexNet got a significantly better score than any of its predecessors, and then in each subsequent year, the quality of the CNN kept on improving as the number of layers got larger and larger.
- ResNet, as described here, got the best score, which was about a fourfold improvement over AlexNet.

Overview of R-CNN

Region-specific CNN (R-CNN) was introduced by Ross Girshick, Jeff Donahue, Trevor Darrell, and Jitendra Malik in a paper titled *Rich feature hierarchies for accurate object detection and semantic segmentation*. It is a simple and scalable object detection algorithm that improves the mean average precision by more than 30% over the previous best result in VOC2012. The paper can be read at `https://arxiv.org/abs/1311.2524`

VOC stands for Visual Object Classes (`http://host.robots.ox.ac.uk/pascal/VOC`) and PASCAL stands for Pattern Analysis Statistical Modeling and Computational Learning. The PASCAL VOC ran challenges from 2005 to 2012 on object-class recognition. The PASCAL VOC annotation is widely used in object detection and it uses `.xml` format.

The entire object detection model is broken down into image segmentation, selective search-based region proposal, feature extraction using CNNs and classification, and bounding box formation using **support vector machine (SVM)**, as shown in the following diagram:

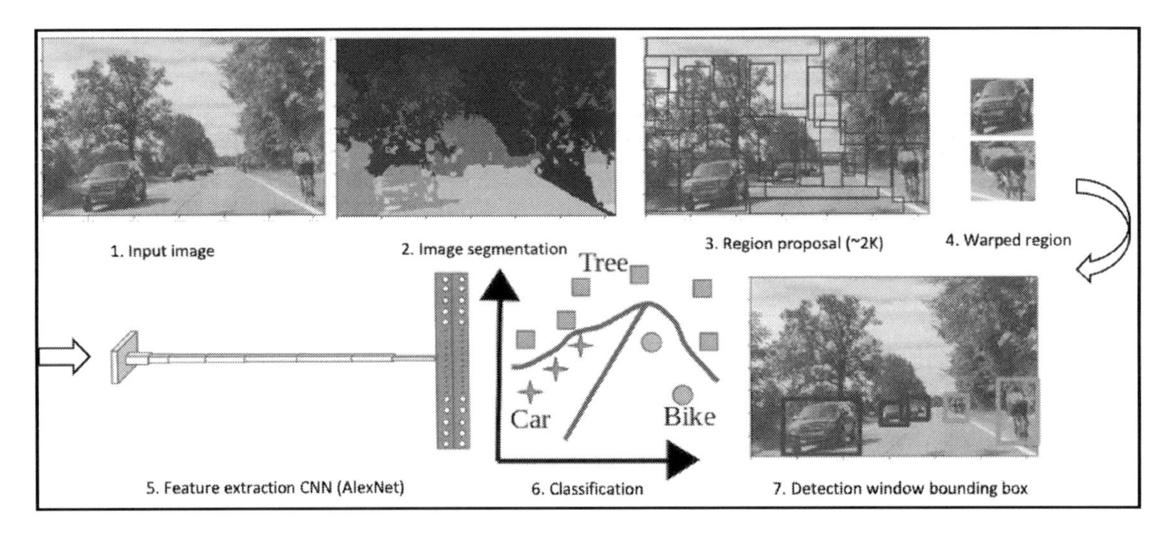

The preceding diagram shows the various steps to convert an input image of a car and a bike on a road to an object detection bounding box.

In the following section, each of these steps will be described in detail.

Image segmentation

Image segmentation is the representation of an image as a number of regions. Each of the regions in the segmented image has similar features, such as color, texture, and intensity.

Clustering-based segmentation

K-means is an unsupervised machine learning technique of separating similar data into groups based on centroids. The key steps in the *K*-means clustering algorithm are outlined as follows:

1. Select *K* data points as the initial number of clusters at an arbitrary location.
2. Find the distance between each cluster centroid and each pixel and assign it to the nearest cluster.
3. Update the averages of every cluster.
4. Repeat this process by changing the cluster centroid until the total distance between each pixel and its associated cluster is minimized.

Graph-based segmentation

There are many graph-based segmentation methods available, but the one described here for R-CNN is the one introduced by Pedro Felzenszwalb and Daniel Huttenlocher in a paper titled *Efficient Graph-Based Image Segmentation*. The paper can be read at `http://people.cs.uchicago.edu/~pff/papers/seg-ijcv.pdf`.

This method involves representing an image as a graph (a detailed explanation is given in the *Overview of GNN* section in this chapter) and then selecting edges from the graph where each pixel is linked to a node in the graph and connected to neighboring pixels through edges. The weights on an edge represent dissimilarity between pixels. The segmentation criteria are based on the degree of variability of neighboring regions of the image separated by a boundary. A boundary is defined by evaluating a threshold function that represents the intensity difference between pixels along the boundary compared to the intensity difference between neighboring pixels. Segmentation is defined as coarse or fine based on the presence of boundaries between the regions.

Selective search

The primary challenge in object detection is to find the precise location of the object in an image. Multiple objects in an image at different spatial orientations make it hard to find the boundary of the object in an image. For example, an object can be covered and only partially visible—an example is a person standing behind a car; we can see the car and the person's body above the car. A selective search is used to solve this problem. It divides the whole image into many segmentation regions. It then uses a bottom-up approach to combine similar regions into larger regions. The selective search uses the generated region to find the object's location. The selective search uses a greedy algorithm to iteratively group regions together based on size, color, and texture. The steps used in the selective search are explained as follows:

1. At first, the two most similar regions are evaluated and grouped together.
2. Next, new similarities are calculated between the resulting region and a new region to form a new group.
3. The process of grouping the most similar regions is repeated until the region covers the whole image.

The selective search is followed by a region proposal, which is described in the following section.

Region proposal

In this stage, the algorithm uses the selective search method described previously to extract around 2,000 category-independent region proposals. The category-independent region proposals are used to identify a number of regions in an image so that each object is well represented by at least one region in the image. Humans do this naturally by localizing objects in an image, but for machines, the location of the object needs to be determined and then it needs to be matched with an appropriate region in an image to detect the object.

Unlike image classification, detection involves image localization so that an appropriate region can be created that encloses the object to detect features within the region. The appropriate region is selected based on the selective search method, which computes a similar region by searching based on color and then searching on the basis of texture, size, and shape.

Feature extraction

Feature extraction is, grouping of similar features, such as edges, corners, and lines, into feature vectors. Feature vectors reduce the dimensionality of the image from 227 x 227 (~51,529) to 4,096, for example. Each region proposal, irrespective of its size, is first converted into a size of 227 x 227 by dilation and warping. This is required as the input image size for AlexNet is 227 x 227. 4,096 feature vectors are extracted from each region using AlexNet. The feature matrix is 4,096 x 2,000, as we have 2,000 region proposals for each image.

In principle, R-CNN can take any CNN model (such as AlexNet, ResNet, Inception, or VGG) as input as long as the input image size is modified to fit the network's image size. The authors of R-CNN compared AlexNet and VGG16 as inputs into R-CNN and found that VGG16 gives 8% higher accuracy, but takes 7 times longer compared to AlexNet.

Classification of the image

After feature extraction through AlexNet, the classification of the image involves passing the feature vector through class-specific linear SVMs to classify the presence of the object within the region proposal. Using SVMs is a supervised machine learning method that assigns weight and bias to each of the feature vectors and then draws a line to separate the objects into specific classes. The separation is done by determining the distance of each vector from the line and then positioning the line so that the separation distance is maximal.

Bounding box regression

Bounding box regression predicts the location of an object within an image. After the SVM, a linear regression model is developed to predict the location and size of the bounding box detection window. The bounding box of an object is defined by four anchor values, [x, y, w, h], where x is the x coordinate of the bounding box origin, y is the y coordinate of the bounding box origin, w is the width of the bounding box, and h is the height of the bounding box.

The regression technique attempts to minimize the errors in bounding box prediction by comparing the predicted value with the ground truth (target) values by adjusting each of the four anchor values.

Overview of Fast R-CNN

R-CNN achieved a more significant improvement in object detection than any of the previous methods, but it was slow, as it performed a forward pass on the CNN for every region proposal. Moreover, training was a multistage pipeline consisting of first optimizing the CNN for region proposal, then running SVMs for object classification, followed by using bounding box regressors to draw the bounding boxes. Ross Girschick, who was also the creator of R-CNN, proposed a model called fast R-CNN to improve detection using a single-stage training method. The following figure shows the architecture of fast R-CNN:

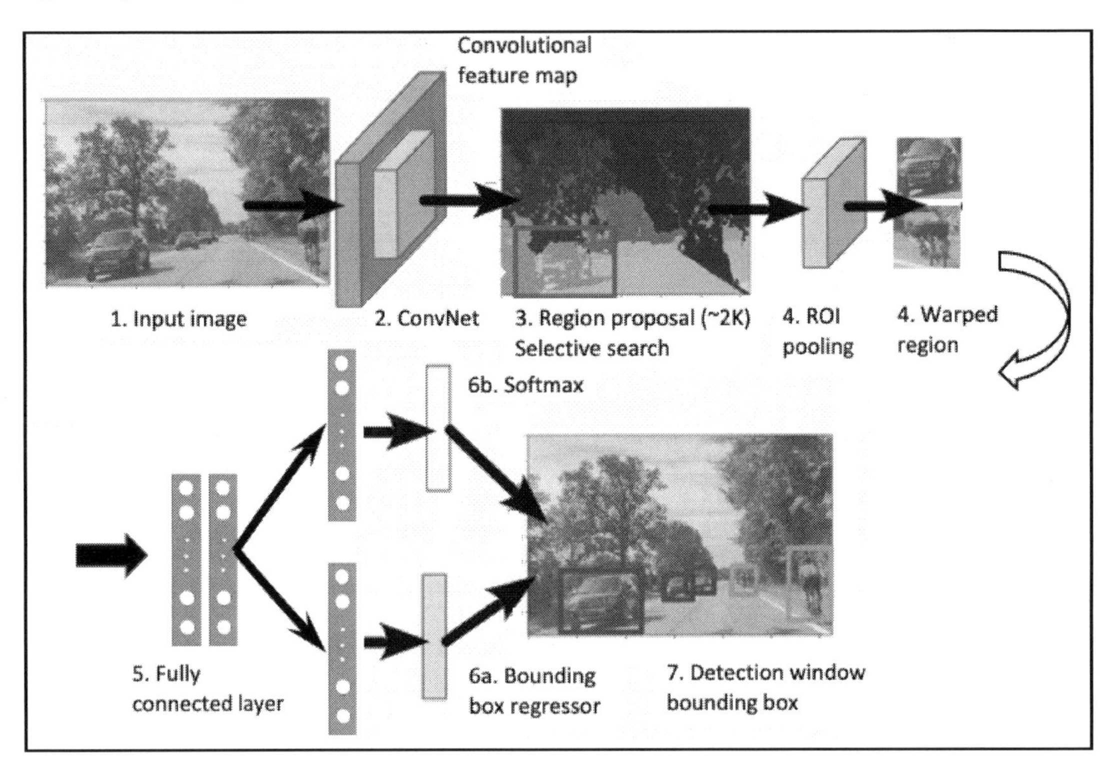

The steps used in fast R-CNN are as follows:

1. The fast R-CNN network processes the whole image with several convolution and max pooling layers to produce a feature map.
2. Feature maps are fed into a selective search to generate region proposals.
3. For each region proposal, a feature vector of fixed length ($h = 7 \times w = 7$) is extracted using **region-of-interest** (**RoI**) max pooling.
4. This feature vector value becomes the input for the **fully connected** (**FC**) layers separated by two branches:
    - Softmax for classification probability
    - Bounding box location and size (x, y, width, height) for each object class.

All network weights are trained using backpropagation, and computation and memory are shared between the forward and backward passes for loss and weight calculation; this reduces the training time in large networks from 84 hrs (R-CNN) to 9.5 hrs (fast R-CNN). Fast R-CNN uses the softmax classifier instead of SVMs (R-CNN). The mean average precision for softmax slightly outperforms that of SVMs, as shown in the following table for small (S), medium (M) and large (L) networks:

VOC07	S	M	L
SVMs	56.3	58.7	66.8
Softmax	57.1	59.2	66.9

The difference in results between SVMs and softmax is small, illustrating that one-shot fine-tuning using softmax is sufficient, compared to multistage training using SVMs. The increasing number of proposals beyond 4,000 results in about a 1% decrease in mean average precision, and when between 2,000 to 4,000, they actually result in around a 0.5% increase in precision.

Overview of Faster R-CNN

Both R-CNN and Fast R-CNN rely on a selective search method to develop a 2,000 region proposal, which results in a detection rate of 2 seconds per image compared to 0.2 seconds per image for most efficient detection methods. Shaoquing Ren, Kaiming He, Ross Girshick, and Jian Sun wrote a paper titled *Faster R-CNN: Towards Real-Time Object Detection with Region Proposal Networks to Improve the R-CNN Speed and Accuracy for Object Detection*. You can read the paper at `https://arxiv.org/abs/1506.01497`.

The following diagram shows the architecture of faster R-CNN:

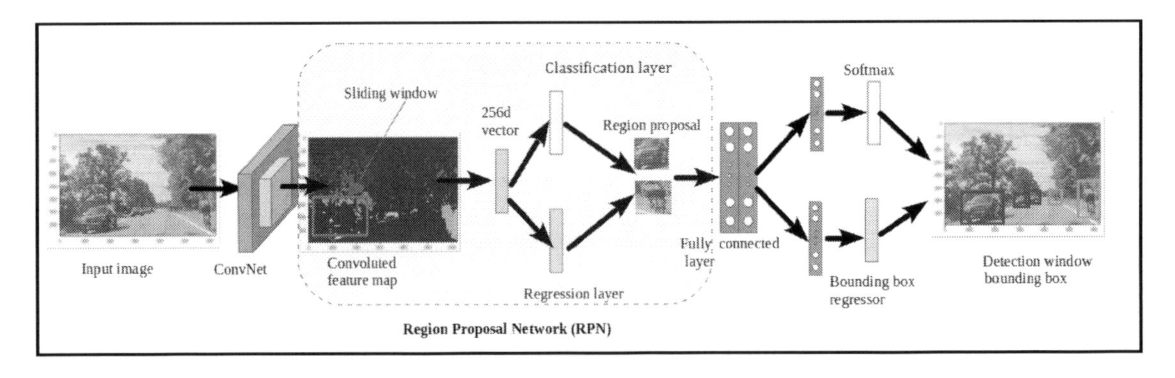

The key concepts are shown in the following list:

- Introduction of the input image to a **Region Proposal Network** (**RPN**), which outputs a set of rectangular region proposals for a given image.
- The RPN shares convolutional layers with state-of-the-art object detection networks.
- The RPN is trained by back propagation and **Stochastic Gradient Descent** (**SGD**).

The object detection network in faster R-CNN is similar to fast R-CNN. The following figure shows some object detection output using faster R-CNN:

Faster R-CNN + Inception ResNet backend
- inference done using pretrained model from TensorFlow Hub

Faster R-CNN + Inception backend
- inference done by training custom model

The preceding figure shows inference using the faster R-CNN model. In `Chapter 10`, *Object Detection Using R-CNN, SSD, and R-FCN*, you will learn how to generate this type of figure yourself. The figure on the left is generated using a pretrained model from TensorFlow Hub, whereas the figure on the right is generated by training our own images and then developing our own model.

The high accuracy illustrated in the preceding figure is obtained by following the technique outlined in the following list:

- Share the convolutional layer between the two networks: RPN for region proposal and fast R-CNN for detection.
- For the faster R-CNN, the input image size is 1,000 x 600.
- The RPN is generated by sliding a small window of size 60 x 40 over the convoluted feature map output.
- Each sliding window is mapped to 9 anchor boxes (3 scales with box area of 128, 256, and 512 pixels and 3 with an aspect ratio of 1:1, 1:2, and 2:1).
- Each anchor box is mapped to a region proposal.
- Each sliding window is mapped to a 256-D feature vector for ZF and 512-D feature vector for the VGG network.
- This vector is then inputted into two fully connected layers—a box-regression layer and a box-classification layer.
- The total number of region proposals is 21,500 (60 x 40 x 9).

For training the RPNs, a binary class label is assigned to each anchor box based on **intersection-over-union (IoU)** overlap with training data. The IoU is used to measure the accuracy of object detection. It is described in detail in `Chapter 7`, *Object Detection Using YOLO*. For now, it's enough for you to know that IoU is measured as a ratio of the area of overlap between two bounding boxes to the area of their union. This means that IOU = 1, which implies two complete bounding box overlaps, so you can only see one, whereas when IoU = 0, this means that two bounding boxes are completely separate from each other.

The binary class level has positive samples and negative samples with the following properties:

- **Positive samples**: IoU is the maximum value or greater than 0.7
- **Negative samples**: IoU is less than 0.3

The features used for regression are of the same spatial size (height and width). In an actual image, the feature size can be different. This is taken into account by using varied bounding box size using a different regression scale and aspect ratio. The convolution features between RPN and object detection are shared using the following principles:

- RPN is trained using the binary class level.
- The detection network is trained by the fast R-CNN method and initialized by an ImageNet pretrained model using RPN training.
- The RPN training is initialized by keeping the shared convolution layers fixed and only fine-tuning the layers unique to the RPN.
- The preceding steps result in the sharing of the two networks.
- Finally, the fully connected layers of the fast R-CNN are fine-tuned by keeping the shared convolution layers fixed.
- The combination of all the preceding steps results in both networks sharing the same convolution layers.

A comparison between R-CNN, fast R-CNN, and faster R-CNN is shown in the following table:

Parameters	**R-CNN**	**Fast R-CNN**	**Faster R-CNN**
Input	Image	Image	Image
Input image processing	Image segmentation based on pixel similarity	An input image is fed to CNN to generate a convolution feature map.	An input image is fed to CNN to generate a convolution feature map.
Region proposal	2K region proposals are generated using a selective search on the segmented image.	2K region proposals are generated using selective search of the convolution feature map.	The region proposals are generated using a **Region Proposal Network (RPN)**. A 60 x 40 sliding window is used for this CNN for each location of the feature map with 9 anchor boxes (3 scales and 3 aspect ratios).

Warping into fixed size	From the region proposal, each region is warped into a fixed size for input to CNN.	The region proposals are warped into a square of fixed size using max-pooling within the RoI pooling layer.	The region proposals are warped into a square of fixed size using the RoI pooling layer.
Feature extraction	2K warped region proposals of fixed size per image are fed to the CNN each time.	The 2K warped region is fed to two branches, each consisting of a fully connected layer.	The 2K warped region is fed to a fully connected layer.
Detection	The output of the CNN is passed to an SVM for classification to a bounding-box regressor to generate a bounding box.	One output of the fully connected layer is passed to a softmax layer for classification and the other one to a bounding box regressor to generate a bounding box.	One output of the fully connected layer is passed to a softmax layer for classification and the other one to a bounding box regressor to generate a bounding box.
CNN type	AlexNet	VGG 16	ZFNet or VGGNet. The ZFNet is a modified version of AlexNet.
Region proposal	Selective search is used to generate ~2,000 region proposals.	Selective search is used to generate ~2,000 region proposals.	CNN is used to generate ~21,500 region proposals (~60 x 40 x 9).
Convolution operation	The convolution operation is done 2K times per image.	The convolution operation is done once per image.	The convolution operation is done once per image.
Region proposal and detection	Region proposal and detection are decoupled.	Region proposal and detection are decoupled.	Region proposal and detection are coupled.
Training time	84 hrs	9 hrs	150 hrs
Test time	49 secs	2.43 secs	0.2 secs
mAP (VOC 2007)	66	66.9	66.9

The preceding table clearly shows the evolution of the R-CNN algorithm and the methods used to speed it up while improving its accuracy. Here are some key points that we learned from the preceding table:

- Image segmentation and selective search to determine pixel similarity is a time-consuming operation, as the operation is a pixel-by-pixel operation.
- The CNN operation that uses a sliding window is much faster in generating a region proposal than the selective search method.
- It is much faster to apply CNN to an entire image than it is to apply it to a region within an image and then repeat the process 2,000 times for a given image.

Overview of GANs

Generative adversarial networks (**GANs**) are a class of CNN that learns to estimate the probability distribution of the data. A GAN consists of two competing connected neural networks called a generator and a discriminator. The generator generates an artificial image based on the noise input of the image feature and the discriminator compares the artificial image with the real image to determine the probability that the image is real. The probability information is passed to the image input to learn in the next stage.
The following image illustrates the mechanism of a GAN:

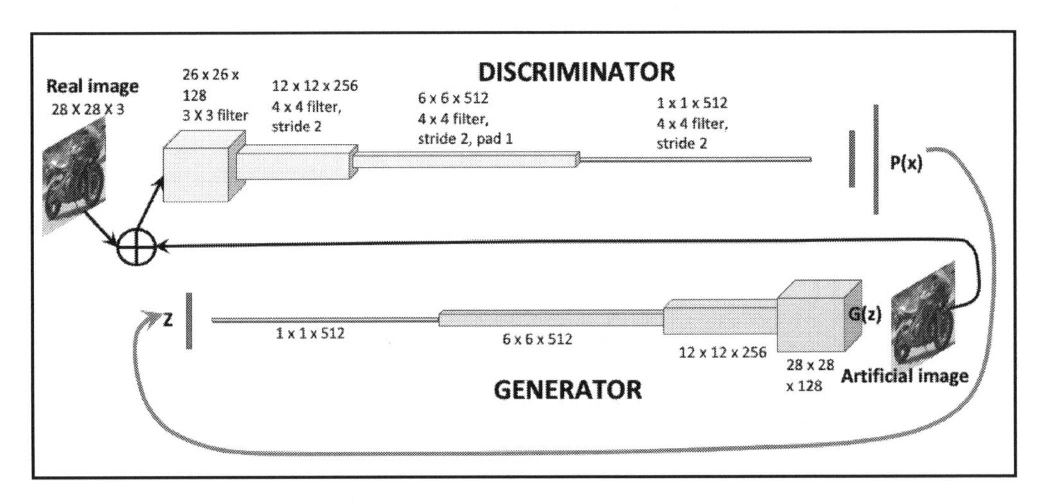

The step-by-step explanation of the GAN algorithm is listed as follows:

1. Given a training set, z, the generator network takes in a random vector representing the feature of the image and runs through a CNN to produce an artificial image, $G(z)$.

2. The discriminator network is a binary classifier; it takes in a real image and the artificial image and generates a probability, *P*(z), of creating an artificial image.
3. The discriminator feeds the probability information to the generator, which uses this information to improve its prediction of image *G*(z).

The binary classifier loss function is called a cross-entropy loss function and is represented as -(y log(p) + (1-y) log(1-p)), where *p* is the probability, and *y* is the expected value.

- **Discriminator objective function**:

$$max\ V(D) = E(x)\left[logD(x)\right] + E(z)\left[log\left(1\ -\ D(z)\right]\right.$$

- **Generator objective function**:

$$min\ V(G) = E(z)\left[log\left(1\ -\ D(z)\right]\right.$$

There are many types of GAN (more than 20) that already exist and more types are developed almost every month. The following list covers two main important variations of the GAN:

- **DCGAN (deep convolutional GAN)**: CNN is used for both discriminator and generator, as described in the original GAN.
- **CGAN (conditional GAN)**: A conditional vector to represent a label is used as an additional input to both the generative and discriminator network. Noise is added to the generative network along with the label vector detect variation in the label.

Some practical use cases of GAN are listed as follows:

- Generating artificial human face image and image datasets
- Combining images to form new datasets
- Generating a cartoon character
- Generating a 3D face and objects from a 2D image
- Semantic image translation
- Generating one set of colored images from a different colored image
- Text-to-image translation
- Human pose estimation
- Photograph editing and inpainting

Overview of GNNs

A **Graph Neural Network** (**GNN**) extends CNN learning to graph data. A graph can be represented as a combination of nodes and edges, where nodes represent the features of the graph and edges joins adjacent nodes, as shown in the following image:

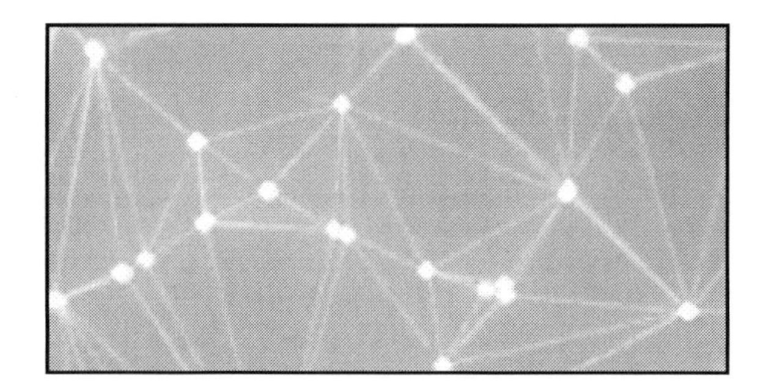

In this image, the nodes are illustrated by solid white points and the edges by the lines joining the points.

The following equations describe the key parameters of the graph:

- $H = (N, E)$
- $N = \{n1, n2, n3, \ldots\}$
- $E \subseteq N x N$

The transformations of the graph into a vector consisting of nodes, edges, and the relationships between the nodes are called the graph embeddings. The embeddings vector can be represented by the following equation:

$$h_{[n]} = f\left(x_{[n]}, x_{e[n],}, h_{ne[n]}, x_{ne[n]}\right)$$

$$o_{[n]} = g\left(h_{[n]}, x_{[n]}\right)$$

The following list describes the elements of the preceding equation:

- $h_{[n]}$ = State embedding for current node n
- $h_{ne[n]}$ = State embedding of the neighborhood of the node n
- $x_{[n]}$ = Feature of the node n
- $x_{e[n]}$ = Feature of the edge of the node n
- $x_{ne[n]}$ = Feature of the neighborhood of the node n
- $o_{[n]}$ = Output of node n

If H, X are the vectors constructed by stacking all the states and all the features, then you can write the following equation for the GNN iterative state:

$$H^{l+1} = F(H^l, X)$$

The general preceding equation is derived into various forms based on the type of GNN. There are two main classifications: spectral GNN and nonspectral GNN.

Spectral GNN

Spectral GNN was first formulated by Joan Bruna, Wojciech Zaremba, Arthus Szlam, and Yann LeCun in the paper titled *Spectral Networks and Deep Locally Connected Networks on Graphs*. You can find the details of the paper at `https://arxiv.org/pdf/1312.6203v3.pdf`.

Spectral GNN is a convolution in the Fourier domain. Spectral GNN can be expressed by the following equation:

$$g_\theta * x = U g_\theta U^T x$$

The following list describes the elements of the preceding equation:

- g_θ= Filter parameter that can also be considered as a convolution weight
- x = Input signal
- U = Matrix of Eigenvectors of the normalized graph Laplacian $L = I_N - D^{-1/2} A D^{-1/2} = U \times \Lambda U^T$

Kipf and Welling (in their article *Semi-Supervised Classification With Graph Convolution Networks, ICLR 2017*) simplified this further to address overfitting issues such as as the following:

$$g_\theta * h \approx \theta \left(I_N + D^{-1/2} A D^{-1/2} \right) h$$

This was simplified even further using the following renormalization:

$$H^{l+1} = \sigma \left[D^{-1/2} A D^{-1/2} H^l W \right]$$

Here, σ represents the activation function.

The following image illustrates the architecture of a GNN:

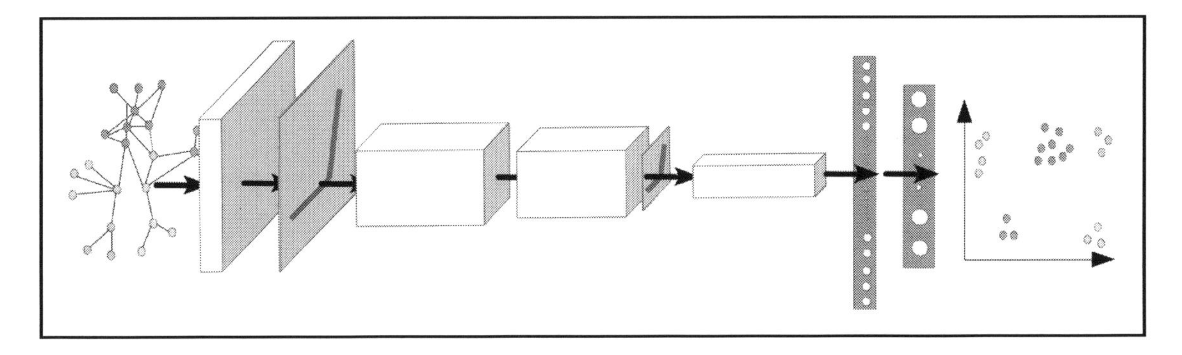

The GNN layer aggregates feature information from its neighbors and applies ReLU activation, pooling, and fully connected and softmax layers to classify different features within the image.

Overview of Reinforcement Learning

Reinforcement learning is a type of machine learning where the agent learns to act in the current environment by predicting a reward (or outcome) based on feedback from cumulative past reward signals. *Q*-learning, introduced by Christopher Watkins in the paper titled *Learning from Delayed Rewards*, is one of the most popular algorithms in reinforcement learning. The *Q* means quality—this is the value of a given action in generating a reward:

- At each learning state, the *Q* table stores the value of the state, action, and corresponding reward.
- The agent searches through the *Q* table to make the next action that maximizes the long-term cumulative reward.
- Reinforced learning differs from supervised and unsupervised learning in one key way: it does not require input labels (supervised) or an underlying structure (unsupervised) to classify objects into classes.

The following image illustrates the concept of reinforcement learning. The agent acts in a state to produce an action, which results in a reward. The action value is improved over time to maximize the reward:

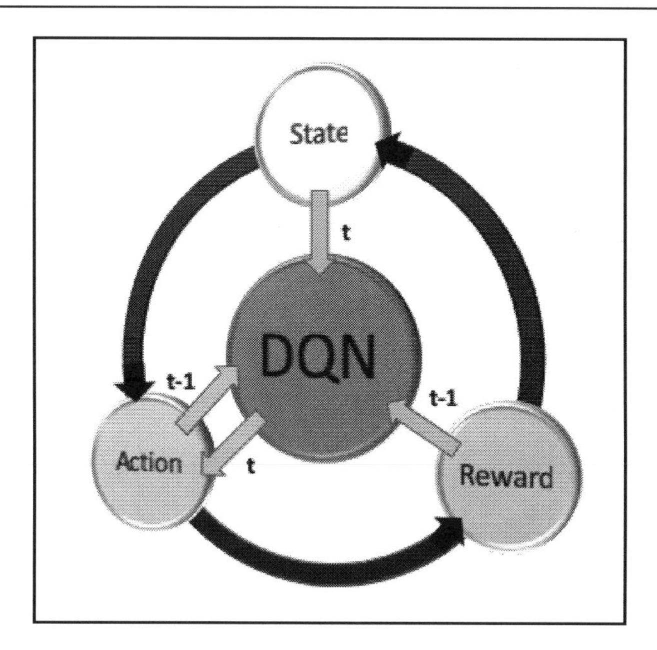

The agent starts in a state (s_t), observes a sequence of observations, takes an action (a_t) and receives a reward.

The following cumulative value function is maximized to find the desired output in the Q-learning method:

$$Q^{new}(s_t, a_t) \leftarrow (1-\alpha) \,.\, Q(s_t, a_t) + \alpha. (r_t + \gamma.\ max\{Q(s_{t+1}, a)\})$$

The following list describes the key features of the preceding equation:

- $Q(st, at)$ is the old value
- α is the learning rate
- γ is the discount factor that trades between the immediate reward and ersuss delayed reward and α is the learning rate
- rt is the reward
- max $Q(st+1, a)$ is the learned value

Since Q-learning includes a maximization step over estimated action values, it tends to overestimate values.

In reinforcement learning, convolutional networks can be used to create an agent's action that is capable of getting positive rewards under complex situations. This concept was first introduced by Mnih et al. in 2015 in a paper titled *Human-level control through deep reinforcement learning*. Details of this paper can be found at `https://web.stanford.edu/class/psych209/Readings/MnihEtAlHassibis15NatureControlDeepRL.pdf`.

This includes three convolution layers and one fully connected hidden layer. Note that in reinforcement learning, the convolutional networks derive different interpretations than in supervised learning. In supervised learning, CNN is used to classify an image into different classes; in reinforced learning, the image represents a state, and CNN is used to create an agent's action to perform in that state.

Overview of Transfer Learning

So far, we have learned to construct CNN architectures by designing the work in isolation to solve specific tasks. Neural network models are depth intensive, require lots of training data, training runs, and expert knowledge of tuning to achieve high accuracy; however as human beings, we don't learn everything from scratch—we learn from others and we learn from the cloud (internet). Transfer learning is useful when data is insufficient for a new class that we are trying to analyze, but there is a large amount of preexisting data on a similar class. Each of the CNN models (AlexNet, VGG16, ResNet, and inception) have been trained on ImageNet ILSVRC competition datasets. ImageNet is a dataset with over 15 million labeled images in 22,000 categories. ILSVRC uses a subset of ImageNet with around 1,000 images in each of the 1,000 categories.

In transfer learning, pretrained models developed for other situations can be modified to be used for our specific situation to predict our own classes. The idea is to pick the CNN architectures that we already studied, such as AlexNet, VGG16, ResNet, and inception, freeze one or two layers, change some weights, and input our own data to make predictions of the classes. In `Chapter 4`, *Deep Learning on Images*, we learned how CNN sees and interprets an image.

These learnings will be used to construct transfer learning, so let's summarize some key points that we learned in CNN visualization in `Chapter 4`, *Deep Learning on Images*:

- The first few layers are basically generic features (such as edge detection, blob detection, and so on) of the car—the middle layers join the edges to form the features of a car, such as tires, door handles, lights, fascia, and so on, and the last few layers are very abstract and very specific for particular objects.
- The fully connected layer flattens the output of its previous layer into a single vector, multiplies it by different weights, and then applies activation coefficients on it. It does its classification using a machine-learning **support vector machine (SVM)** type of approach.

Now that we understand the concepts, we will be able to appreciate the following commonly used method for transfer learning:

1. Remove and swap the softmax layer:

    1. Take a CNN that is pretrained on ImageNet, such as VGG16, AlexNet, ResNet, or inception, using TensorFlow.
    2. Remove the last softmax layer and treat the rest of the CNN as a fixed feature extractor for the new dataset.
    3. Replace the softmax layer with your own custom softmax defining your number of classes and train the resulting model with your dataset.

2. Fine-tune the ConvNet. To reduce the overfitting, keep some of the earlier layers fixed and only fine-tune a higher-level portion of the network. As we have seen in the visualization example in `Chapter 4`, *Deep Learning on Images*, the last layers are very abstract and are tuned for a particular dataset, so freezing the entire model and changing the softmax to a new softmax for *Step 1* will likely result in higher inaccuracy. For increased accuracy, it is better to train your custom image from the middle of the CNN—this way, the last few layers before the fully connected layers will have features specific to your application, which will lead to higher prediction accuracy. In `Chapter 6`, *Visual Search Using Transfer Learning*, we will perform coding on this concept and see the accuracy increase for initiating training from near the middle of the CNN.

Summary

In this chapter, we learned about the architectures of different convolution networks (ConvNet) and how different layers of a ConvNet are stacked together to classify various inputs into predefined classes. We learned different image classification models, such as AlexNet, VGGNet, Inception, and ResNet, why they are different, what problems they solve, and their overall similarities.

We learned about object detection methods, such as R-CNN, and how it got transformed over time into fast and faster R-CNN for bounding-box detection. The chapter introduced two new models, GAN and GNN, as two new sets of neural networks. The chapter ended with an introduction to reinforcement learning and transfer learning. We learned that in reinforcement learning, an agent interacts with the environment to learn an optimal policy (such as turning left or right at an intersection) based on a reward, whereas in transfer learning, a pre-trained model, such as VGG16, can be used to derive a new class based on new data by optimizing the later layers of the CNN.

In the next chapter, you will learn how to use transfer learning to train your own neural network and then perform a visual search with the trained network.

6
Visual Search Using Transfer Learning

Visual search is a method of displaying similar images to one uploaded by a user to a retail website. Similar images are found by transforming an image into a feature vector using a CNN. Visual search has a lot of applications in online shopping as it compliments textual search for a better and more refined way of expressing a user's choice of product. Shoppers like visual discovery and find it something unique that is not available in a traditional shopping experience.

In this chapter, we will use the concepts of deep neural networks learned in `Chapter 4`, *Deep Learning on Images*, and `Chapter 5`, *Neural Network Architecture and Models*. We will use transfer learning to develop a neural network model for our image classes and apply it for visual search. The exercises in this chapter will help you to develop sufficient practical knowledge to write your own code for neural networks and transfer learning.

The topics covered in this chapter are as follows:

- Coding deep learning models using TensorFlow
- Developing a transfer learning model using TensorFlow
- Understanding the architecture and applications of visual search
- Working with a visual search input data pipeline using `tf.data`

Coding deep learning models using TensorFlow

We learned about the architecture of various deep learning models in `Chapter 5`, *Neural Network Architecture and Models*. In this section, we will learn how to use TensorFlow/Keras to load images, explore and preprocess the data, and then apply three CNN models' (VGG16, ResNet, and Inception) pre-trained weights to predict object class.

Note that no training will be required in this section, as we are not building the model but will be using an already built model (that is, one with pre-trained weights) to predict image class.

The code for this section can be found at: `https://github.com/PacktPublishing/Mastering-Computer-Vision-with-TensorFlow-2.0/blob/master/Chapter06/Chapter6_CNN_PretrainedModel.ipynb`

Let's dive deep into the code and understand the purpose of each of its lines.

Downloading weights

The code for downloading the weights is as follows:

```
from tensorflow.keras.applications import VGG16
from keras.applications.vgg16 import preprocess_input
from tensorflow.keras.applications.resnet50 import ResNet50,
preprocess_input
from tensorflow.keras.applications import InceptionV3
from keras.applications.inception_v3 import preprocess_input
```

The preceding code performs the following two tasks:

1. The weights will be downloaded as follows as part of the output from the preceding code:

    - `Download VGG16 weight, the *.h5 file`
    - `Download Resnet50 weight, the *.h5 file`
    - `Download InceptionV3 weight, the *.h5 file`

2. It does the preprocessing of the image to normalize the current image to the `ImageNet RGB` dataset. Since the model is developed on the `ImageNet` dataset, without this step, the model will likely result in the wrong prediction of classes.

Decoding predictions

The ImageNet data has 1,000 different classes. A neural network such as Inception trained on ImageNet will output the class as an integer. We need to convert the integer to a corresponding class name using decoding. For example, if the integer value output is `311`, we need to decode what `311` means. With decoding, we will know that `311` corresponds to a folding chair.

The code for decoding predictions is as follows:

```
from tensorflow.keras.applications.vgg16 import decode_predictions
from tensorflow.keras.applications.resnet50 import decode_predictions
from tensorflow.keras.applications.inception_v3 import decode_predictions
```

The preceding code maps the class integers to class names using the `decode_predictions` command. Without this step, you will not be able to predict the class names.

Importing other common features

This section is about importing Keras and Python's common package. Keras `preprocessing` is the image processing module of Keras. The code for other common import functions is shown here:

```
from keras.preprocessing import image
import numpy as np
import matplotlib.pyplot as plt
import os
from os import listdir
```

You can observe the following in the preceding code:

- We loaded the Keras image preprocessing function.
- `numpy` is a Python array processing function.
- `matplotlib` is a Python plotting function.
- The `os` module is required to access the directory for file input.

Constructing a model

In this section, we will import a model. The code for model construction is shown as follows (the explanation of each code snippet is just underneath the code):

```
model = Modelx(weights='imagenet',
include_top=True,input_shape=(img_height, img_width, 3))
Modelx = VGG16 or ResNet50 or InceptionV3
```

The model construction has three important parameters:

- `weights` is the pre-trained model we used on ImageNet images that were downloaded before.
- The `include_top` function indicates whether the final dense layer should be included or not. For class prediction for a pre-trained model, this is always `True`; however, in a later part of the chapter (the *Developing a transfer learning model using TensorFlow* section), we will learn that, during transfer learning, this function is set to `False` to only include convolutional layers.
- `input_shape` is the height, width, and number of channels. Since we are dealing with color images, the number of channels is set to `3`.

Inputting images from a directory

The code for inputting images from a directory is shown here:

```
folder_path = '/home/.../visual_search/imagecnn/'
images = os.listdir(folder_path)
fig = plt.figure(figsize=(8,8))
```

The preceding code specifies the image folder path and defines image properties to be able to download the image in a later part. It also specifies the figure size as 8 x 8.

Loop function for importing multiple images and processing using TensorFlow Keras

This section describes how to import multiple images in a batch to process all of them together rather than importing them one by one. This is a critical skill to learn as, in most production applications, you will not be importing images one by one. The code for a loop function for importing and processing multiple images using TensorFlow Keras is as follows:

```
for image1 in images:
 i+=1
 im = image.load_img(folder_path+image1, target_size=(224, 224))
 img_data = image.img_to_array(im)
img_data = np.expand_dims(img_data, axis=0)
img_data = preprocess_input(img_data)
resnet_feature = model_resnet.predict(img_data,verbose=0)
 label = decode_predictions(resnet_feature)
 label = label[0][0]
 fig.add_subplot(rows,columns,i)
 fig.subplots_adjust(hspace=.5)
 plt.imshow(im)
 stringprint ="%.1f" % round(label[2]*100,1)
 plt.title(label[1] + " " + str(stringprint) + "%")
plt.show()
```

The preceding code performs the following steps:

1. Loops through the `images` property with `image1` as the loop's intermediate value.
2. The `image.load` function adds each new image to the folder path. Note the target size is `224` for VGG16 and ResNet and `299` for Inception.
3. Converts an image to an array function and expands its dimensions using a NumPy array and then applies the `preprocessing` function as explained in the *Downloading weights* section.
4. Next, it calculates the feature vector using the `model.predict()` function.
5. Then, the prediction decodes the class label name.
6. The `label` function is stored as an array and it has two elements: a class name and confidence, `%`.

7. The next few sections involve plotting using the `matplotlib` library:
    - `fig.add_subplot` has three elements: `rows`, `columns`, and `i` – for example, with a total of 9 images arranged as three columns and three rows, the `i` term will go from `1` to `9` with `1` being the first image and `9` the last image.
    - `fig.subplots_adjust` adds vertical space between images.
    - `plt.title` adds the title to each image.

Please note that the complete code can be found in the GitHub link of the book at `https://github.com/PacktPublishing/Mastering-Computer-Vision-with-TensorFlow-2.0/blob/master/Chapter06/Chapter6_CNN_PretrainedModel.ipynb`

To validate the model, nine different images were stored in a directory and passed through each of the models one by one to generate predictions. The final prediction output for each target image using three different neural network models is shown in the following table:

Target image	**VGG16**	**ResNet**	**Inception**
Dining table	Dining Table 58%	Pool table 30.1%	Desk 51%
Wok	Ladle 55%	Ladle 87%	Ladle 30%
Sofa	Studio couch 42%	Studio couch 77%	Studio couch 58%
Bed	Studio couch 35%	Four-poster 53%	Studio couch 44%
Water bottle	Water bottle 93%	Water bottle 77%	Water bottle 98%
Luggage	Folding chair 39%	Backpack 66%	Mailbag 35%
Backpack	Backpack 99.9%	Backpack 99.9%	Backpack 66%
Couch	Studio couch 79%	Studio couch 20%	Studio couch 48%
SUV	Minivan 74%	Minivan 98%	Minivan 52%

The following figure shows the VGG16 output for the nine classes:

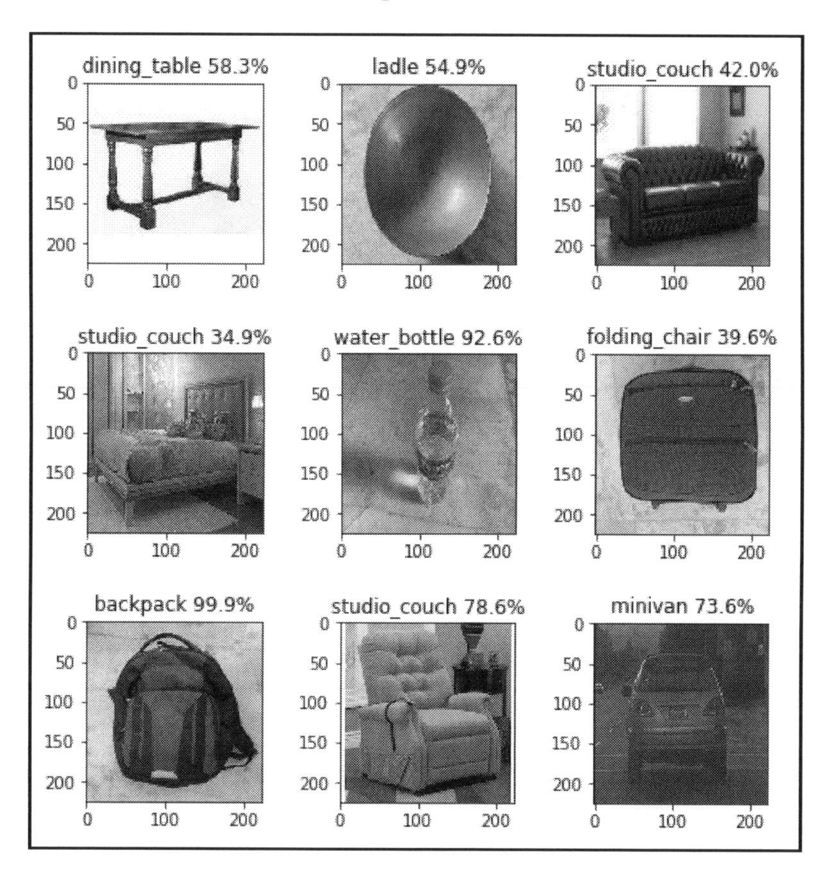

In the preceding figure, you can observe the following:

- Each figure dimension is 224 x 224 with labels printed at the top with a confidence percentage.
- There are three incorrect predictions: the wok (predicted as a ladle), the bed (predicted as a studio couch), and the luggage (predicted as a folding chair).

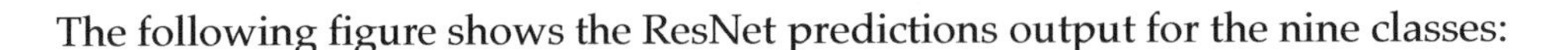

The following figure shows the ResNet predictions output for the nine classes:

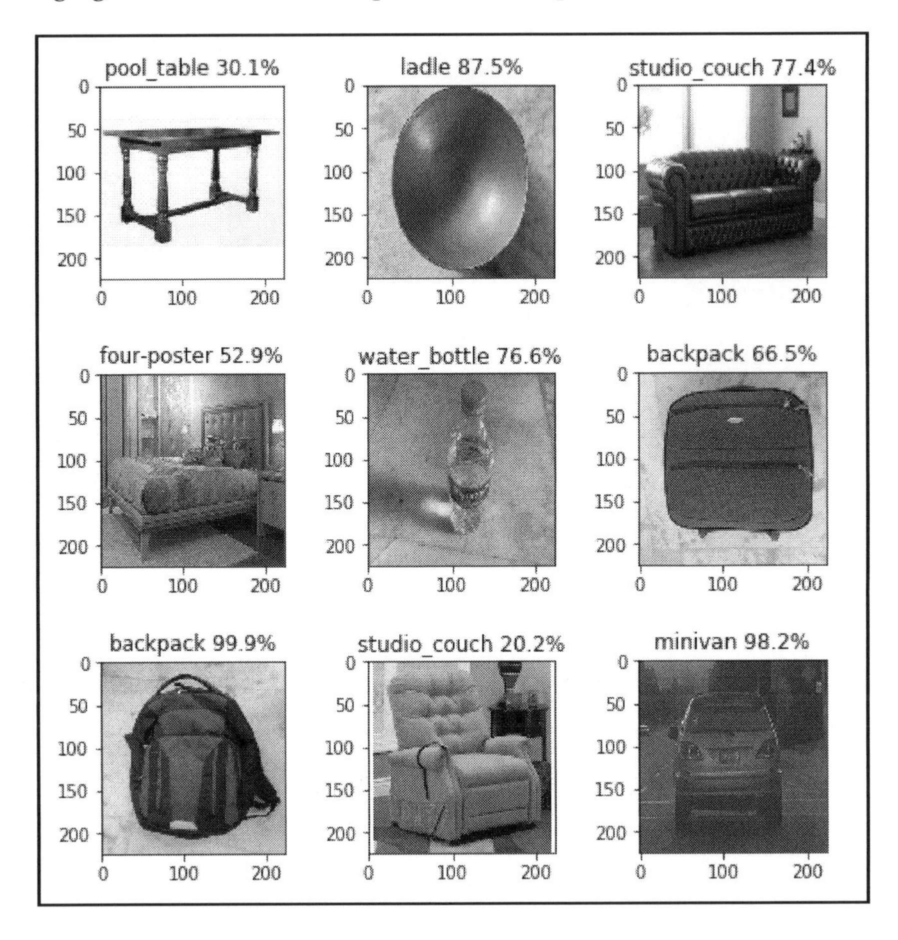

In the preceding figure, you can observe the following:

- Each figure dimension is 224 x 224 with labels printed at the top with a confidence percentage.
- There are two incorrect predictions: the wok (predicted as a ladle) and the luggage (predicted as a backpack).

The following figure shows the Inception predictions output for the nine classes:

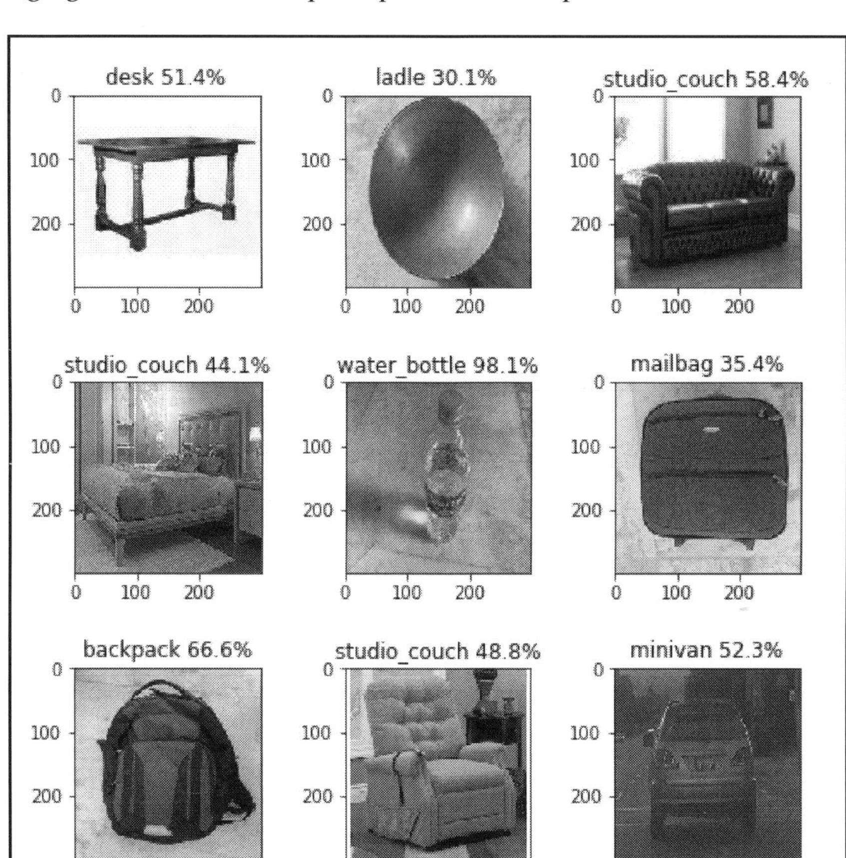

From this, you can observe the following:

- Each figure dimension is 224 x 224 with labels printed at the top with a confidence percentage.
- There are two incorrect predictions: the wok (predicted as a ladle) and the bed (predicted as a studio couch).

With this exercise, we now understand how to predict well-known class objects using a pre-trained model without training a single image. The reason we can do this is that each of the models is trained using the ImageNet database with 1,000 classes and the resulting weights from the model are made available by the computer vision community, ready for the use of others.

In the next section, we will learn how to use transfer learning to train our model for our custom images to make predictions instead of inferring from models developed directly from ImageNet datasets.

Developing a transfer learning model using TensorFlow

We introduced the concept of transfer learning in `Chapter 5`, *Neural Network Architecture and Models*, and how to predict image classes based on pre-trained models was demonstrated in the *Coding deep learning model using TensorFlow* section. We have observed that the pre-trained model gets reasonable accuracy on large datasets, but we can improve on this by training the model on our own datasets. One approach is to build the entire model (ResNet for example) and train it on our datasets—but this process will likely require a significant amount of time to run the model and then optimize the model parameters for our own datasets.

The other more efficient approach (called **transfer learning**) is to extract the feature vector from the base model without the top layer trained on an ImageNet dataset and then add our custom fully connected layer, including activation, dropout, and softmax, to constitute our final model. We freeze the base model, but the top layer of the newly added components remains unfrozen. We train the newly created model on our own datasets to generate predictions. This entire process of transferring learned feature maps from a large model and then customizing them on our own datasets by fine-tuning the higher-order model parameters is called transfer learning. The transfer learning workflow, along with the relevant TensorFlow/Keras code is explained in the next few sections, starting with *Analyzing and storing data*.

Analyzing and storing data

First, we will start by analyzing and storing the data. Here, we are constructing a furniture model with three different classes: `bed`, `chair`, and `sofa`. Our directory structure is as follows. Each image is a color image of size 224 x 224.

`Furniture_images`:

- `train` (2,700 images)
    - `bed` (900 images)
    - `chair` (900 images)
    - `sofa` (900 images)
- `val` (300 images)
    - `bed` (100 images)
    - `chair` (100 images)
    - `sofa` (100 images)

Note the number of images is just an example; it is unique in every situation. The important thing to note is, for good detection, we need about 1,000 images per class and a train and validation split of 90%:10%.

Importing TensorFlow libraries

Our next step is to import the TensorFlow libraries. The following code imports the ResNet model weights and preprocessed input, similar to what we did in the last section. We learned about each of these concepts in `Chapter 5`, *Neural Network Architecture and Models*:

```
from tensorflow.keras.applications.resnet50 import ResNet50,
preprocess_input
from tensorflow.keras.layers import Dense, Activation, Flatten, Dropout
from tensorflow.keras.models import Sequential, Model
from tensorflow.keras.optimizers import SGD, Adam
img_width, img_height = 224, 224
```

The code also imports several deep learning parameters, such as `Dense` (a fully connected layer), `Activation`, `Flatten`, and `Dropout`. We then import the Sequential model API to create a layer-by-layer model, and **stochastic gradient descent** (**SGD**) and the Adam optimizer. The image height and width are `224` for ResNet and VGG and `299` for the Inception model.

Setting up model parameters

For our analysis, we set the model parameters as shown in the following block of code:

```
NUM_EPOCHS = 5
batchsize = 10
num_train_images = 900
num_val_images = 100
```

The base model is then constructed similar to our example in the last section, except we do not include the top model by setting `include_top=False`:

```
base_model =
ResNet50(weights='imagenet',include_top=False,input_shape=(img_height,
img_width, 3))
```

In this code, we used the base model to generate the feature vector by using only convolutional layers.

Building an input data pipeline

We will import an image data generator that generates tensor images using data augmentation such as rotation, horizontal flip, vertical flip, and data preprocessing. The data generator will be repeated for the training and validation data.

Training data generator

Let's have a look at the following code for the training data generator:

```
from keras.preprocessing.image import ImageDataGenerator
train_dir = '/home/.../visual_search/furniture_images/train'
train_datagen =
ImageDataGenerator(preprocessing_function=preprocess_input,rotation_range=9
0,horizontal_flip=True,vertical_flip=True)
```

Flow for directory API—this is used to import data from directories. It has the following parameters:

- `Directory`: This is a folder path, and should be set to the path where images for all three classes are present. An example, in this case, would be a path for the `train` directory. To get the path, you can drag the folder to the Terminal and it will show you the path, which you can then copy and paste.
- `Target_size`: Set it equal to the size of the image that the model takes, for example, 299 x 299 for Inception and 224 x 224 for ResNet and VGG16.
- `Color_mode`: Set to `grayscale` for b/w images and `RGB` for color images.
- `Batch_size`: Number of images per batch.
- `class_mode`: Set to binary if you have only two classes to predict; if not, set to `categorical`.
- `shuffle`: Set to `True` if you want to reorder the images; otherwise, set to `False`.
- `seed`: A random seed for applying random image augmentation and shuffling the order of the images.

The following code shows how to write the final training data generator, which will be imported into the model:

```
train_generator =
train_datagen.flow_from_directory(train_dir,target_size=(img_height,
img_width), batch_size=batchsize)
```

Validation data generator

Next, we will repeat the process for validation in the following code. The process is the same as for the training generator, except we'll validate the image directory instead of training the image directory:

```
from keras.preprocessing.image import ImageDataGenerator
val_dir = '/home/.../visual_search/furniture_images/val'
val_datagen =
ImageDataGenerator(preprocessing_function=preprocess_input,rotation_range=9
0,horizontal_flip=True,vertical_flip=True)
val_generator =
val_datagen.flow_from_directory(val_dir,target_size=(img_height,
img_width),batch_size=batchsize)
```

The preceding code shows the final validation data generator.

Constructing the final model using transfer learning

We start by defining a function called `build_final_model()`, which takes in the base model and model parameters such as dropout, fully connected layers, and the number of classes. We first freeze the base model by using `layer.trainable = False`. We then flatten the base model output feature vector for subsequent processing. Next, we add a fully connected layer and dropout to the flattened feature vector to predict the new class using the softmax layer:

```
def build_final_model(base_model, dropout, fc_layers, num_classes):
 for layer in base_model.layers:
    layer.trainable = False
    x = base_model.output
    x = Flatten()(x)
    for fc in fc_layers:
    # New FC layer, random init
    x = Dense(fc, activation='relu')(x)
    x = Dropout(dropout)(x)
    # New softmax layer
    predictions = Dense(num_classes, activation='softmax')(x)
    final_model = Model(inputs=base_model.input, outputs=predictions)
        return final_model
    class_list = ["bed", "chair", "sofa"]
    FC_LAYERS = [1024, 1024]
    dropout = 0.3
    final_model =
build_final_model(base_model,dropout=dropout,fc_layers=FC_LAYERS,num_classe
s=len(class_list))
```

The model is compiled using the `adam` optimizer with categorical cross-entropy loss:

```
adam = Adam(lr=0.00001)
final_model.compile(adam, loss='categorical_crossentropy',
metrics=['accuracy'])
```

The final model is developed and run using the `model.fit_generator` command. The history stores epochs, time per step, loss, accuracy, validation loss, and validation accuracy:

```
history =
final_model.fit(train_dir,epochs=NUM_EPOCHS,steps_per_epoch=num_train_image
s // batchsize,callbacks=[checkpoint_callback],validation_data=val_dir,
validation_steps=num_val_images // batchsize)
```

The various parameters of `model.fit()` are explained here. Note `mode.fit_generator` will be deprecated in the future and will be replaced by the `model.fit()` function, shown previously:

- `train_dir`: This inputs training data; details of its operation were explained in the previous section.
- `epochs`: An integer indicating the number of epochs to train the model. The epoch increments from `1` to the value of `epochs`.
- `steps_per_epoch`: This is an integer. It shows the total number of steps (batches of samples) before training is completed and training the next epoch is started. Its maximum value is equal to (number of training images / `batch_size`). So, if there are 900 training images and the batch size is 10, then the number of steps per epoch is 90.
- `workers`: A high value ensures that the CPU creates enough batches for the GPU to process and the GPU never remains idle.
- `shuffle`: This is of a Boolean type. It indicates the reordering of the batches at the beginning of each epoch. It is only used with `Sequence` (`keras.utils.Sequence`). It has no effect when `steps_per_epoch` is not `None`.
- `Validation_data`: This is a validation generator.
- `validation_steps`: This is the total number of steps (batches of samples) used in the `validation_data` generator and is equal to the number of samples in your validation dataset divided by the batch size.

Saving a model with checkpoints

A TensorFlow model can run for a long time as each epoch takes several minutes to complete. TensorFlow has a command called `Checkpoint` that enables us to save the intermediate model at the completion of every epoch. Thus, if you have to interrupt the model in the middle because the loss has saturated or to use your PC for something else, then you do not have to start from scratch—you can use the model developed so far for your analysis. The following code block shows an addition to the previous code block to execute checkpoints:

```
from tensorflow.keras.callbacks import ModelCheckpoint
filecheckpath="modelfurn_weight.hdf5"
checkpointer = ModelCheckpoint(filecheckpath, verbose=1,
save_best_only=True)

history = final_model.fit_generator(train_generator, epochs=NUM_EPOCHS,
workers=0,steps_per_epoch=num_train_images // batchsize, shuffle=True,
validation_data=val_generator,validation_steps=num_val_images // batchsize,
callbacks = [checkpointer])
```

The output from the preceding code is the following:

```
89/90 [============================>.] - ETA: 2s - loss: 1.0830 - accuracy:
0.4011 Epoch 00001: val_loss improved from inf to 1.01586, saving model to
modelfurn_weight.hdf5 90/90 [==============================] - 257s 3s/step
- loss: 1.0834 - accuracy: 0.4022 - val_loss: 1.0159 - val_accuracy: 0.4800
 Epoch 2/5 89/90 [============================>.] - ETA: 2s - loss: 1.0229
- accuracy: 0.5067 Epoch 00002: val_loss improved from 1.01586 to 0.87938,
saving model to modelfurn_weight.hdf5 90/90
[==============================] - 253s 3s/step - loss: 1.0220 - accuracy:
0.5067 - val_loss: 0.8794 - val_accuracy: 0.7300
 Epoch 3/5 89/90 [============================>.] - ETA: 2s - loss: 0.9404
- accuracy: 0.5719 Epoch 00003: val_loss improved from 0.87938 to 0.79207,
saving model to modelfurn_weight.hdf5 90/90
[==============================] - 256s 3s/step - loss: 0.9403 - accuracy:
0.5700 - val_loss: 0.7921 - val_accuracy: 0.7900
 Epoch 4/5 89/90 [============================>.] - ETA: 2s - loss: 0.8826
- accuracy: 0.6326 Epoch 00004: val_loss improved from 0.79207 to 0.69984,
saving model to modelfurn_weight.hdf5 90/90
[==============================] - 254s 3s/step - loss: 0.8824 - accuracy:
0.6322 - val_loss: 0.6998 - val_accuracy: 0.8300
 Epoch 5/5 89/90 [============================>.] - ETA: 2s - loss: 0.7865
- accuracy: 0.7090 Epoch 00005: val_loss improved from 0.69984 to 0.66693,
saving model to modelfurn_weight.hdf5 90/90
[==============================] - 250s 3s/step - loss: 0.7865 - accuracy:
0.7089 - val_loss: 0.6669 - val_accuracy: 0.7700
```

The output displays the loss and accuracy from every epoch and the corresponding file is saved as an `hdf5` file.

Plotting training history

The line plot showing training accuracy and training loss per epoch is shown using the Python `matplotlib` function. We will import `matplotlib` first and then define parameters for training and validation loss and accuracy:

```
import matplotlib.pyplot as plt
acc = history.history['accuracy']
val_acc = history.history['val_accuracy']
loss = history.history['loss']
val_loss = history.history['val_loss']
```

The following code is standard for plotting the model output with Keras and TensorFlow. We first define the figure size (8 x 8) and use the subplot function shows `(2,1,1)` and `(2,1,2)`. We then define the label, limit, and title:

```
plt.figure(figsize=(8, 8))
plt.subplot(2, 1, 1)
plt.plot(acc, label='Training Accuracy')
plt.plot(val_acc, label='Validation Accuracy')
plt.legend(loc='lower right')
plt.ylabel('Accuracy')
plt.ylim([min(plt.ylim()),1])
plt.title('Training and Validation Accuracy')
plt.subplot(2, 1, 2)
plt.plot(loss, label='Training Loss')
plt.plot(val_loss, label='Validation Loss')
plt.legend(loc='upper right')
plt.ylabel('Cross Entropy')
plt.ylim([0,5.0])
plt.title('Training and Validation Loss')
plt.xlabel('epoch')
plt.show()
```

Let's have a look at the output of the preceding code. The accuracy comparison between different models is shown in the following screenshot. It shows the training parameter of Inception:

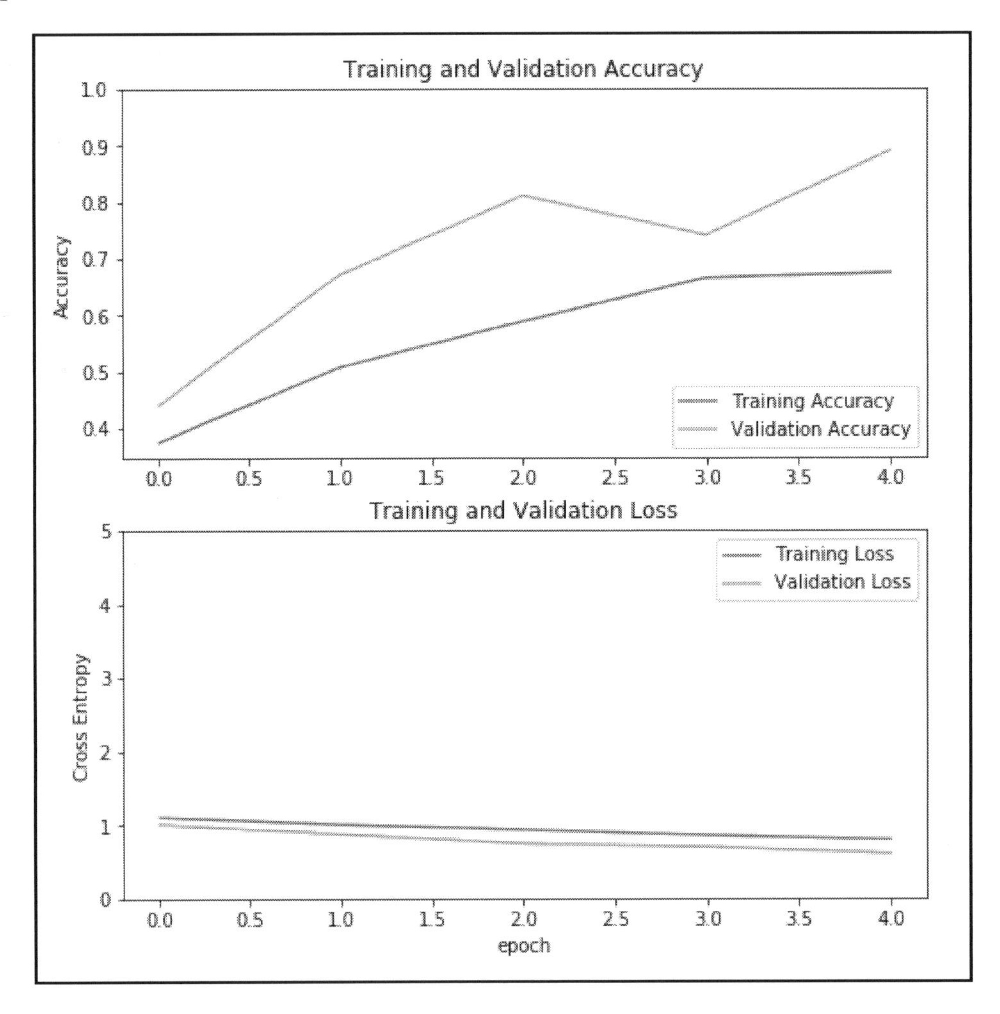

In the preceding screenshot, you can observe that the accuracy of Inception goes to about 90% in five epochs. Next, we plot the training parameter for VGG16:

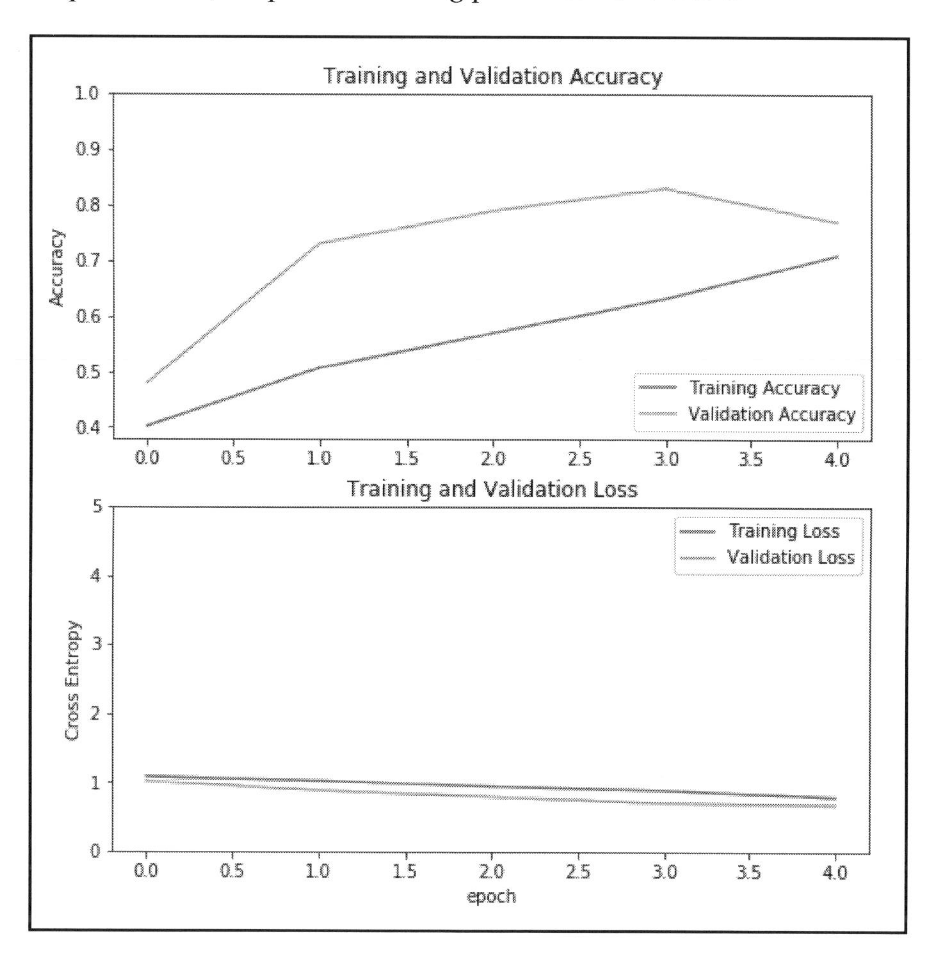

The preceding figure shows the accuracy of VGG16 goes to about 80% in five epochs. Next, we plot the training parameter for ResNet:

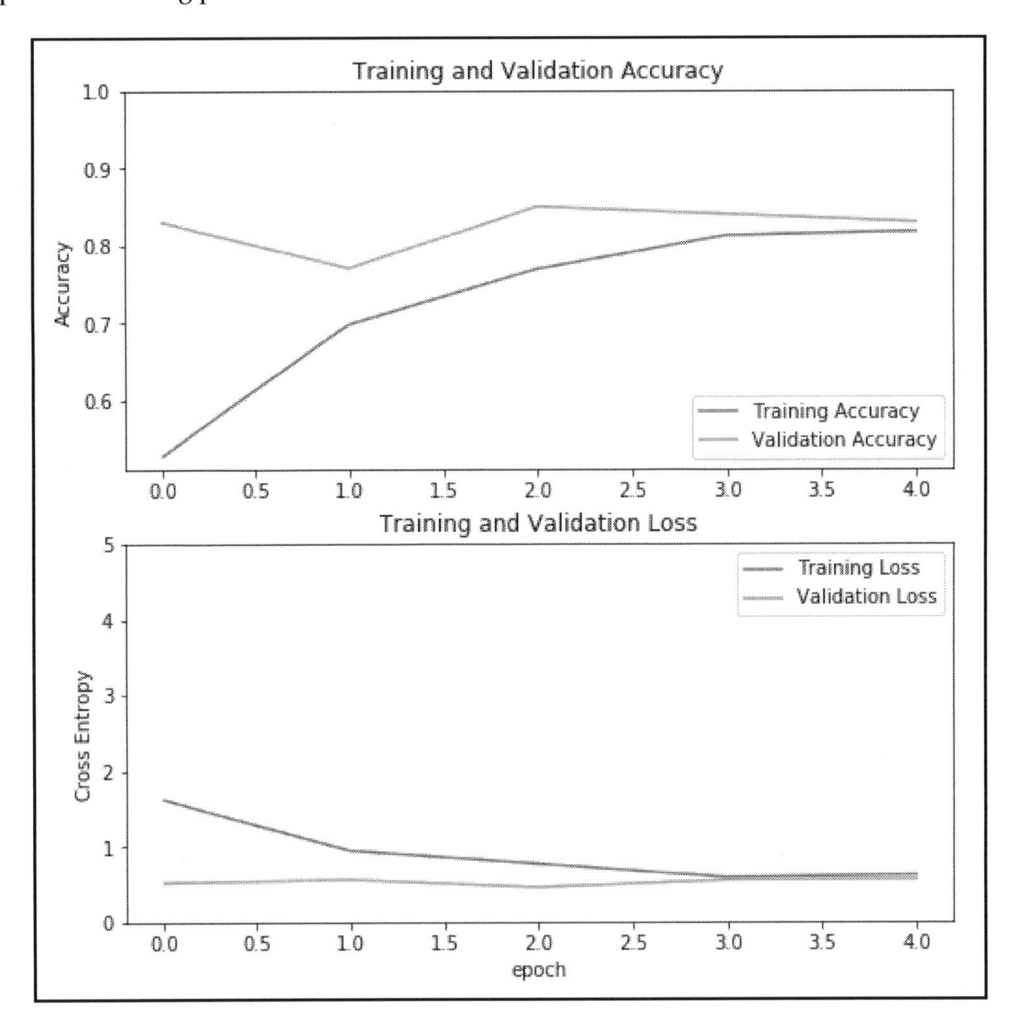

The preceding screenshot shows the accuracy of ResNet goes to about 80% in four epochs.

The accuracy consistently reached at least 80% in four epochs for all three models. The Inception model's result has the highest accuracy.

Understanding the architecture and applications of visual search

Visual search uses deep neural network technology to detect and classify an image and its contents and use it to search within an image database to return a list of matching results. Visual search is particularly relevant to the retail industry as it allows retailers to display a host of images similar to a customer's uploaded image to increase sales revenue.Visual search can be combined with voice search to enhance the search further. Visual information is more relevant than textual information and this results in the greater popularity of visual search. A host of different companies, including Google, Amazon, Pinterest, Wayfair, Walmart, Bing, ASOS, Neiman Marcus, IKEA, Argos, and others have all built powerful visual search engines to improve their customer experience.

The architecture of visual search

Deep neural network models such as ResNet, VGG16, and Inception can essentially be broken down into two components:

- The first component identifies the low-level content of an image, such as feature vectors (edges).
- The second component represents the high-level content of an image, such as the final image characteristics, which are an ensemble of various low-level contents. The following diagram illustrates a convolutional neural network that classifies seven classes:

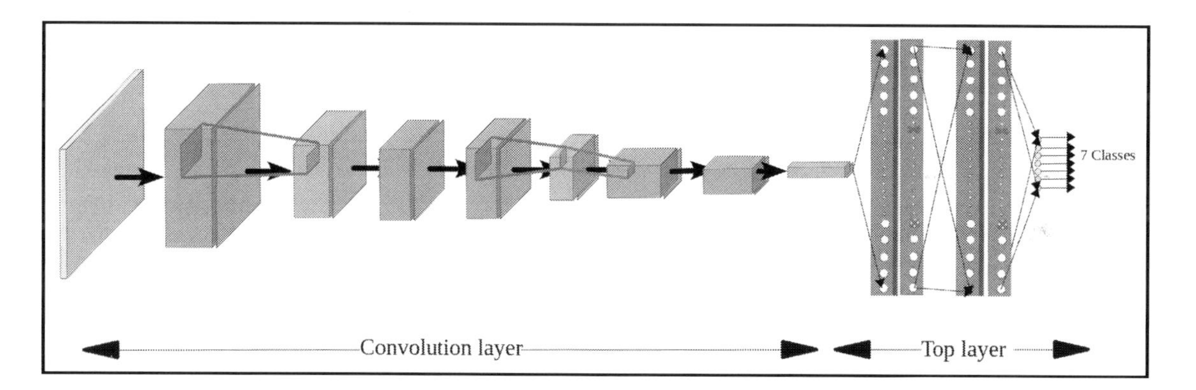

The preceding diagram shows that the entire image classification neural network model can be divided into two: the convolution layer and the top layer. The last convolution layer before the fully connected layer is a feature vector of shape (*# of images, X, Y, # of channels*), which is flattened (*# of images, X*Y*# of channels*) to generate an n-dimensional vector.

The feature vector shape has four components:

# of images indicates the number of training images. So if you have 1,000 training images, the value will be 1,000.
X indicates the width of the layer. A typical value is 14.
Y indicates the height of the layer, it can be something like 14.
# of channels indicates the number of filters or depth of the Conv2D. A typical value is 512.

In visual search, we calculate the similarity of two images by comparing the similarity of their feature vectors using tools such as Euclidean distance or cosine similarity. The architecture of visual search is shown here:

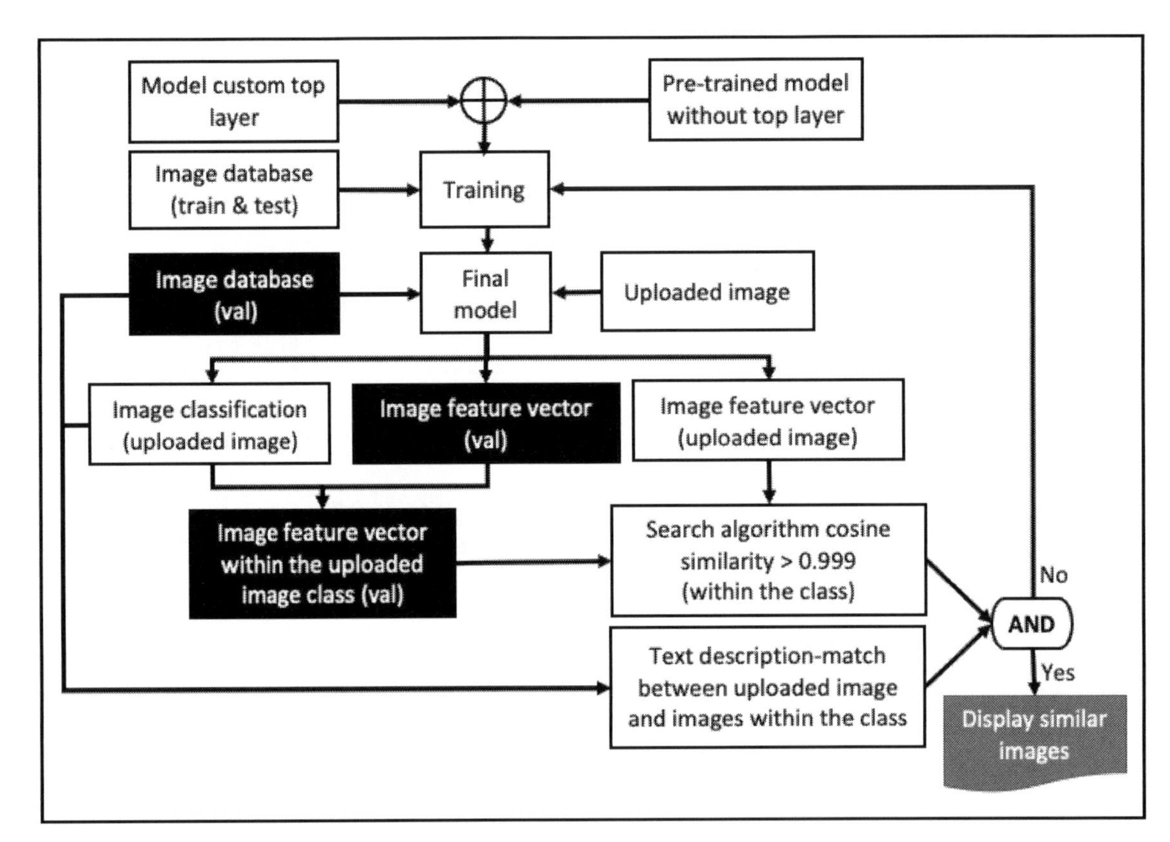

The various steps are listed here:

1. Use transfer learning to develop a new model by detaching the top layer from well-known models such as ResNet, VGG16, or Inception and then add custom top layers including a fully connected layer, dropout, activation, and a softmax layer.
2. Train the new model with your new datasets.
3. Upload an image and find its feature vector and image class by running the image through the new model we just developed.
4. To save time searching, search only within the directory class that corresponds to the uploaded image.
5. Search using an algorithm such as Euclidean distance or cosine similarity.
6. Display search results if cosine similarity > 0.999; if not, retrain the model with the uploaded image or adjust the model parameter and rerun the process.
7. To speed up the search even further, detect the location of objects within the uploaded image and within the search image database and directory using the bounding box generated.

The aforementioned flow chart has several key components:

- **Model development:** This consists of choosing an appropriate pre-trained model, removing the layers near its top, freezing all layers before that, and adding a new top layer to match our class. This means, if we use a pre-trained model trained on ImageNet datasets of 1,000 classes, we will remove its top layers and replace it with our new top layer with only 3 classes–`bed`, `chair`, and `sofa`.
- **Model training:** This involves first compiling the model and then beginning training using the `model.fit()` function.
- **Model output**: The uploaded image and each image in the test image database are passed through the model to generate the feature vector. The uploaded image is also used to determine the model class.
- **Search algorithm**: The search algorithm is executed within the test image folder specified by the given class and not the entire set of test images, thus saving time. The search algorithm relies on the correct class being selected by the CNN model. If the class matching is not correct, then the resulting visual search will result in an incorrect result. To solve this problem, several steps can be taken:

    1. Rerun the model with a new image set, increase the training image size, or improve the model parameters.

2. However, no matter how much data is used, the CNN model never has 100% accuracy. So, to fix this issue, the visual search result is often supplemented by textual keyword searches. For example, a customer may write *can you find a bed that is similar to the one shown in the uploaded image?* In this case, we know that the uploaded class is a bed. This is accomplished using **Natural Language Processing** (**NLP**).
3. The other alternative to fix the issue is to run the same uploaded image against multiple pre-trained models and if the class predictions differ from each other, then take the mode value.

Next, we will explain in detail the code used for visual search.

Visual search code and explanation

In this section, we will explain the TensorFlow code for visual search and its functions:

1. First, we will specify a folder for the uploaded image (there are three folders, which we switch for each image type). Note the images shown here are just examples; your images might be different:

```
#img_path = '/home/.../visual_search/ test/bed/bed1.jpg'
#img_path ='/home/.../visual_search/test/chair/chair1.jpg'
#img_path ='/home/.../visual_search/test/sofa/sofa1.jpg'
```

2. Then, we will upload the image, convert the image to an array, and preprocess the image similarly to what we did before:

```
img = image.load_img(img_path, target_size=(224, 224))
img_data = image.img_to_array(img)
img_data = np.expand_dims(img_data, axis=0)
img_data = preprocess_input(img_data)
```

The preceding code is the standard code to convert the image to an array before further processing.

Predicting the class of an uploaded image

Once a new image is uploaded, our task will be to find out which class it belongs to. To do that, we calculate the probability for each class that the image could belong to and pick the class with the highest probability. The example here illustrates a calculation using the VGG pre-trained model, but the same concept applies elsewhere:

```
vgg_feature = final_model.predict(img_data,verbose=0)
vgg_feature_np = np.array(vgg_feature)
vgg_feature1D = vgg_feature_np.flatten()
print (vgg_feature1D)
y_prob = final_model.predict(img_data)
y_classes = y_prob.argmax(axis=-1)
print (y_classes)
```

In the preceding code, we calculated the probability of the image belonging to a particular class using the `model.predict()` function and the class name using `probability.argmax` to indicate the class with the highest probability.

Predicting the class of all images

The following function imports the necessary packages to get files from the directory and the similarity calculation. We then specify which folder to target based on the input class of the uploaded image:

```
import os
from scipy.spatial import distance as dist
from sklearn.metrics.pairwise import cosine_similarity
if y_classes == [0]:
    path = 'furniture_images/val/bed'
elif y_classes == [1]:
    path = 'furniture_images/val/chair'
else:
    path = 'furniture_images/val/sofa'
```

The following function loops through each image in the test directory and converts the image into an array, which is then used to predict the feature vector using the trained model:

```
mindist=10000
maxcosine =0
i=0
for filename in os.listdir(path):
    image_train = os.path.join(path, filename)
    i +=1
```

```
        imgtrain = image.load_img(image_train, target_size=(224, 224))
        img_data_train = image.img_to_array(imgtrain)
        img_data_train = np.expand_dims(img_data_train, axis=0)
        img_data_train = preprocess_input(img_data_train)
        vgg_feature_train = final_model.predict(img_data_train)
        vgg_feature_np_train = np.array(vgg_feature_train)
        vgg_feature_train1D = vgg_feature_np_train.flatten()
        eucldist = dist.euclidean(vgg_feature1D,vgg_feature_train1D)
        if mindist > eucldist:
            mindist=eucldist
            minfilename = filename
            #print (vgg16_feature_np)
        dot_product = np.dot(vgg_feature1D,vgg_feature_train1D)#normalize the
    results, to achieve     similarity measures independent #of the scale of
    the vectors
        norm_Y = np.linalg.norm(vgg_feature1D)
        norm_X = np.linalg.norm(vgg_feature_train1D)
        cosine_similarity = dot_product / (norm_X * norm_Y)
        if maxcosine < cosine_similarity:
            maxcosine=cosine_similarity
            cosfilename = filename
        print ("%s filename %f euclediandist %f cosine_similarity"
    %(filename,eucldist,cosine_similarity))
        print ("%s minfilename %f mineuclediandist %s cosfilename %f
    maxcosinesimilarity" %(minfilename,mindist, cosfilename, maxcosine))
```

You can observe the following in the preceding code:

- Each feature vector is compared with the uploaded image feature vector to calculate the Euclidean distance and cosine similarity.
- The image similarity is calculated by determining the minimum value for the Euclidean distance and the maximum value for cosine similarity.
- The image file corresponding to the minimum distance is determined and displayed.

The complete code including transfer learning and visual search can be found in the GitHub repository of the book, at: `https://github.com/PacktPublishing/Mastering-Computer-Vision-with-TensorFlow-2.0/blob/master/Chapter06/Chapter6_Transferlearning_VisualSearch.ipynb`.

The following figure shows the visual search prediction for an uploaded image of a bed using three different models and two different search algorithms—Euclidean distance and cosine similarity:

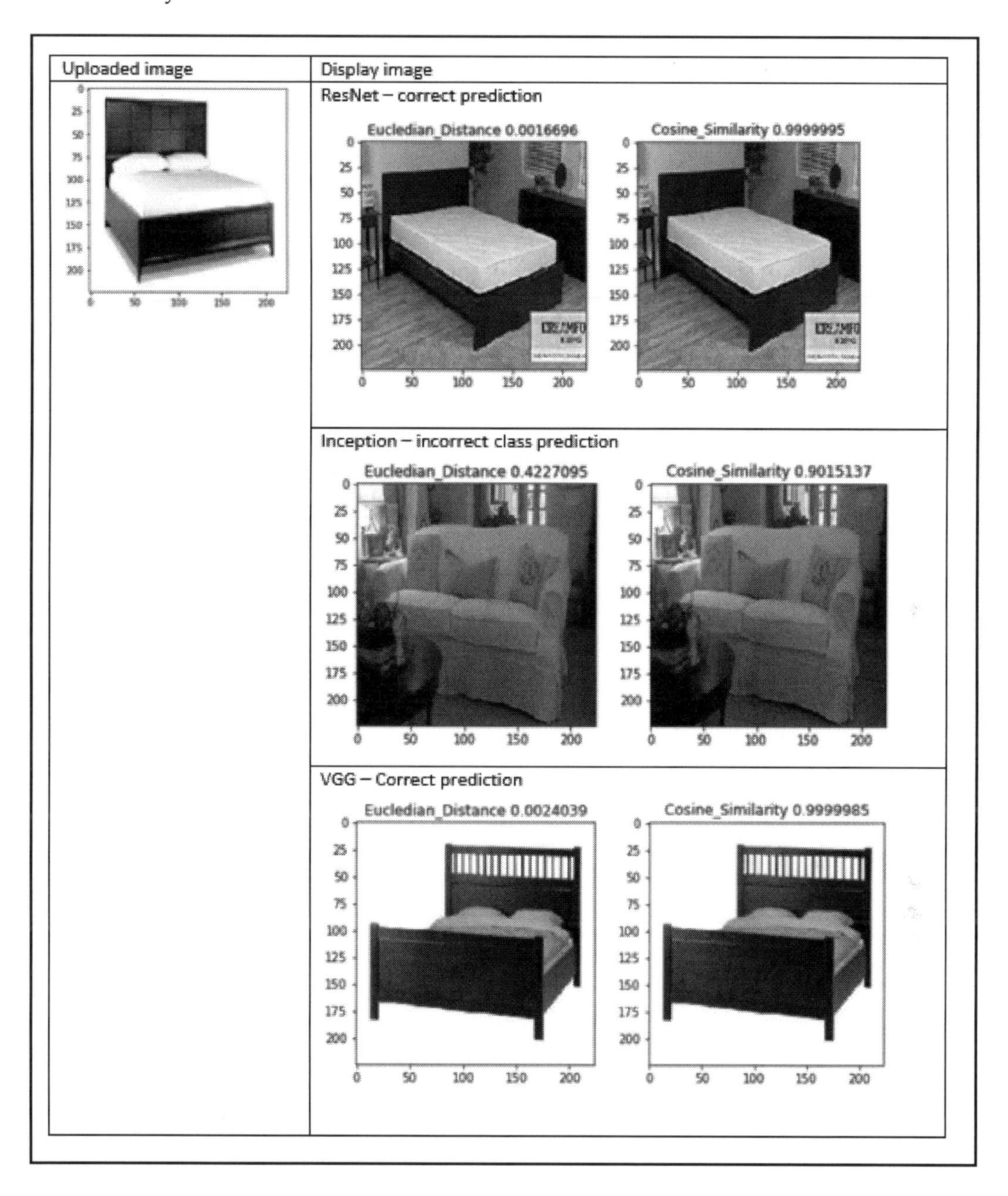

In the preceding figure, the following can be observed:

- The Inception model predicted an inaccurate class, which resulted in the visual search model predicting the wrong class.
- Note that the visual search model is not able to catch the neural network predicting the wrong class. We can also check the class prediction using other models for the same uploaded image to see the mode (majority) value—in this case, it is `bed` as ResNet and VGG predicts `bed`, while Inception predicts `sofa`.
- So to summarize, since we do not know if a given model will predict the class correctly, our recommended method is to predict the class of the uploaded image using three or more different models simultaneously and then choose the predicted class with majority value. Using this method, we will increase the confidence in our prediction.

The following figure shows the prediction using a different uploaded image and this seems to be correct:

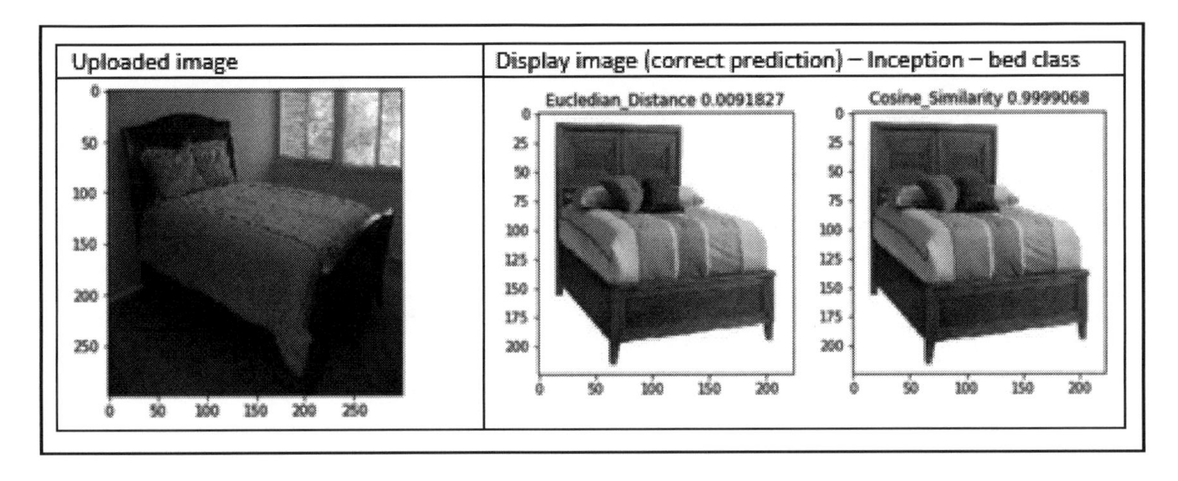

The following figure shows the visual search prediction for an uploaded image of a chair using three different models and two different search algorithms—Euclidean distance and cosine similarity:

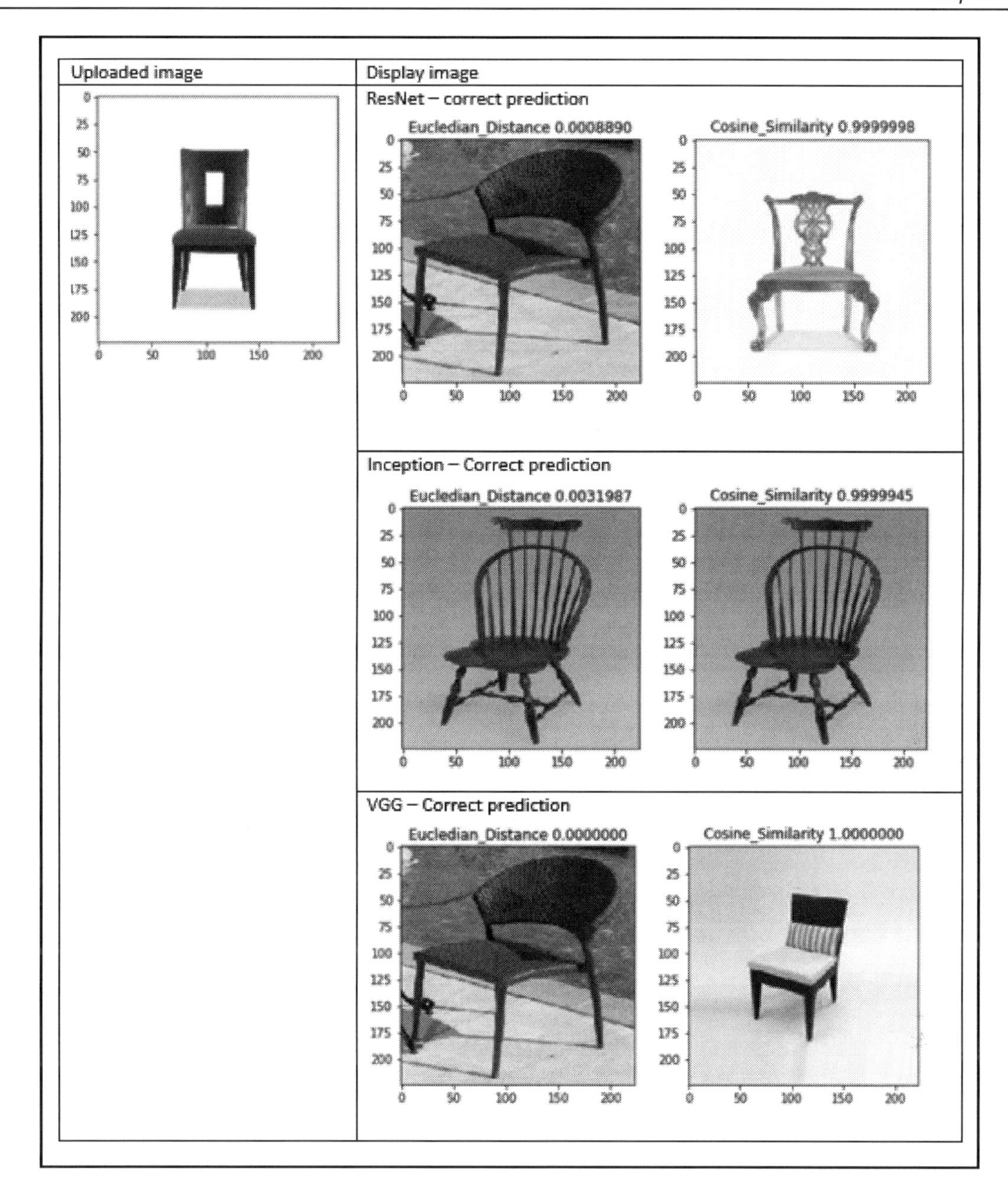

You can observe the following in the preceding figure:

- The prediction is correct in all cases, although the image displayed by the cosine similarity function differs from that of the Euclidean distance function.

- Both seem to be pretty close and the two methods of display provide us with a method to display multiple images. This means that if a user uploads an image of a chair and wants to find a similar chair in the online catalog, our system will display two images to the user to choose from, rather than just one image, which will increase our chance of selling the chair. If the two images are the same, the algorithm will just display one image, otherwise it will display two images. The other option would be to display the first two matches using the same algorithm.

The following image shows the visual search prediction for an uploaded image of a sofa using three different models and two different search algorithms—Euclidean distance and cosine similarity:

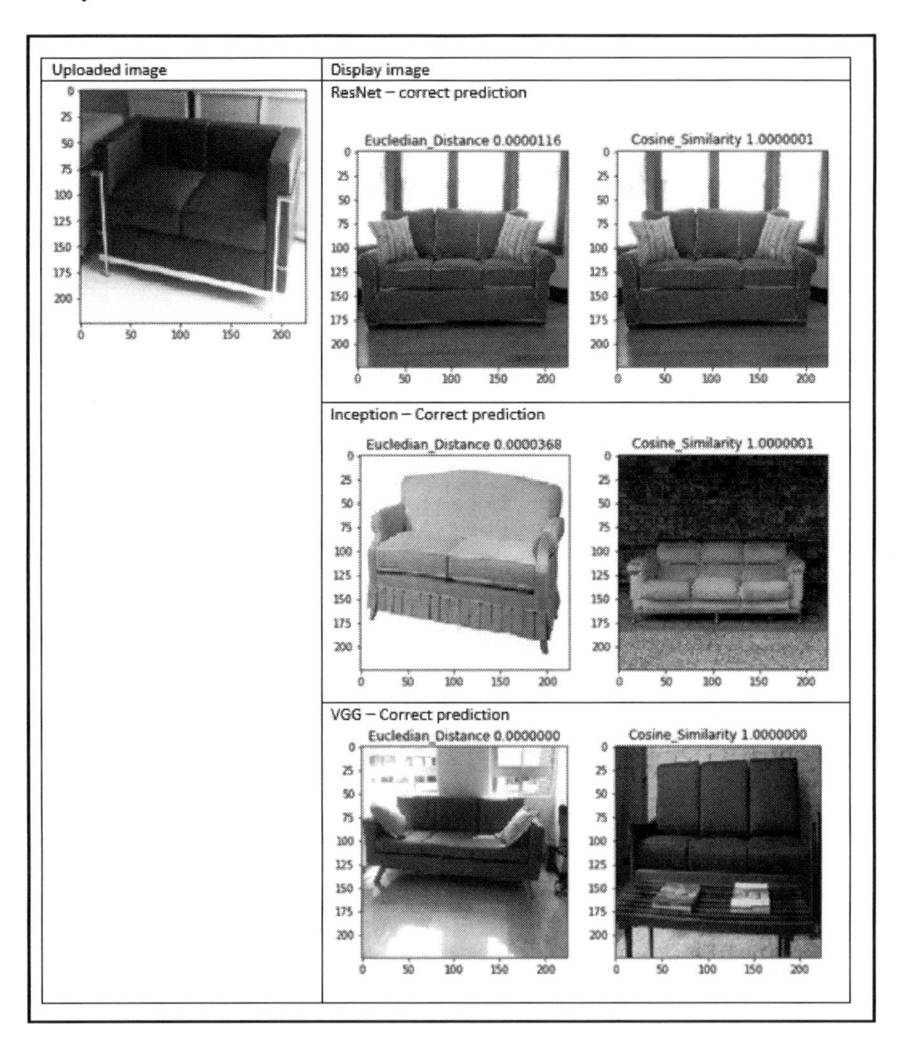

You can observe the following in the preceding figure:

- The prediction is correct in all cases, although the image displayed by the cosine similarity function differs from that of the Euclidean distance function.
- Both seem to be pretty close and the two methods of the display provide us with a method to display multiple images. As explained previously, with two similar images to the uploaded image, the user has more options to select from.

Working with a visual search input pipeline using tf.data

The TensorFlow `tf.data` API is a highly efficient data pipeline that processes data an order of magnitude faster than the Keras data input process. It aggregates data in a distributed filesystem and batch processes it. For further details, refer to: `https://www.tensorflow.org/guide/data`.

The following screenshot shows an image upload time comparison of `tf.data` versus the Keras image input process:

```
timeit(train_generator)

.............................................
1000 batches: 142.58274674415588 s
70.13471 Images/s

timeit(train_ds)

.............................................
1000 batches: 1.5855846405029297 s
6306.82194 Images/s
```

Note that 1,000 images take about 1.58 seconds, which is about 90 times faster than the Keras image input process.

Here is some common features for `tf.data`:

- For this API to work, you need to import the `pathlib` library.
- `tf.data.Dataset.list_files` is used to create a dataset of all files matching a pattern.
- `tf.strings.splot` splits the file path based on a delimiter.

- `tf.image.decode_jpeg` decodes a JPEG image into a tensor (note the conversion must not have a file path).
- `tf.image.convert_image_dtype` converts the image to a dtype float 32.

The following link provides the updated visual search code:

`https://github.com/PacktPublishing/Mastering-Computer-Vision-with-TensorFlow-2.0/blob/master/Chapter06/Chapter6_Transferlearning_VisualSearch_tfdata_tensor.ipynb`

This code includes `tf.data`, as explained previously. Besides `tf.data`, it also unfreezes the top part of the model by making the following changes in `build_final_model`:

```
layer.trainable = True
layer_adjust = 100
for layer in base_model.layers[:layer_adjust]:
    layer.trainable = False
```

The preceding change enables the model to start training after the one-hundredth layer, as opposed to just training the last few layers. This change increases the accuracy, as you can see in the following figure:

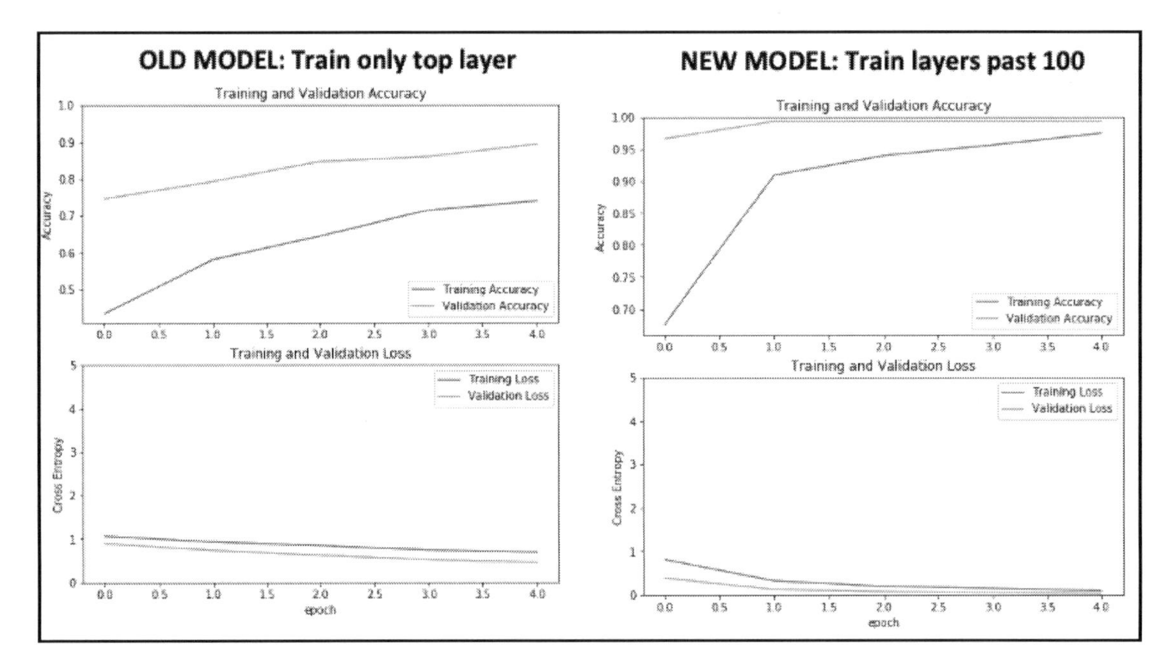

Training takes more time but the model accuracy is close to 100% as opposed to about 90%.

Before we conclude the chapter let's recap two important concept for training a CNN: Accuracy and loss. Keras define `y-pred` and `y-true` as the model predicted value and the ground truth value. Accuracy is defined as defined as comparing the `y-pred` to `y-true` and then averaging the difference. The loss term also known as entropy is defined as the negative sum of the product class probability and the classification index. There can be other loss term such as rms prop. In general, training gives correct output if `accuracy > 0.9` and `loss < 1`.

Summary

In this chapter, we learned how to use TensorFlow/Keras to develop transfer learning code for deep learning models we studied in the last chapter. We learned how to import trained images from a directory consisting of multiple classes and use them to train the models and make predictions with them. We then learned how to keep the base layer of the model frozen, remove the top layer, and replace it with our own top layer and train the resultant model with it.

We studied the importance of visual search and how transfer learning can be used to augment visual search methods. Our example consists of furniture of three different classes—we understood the accuracy of the model and how to improve the resulting losses. In this chapter, we also learned how to use the TensorFlow `tf.data` input pipeline for faster image processing during training.

In the next chapter, we will study YOLO to draw bounding-box object detection on images and videos and use it to improve visual search even further.

7
Object Detection Using YOLO

In the previous chapter, we discussed, in detail, the various neural network image classification and object detection architectures that utilize multiple steps for the object detection, classification, and refinement of a bounding box. In this chapter, we will be introducing two single-stage, fast object detection methods—**You Only Look Once** (**YOLO**) and RetinaNet. We will be discussing the architectures of each model and then perform inference in real images and videos using YOLO v3. We will show you how to optimize configuration parameters and train your own custom images using YOLO v3.

The topics covered in this chapter are as follows:

- An overview of YOLO
- An introduction to Darknet for object detection
- Real-time prediction using Darknet and Tiny Darknet
- Comparing YOLOs – YOLO versus YOLO v2 versus YOLO v3
- When to train a model?
- Training your own image set with YOLO v3 to develop a custom model
- An overview of feature pyramids and RetinaNet

An overview of YOLO

We learned in `Chapter 5`, *Neural Network Architecture and Models*, that each published neural network architecture improves on the preceding one by learning its architecture and features and then developing a whole new classifier to improve the accuracy and detection time. YOLO was at the **Computer Vision and Pattern Recognition Conference (CVPR)** 2016 by Joseph Redmon, Santosh Divvala, Ross Girshick, and Ali Farhadi in the *You Only Look Once: Unified, Real-Time Object Detection* paper `https://arxiv.org/pdf/1506.02640.pdf`. YOLO is an extremely fast neural network that detects multiple classes of objects all at once at the astounding speed of 45 frames per second (base YOLO) to 155 frames per second (fast YOLO). As a comparison, most cell phone cameras capture videos at around 30 frames per second, while high-speed cameras capture videos at around 250 frames per second. The YOLO's frames per second rate is equivalent to the detection time of around 6 to 22 ms. Compare this to the time taken for the human brain to detect images of around 13 ms—YOLO recognizes images instantly in a similar way to how humans do. So, it provides machines with instantaneous object detection capability.

Before looking further at the details, we will first look at the concept of **Intersection Over Union (IOU)**.

The concept of IOU

IOU is an object detection evaluation metric based on the degree of overlap between the predicted bounding box and the ground truth bounding box (hand labeled). Let's have a look at the following derivative of IOU:

$$IOU = \frac{Overlap\ area}{Union\ area} = \frac{Common\ area\ of\ the\ bounding\ boxes}{Total\ area\ covering\ both\ the\ bounding\ boxes}$$

The following image illustrates IOU, showing the predicted and ground truth bounding box of a large van:

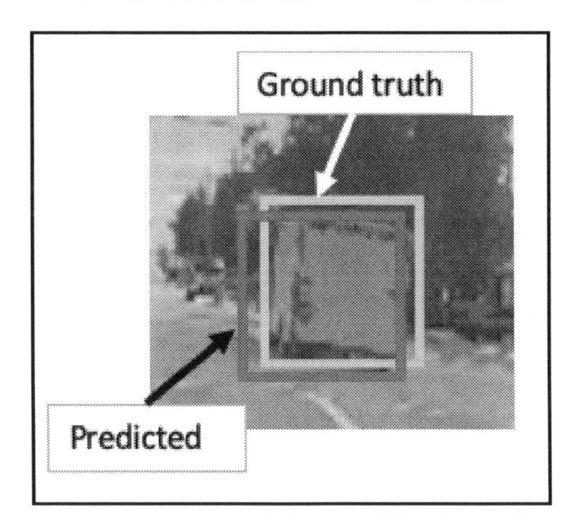

In this case, the IOU value is close to around `0.9` as the overlap area is very high. If the two bounding boxes do not overlap, then the IOU value is `0`, and if they do overlap by 100%, then the IOU value is `1`.

How does YOLO detect objects so fast?

YOLO's detection mechanism is based on a single **Convolutional Neural Network** (**CNN**) that simultaneously predicts multiple bounding boxes for objects and the probability of detection of a given object class in each bounding box. The following images illustrate this methodology:

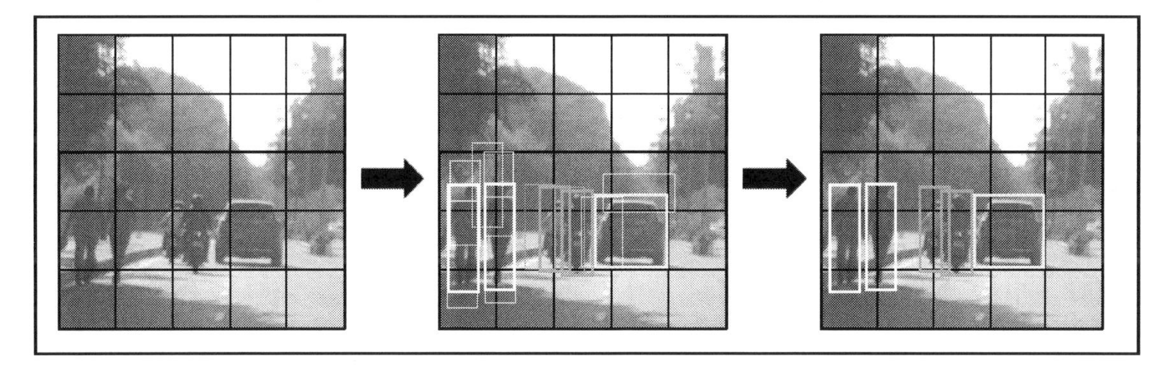

The preceding photos show the three major steps, from the development of bounding boxes to the use of non-max suppression and the final bounding boxes. The detailed steps to this are as follows:

1. The CNN in YOLO uses features from the entire image to predict each bounding box. So, the prediction is global, rather than local.
2. The entire image is divided into S x S grid cells and each grid cell predicts B bounding boxes and the probability (P) that the bounding box contains an object. So, there is a total of S x S x B bounding boxes, with corresponding probabilities for each bounding box.
3. Each bounding box contains five predictions (*x*, *y*, *w*, *h*, and *c*), where the following applies:
    - o (*x*, *y*) is the coordinate of the center of the bounding box, relative to the grid cell coordinate.
    - o (*w*, *h*) is the width and height of the bounding box, relative to the image dimension.
    - o (*c*) is the confidence prediction, representing IOU between the predicted box and ground truth box.
4. The probability that a grid cell contains an object is defined as the probability of the class multiplied by the IOU value. This means that if a grid cell only partially contains an object, its probability will be low and the IOU value will remain low. It will have two effects on the bounding box from that grid cell:
    - The bounding box shape will be smaller than the size of the bounding box from a grid cell that completely includes the object because the grid cell only sees part of the object and infers its shape from it. If the grid cell contains a very small part of an object, then it may not recognize the object at all.
    - The bounding box class confidence level will be low because the IOU value resulting from the partial image will not fit the ground truth prediction.

5. In general, each grid cell can contain only one class but using an anchor box principle, multiple classes can be assigned to a grid cell. An anchor box is a predefined shape that represents the shape of the classes being detected. For example, if we are detecting three classes—car, motorcycle, and human—then we can probably get by with two anchor box shapes—one representing the motorcycle and human, and the another representing the car. This can be confirmed by looking at the right-most image in the preceding images. We can determine the anchor box shape to form the training CSV data by analyzing the shape of each class using algorithms such as k-means clustering.

Let's take the example of the preceding images. Here, we have three classes: `car`, `motorcycle`, and `human`. We are assuming a 5 x 5 grid with 2 anchor boxes and 8 dimensions (5 bounding box parameters (*x, y, w, h,* and *c*) and 3 classes (c1, c2, and c3)). So, the output vector size is 5 x 5 x 2 x 8.

We repeat the `Y = [x, y, w, h, c, c1, c2, c3, x, y, w, h, c, c1, c2, c3]` parameter twice for each anchor box. The following images illustrates the calculation of the bounding box coordinates:

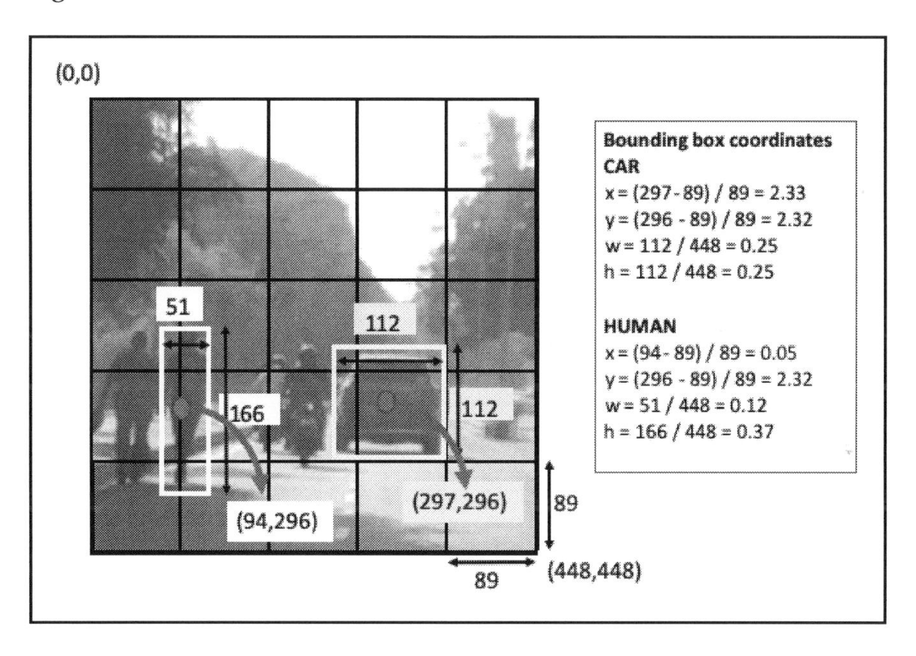

The size of the image is 448 x 448. Here, for illustration purposes, the calculation methodology for two classes—`human` and `car`—is shown. Note that each anchor box size is 448/5 ~ 89.

The YOLO v3 neural network architecture

TYOLO v3 was introduced in 2018 by Joseph Redmon and Ali Farhadi in the paper *YOLOv3: An Incremental Improvement* `https://pjreddie.com/media/files/papers/YOLOv3.pdf`. The YOLO v3 neural network architecture is shown in the following diagram. The network has 24 convolutional layers with 2 fully connected layers; it does not have any softmax layers.

The following diagram illustrates the YOLO v3 architecture graphically:

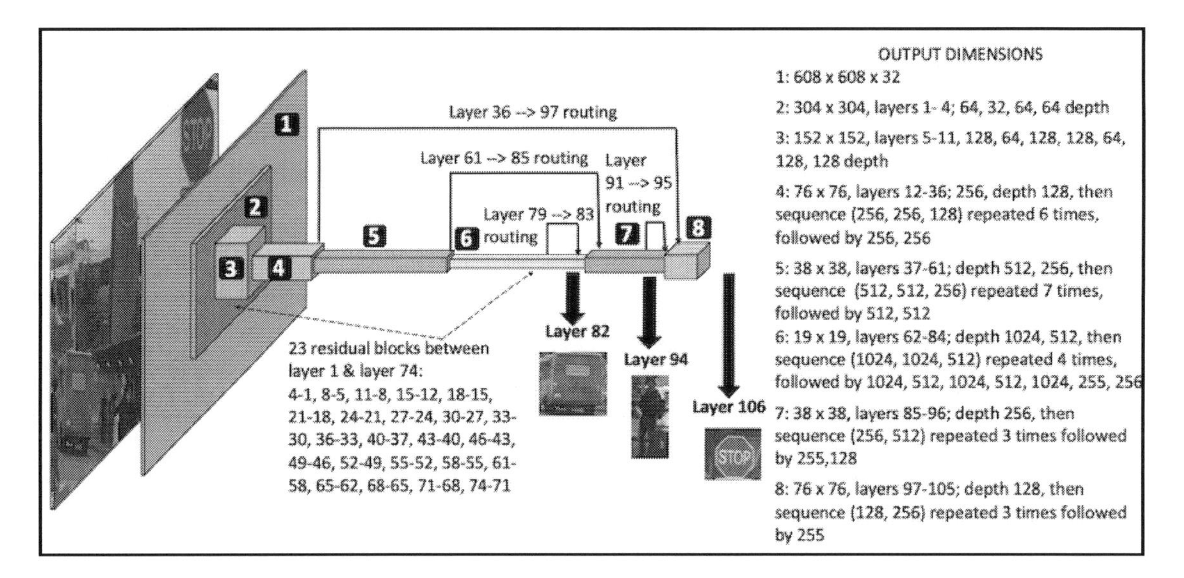

The most important feature of YOLO v3 is its detection mechanism and this is done at three different scales—at layers 82, 94, and 106:

- The network consists of 23 convolution and residual blocks between layers 1 and 74, where the input image size drops from `608` to `19` and the depth increases from `3` to `1,024` through the alternate 3 x 3 and 1 x 1 filters.
- The stride is kept as `1` most of the time, except in 5 cases, where a stride value of `2` is used for size reduction, along with a 3 x 3 filter.
- The residual block is succeeded by a pre-convolution block of alternate 1 x 1 and 3 x 3 filters until the first detection at layer 82. Two short circuits have been used—one between layers 61 and 85, and another between layers 36 and 97.

A comparison of YOLO and Faster R-CNN

The similarities between YOLO and Faster R-CNN are shown in the following table:

YOLO	R-CNN
Predicts the bounding box per grid cell.	Selective search generates the bounding box for each region proposal (which is essentially a grid cell).
Uses bounding box regression.	Uses bounding box regression.

The differences between YOLO and Faster R-CNN are shown in the following table:

YOLO	R-CNN
Classification and bounding box regression occur simultaneously.	Selective search generates a bounding box for each region proposal—these are separate events.
98 bounding boxes per image.	About 2,000 region proposal bounding boxes per image.
2 anchors per grid cell.	9 anchors per grid cell.
It cannot detect small objects and objects that are next to each other.	Detects small objects and objects that are next to each other.
Fast algorithm.	Faster R-CNN is slower than YOLO.

So, in summary, if you need production-level accuracy and do not care so much about speed, choose Faster R-CNN. However, if you need fast detection, choose YOLO. Like any neural network model, you need to have enough samples (around 1,000) oriented at different angles and with different colors and shapes to make a good prediction. Once this is done, based on my personal experience, YOLO v3 gives a very reasonable and fast prediction.

An introduction to Darknet for object detection

Darknet is an open neural network framework that is written in C and managed by Joseph Redmon, the first author of YOLO. Detailed information about Darknet can be found at `pjreddie.com`. In this section, we will discuss Darknet and Tiny Darknet for object detection.

Detecting objects using Darknet

In this section, we will install Darknet from the official Darknet site and use it for object detection. Follow these steps to install Darknet on your PC and make an inference:

1. The following five lines should be entered in the terminal. Hit *Enter* after each command line. These steps will clone Darknet from GitHub, which will create a Darknet directory in your PC as well as get the YOLO v3 weights and then detect the objects in an image:

```
git clone https://github.com/pjreddie/darknet.git
cd darknet
make
wget https://pjreddie.com/media/files/yolov3.weights
./darknet detect cfg/yolov3.cfg yolov3.weights
data/carhumanbike.png
```

2. Once you execute the `git clone` command, you get the following output in the terminal:

```
Cloning into 'darknet'...
remote: Enumerating objects: 5901, done.
remote: Total 5901 (delta 0), reused 0 (delta 0), pack-reused 5901
Receiving objects: 100% (5901/5901), 6.16 MiB | 8.03 MiB/s, done.
Resolving deltas: 100% (3916/3916), done.
```

3. After you enter the `wget yolov3` weight, you get the following output in the terminal:

```
Resolving pjreddie.com (pjreddie.com)... 128.208.4.108
 Connecting to pjreddie.com (pjreddie.com)|128.208.4.108|:443...
connected.
HTTP request sent, awaiting response... 200 OK
Length: 248007048 (237M) [application/octet-stream]
Saving to: 'yolov3.weights'
yolov3.weights
100%[=========================================================>]
236.52M  8.16MB/s    in 29s
... (8.13 MB/s) - 'yolov3.weights' saved [248007048/248007048]
```

4. Then, once you enter `darknet$ ./darknet detect cfg/yolov3.cfg yolov3.weights data/carhumanbike.png`, you get the following output in the terminal:

```
layer filters    size              input                output
 0 conv     32  3 x 3 / 1   608 x 608 x   3   ->   608 x 608 x  32
```

```
0.639 BFLOPs --> image size 608x608
 1 conv     64  3 x 3 / 2   608 x 608 x  32   ->   304 x 304 x  64
3.407 BFLOPs
 2 conv     32  1 x 1 / 1   304 x 304 x  64   ->   304 x 304 x  32
0.379 BFLOPs
 3 conv     64  3 x 3 / 1   304 x 304 x  32   ->   304 x 304 x  64
3.407 BFLOPs
 4 res    1                 304 x 304 x  64   ->   304 x 304 x  64
--> this implies residual block connecting layer 1 to 4
 5 conv    128  3 x 3 / 2   304 x 304 x  64   ->   152 x 152 x 128
3.407 BFLOPs
 6 conv     64  1 x 1 / 1   152 x 152 x 128   ->   152 x 152 x  64
0.379 BFLOPs
 7 conv    128  3 x 3 / 1   152 x 152 x  64   ->   152 x 152 x 128
3.407 BFLOPs
 8 res    5                 152 x 152 x 128   ->   152 x 152 x 128
--> this implies residual block connecting layer 5 to 8
 ...
 ...
 ...
 83 route 79 --> this implies layer 83 is connected to 79, layer
80-82 are prediction layers
 84 conv 256 1 x 1 / 1 19 x 19 x 512 -> 19 x 19 x 256 0.095 BFLOPs
 85 upsample 2x 19 x 19 x 256 -> 38 x 38 x 256 --> this implies
image size increased by 2X
 86 route 85 61 --> this implies shortcut between layer 61 and 85
 87 conv 256 1 x 1 / 1 38 x 38 x 768 -> 38 x 38 x 256 0.568 BFLOPs
 88 conv 512 3 x 3 / 1 38 x 38 x 256 -> 38 x 38 x 512 3.407 BFLOPs
 89 conv 256 1 x 1 / 1 38 x 38 x 512 -> 38 x 38 x 256 0.379 BFLOPs
 90 conv 512 3 x 3 / 1 38 x 38 x 256 -> 38 x 38 x 512 3.407 BFLOPs
 91 conv 256 1 x 1 / 1 38 x 38 x 512 -> 38 x 38 x 256 0.379 BFLOPs
 92 conv 512 3 x 3 / 1 38 x 38 x 256 -> 38 x 38 x 512 3.407 BFLOPs
 93 conv 255 1 x 1 / 1 38 x 38 x 512 -> 38 x 38 x 255 0.377 BFLOPs
 94 yolo --> this implies prediction at layer 94
 95 route 91 --> this implies layer 95 is connected to 91, layer
92-94 are prediction layers
 96 conv 128 1 x 1 / 1 38 x 38 x 256 -> 38 x 38 x 128 0.095 BFLOPs
 97 upsample 2x 38 x 38 x 128 -> 76 x 76 x 128 à this implies image
size increased by 2X
 98 route 97 36. --> this implies shortcut between layer 36 and 97
 99 conv 128 1 x 1 / 1 76 x 76 x 384 -> 76 x 76 x 128 0.568 BFLOPs
 100 conv 256 3 x 3 / 1 76 x 76 x 128 -> 76 x 76 x 256 3.407 BFLOPs
 101 conv 128 1 x 1 / 1 76 x 76 x 256 -> 76 x 76 x 128 0.379 BFLOPs
 102 conv 256 3 x 3 / 1 76 x 76 x 128 -> 76 x 76 x 256 3.407 BFLOPs
 103 conv 128 1 x 1 / 1 76 x 76 x 256 -> 76 x 76 x 128 0.379 BFLOPs
 104 conv 256 3 x 3 / 1 76 x 76 x 128 -> 76 x 76 x 256 3.407 BFLOPs
 105 conv 255 1 x 1 / 1 76 x 76 x 256 -> 76 x 76 x 255 0.754 BFLOPs
 106 yolo --> this implies prediction at layer 106
```

You will see the full model after executing the code. For brevity, we only showed the beginning of the model in the preceding snippet.

The preceding output describes the detailed neural network building blocks of YOLO v3. Take some time to understand all 106 convolution layers and their purpose. An explanation of all the unique code lines is provided in the preceding section. The preceding code results in the following output of the image:

```
Loading weights from yolov3.weights...Done!
data/carhumanbike.png: Predicted in 16.140244 seconds.
car: 81%
truck: 63%
motorbike: 77%
car: 58%
person: 100%
person: 100%
person: 99%
person: 94%
```

The prediction output is shown here:

The YOLO v3 model does a very good job of prediction. Even the very-distant car is detected correctly. The car at the front is categorized as both a car (the label can't be seen in the image) and a truck. All four people—two walking and two riding motorcycles—are detected. Out of the two motorcycles, one motorcycle is detected. Note that although the color of the car is black, the model doesn't falsely detect the shadow as a car.

Detecting objects using Tiny Darknet

Tiny Darknet is a small and fast network that can detect objects very quickly. It has a size of 4 MB, compared to Darknet's size of 28 MB. You can find details of its implementation at `wget https://pjreddie.com/media/files/tiny.weights`.

After following the preceding steps, Darknet should already be installed on your PC. Execute the following command in the terminal:

```
$ cd darknet
darknet$ wget https://pjreddie.com/media/files/tiny.weights
```

The preceding command will install Darknet weights in your `darknet` folder. You should also have `tiny.cfg` in your `cfg` folder. Then, execute the following command to detect objects. Here, we will use the same image for detection that we used for the referenced Darknet model; we just change the weights and the `cfg` file from Darknet to Tiny Darknet:

```
darknet$ ./darknet detect cfg/tiny.cfg tiny.weights data /carhumanbike.png
```

Just as with Darknet, the preceding command will display all 21 layers (as opposed to 106 for Darknet) of the Tiny Darknet model, as shown:

```
layer filters size input output
 0 conv 16 3 x 3 / 1 224 x 224 x 3 -> 224 x 224 x 16 0.043 BFLOPs
 1 max 2 x 2 / 2 224 x 224 x 16 -> 112 x 112 x 16
 2 conv 32 3 x 3 / 1 112 x 112 x 16 -> 112 x 112 x 32 0.116 BFLOPs
 3 max 2 x 2 / 2 112 x 112 x 32 -> 56 x 56 x 32
 4 conv 16 1 x 1 / 1 56 x 56 x 32 -> 56 x 56 x 16 0.003 BFLOPs
 5 conv 128 3 x 3 / 1 56 x 56 x 16 -> 56 x 56 x 128 0.116 BFLOPs
 6 conv 16 1 x 1 / 1 56 x 56 x 128 -> 56 x 56 x 16 0.013 BFLOPs
 7 conv 128 3 x 3 / 1 56 x 56 x 16 -> 56 x 56 x 128 0.116 BFLOPs
 8 max 2 x 2 / 2 56 x 56 x 128 -> 28 x 28 x 128
 9 conv 32 1 x 1 / 1 28 x 28 x 128 -> 28 x 28 x 32 0.006 BFLOPs
 10 conv 256 3 x 3 / 1 28 x 28 x 32 -> 28 x 28 x 256 0.116 BFLOPs
 11 conv 32 1 x 1 / 1 28 x 28 x 256 -> 28 x 28 x 32 0.013 BFLOPs
 12 conv 256 3 x 3 / 1 28 x 28 x 32 -> 28 x 28 x 256 0.116 BFLOPs
 13 max 2 x 2 / 2 28 x 28 x 256 -> 14 x 14 x 256
 14 conv 64 1 x 1 / 1 14 x 14 x 256 -> 14 x 14 x 64 0.006 BFLOPs
 15 conv 512 3 x 3 / 1 14 x 14 x 64 -> 14 x 14 x 512 0.116 BFLOPs
 16 conv 64 1 x 1 / 1 14 x 14 x 512 -> 14 x 14 x 64 0.013 BFLOPs
 17 conv 512 3 x 3 / 1 14 x 14 x 64 -> 14 x 14 x 512 0.116 BFLOPs
 18 conv 128 1 x 1 / 1 14 x 14 x 512 -> 14 x 14 x 128 0.026 BFLOPs
 19 conv 1000 1 x 1 / 1 14 x 14 x 128 -> 14 x 14 x1000 0.050 BFLOPs
 20 avg 14 x 14 x1000 -> 1000
 21 softmax 1000
Loading weights from tiny.weights...Done!
data/carhumanbike.png: Predicted in 0.125068 seconds.
```

However, the model was not able to detect objects in the image. I changed the detection to classification, as shown:

```
darknet$ ./darknet classify cfg/tiny.cfg tiny.weights data/dog.jpg
```

The preceding command generates a result that is similar to what was published in the Tiny YOLO link (`wget https://pjreddie.com/media/files/tiny.weights`):

```
Loading weights from tiny.weights...Done!
data/dog.jpg: Predicted in 0.130953 seconds.
14.51%: malamute
 6.09%: Newfoundland
 5.59%: dogsled
 4.55%: standard schnauzer
 4.05%: Eskimo dog
```

However, the same image, when passed through object detection, returns no bounding box.

Next, we will discuss real-time prediction on videos using Darknet.

Real-time prediction using Darknet

Prediction involving Darknet can all be done using the command line in the terminal. For more details, refer to `https://pjreddie.com/darknet/yolo/`.

Up to now, we have made inferences using Darknet on an image. In the following steps, we will learn how to make inferences using Darknet on a video file:

1. Go to the `darknet` directory (already installed in the previous steps) by typing **`cd darknet`** in the terminal.
2. Make sure OpenCV is installed. Even though you have OpenCV installed, it may still create an error flag. Use the **`sudo apt-get install libopencv-dev`** command to install OpenCV in the `darknet` directory.
3. In the `darknet` directory, there is a file called `Makefile`. Open that file, set `OpenCV = 1`, and save.
4. Download the weights from the terminal by going to `https://pjreddie.com/media/files/yolov3.weights`.
5. At this point, you have to recompile since `Makefile` was changed. You do that by typing **`make`** in the terminal.

6. Then, download the video file by typing the following command in the terminal:

```
./darknet detector demo cfg/coco.data cfg/yolov3.cfg yolov3.weights
data/road_video.mp4
```

7. Here, the YOLO model with 106 layers, as explained before, will be compiled and the video will be played. You will notice that the video plays extremely slowly. This can be fixed in the following two steps that we will execute. They should be executed one by one, as each step has ramifications.
8. Open `Makefile` again. Change `GPU` to `1`, save `Makefile`, and repeat steps 4 to 6. At this point, I noticed that step 6 provided the following CUDA `out of memory` error:

```
 .......
 57 conv    512  3 x 3 / 1    38 x  38 x 256   ->    38 x  38 x 512
3.407 BFLOPs
 58 res    55                 38 x  38 x 512   ->    38 x  38 x 512
 59 conv    256  1 x 1 / 1    38 x  38 x 512   ->    38 x  38 x 256
0.379 BFLOPs
 60 CUDA Error: out of memory
 darknet: ./src/cuda.c:36: check_error: Assertion `0' failed.
 Aborted (core dumped)
```

The error was solved with the help of two mechanisms:

- Changing the image size.
- Changing the NVIDIA CUDA version from 9.0 to 10.1. Refer to the NVIDIA site to change the NVIDIA version (`https://docs.nvidia.com/deploy/cuda-compatibility/index.html`).

First, try changing the image size. If this does not work, then check the CUDA version and update it if you are still using version 9.0.

9. In the `darknet` directory, there is a file called `yolov3.cfg` under the `cfg` directory. Open that file and change the width and height from `608` to either `416` or `288`. I found that when the value is set to `304`, it still fails. Save the file and repeat steps 5 and 6.

Here's the error code you will get when the image size is set to `304`:

```
 .....
 80 conv   1024  3 x 3 / 1    10 x  10 x 512   ->    10 x  10 x1024
0.944 BFLOPs
 81 conv    255  1 x 1 / 1    10 x  10 x1024   ->    10 x  10 x 255
0.052 BFLOPs
```

```
 82 yolo
 83 route  79
 84 conv    256  1 x 1 / 1    10 x  10 x 512   ->    10 x  10 x 256
0.026 BFLOPs
 85 upsample            2x    10 x  10 x 256   ->    20 x  20 x 25
 86 route  85 61
 87 Layer before convolutional layer must output image.: File
exists
 darknet: ./src/utils.c:256: error: Assertion `0' failed.
 Aborted (core dumped)
```

The following image shows a screenshot of a video file with traffic sign labels and car detection at the same time:

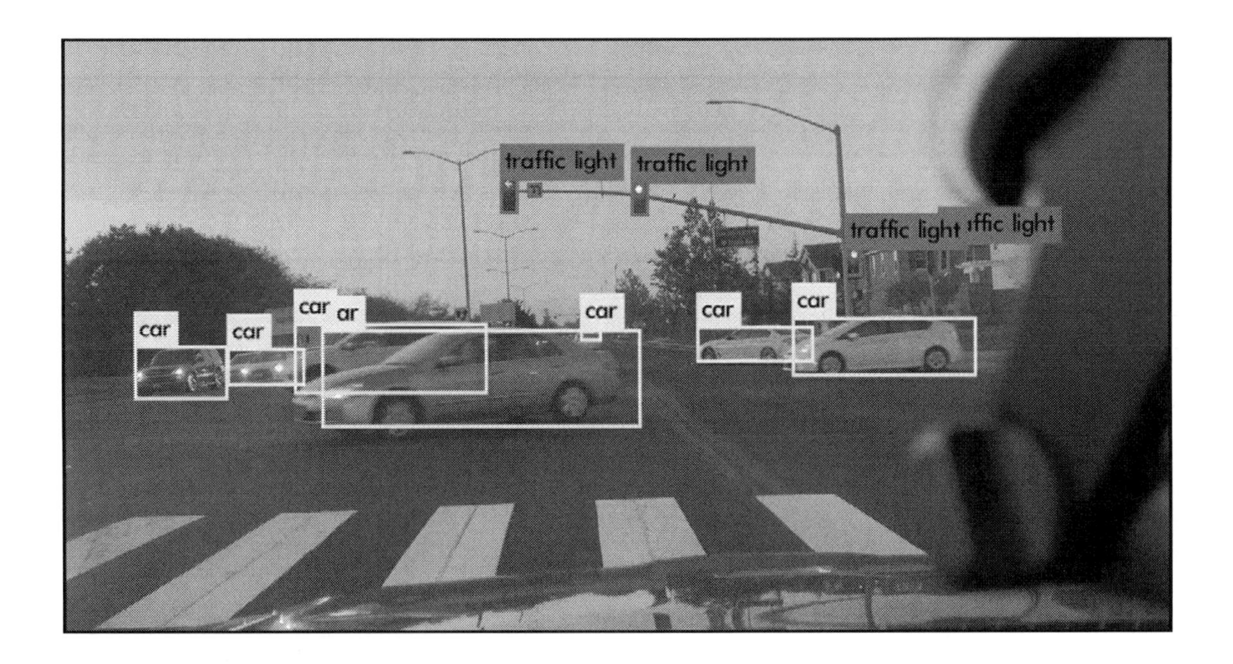

Note that all the cars are detected correctly and even the main and side traffic lights are detected.

We discussed the YOLO v3 layer with a default size of `608` previously. The following is the same output, with the size changed to `416` in order to display the video file correctly:

```
 layer     filters    size              input                output
 0 conv     32  3 x 3 / 1   416 x 416 x   3   ->   416 x 416 x  32
0.299 BFLOPs
 1 conv     64  3 x 3 / 2   416 x 416 x  32   ->   208 x 208 x  64
1.595 BFLOPs
 2 conv     32  1 x 1 / 1   208 x 208 x  64   ->   208 x 208 x  32
0.177 BFLOPs
 3 conv     64  3 x 3 / 1   208 x 208 x  32   ->   208 x 208 x  64
1.595 BFLOPs
 4 res    1                 208 x 208 x  64   ->   208 x 208 x  64
 5 conv    128  3 x 3 / 2   208 x 208 x  64   ->   104 x 104 x 128
1.595 BFLOPs
 6 conv     64  1 x 1 / 1   104 x 104 x 128   ->   104 x 104 x  64
0.177 BFLOPs
 7 conv    128  3 x 3 / 1   104 x 104 x  64   ->   104 x 104 x 128
1.595 BFLOPs
 8 res    5                 104 x 104 x 128   ->   104 x 104 x 128
 ...
 ...
 ...
 94 yolo
 95 route  91
 96 conv    128  1 x 1 / 1    26 x  26 x 256   ->    26 x  26 x 128
0.044 BFLOPs
 97 upsample            2x    26 x  26 x 128   ->    52 x  52 x 128
 98 route  97 36
 99 conv    128  1 x 1 / 1    52 x  52 x 384   ->    52 x  52 x 128
0.266 BFLOP
 100 conv    256  3 x 3 / 1    52 x  52 x 128   ->    52 x  52 x 256
1.595 BFLOPs
 101 conv    128  1 x 1 / 1    52 x  52 x 256   ->    52 x  52 x 128
0.177 BFLOPs
 102 conv    256  3 x 3 / 1    52 x  52 x 128   ->    52 x  52 x 256
1.595 BFLOPs
 103 conv    128  1 x 1 / 1    52 x  52 x 256   ->    52 x  52 x 128
0.177 BFLOPs
 104 conv    256  3 x 3 / 1    52 x  52 x 128   ->    52 x  52 x 256
1.595 BFLOPs
 105 conv    255  1 x 1 / 1    52 x  52 x 256   ->    52 x  52 x 255
0.353 BFLOPs
 106 yolo
 Loading weights from yolov3.weights...Done!
 video file: data/road_video.mp4
```

You will see the full model after executing the preceding code. For brevity, we only showed the beginning of the model in the preceding snippet.

The following table summarizes the output for two different image sizes:

Layer	**608 size**	**416 size**
82	19 x 19	13 x 13
94	38 x 38	26 x 26
106	76 x 76	52 x 52

Note that a ratio of 32 is maintained between the original image size and the 82nd layer output size. So far, we have compared inferences using Darknet and Tiny Darknet. Now, we will compare different YOLO models.

YOLO versus YOLO v2 versus YOLO v3

A comparison of the three YOLO versions is shown in this table:

	YOLO	**YOLO v2**	**YOLO v3**
Input size	224 x 224	448 x 448	
Framework	Darknet trained on ImageNet—1,000.	Darknet-19 19 convolution layers and 5 max pool layers.	Darknet-53 53 convolutional layers. For detection, 53 more layers are added, giving a total of 106 layers.
Small size detection	It cannot find small images.	Better than YOLO at detecting small images.	Better than YOLO v2 at small image detection.
		Uses anchor boxes.	Uses a residual block.

The following diagram compares the architectures of YOLO v2 and YOLO v3:

YOLOV2

Type	Filters	Size	Output
Convolutional	32	3 x 3	224 x 224
Maxpool		2 x 2 / 2	112 x 112
Convolutional	64	3 x 3	112 x 112
Maxpool		2 x 2 / 2	56 x 56
Convolutional	128	3 x 3	56 x 56
Convolutional	64	1 x 1	56 x 56
Convolutional	128	3 X 3	56 X 56
Maxpool		2 x 2 / 2	28 X 28
Convolutional	256	3 x 3	28 X 28
Convolutional	128	1 x 1	28 X 28
Convolutional	256	3 X 3	28 X 28
Maxpool		2 x 2 / 2	14 X 14
Convolutional	512	3 x 3	14 X 14
Convolutional	256	1 x 1	14 X 14
Convolutional	512	3 X 3	14 X 14
		2 x 2 / 2	7 X 7
Convolutional	1024	3 x 3	7 X 7
Convolutional	512	1 x 1	7 X 7
Convolutional	1024	3 X 3	7 X 7
Convolutional	512	1 x 1	7 X 7
Convolutional	1024	3 X 3	7 X 7
Convolutional	1000	1 X 1	7 X 7
Avgpool		Global	1000

YOLOV3

	Type	Filters	Size	Output
	Convolutional	32	3 x 3	256 x 256
	Convolutional	64	3 x 3 / 2	128 x 128
	Convolutional	32	1 x 1	
1 x	Convolutional	64	3 X 3	
	Residual			128 X 128
	Convolutional	128	3 x 3 / 2	64 x 64
	Convolutional	64	1 x 1	
2 x	Convolutional	128	3 x 3	
	Residual			64 X 64
	Convolutional	256	3 x 3 / 2	32 x 32
	Convolutional	128	1 x 1	
8 x	Convolutional	256	3 x 3	
	Residual			32 x 32
	Convolutional	512	3 x 3 / 2	32 x 32
	Convolutional	256	1 x 1	
8 x	Convolutional	512	3 x 3	
	Residual			16 x 16
	Convolutional	1024	3 x 3 / 2	32 x 32
	Convolutional	512	1 x 1	
4 x	Convolutional	1024	3 x 3	
	Residual			8 x 8
	Avgpool		Global	
	Connected		1000	
	Softmax			

The basic convolution layers are similar, but YOLO v3 carries out detection at three separate layers: 82, 94, and 106.

The most critical item that you should take from YOLO v3 is its object detection at three different layers and at three different scales: 82 (the largest), 94 (intermediate), and 106 (the smallest).

When to train a model?

In transfer learning, the trained model is developed by training on a lot of data. So, if your class belongs to one of the following, there is no reason to train the model for these classes. The 80 classes trained for YOLO v3 are as follows:

```
Person, bicycle, car, motorbike, airplane, bus, train, truck, boat, traffic
light, fire hydrant, stop sign, parking meter, bench, bird, cat, dog,
horse, sheep, cow, elephant, bear, zebra, giraffe, backpack, umbrella,
handbag, tie, suitcase, frisbee, skis, snowboard, sports ball, kite,
baseball bat, baseball glove, skateboard, surfboard. tennis racket, bottle,
wine glass, cup, fork, knife, spoon, bowl, banana, apple, sandwich, orange,
broccoli, carrot, hot dog, pizza, donut, cake, chair, sofa, potted plant,
bed, dining table, toilet, tv monitor, laptop, mouse, remote, keyboard,
cell phone, microwave, oven, toaster, sink, refrigerator, book, clock,
vase, scissors, teddy bear, hair drier, toothbrush
```

So, if you are trying to detect the type of food, YOLO v3 will do a good job at detecting `banana`, `apple`, `sandwich`, `orange`, `broccoli`, `carrot`, `hot dog`, `pizza`, `donut`, and `cake`, but it won't be able to detect `hamburger`.

Similarly, YOLO v3 trained on the PASCAL VOC dataset will be able to detect all of the 20 classes, which are `airplane`, `bicycle`, `bird`, `boat`, `bottle`, `bus`, `car`, `cat`, `chair`, `cow`, `dining table`, `dog`, `horse`, `motorbike`, `person`, `potted plant`, `sheep`, `sofa`, `train`, and `tv monitor`, but it won't be able to detect a new class, `hot dog`.

So, this is where training your own image set comes in, which is described in the next section.

Training your own image set with YOLO v3 to develop a custom model

In this section, we will learn how to use YOLO v3 to train your own custom detector. The training process involves a number of different steps. For the sake of clarity, the input and output from each step are indicated in the following flowchart. Many of the training steps are included in YOLO's *YOLOv3: An Incremental Improvement* publication by Redmon, Joseph, Farhadi, and Ali, published on arXiv in 2018. They are also included under the *Training YOLO on VOC* section at `https://pjreddie.com/darknet/yolo/`.

The following image shows you how to use YOLO v3 to train a VOC dataset. In our case, we will use our own custom furniture data that we used to classify images using Keras in `Chapter 6`, *Visual Search Using Transfer Learning*:

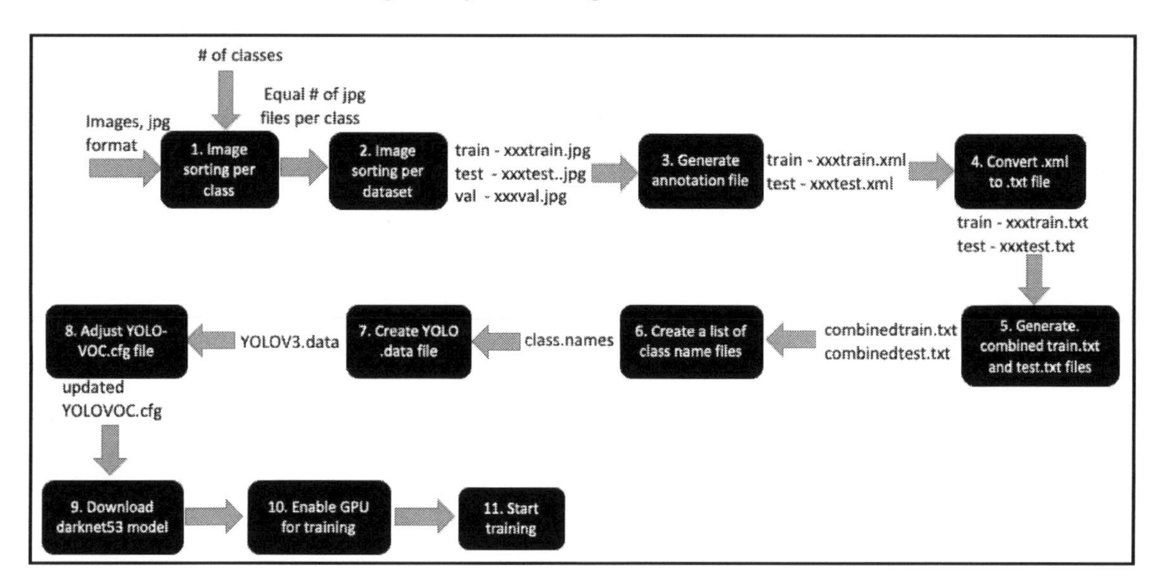

A detailed description of sections 1 to 11 is described here.

Preparing images

Follow these steps to prepare your image:

1. Study how many classes you want to detect—in this example, we will consider the `bed`, `chair`, and `sofa` classes discussed in Chapter 6, *Visual Search Using Transfer Learning*.
2. Ensure that you have the same number of images per class.
3. Make sure your class name does not have white spaces in it; for example, use `caesar_salad` instead of `caesar salad`.
4. Collect at least 100 images per class to start the initial training (hence, complete steps 1 to 10 to develop the model) and then increase the number as you have more and more images. Ideally, 1,000 images is a good number for training.

5. Bulk resize all the images to 416 x 416—you can select **options** in the macOS **preview** pane, then select multiple images, and then bulk resize, or you can use a program such as ImageMagick in Ubuntu to bulk resize in the terminal. The reason this step is needed is that YOLO v3 expects images to be sized to 416 x 416 and so will resize images by itself, but this may cause the bounding box to appear differently for that image, resulting in no detection in some cases.

Generating annotation files

This step involves creating bounding box coordinates for each object in each image in the dataset. This bounding box coordinate is typically represented by four parameters: (x,y) to determine initial location and the width and height. The bounding box can be expressed as `.xml` or in `.txt` form. This coordinate file is also known as an annotation file. Follow these steps to complete this section:

1. A lot of image annotation software applications are being used for labeling images. We have already covered VGG Image Annotator in `Chapter 3`, *Facial Detection Using OpenCV and CNN*, during facial key-point detection. In `Chapter 11`, *Deep Learning on Edge Devices with CPU/GPU Optimization*, we will cover CVAT tool for automated image annotation. In this chapter, we will introduce an annotation tool called `labelImg`.
2. Download the `labelImg` annotation software from `pypi` at `https://pypi.org/project/labelImg/`. You can follow the instructions on there to install `labelImg` for your operating system—if you have any issues, a simple way to install this is to type `pip3 install lableImg` in the terminal. Then, to run it, all you have to do is type `labelImg` in the terminal.
3. In `labelImg`, click on the directory of images in the **Open Dir** box. Select each image and create a bounding box around it by clicking on **Create/RectBox**, and then add a class name for the bounding box, such as `bed`, `chair`, or `sofa`. Save the annotation and go to the next image by clicking on the right arrow.
4. If there are multiple classes or multiple positions of the same class within your image in the picture, draw rectangles around each of them. Examples of multiple classes are cars and pedestrians in the same image. Examples of multiple positions within the same class are different cars at different positions in the same image. So, if an image consists of multiple chairs and a sofa, draw rectangles around each of the chairs and, in the class name, type `chair` for each and for the sofa, draw a rectangle around it and type `sofa`. If the image consists of only a sofa, then draw a rectangle around the sofa and type `sofa` as the class name. The following diagram illustrates this:

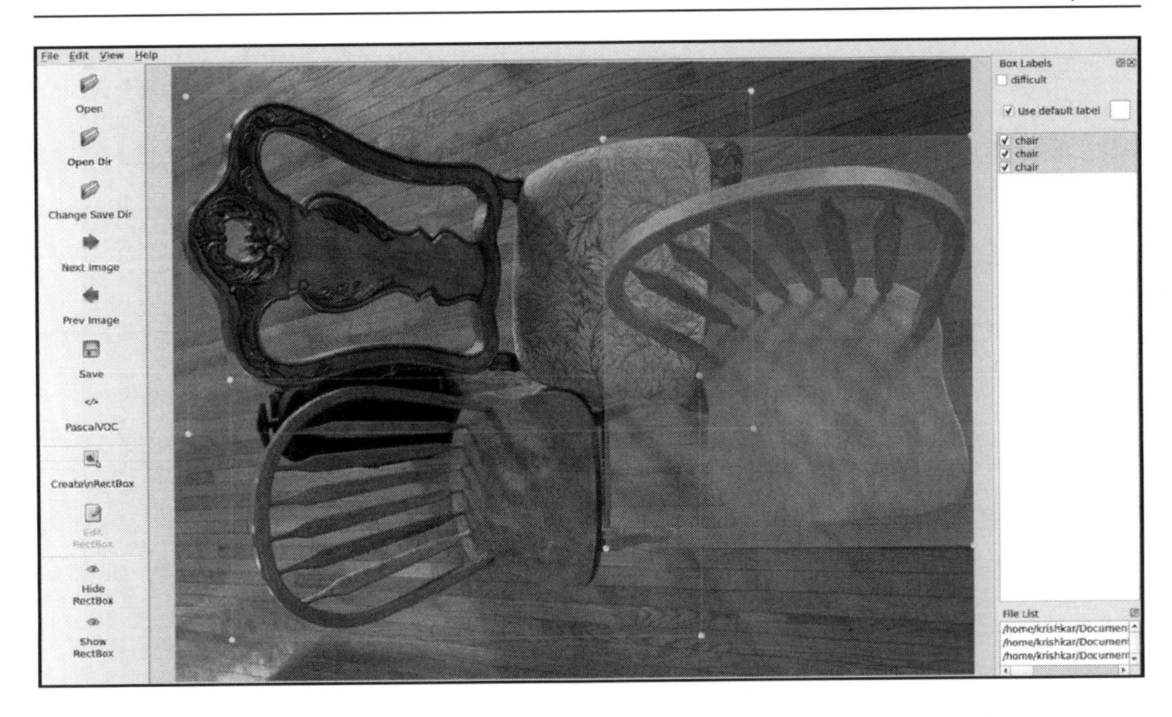

This diagram shows you how to label multiple images belonging to the same class.

Converting .xml files to .txt files

YOLO v3 needs an annotation file to be saved as a `.txt` file and not as a `.xml` file. This section describes how to convert and arrange a `.txt` file for input to the model. There are many tools available for such a conversion—we will mention two tools here:

- `RectLabel`: This has a built-in converter to convert a `.xml` file to a `.txt` file.
- The command-line `xmltotxt` tool: You can find this tool at the `https://github.com/Isabek/XmlToTxt` GitHub page.

The output of this process will be a directory containing the `.jpg`, `.xml`, and `.txt` files. Every image `.jpg` file will have a corresponding `.xml` and `.txt` file. You can delete the `.xml` file from the directory as we won't need these anymore.

Creating a combined train.txt and test.txt file

This step involves, as the name suggests, one `.txt` file representing all the images. For this, we will run a simple Python file—one each for training and test images—to create a `combinedtrain.txt` and `combinedtest.txt` file. Go to `https://github.com/PacktPublishing/Mastering-Computer-Vision-with-TensorFlow-2.0/blob/master/Chapter07/Chapter7_yolo_combined_text.py` for the Python file.

The sample output from the Python code is shown in the following screenshot:

train.txt

```
/home/krishkar/Documents/chapter7_yolo/furniture_data/trainyolo/sofa_316.jpg
/home/krishkar/Documents/chapter7_yolo/furniture_data/trainyolo/bed_418.jpg
/home/krishkar/Documents/chapter7_yolo/furniture_data/trainyolo/chair_169.jpg
/home/krishkar/Documents/chapter7_yolo/furniture_data/trainyolo/sofa_102.jpg
/home/krishkar/Documents/chapter7_yolo/furniture_data/trainyolo/chair_227.jpg
/home/krishkar/Documents/chapter7_yolo/furniture_data/trainyolo/bed_144.jpg
/home/krishkar/Documents/chapter7_yolo/furniture_data/trainyolo/chair_312.jpg
```

Each text file consists of several rows—each row consists of the path of the image file, as shown earlier.

Creating a list of class name files

This file consists of lists of all the classes. So, in our case, it is a simple text file with a `.names` extension, as shown:

```
bed
chair
sofa
```

Creating a YOLO .data file

These steps involve the path of the `train` and `valid` folders. Before beginning, copy the combined `train`, combined `test`, and `.names` files to your `darknet` directory. The following code block shows how a typical `.data` file (in this example, `furniture.data`) will look:

```
classes= 3
train = /home/krishkar/darknet/furniture_train.txt
valid = /home/krishkar/darknet/furniture_test.txt
names = /home/krishkar/darknet/furniture_label.names
backup = backup
```

Here, we have three classes (bed, chair, and sofa), so the value of classes is set to 3. The train, valid, and names folders show the combined train, combined test, and label .names file. Keep this file in the cfg directory.

Adjusting the YOLO configuration file

After completing these steps, the file arrangement part is complete and we will now work on optimizing the parameters in the YOLO configuration file. To do that, open YOLO-VOC.cfg under the Darknet cfg directory and make the following changes. The resulting code can also be downloaded from https://github.com/PacktPublishing/Mastering-Computer-Vision-with-TensorFlow-2.0/blob/master/Chapter07/yolov3-furniture.cfg:

Note that in the following section, we will be describing various line numbers and values to change – these line numbers correspond to the YOLO-VOC.cfg file.

1. Line 6—the batch size. Set this to 64. This means 64 images will be used in every training step to update the CNN parameters.
2. Line 7—subdivisions. This splits the batches by batch size/subdivisions, which are then fed into the GPU for processing. The process will be repeated for the number of subdivisions until the batch size (64) is completed and a new batch is started. So, if subdivisions is set to 1, then all 64 images are sent to the GPU for processing simultaneously in a given batch. If the batch size is set to 8, then 8 images are sent to the GPU for processing and the process is repeated 8 times before the next batch is started. Setting the value to 1 may cause the GPU to fail, but may increase the accuracy of detection. For the initial run, set the value to 8.
3. Line 11—momentum. This is used to minimize large weight changes between batches as only a small batch (64, in this example) of the image is processed at any point in time. The default value of 0.9 is OK.
4. Line 12—decay. This is used to minimize overfitting by controlling the weight value to gain a large value. The default value of 0.005 is OK.

5. Line 18—`learning_rate`. This indicates how fast the current batch is learned. The following figure shows the learning rate as a function of batches, which will be explained next. The default value of `0.001` is a reasonable start and can be decreased if the values are **Not a Number** (**NaN**):

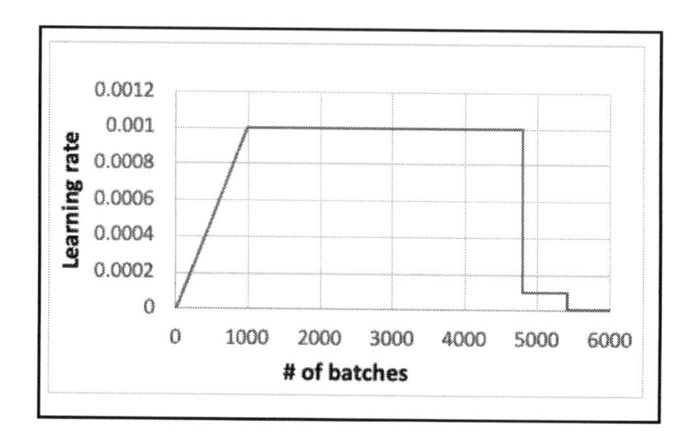

6. Line 19—`burn_in`.This indicates the initial period that the learning rate ramps up. Set it to `1000` and lower it if `max_batches` is reduced.

Note that if you set the code as in the previous steps and you notice that you are not learning much when the epochs are around `200` to `300`, the reason may be that your learning rate is very low at the time. You will start to see the learning rate creep up past `1000` epochs.

7. Line 20—`max_batches`. The maximum number of batches. Set it to 2,000 multiplied by the number of classes. For `3` classes, a value of `6000` is reasonable. Note that the default value is `500200`, which is very high and, if left unchanged, the training will run for days.
8. Line 22—`steps`. This is the step after which the learning rate is multiplied by scales in line 23. Set it equal to 80% and 90% of `max_batches`. So, if the batch size is `6000`, set the value to `4800` and `5400`.
9. Lines 611, 695, 779. Change the `classes` value from its default (`20` or `80`) to your class value (`3`, in this example).
10. Lines 605, 689, 773. These are the last convolution layers before the YOLO prediction. Set the `filters` value from its default of `255` to `(5+ # of classes)x3`. So, for 3 classes, the filter value should be 24.

11. Lines 610, 694, 778. These are anchors, a preset bounding box with a height-to-width ratio as shown here. The anchor sizes are represented by (width, height), their value do not need to change, but it is important to understand its context. (10, 13), (16, 30), (32, 23), (30, 61), (62, 45), (59, 119), (116, 90), (156, 198), (373, 326). Altogether, there are nine anchors ranging from a height of `10` to a height of `373`. This represents the smallest to the largest image detection. For this exercise, we do not need to change the anchors.
12. Lines 609, 693, 777. These are masks. They specify which of the anchor boxes we will need to select for training. If the value of the lower level is `0, 1, 2` and you continue to observe NaN in the output for regions `94` and `106`, consider increasing the value. The best way to select the value is to review your training image bounding box proportion for the smallest to the largest image, understand where they fall, and select appropriate masks to represent that. In our test case, the bounding box for the smallest dimension starts around `62, 45, 40`, so we select `5, 6, 7` for the smallest value. The following table shows the default value of the mask and the adjusted value:

Default value	**Adjusted value**
6, 7, 8	7, 8, 9
3, 4, 5	6, 7, 8
0, 1, 2	6, 7, 8

The maximum value of `9` represents `bed`, and the smallest value of `6` represents `chair`.

Note that if your bounding box in an image is different, your `mask` value can be adjusted to get the desired result. So, start with the default value and adjust to avoid a NaN result.

Enabling the GPU for training

Open `Makefile` in your `darknet` directory and set the parameters as follows:

```
GPU = 1
CUDNN = 1
```

Start training

Execute the following commands in the terminal one by one:

1. Download the pretrained `darknet53` model weights to speed up training. Run the command found at `https://pjreddie.com/media/files/darknet53.conv.74` in the terminal.

2. After the download of the pretrained weights is complete, execute the following command in the terminal:

```
./darknet detector train cfg/furniture.data cfg/yolov3-
furniture.cfg darknet53.conv.74 -gpus 0
```

The training will start and will continue until maximum batches are created with values written for the 82, 94, and 106 layers. In the following code, we will show two outputs—one for when everything goes correctly, and the other one for when training does not go correctly:

```
Correct training
Region 82 Avg IOU: 0.063095, Class: 0.722422, Obj: 0.048252, No Obj:
0.006528, .5R: 0.000000, .75R: 0.000000, count: 1
Region 94 Avg IOU: 0.368487, Class: 0.326743, Obj: 0.005098, No Obj:
0.003003, .5R: 0.000000, .75R: 0.000000, count: 1
Region 106 Avg IOU: 0.144510, Class: 0.583078, Obj: 0.001186, No Obj:
0.001228, .5R: 0.000000, .75R: 0.000000, count: 1
298: 9.153068, 7.480968 avg, 0.000008 rate, 51.744666 seconds, 298 images

Incorrect training
Region 82 Avg IOU: 0.061959, Class: 0.404846, Obj: 0.520931, No Obj:
0.485723, .5R: 0.000000, .75R: 0.000000, count: 1
Region 94 Avg IOU: -nan, Class: -nan, Obj: -nan, No Obj: 0.525058, .5R: -
nan, .75R: -nan, count: 0
Region 106 Avg IOU: -nan, Class: -nan, Obj: -nan, No Obj: 0.419326, .5R: -
nan, .75R: -nan, count: 0
```

In the preceding code, `IOU` describes intersection over union and `Class` signifies object classification—a `Class` value close to `1` is desirable. `Obj` is the probability of detecting an object and its value should be close to `1`. The value of `NoObj` should be close to `0. 0.5.R` is the ratio of positive samples detected divided by the actual sample in the image.

So far, we have learned how to use Darknet to make an inference with a pretrained YOLO model and trained our own YOLO model for our custom images. In the next section, we will get an overview of another neural network model, called **RetinaNet**.

An overview of the Feature Pyramid Network and RetinaNet

We have learned from `Chapter 5`, *Neural Network Architecture and Models*, that each layer of a CNN is a feature vector in itself. There are two critical and interdependent parameters associated with this, as explained here:

- As we go up the CNN of the image through various convolution layers to the fully connected layer, we identify more features (semantically strong), from a simple edge to a feature of an object to a complete object. However, in doing so, the resolution of the image decreases as the feature width and height decreases while its depth increases.
- Objects of different scales (small versus large) are affected by this resolution and dimension. As the following diagram shows, a smaller object will be harder to detect at the highest layer because its features will be so blurred that the CNN will not be able to detect it very well:

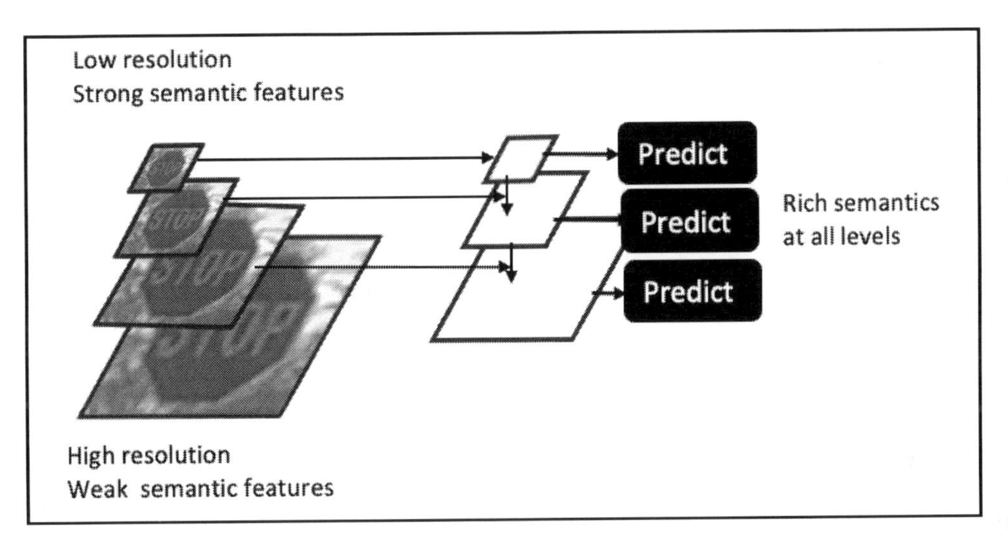

Detecting multiple images at different scales is difficult to do simultaneously due to the resolution issues for a small object, as explained previously. So, instead of images, we stack features in a pyramid form with smaller dimensions at the top and larger features at the bottom, as illustrated in the preceding figure. This is called a pyramid of features.

A **Feature Pyramid Network** (**FPN**) consists of a pyramid of features, consisting of a higher dimension and lower resolution between each CNN layer. This pyramid of features is used in an FPN to make detections of different objects of scale. The FPN uses the last fully connected layer feature, which applies an upsampling of 2x based on its nearest neighbors, and adds it to its previous feature vector and then applies a 3 x 3 convolution to the merged layer. This process is repeated all the way to the second convolution layer. The result is a rich semantic at all levels, leading to object detection at different scales.

RetinaNet (`https://arxiv.org/abs/1708.02002`) was introduced in *Focal Loss for Dense Object Detection* by Tsung-Yi Lin, Priya Goyal, Ross Girshick, Kaiming He, and Piotr Dollár. RetinaNet is a dense, one-stage network composed of a base ResNet-type network and two task-specific subnetworks. The base network computes a convolutional feature map for different image scales using FPN. The first subnet performs object classification and the second subnet performs convolutional bounding box regression.

Most CNN object detectors can be classified into two categories—one-stage and two-stage networks. In a one-stage network, such as YOLO and SSD, a single stage is responsible for both classification and detection. In a two-stage network, such as R-CNN, the first stage generates object location and the second stage evaluates its classification. The one-stage network is known for its speed, whereas the two-stage network is known for its accuracy.

The one-stage network is known to suffer from class imbalance arising from the fact that only a few of the candidate locations actually contain an object. This class imbalance makes the training ineffective in the majority of the sections of the image. RetinaNet addresses the class imbalance by introducing **Focal Loss** (**FL**), which fine-tunes the loss **Cross-Entropy** (**CE**) to focus on difficult detection problems. The fine-tuning of the loss CE is done by applying a modulating factor (*g*) on the probability of detection (*pt*) to the loss CE, as shown:

$$FL(pt) = -(1 - pt)\gamma log(pt) = CE.(1 - pt)\gamma$$

RetinaNet matches the speed of the one-stage network while matching the accuracy of the two-stage network by utilizing the FL concept.

The Keras version of RetinaNet can be downloaded in the terminal by executing the following command:

```
pip install keras-retinanet
```

In terms of precision and speed, YOLO v3 maintains an average precision of over 50 and is faster compared to RetinaNet.

Summary

In this chapter, we learned the building blocks of the YOLO object detection method and learned how it can detect an object so quickly and accurately compared to other object detection methods. We learned about different evolutions of YOLO—the original version of YOLO, YOLO v2, and YOLO v3—and their differences. We used YOLO to detect an object in an image and video file, such as traffic signs.

We learned how to debug YOLO v3 so that it can generate correct outputs without crashing. We understood how to use pretrained YOLO to make an inference and learned the detailed process for using our custom image to develop a new YOLO model and how to tune CNN parameters to generate correct results. This chapter also introduced you to RetinaNet and how it uses the concept of a feature pyramid to detect objects of different scales.

In the next chapter, we will be learning about content filling on images using semantic segmentation and image inpainting.

8
Semantic Segmentation and Neural Style Transfer

The application of a deep neural network is not only restricted to finding an object in an image (which we learned about in the previous chapters) – it can also be used to segment images into spatial regions, thereby producing artificial images and transferring style from one image to another.

In this chapter, we will use TensorFlow Colab to perform all these tasks. Semantic segmentation predicts whether each pixel of an image belongs to a certain class. It is a useful technique for image overlaying. You will learn about TensorFlow DeepLab so that you can perform semantic segmentation on images. **Deep Convolutional Generative Adversarial Networks** (**DCGANs**) are powerful tools that are used to produce artificial images such as human faces and handwritten digits. They can also be used for image inpainting. We will also discuss how to use CNNs to transfer style from one image to another.

In this chapter, we will cover the following topics:

- Overview of TensorFlow DeepLab for semantic segmentation
- Artificial image generation using DCGANs
- Image inpainting using OpenCV
- Understanding neural style transfer

Overview of TensorFlow DeepLab for semantic segmentation

Semantic segmentation is the task of understanding and classifying the content of an image at the pixel level. Unlike object detection, where a rectangular bounding box is drawn over multiple object classes (similar to what we learned about YOLOV3), semantic segmentation learns the whole image and assigns a class of the enclosed object to the corresponding pixels in the image. Thus, semantic segmentation can be more powerful than object detection. The foundational architecture of semantic segmentation is based on the encoder-decoder network, where the encoder creates a high-dimensional feature vector and aggregates it at different levels, while the decoder creates a semantic segmentation mask at a different level of the neural network. Whereas the encoder uses a traditional CNN, the decoder uses unpooling, deconvolution, and upsampling. DeepLab is a special type of semantic segmentation introduced by Google, that uses Atrous Convolution, spatial pyramid pooling instead of regular max pooling, and an encoder-decoder network. DeepLabV3+ was introduced by Liang-Chieh Chen, Yukun Zhu, George Papandreou, Florian Schro, and Hartwig Adam in their paper *Encoder-Decoder with Atrous Separable Convolution for Semantic Image Segmentation* (`https://arxiv.org/abs/1802.02611`).

DeepLab started with V1 in 2015 and quickly moved to V3+ as of 2019. A comparison of the different DeepLab versions can be seen in the following table:

	DeepLab V1	**DeepLab V2**	**DeepLab V3**	**DeepLab V3+**
Paper	*Semantic Image Segmentation with Deep Convolutional Nets and Fully Connected CRFs*, 2015	*DeepLab: Semantic Image Segmentation with Deep Convolutional Nets, Atrous Convolution, and Fully Connected CRFs*, 2017	*Rethinking Atrous Convolution for Semantic Image Segmentation*, 2017	*Encoder-Decoder with Atrous Separable Convolution for Semantic Image Segmentation*, 2018
Authors	Liang-Chieh Chen, George Papandreou, Iasonas Kokkinos, Kevin Murphy, and Alan L. Yuille	Liang-Chieh Chen, George Papandreou, Iasonas Kokkinos, Kevin Murphy, and Alan L. Yuille	Liang-Chieh Chen, George Papandreou, Florian Schroff, and Hartwig Adam	Liang-Chieh Chen, Yukun Zhu, George Papandreou, Florian Schro, and Hartwig Adam
Key Concepts	Atrous convolution, fully connected **conditional random fields** (**CRFs**)	**Atrous spatial pyramid pooling** (**ASPP**)	ASPP, image-level features, and batch normalization	ASPP and encoder/decoder modules

DeepLabV3+ uses the concept of **spatial pyramid pooling** (**SPP**) to define its architecture.

Spatial Pyramid Pooling

Most of the CNN models we introduced in `Chapter 5`, *Neural Network Architecture and Models*, require a fixed input image size, which limits the aspect ratio and scale of an input image. The fixed size constraint does not come from the convolution operation; instead, it comes from the fully connected layer, which requires a fixed input size. The convolution operation generates feature maps from the edges, corners, and different shapes of the images in different layers of the CNN. The feature maps are different in different layers and are a function of the shape within the image. They don't change considerably as a function of input size. SPP replaces the last pooling layer, just before the fully connected layer, and consists of parallelly arranged spatial bins whose sizes are proportional to the input image size, but whose total numbers are fixed to the number of fully connected layers. The spatial pooling layer removes the fixed size constraint of the input image by keeping the filter size fixed but changing the scale of the feature vector.

The architecture of DeepLabV3 is based on two types of neural networks - Atrous convolution and the encoder-decoder network.

Atrous convolution

We introduced the concept of convolution in `Chapter 4`, *Deep Learning on Images*, but we did not get into the various types of Atrous convolution. Atrous convolution, also known as dilated convolution, increases the field of view of convolution. The traditional CNN uses max pooling and stride to quickly reduce the size of a layer but in doing so, it also reduces the spatial resolution of the feature maps. Atrous convolution is a method that's used to get past this problem. It does this by modifying the stride using the Atrous value, thus effectively changing the filter's field of values, as shown in the following diagram:

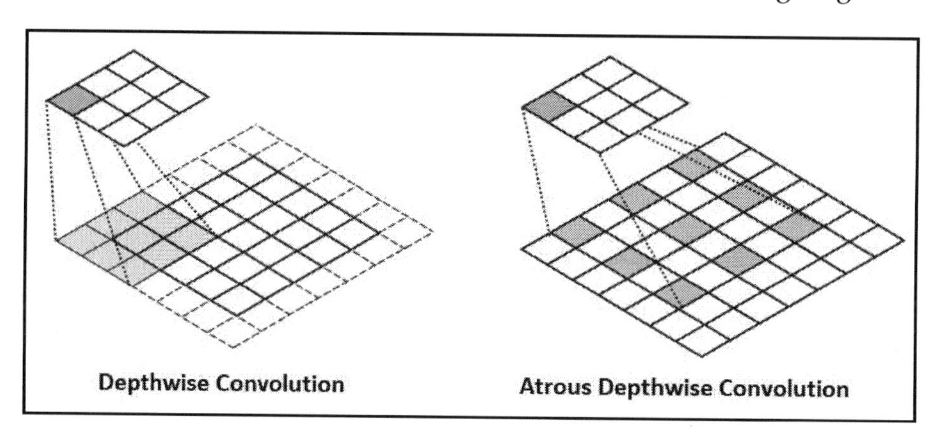

The preceding diagram shows the Atrous convolution with rate = 2. It skips every other cell compared to a depthwise convolution. Effectively, a 3 x 3 kernel is a 5 x 5 kernel if we apply stride = 2. Compared to a simple depthwise smaller feature map, the Atrous convolution increases the field of view and also captures boundary information (compared to max pooling, where the object boundary is missing), thus resulting in a rich image context. Because of its property of keeping the field of view the same in each subsequent layer, Atrous convolution is used for image segmentation.

DeepLabV3 performs several parallel Atrous convolutions, all of which operate at a different rate, like in the spatial pooling layer concept we described previously. The preceding diagram illustrates the Atrous convolution and parallel modules being stacked next to each other to form SPP. Unlike traditional convolution, where the depth and width of the final feature vector are reduced compared to the original image, Atrous convolution preserves the image size. Due to this, the image's finer details are not lost. This is helpful when it comes to building a segmentation map with a rich image context.

Encoder-decoder network

An encoder is a neural network that takes an image and generates a feature vector. The decoder does the reverse of the encoder; it takes a feature vector and generates an image from it. The encoder and decoder are trained together to optimize a combined loss function.

An encoder-decoder network results in faster computation in the encoder path as features do not have to be dilated in the encoder path and sharp objects are recovered in the decoder path. The encoder-decoder network contains an encoder module that captures higher semantic information such as shape within the image. It does this by gradually reducing the feature maps. The decoder module, on the other hand, preserves the spatial information and sharper image segmentation.

The encoder and decoder mainly use 1 x 1 and 3 x 3 Atrous convolutions at multiple scales. Let's take a look at them in more detail.

Encoder module

The key features of the encoder module are as follows:

- Atrous convolution to extract features.
- The output stride is the ratio of the input image's resolution to the final output resolution. A typical value for this is 16 or 8, which results in denser feature extraction.
- An Atrous convolution with a rate of 2 and 4 is used in the last two blocks.
- An ASPP module is used to apply convolution operations at multiple scales.

Decoder module

The key features of the decoder module are as follows:

- 1 x 1 convolution is used to reduce the channels of the low-level feature map from the encoder module.
- 3 x 3 convolution is used to obtain sharper segmentation results.
- Upsampling by 4.

Semantic segmentation in DeepLab – example

The detailed code for training DeepLab using TensorFlow can be found at the following GitHub page, which is managed by TensorFlow: `https://github.com/tensorflow/models/tree/master/research/deeplab`.

Google Colab contains built-in DeepLab Python code based on several pre-trained models. This can be found at `https://colab.research.google.com/github/tensorflow/models/blob/master/research/deeplab/deeplab_demo.ipynb`.

Google Colab, Google Cloud TPU, and TensorFlow

Before we get into the details of the example code, let's understand some of the basic features of Google machine learning, all of which are available for free, so that we can develop powerful computer vision and machine learning code:

- **Google Colab**: You can open Google Colab from your Google Drive, as shown in the following screenshot. If you're using this for the first time, you have to click on **New** and then **More** to install Google Colab to your Drive. Google Colab lets you open Jupyter Notebook without the need to install it. It also has TensorFlow built into it, which means it's far easier to work with all the TensorFlow dependencies that have been included for you:

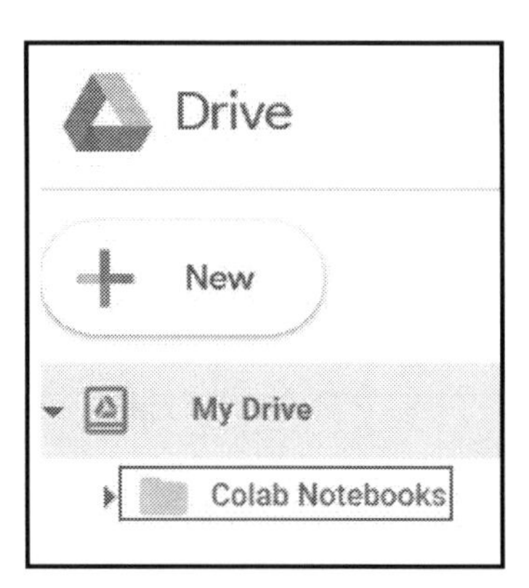

The preceding screenshot shows the location of the Google Colab folder, relative to Google Drive. It lets you work with `.ipynb` files and then store them.

- **Google Cloud TPU:** This is a tensor processing unit. It allows you to run your neural network code much faster. Once you are in a Google Colab Notebook, you can activate TPU for your Python `.ipynb` file, as shown in the following screenshot:

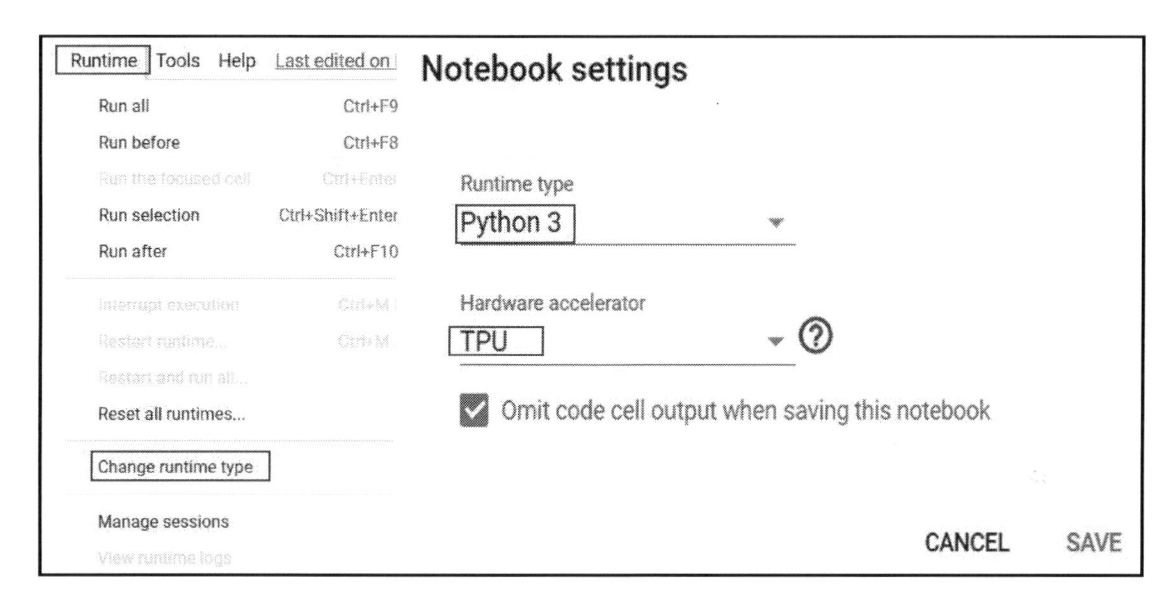

Turning on Cloud TPU, as illustrated in the preceding screenshot, will help speed up how you process the neural network's training and prediction phases.

The Google Colab DeepLab notebook contains three sample images, and also provides you with the option to get a URL so you can load a custom image. When you get the URL of the image, make sure that the URL has `.jpg` at the end. Many images that are pulled from the internet do not have this extension, and the program will say it cannot find it. If you have images of your own that you wish to use, store them on your GitHub page and then download the URL. The following screenshot shows the output received based on `mobilenetv2_coco_voctrainaug`:

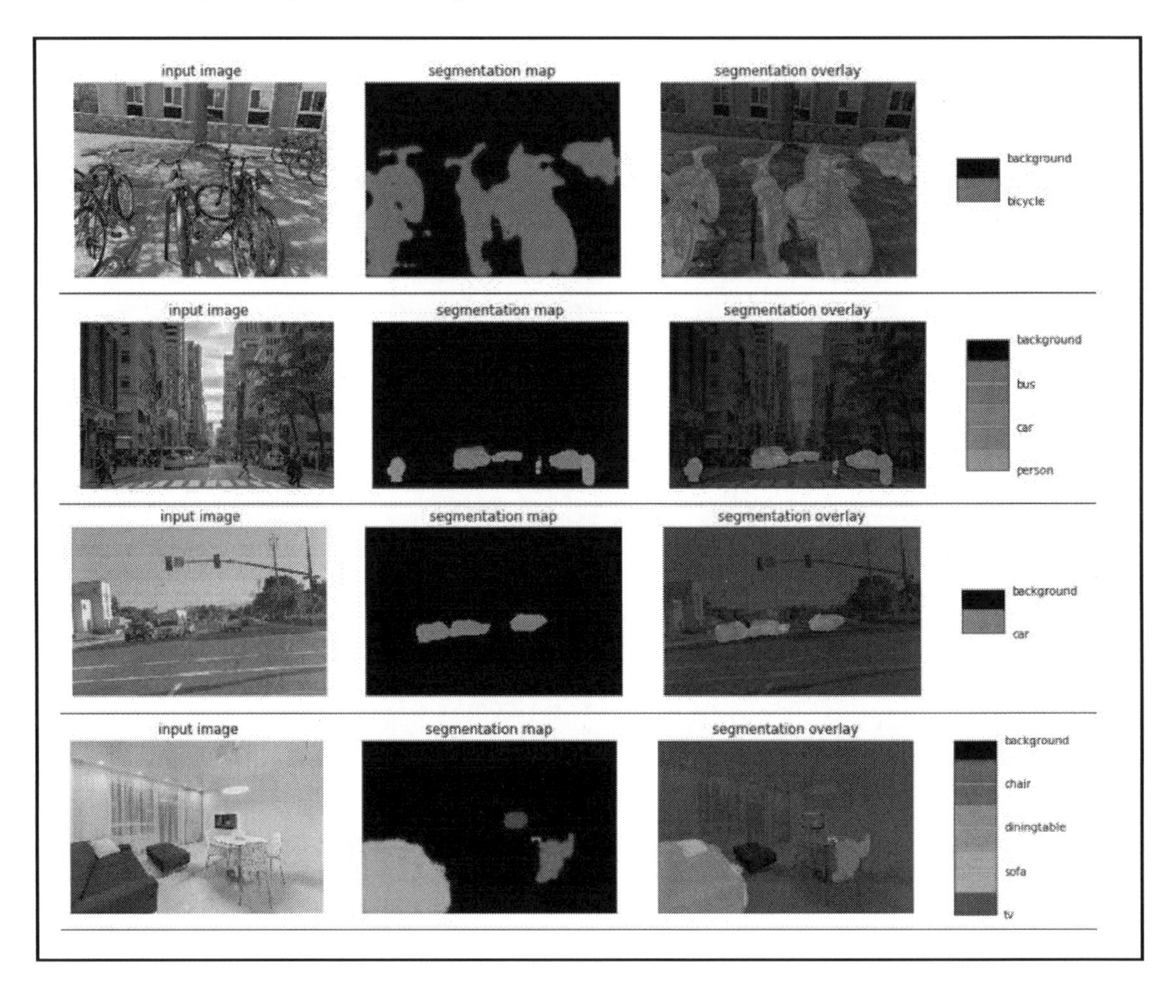

The preceding screenshot shows four different images – parked bicycle, busy New York street, city road, and a room with furniture. The detection is pretty good in all cases. It should be noted that the model only detects the following 20 classes, plus a background class: *background, aeroplane, bicycle, bird, boat, bottle, bus, car, cat, chair, cow, diningtable, dog, horse, motorbike, person, pottedplant, sheep, sofa, train, tv*. The following screenshot shows the same four images being run using a different model, that is, `xception_coco_voctrainval`:

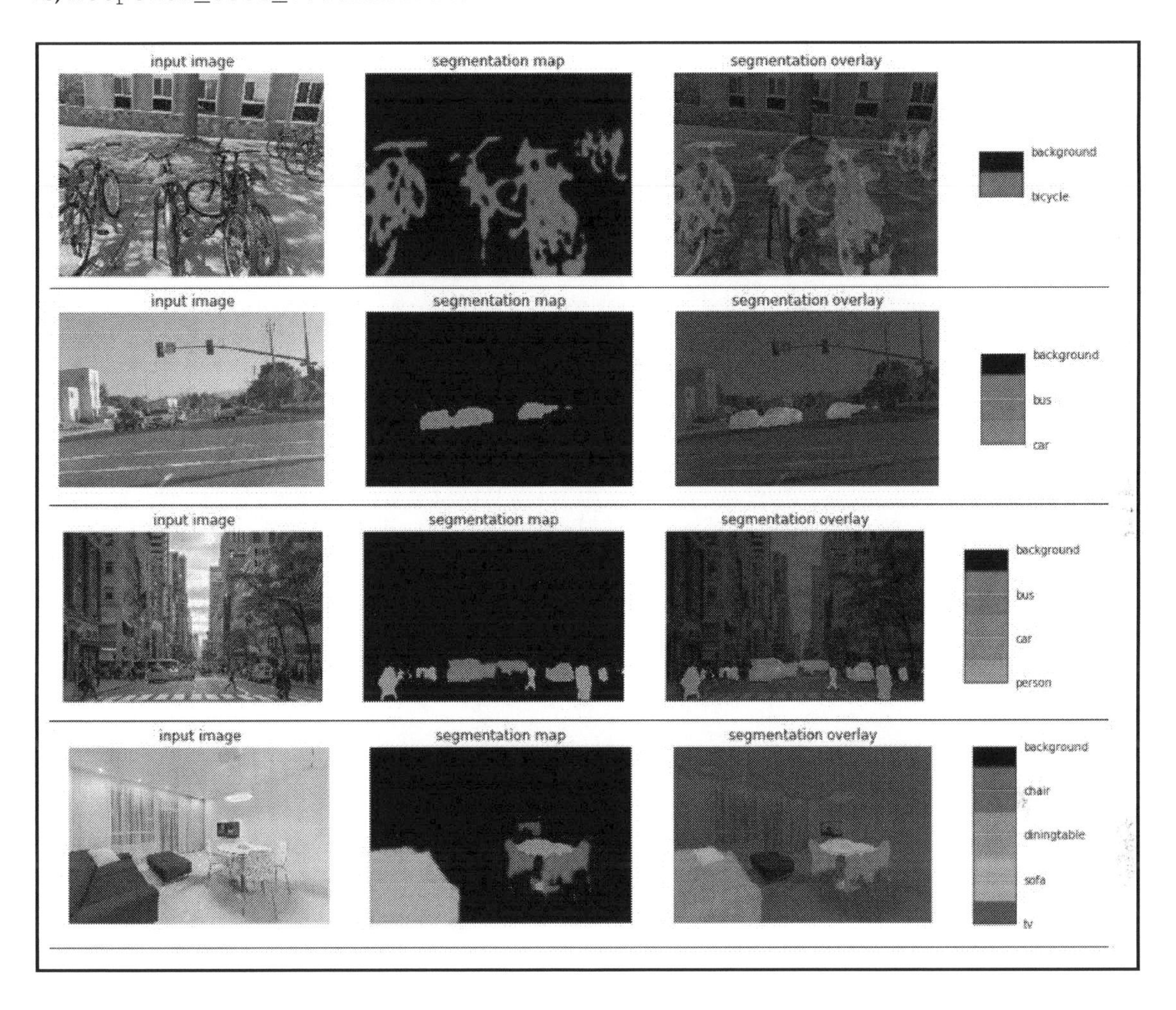

The object's prediction for the exception model shows far more improvement compared to the MobileNet model. The segmentation for the bicycle, the human, and the table has been clearly detected for the exception model compared to the MobileNet model.

MobileNet is an efficient neural network model that's used for mobile phones and edge devices. It uses depthwise convolution as opposed to normal convolutions. For a detailed understanding of MobileNet and depthwise convolution, please refer to `Chapter 11`, *Deep Learning on Edge with GPU/CPU Optimization*.

Artificial image generation using DCGANs

In `Chapter 5`, *Neural Network Architecture and Models*, we learned about DCGANs. They consist of a generator model and a discriminator model. The generator model takes in a random vector representing the feature of an image and runs through a CNN to produce an artificial image, *G(z)*. Due to this, the generator model returns the absolute probability *G(z)*, of generating a new image and its class. The **discriminator** (**D**) network is a binary classifier. It takes in the real image from a sample probability, distribution of images (p-data) and the artificial image from the generator in order to generate a probability, *P(z)*, that the final image has been sampled from a real image distribution. Thus, the discriminator model returns the conditional probability that the class of the final image is from a given distribution.

The discriminator feeds the probability information of generating the real image to the generator, which uses this information to improve its prediction in order to create the artificial image, *G(z)*. As training progresses, the generator gets better at creating an artificial image that can fool the discriminator, and the discriminator will find it harder to distinguish the real image from the artificial image. The two models oppose each other – hence the name adversarial network. The model converges when the discriminator can no longer separate the real image from the artificial image.

GAN training follows an alternative pattern of discriminator and generator training for several epochs, which is then repeated until convergence is achieved. During each training period, the other component is kept fixed, meaning that when we train a generator, the discriminator is kept fixed, and when training a discriminator, the generator is kept fixed, to minimize the chances of the generator and discriminator chasing each other.

The preceding description should have provided you with a high-level understanding of GANs. However, in order to code a GAN, we need to know more about the model architecture. Let's get started.

Generator

The architecture of the generator network of the DCGAN is shown in the following diagram:

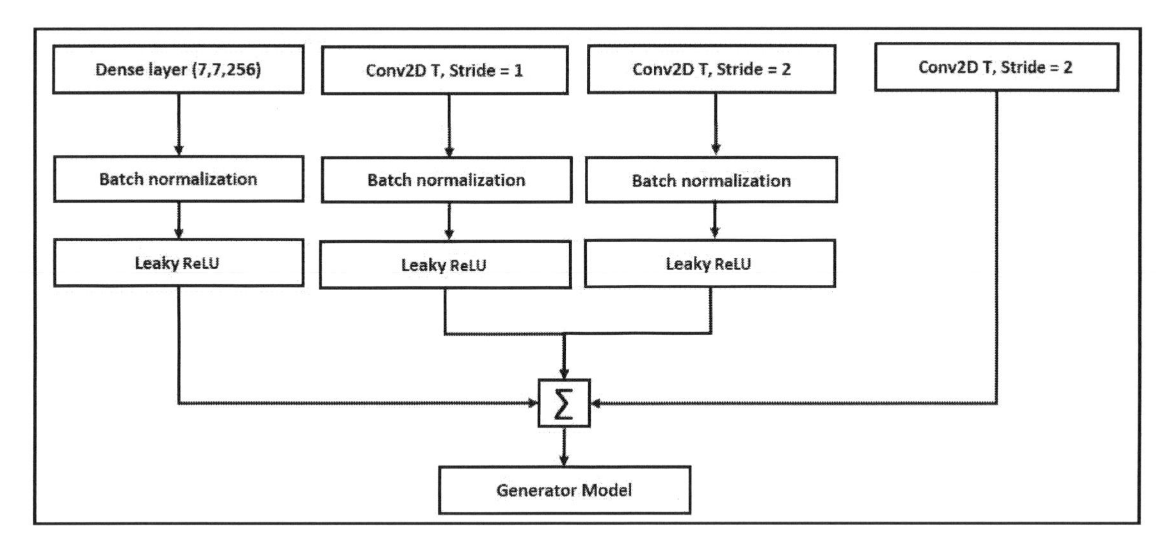

From the preceding diagram, we can see the following:

- All convolutional networks with stride but without max pooling allow the network to learn its own up-sampling in a generator. Note that max pooling is replaced by strided convolution.
- The first layer, which takes in the probability P(z) from the discriminator, is connected to the next convolutional layer through matrix multiplication. This means that no formal fully connected layer is used. However, the network serves its purpose.
- We apply batch normalization to all the layers to rescale the input, except the generator output layer to improve stability in learning.

Discriminator

The architecture of the discriminator network of the DCGAN is shown in the following diagram:

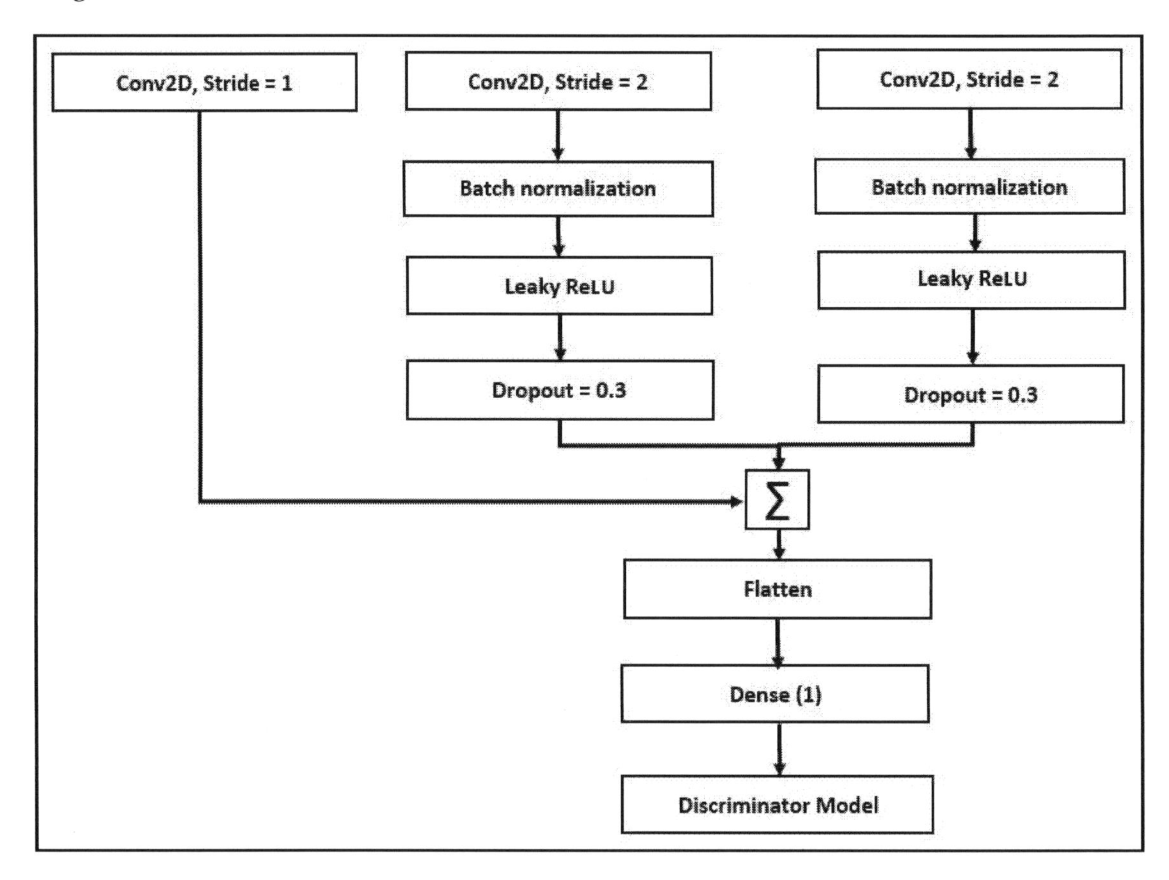

From the preceding diagram, we can see the following:

- All convolutional networks with stride but without max pooling allow the network to learn its own downsampling in the discriminator.
- We eliminate the fully connected layer. The last convolutional layer is flattened and directly connected to a single sigmoid output.
- We apply batch normalization to all the layers except the discriminator input layer to improve stability in learning.

Training

The key features to take into account while training are as follows:

- Activation: Tanh
- **Stochastic gradient descent** (**SGD**) with a mini-batch size of 128
- Leaky ReLU: Slope = 0.2
- Adam optimizer with a learning rate of 0.0002
- Momentum term of 0.5: A value of 0.9 causes oscillation

The following diagram shows the loss term of the DCGAN during the training phase:

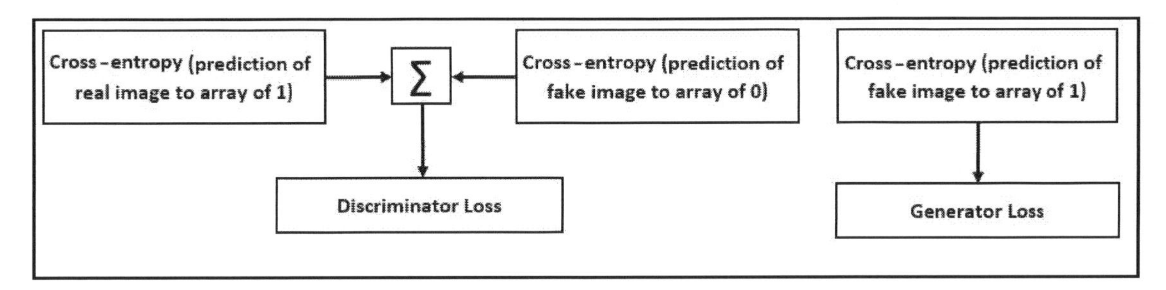

Training starts when the generator receives a random input and the generator loss is defined as its ability to produce fake output. The discriminator loss is defined as its ability to separate the real output from the fake output. Gradients are used to update the generator and the discriminator. During training, both the generator and the discriminator are trained simultaneously. The training process is usually as long as we need it to be to train two models simultaneously. Keep in mind that both models are in sync with each other.

Image inpainting using DCGAN

Image inpainting is the process of filling missing parts of an image or video based on information from neighboring points. The image inpainting workflow involves the following steps:

1. Having an image with missing parts in it.
2. Gathering pixel information of the corresponding missing parts. This is called a layer mask.
3. Feeding the neural network with images described in steps 1 and 2 to determine what part of the image needs to be filled in. This means the neural network is processed first with the image with the missing part and then with the layer mask.

4. The input image goes through a similar DCGAN, as explained previously (convolution and deconvolution). The layer mask allows the network to focus only on missing parts based on its neighboring pixel data and discards portions of the image that are already complete. The generator network produces a fake image, whereas the discriminator network ensures that the final painting appears as real as possible.

TensorFlow DCGAN – example

TensorFlow.org has an excellent example of image inpainting that you can run in Google Colab or on your own local machine. The example can be run in Google Colab at `https://colab.research.google.com/github/tensorflow/docs/blob/master/site/en/tutorials/generative/dcgan.ipynb#scrollTo=xjjkT9KAK6H7`.

This example shows training a GAN based on the MNIST dataset and then the production of artificial numbers. The model that's used is similar to what we described in the preceding sections.

Image inpainting using OpenCV

OpenCV provides two image inpainting methods, as follows:

- `cv.INPAINT_TELEA` is based on the paper *An Image Inpainting Technique Based on the Fast Marching Method*, by Alexandru Telea in 2004. This method replaces the pixel in the neighborhood to be inpainted by the normalized weighted sum of all the known pixels in the neighborhood. More weight is given to those pixels lying near to the point and on the boundary contours. Once a pixel has been inpainted, it moves to the next nearest pixel using the fast marching method:

```
import numpy as np
import cv2 as cv
img = cv.imread('/home/.../krishmark.JPG')
mask = cv.imread('/home/.../markonly.JPG',0)
dst = cv.inpaint(img,mask,3,cv.INPAINT_TELEA)
cv.imshow('dst',dst)
cv.waitKey(0)
cv.destroyAllWindows()
```

- `cv.INPAINT_NS` is based on the paper *Navier-Stokes, Fluid Dynamics, and Image and Video Inpainting*, by Bertalmio, Marcelo, Andrea L. Bertozzi, and Guillermo Sapiro in 2001. It joins points with the same intensity while matching gradient vectors at the boundary of the inpainting region. This method uses the fluid dynamics algorithm:

```
import numpy as np
import cv2 as cv
img = cv.imread('/home/.../krish_black.JPG')
mask = cv.imread('/home/.../krish_white.JPG',0)
dst = cv.inpaint(img,mask,3,cv.INPAINT_NS)
cv.imshow('dst',dst)
cv.waitKey(0)
cv.destroyAllWindows()
```

The final output can be seen in the following image:

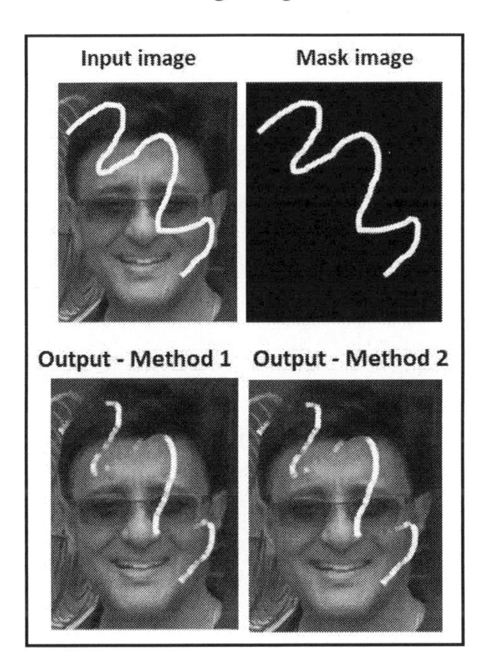

As we can see, both predictions were partially successful but did not delete the line completely.

Understanding neural style transfer

Neural style transfer is a technique where you blend a content image and a styled image by matching their feature distributions in order to generate a final image that's similar to the content image but that's artistically painted with the style of the styled image. Style transfer can be done in TensorFlow in two different ways:

- Using the pre-trained model in TensorFlow Hub. This is where you upload your image and style and the kit will generate your styled output. You can upload your image at `https://colab.research.google.com/github/tensorflow/hub/blob/master/examples/colab/tf2_arbitrary_image_stylization.ipynb`. Note that TensorFlow Hub is a source of many pre-trained networks.
- Develop your own model by training the neural network. To do this, follow these steps:
    1. Select the VGG19 network – it has five convolution (Conv2D) networks with four layers per Conv2D, followed by fully connected layers.
    2. Load your content image through the VGG19 network.
    3. Predict the top five convolutions.
    4. Load the VGG19 model without the top layer (similar to what we did in `Chapter 6`, *Visual Search Using Transfer Learning*) and list the layer's name.
    5. The convolution layer in VGG19 does feature extraction, whereas the fully connected layer performs the classification task. Without the top layer, the network will only have the top five convolution layers. We know from the previous chapters that the initial layers convey the input pixels of the raw image, whereas the final layers capture the defining features and patterns of the image.
    6. By doing this, the content of an image is represented by the intermediate feature map – in this case, this is the fifth convolution block.

7. A **maximum mean discrepancy** (**MMD**) is used to compare two vectors. In their original paper on *Demystifying Neural Style Transfer*, Yanghao Li, Naiyan Wang, Jiaying Liu, and Xiaodi Hou showed that matching gram matrices of image feature maps is equivalent to minimizing the MMD of the feature vector. The style of the image is represented by the gram matrix of the feature map of the styled image. The gram matrix gives us the relationship between feature vectors and is represented by the dot product. This can also be thought of as a correlation between the feature vectors and the average value over the entire image.

8. The total loss = style loss + content loss. The loss is calculated as the weighted sum of the mean square error of the output image relative to the target image.

A gram matrix is a matrix of the inner product of vector $G = I_i^T I_j$. Here, I_i and I_j are the feature vectors of the original image and the styled image. The inner product represents the covariance of the vectors, which represents correlation. This can be represented by style.

The following code inputs a VGG model and extracts the style and content layers from the model:

```
vgg = tf.keras.applications.VGG19(include_top=False, weights='imagenet')
vgg.trainable = False
for layer in vgg.layers:
print(layer.name)
```

The following result displays the convolution block and its sequence:

```
input_2
 block1_conv1
 block1_conv2
 block1_pool
 block2_conv1
 block2_conv2
 block2_pool
 block3_conv1
 block3_conv2
 block3_conv3
 block3_conv4
 block3_pool
 block4_conv1
 block4_conv2
```

```
block4_conv3
block4_conv4
block4_pool
block5_conv1
block5_conv2
block5_conv3
block5_conv4
block5_pool
```

We will use the convolution results we generated from the preceding output to develop the content layers and style layers, as shown in the following code:

```
#Content layer:
content_layers = ['block5_conv2']
#Style layer:
style_layers = ['block1_conv1','block2_conv1','block3_conv1',
'block4_conv1', 'block5_conv1']
style_outputs = [vgg.get_layer(name).output for name in style_layers]
content_outputs = [vgg.get_layer(name).output for name in content_layers]
vgg.input = style_image*255
```

The four dimensions of the input are batch size, the width of the image, the height of the image, and the number of image channels. The 255 multiplier converts the image intensity into a scale of 0 to 255:

```
model = tf.keras.Model([vgg.input], outputs)
```

As described previously, this style can be expressed in terms of the gram matrix. In TensorFlow, the gram matrix can be expressed as `tf.linalg.einsum`.

Thus, we can write the following:

```
for style_output in style_outputs:
gram_matrix = tf.linalg.einsum('bijc,bijd->bcd',
style_outputs,style_outputs)/tf.cast(tf.shape(style_outputs[1]*style_output
s[2]))
```

The loss calculation is as follows:

```
style_loss = tf.add_n([tf.reduce_mean((style_outputs[name]-
style_targets[name])**2) for name in style_outputs.keys()])
style_loss *= style_weight / num_style_layers

content_loss = tf.add_n([tf.reduce_mean((content_outputs[name]-
content_targets[name])**2) for name in content_outputs.keys()])
content_loss *= content_weight / num_content_layers
loss = style_loss + content_loss
```

The final code for this can be obtained from the TensorFlow tutorial at `https://www.tensorflow.org/tutorials/generative/style_transfer`. The code structure is as described here. I ran it on the following image, where the output is as follows:

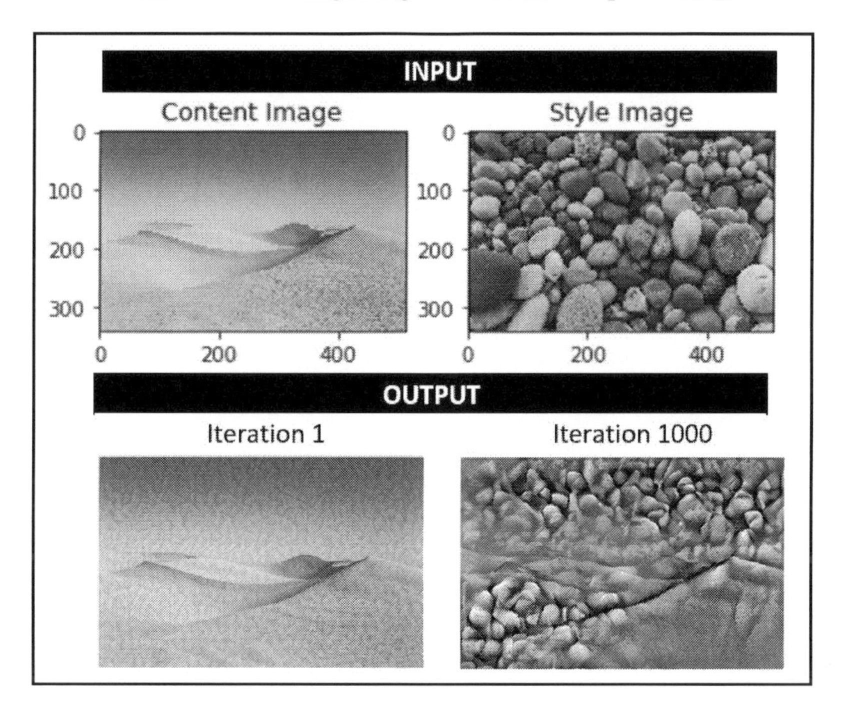

Note how the image output transitioned from a small amount of stone grain in the desert to being completely filled with stone, all while maintaining some of the desert's structure. The final iteration (iteration 1,000) really shows an artistic blend.

Summary

In this chapter, we learned how to use TensorFlow 2.0 and Google Colab to train a neural network to perform a lot of complex image manipulation tasks such as semantic segmentation, image inpainting, generating an artificial image, and neural style transfer. We learned about the functionality of generative and discriminator networks, as well as how neural networks can be trained simultaneously in a balanced fashion to create fake output images. We also learned how to use Atrous convolution, spatial pooling, and encoder-decoder networks to develop semantic segmentation. Finally, we used Google Colab to train a neural network to perform neural style transfer.

In the next chapter, we will use a neural network for activity recognition.

3
Section 3: Advanced Implementation of Computer Vision with TensorFlow

In this section, you will build on your understanding acquired from the previous sections and develop newer concepts and learn new techniques for action recognition and object detection. Throughout this section, you will learn different TensorFlow tools, such as TensorFlow Hub, TFRecord, and TensorBoard. You will also learn how to use TensorFlow to develop machine learning models for action recognition.

By the end of this section, you will be able to do the following:

- Understand the theory and develop an intuition behind various action recognition methods such as OpenPose, Stacked HourGlass, and PoseNet (chapter 9)
- Analyze the OpenPose and Stacked HourGlass code to develop an understanding of how to build a very complex neural network and connect its different blocks. Hopefully, you can use this learning to build your own complex network (chapter 9)
- Use TensorFlow PoseNet for action recognition via webcam (chapter 9)
- Understand various types of object detectors, such as SSD, R-FCN, faster R-CNN, and MaskR-CNN (chapter 10).
- Learn how to convert image and annotation files in TFRecord for input into the TensorFlow object detection API (chapter 10)
- Learn how to use your own images to train a model using the TensorFlow object detection API and make inferences with them (chapter 10)

- Learn how to use the TensorFlow hub for object detection and how to use TensorBoard to visualize training progress (chapter 10)
- Develop an understanding of IOU, ROI, RPN, and ROI align in relation to object detection (chapter 10).
- Learn how to perform segmentation on images using Mask R-CNN (chapter 10)
- Learn different OpenCV as well as Siamese network-based object tracking methods and use them on video files (chapter 10)

This section comprises the following chapters:

- `Chapter 9`, *Action Recognition Using Multitask Deep Learning*
- `Chapter 10`, *Object Detection Using R-CNN, SSD, and R-FCN*

9
Action Recognition Using Multitask Deep Learning

Action recognition is a key part of computer vision and involves recognizing human hand, leg, head, and body positions to detect specific movements and classify them into well-known categories. The difficulty comes in there being variations in visual inputs (such as the body being cluttered or covered with clothing), similar actions but different categories such as drinking water or talking using a handheld cell phone, and getting representative training data.

This chapter provides a detailed overview of the key methods we can use for human pose estimation, as well as action recognition. Action recognition combines the pose estimation method with acceleration-based activity recognition, as well as video and three-dimensional point cloud-based action recognition. The theory will be supplemented by an explanation of its implementation using TensorFlow 2.0.

The chapter is broken down into four sections. The first three talk about the three different methods we can use for human pose estimations, while the fourth one is all about action recognition:

- Human pose estimation – OpenPose
- Human pose estimation – stacked hourglass model
- Human pose estimation – PoseNet
- Action recognition using various methods

Human pose estimation – OpenPose

Human pose estimation is another area of the remarkable success of the deep neural networks and has had rapid growth in recent years. In the last few chapters, we learned that deep neural networks use a combination of linear (convolution) and nonlinear (ReLU) operations to predict the output for a given set of input images. In the case of pose estimation, the deep neural network predicts the joint locations, when given a set of input images. The labeled dataset in an image consists of a bounding box determining *N* persons in the image and *K* joints per person. As the pose changes, the orientation of the joints change, so different positions are characterized by looking into the relative position of the joints. In the following sections, we'll describe the different pose estimation methods we can use.

Theory behind OpenPose

OpenPose is the first open source real-time two-dimensional pose estimation system for multiple people in an image or video. It was mainly developed by the students and faculties of **Carnegie Mellon University** (**CMU**). The title of the paper is *OpenPose: Realtime Multi-Person 2D Pose Estimation Using Part Affinity Fields*, and the authors are Zhe Cao, Gines Hidalgo, Tomas Simon, Shih-En-Wei, and Yaser Sheikh. You can find the paper at `https://arxiv.org/abs/1812.08008`.

Note that OpenPose was first presented in CVPR 2017 in the paper titled *Real-Time Multi-Person 2D Pose Estimation Using Part Affinity Fields*, which can be found at `https://arxiv.org/abs/1611.08050`. This is followed by the 2018 paper *OpenPose: Realtime Multi-Person 2D Pose Estimation using Part Affinity Fields*, where the network is further improved upon.

The key findings of this paper were as follows:

- The input to the network consists of the first 10 layers of the VGG-19 model, which are used to generate a set of feature maps, *F*. The architecture of the OpenPose network can be seen in the following diagram:

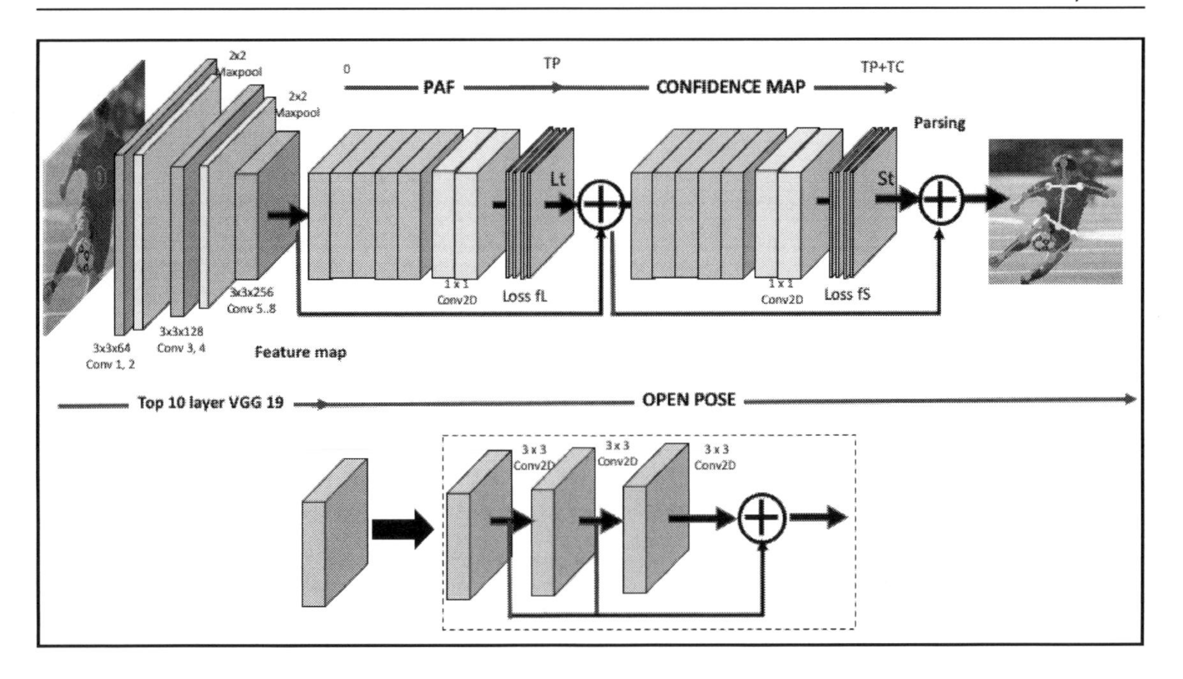

- The OpenPose network takes the feature map as input and consists of two stages of CNN: the first stage predicts **Part Affinity Fields** (**PAF**) with a T_p number of iterations, while the second stage predicts a confidence map with a T_c number of iterations. The OpenPose model presented in 2018 is a general improvement over the earlier model presented in 2017 due to two key metrics:
    - Reduces computation time by half by calculating PAF and then a confidence map. This differs from the simultaneous calculation of both and replacing the 7 x 7 convolution with a 3 x 3 convolution.
    - Improves accuracy as the refined PAF estimation (2018 paper) improves the confidence map over the regular PAF (2017) by increasing the depth of the neural network.
- In the next stage, the predictions from the previous stage and the original image features, *F*, are concatenated to produce two-dimensional keypoint prediction for all the people in the image. A loss function is applied at the end of each stage between the estimated prediction, the ground truth feature map, and the PAF. This process is repeated for several iterations, resulting in the most updated feature map and PAF detection.
- The bottom-up approach based on feature vectors is used, which leads to high accuracy, irrespective of the number of people in the image.

- A confidence map is a two-dimensional representation of the probability that a particular feature (body part) can be located in any given pixel. On the other hand, a feature map represents the output map for a given filter in a given layer of the CNN.
- The network architecture consists of several 1 x 1 and 3 x 3 kernels. The output of each 3 x 3 kernel is concatenated.
- OpenPose is the first real-time multi-person system that detects 135 keypoints using three separate CNN blocks: (a) body and foot detection, (b) hand detection, and (c) face detection.
- In the object detection discussion (`Chapter 5`, *Neural Network Architecture and Models*, and `Chapter 7`, *Object Detection Using YOLO*), we found that region proposal methods such as Faster R-CNN lead to higher accuracy but lower speed compared to single-shot detection methods such as SSD or YOLO. Similarly, for human pose estimation, the top-down approach achieves higher accuracy but lower speed compared to the bottom-up approach. The top-down approach individually feeds each bounding box consisting of a person in an image. The bottom-up approach feeds the whole image consisting of several bounding boxes of a person, resulting in a smaller resolution image of the person.

In 2019, the authors of OpenPose, along with a few others (Gines Hidalgo, Yaadhav Raaj, Haroon Idrees, Donglai Xiang, Hanbyul Joo, Tomas Simon1, and Yaser Sheikh), improved the accuracy and detection time in OpenPose in a paper titled *Single-Network Whole-Body Pose Estimation*. You can find this paper at `https://arxiv.org/abs/1909.13423`.

The key features are as follows:

- The network doesn't need to be repeated for hand and face pose detection, thus making it faster compared to OpenPose. **Multi-task learning** (**MTL**) is used to train a single whole-body estimation model out of the four different tasks: body, face, hand, and foot detection.
- The keypoint confidence map is augmented by concatenating the confidence map of the face, hand, and feet. With this method, all the key points are defined under the same model architecture.
- The network architecture input resolution and number of convolution layers is increased to improve overall accuracy.
- The detection time output is about 10% faster than OpenPose for images with a single person in them.

Understanding the OpenPose code

CMU uses the OpenPose model, while OpenCV integrates the pre-trained OpenPose model in its new **deep neural network** (**DNN**) framework. The entire code block can be downloaded from the following GitHub page. This model uses the TensorFlow example instead of the Caffe model that was originally used by the OpenPose authors, can be found at `https://github.com/quanhua92/human-pose-estimation-opencv`.

OpenCV's OpenPose code can be executed in a Terminal using the following command:

```
python openpose.py --input image.jpg
```

To get started using your PC's web camera, just type the following in your Terminal:

```
python openpose.py
```

The following image shows the implementation of OpenPose for an image of a soccer player:

The algorithm is susceptible to background images, as shown in the following image of a baseball player:

The algorithm's prediction is pretty good when the background has been removed.

Let's go over the main features of the code. We will define the key points and then construct the model for prediction:

1. The model inputs 18 body parts and pose pairs, as shown here:

```
BODY_PARTS = { "Nose": 0, "Neck": 1, "RShoulder": 2, "RElbow": 3,
"RWrist": 4,"LShoulder": 5, "LElbow": 6, "LWrist": 7, "RHip": 8,
"RKnee": 9,"RAnkle": 10, "LHip": 11, "LKnee": 12, "LAnkle": 13,
"REye": 14,"LEye": 15, "REar": 16, "LEar": 17, "Background": 18 }

POSE_PAIRS = [ ["Neck", "RShoulder"], ["Neck", "LShoulder"],
["RShoulder", "RElbow"],["RElbow", "RWrist"], ["LShoulder",
"LElbow"], ["LElbow", "LWrist"],["Neck", "RHip"], ["RHip",
"RKnee"], ["RKnee", "RAnkle"], ["Neck", "LHip"],["LHip", "LKnee"],
["LKnee", "LAnkle"], ["Neck", "Nose"], ["Nose", "REye"],["REye",
"REar"], ["Nose", "LEye"], ["LEye", "LEar"] ]
```

2. Next, OpenPose is implemented through TensorFlow using the following code:

```
net = cv.dnn.readNetFromTensorflow("graph_opt.pb")
```

OpenPose is implemented in TensorFlow using tf-pose-estimation. The actual GitHub page for TensorFlow/model/graph can be found at `https://github.com/ildoonet/tf-pose-estimation/blob/master/models/graph/mobilenet_thin/graph_opt.pb`. *Note that a description of MobileNetV1 can be found at* `https://arxiv.org/abs/1704.04861`.

3. Next, the image is preprocessed (subtraction and scaling are performed) using `cv.dnn.blobFromImage`:

```
net.setInput(cv.dnn.blobFromImage(frame, 1.0, (inWidth, inHeight),
(127.5, 127.5, 127.5), swapRB=True, crop=False))
```

4. Next, we predict the model's output using `out = net.forward()` and get the first 19 elements of the MobileNetV1 output:

```
out = out[:, :19, :, :] .
```

5. The following code calculates a heat map, finds the point value using OpenCV's `minMaxLoc` function, and adds a point if its confidence is higher than the threshold. A heat map is a data graph represented in color:

```
for i in range(len(BODY_PARTS)):
    # Slice heatmap of corresponding body's part.
    heatMap = out[0, i, :, :]
    # Originally, we try to find all the local maximums. To
simplify a     sample
    # we just find a global one. However only a single pose at the
same     time
    # could be detected this way.
    _, conf, _, point = cv.minMaxLoc(heatMap)
    x = (frameWidth * point[0]) / out.shape[3]
    y = (frameHeight * point[1]) / out.shape[2]
    # Add a point if it's confidence is higher than threshold.
    points.append((int(x), int(y)) if conf > args.thr else None)
```

6. The following code block displays the key points using `cv.line` and `cv.ellipse` in the original image:

```
for pair in POSE_PAIRS:
    partFrom = pair[0]
    partTo = pair[1]
    assert(partFrom in BODY_PARTS)
    assert(partTo in BODY_PARTS)
```

```
        idFrom = BODY_PARTS[partFrom]
        idTo = BODY_PARTS[partTo]
        if points[idFrom] and points[idTo]:
            cv.line(frame, points[idFrom], points[idTo], (0, 255, 0), 3)
            cv.ellipse(frame, points[idFrom], (3, 3), 0, 0, 360, (0, 0,
255),        cv.FILLED)
            cv.ellipse(frame, points[idTo], (3, 3), 0, 0, 360, (0, 0,
255),         cv.FILLED)
```

So far, we have used OpenPose to determine multiple body poses using a bottom-up approach. In the next section, we will be using a stacked hourglass method, which uses both top-down and bottom-up approaches.

Human pose estimation – stacked hourglass model

The stacked hourglass model was developed in 2016 by Alejandro Newell, Kaiyu Yang, and Jia Deng in their paper titled *Stacked Hourglass Networks for Human Pose Estimation*. The details of the model can be found at `https://arxiv.org/abs/1603.06937`.

The architecture of the model is illustrated in the following diagram:

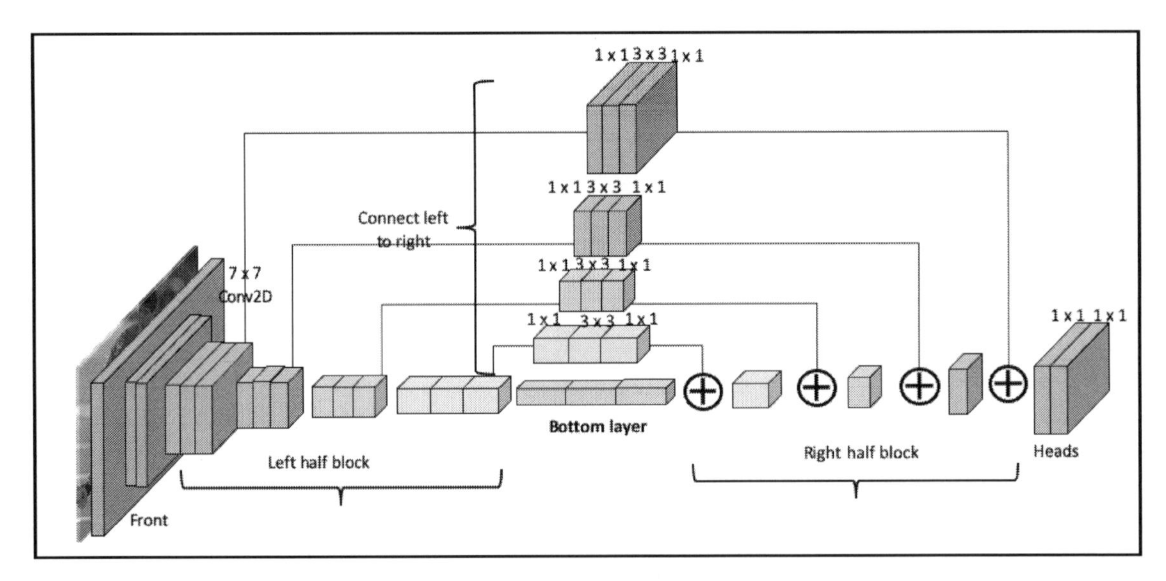

The key features of this model are as follows:

- Bottom-up and top-down processing of the feature is repeated across all scales by stacking multiple hourglasses together. This method results in being able to verify the initial estimates and features across the whole image.
- The network uses multiple convolutions and a max pooling layer, which results in a low final resolution, before upsampling to bring the resolution back up.
- At each max pooling step, additional convolutional layers are added parallel to the main network.
- The output results in heatmaps representing the probability of a joint's presence per pixel.
- The architecture makes extensive use of the residual model. Each residual has three layers:
    - 1 x 1 Conv2D for dimensional reduction from 256 to 128 channels
    - 3 x 3 Conv2D of 128 channels
    - 1 x 1 Conv2D for dimensional increase from 128 to 256 channels
- The architecture starts with 7 x 7 convolutions with a stride of 2 to bring the input image from 256 x 256 to 64 x 64 so that it can effectively use GPU memory.
- Max pooling of 2 x 2 with a stride of 2 is used to downsample the image. Before and after every max pooling is performed, the residual block is added and then added back to the main block after upsampling to the original size.
- The final header block consists of two 1 x 1 Conv2D.
- The best performing result has eight hourglass modules stacked together; each hourglass module has a single residual module at each resolution.
- The model takes about 40,000 iterations to get an accuracy above 70%.
- The training process requires about 5,000 images (4,000 for training and 1,000 for testing) for FLIC and 40,000 annotated samples for MPII (28,000 for training and 12,000 for testing). Frames Labeled in Cinema (FLIC, available from `https://bensapp.github.io/flic-dataset.html`) and MPII (`http://human-pose.mpi-inf.mpg.de`) are two pose estimation databases. FLIC is composed of 5,003 images (3,987 for training and 1,016 for testing) taken from films, whereas MPII consists of 40,000 annotated samples (28,000 for training and 12,000 for testing).
- The network is trained on Torch 7 with a learning rate of 2.5e-4. Training takes about 3 days on a 12 GB NVIDIA Titan X GPU.

Understanding the hourglass model

The hourglass model achieves the state of the art results across all joints in the MPII human pose datasets, but this comes at the cost of resource-intensive network bandwidth usage. This results from the difficulty in training due to the high number of channels per layer. The **FastPose distillation** (**FPD**) was introduced in CVPR 2019 by Feng Zhang, Xiatian Zhu, and Mao Ye in their paper titled *Fast Human Pose Estimation*. Compared to the hourglass model, FPD results in faster and cost-effective model inference while reaching identical model performance. The key features are as follows:

- Four hourglasses (instead of eight) are sufficient to predict 95% model accuracy.
- Dropping from 256 to 128 channels results in only a 1% drop in accuracy.
- At first, training is performed on the large hourglass model (also called the teacher pose model). Then, the target student model (four hourglasses, 128 channels) is trained with the aid of the teacher pose model. A distillation loss function is defined to extract knowledge from the teacher model and pass it to the student model.
- The pose distillation loss function is as follows:

$$L_{pd} = \frac{1}{K}\sum_{k=1}^{K}\|m_{ks} - m_{kt}\|_2^2$$

  Here, K is the total number of joints, L_{pd} is the predicted joint confidence map for FPD, m_{ks} is the confidence map for the k_{th} joint predicted by the student's model, and m_{kt} is the confidence map for the k_{th} joint predicted by the teacher's model.

- The overall loss function is as follows:

$$L_{fpd} = \mu L_{pd} + (1 - \mu)\, L_{gt}$$

  Here, L_{fpd} is the overall FPD loss function, L_{gt} is the confidence map for ground truth annotation, and M is the weight function.

- The teacher model and the target model are trained separately using the loss function described previously.

The Keras implementation of the model can be found at `https://github.com/yuanyuanli85/Stacked_Hourglass_Network_Keras`

Note that the purpose of the next section is to explain the hourglass network's code in detail. This is a complicated neural network model and the idea is that once you have a grasp of this code, you should be able to construct a very complicated neural network model on your own. We will not be emphasizing how to run the code as that is explained in detail at the preceding GitHub page.

In the next section, we will describe the architecture of the model and explain it in detail.

Coding an hourglass model

The coding blocks of the hourglass model can be seen in the following diagram:

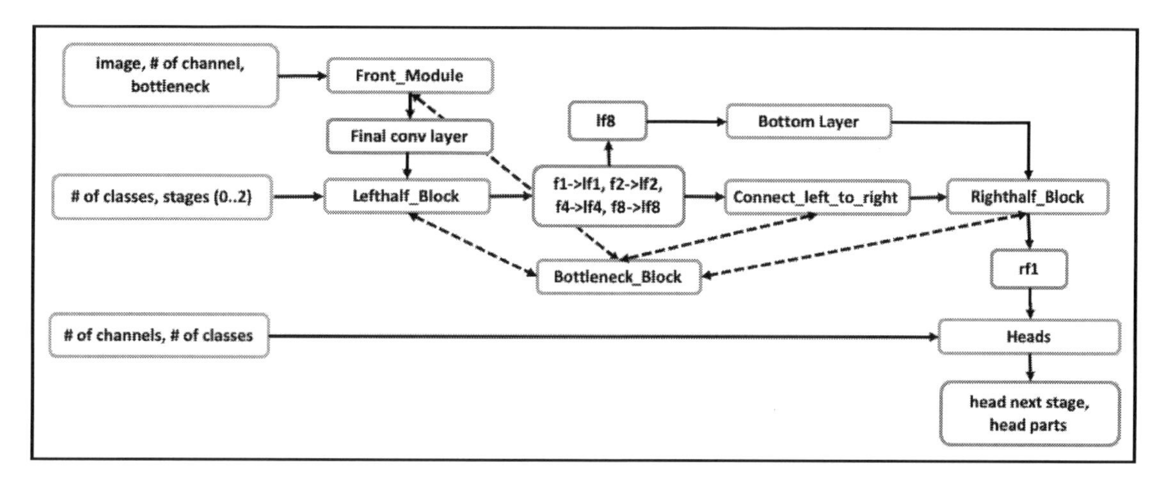

Let's take a moment to understand the preceding diagram since we will be coding it in the following section:

- The front module takes the image as input and the number of channels (the third dimension of each layer, with the first two dimensions being width and height).
- The image passes through the different layers of the front module and the final module is connected to the left half-block.
- The left half-block has four bottleneck convoluted blocks – f1, f2, f4, and f8 – each at 1, 1/2, 1/4, and 1/8 resolutions respectively. This should be clear if you look at the architecture diagram, just under the stacked hourglass induction.
- The last layer from each of the blocks – f1, f2, f4, and f8 – creates a corresponding feature map, that is, lf1, lf2, lf4, and lf8.

- The feature maps – lf1, lf2, lf4, and lf8 – are connected to the right half-block. The output of this block is rf1.
- The bottom layer is also connected to the lf8 feature map from the left half-block.
- The head block is connected to rf1. There are two head blocks in total. Each uses a 1 x 1 convolution.

Let's take a look at the different code blocks.

argparse block

The Python command-line argument (entered via the Terminal) allows the program to take different instructions about neural network operations through the `parser.add_argument` command. This can be imported from the `argparse` function package.

The 16 different classes are shown in the following diagram:

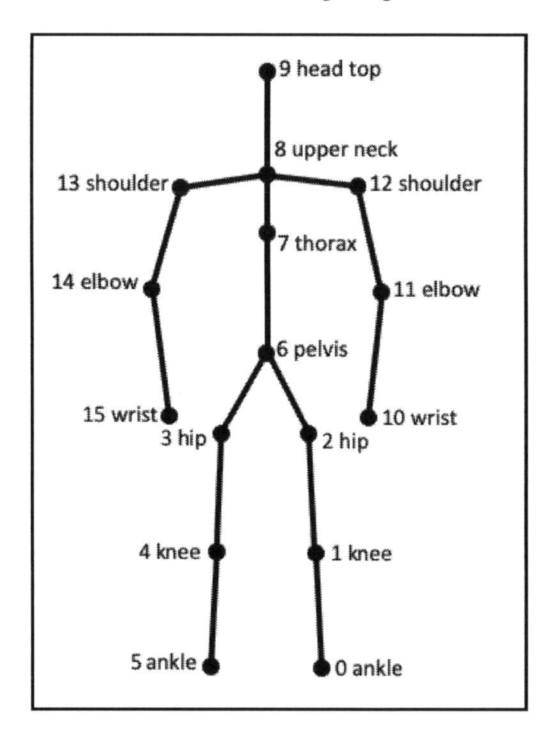

The code block that was used for the preceding diagram is as follows:

```
0 - r ankle, 1 - r knee, 2 - r hip, 3 - l hip, 4 - l knee, 5 - l ankle, 6 -
pelvis, 7 - thorax, 8 - upper neck, 9 - head top, 10 - r wrist, 11 - r
elbow, 12 - r shoulder, 13 - l shoulder, 14 - l elbow, 15 - l wrist
```

The following code imports the `argparse` module, TensorFlow, and the HourglassNet model. It has two types of user-selectable models: 128 channels for tiny networks and 256 channels for large networks:

```
import argparse
import os
import tensorflow as tf
from keras import backend as k
from hourglass import HourglassNet
parser.add_argument("--resume", default=False, type=bool, help="resume
training or not")
parser.add_argument("--resume_model", help="start point to retrain")
parser.add_argument("--resume_model_json", help="model json")
parser.add_argument("--init_epoch", type=int, help="epoch to resume")
parser.add_argument("--tiny", default=False, type=bool, help="tiny network
for speed, inres=[192x128], channel=128")
args = parser.parse_args()
if args.tiny:
    xnet = HourglassNet(num_classes=16, num_stacks=args.num_stack,
num_channels=128, inres=(192, 192),outres=(48, 48))
else:
xnet = HourglassNet(num_classes=16, num_stacks=args.num_stack,
num_channels=256, inres=(256, 256),outres=(64, 64))
if args.resume:
    xnet.resume_train(batch_size=args.batch_size,
model_json=args.resume_model_json,model_weights=args.resume_model,init_epoc
h=args.init_epoch, epochs=args.epochs)
else:
xnet.build_model(mobile=args.mobile, show=True)
xnet.train(epochs=args.epochs, model_path=args.model_path,
batch_size=args.batch_size)
```

Training an hourglass network

The hourglass network has already been described. In this section, we will explain the code behind training the network.

If you want to train your own hourglass network, follow the instructions at https://github.com/yuanyuanli85/Stacked_Hourglass_Network_Keras.

The code for training an hourglass network is as follows:

```
def build_model(self, mobile=False, show=False):
if mobile:
   self.model = create_hourglass_network(self.num_classes, self.num_stacks,
self.num_channels, self.inres, self.outres, bottleneck_mobile)
 else:
    self.model = create_hourglass_network(self.num_classes,
self.num_stacks,self.num_channels, self.inres, self.outres,
bottleneck_block)
# show model summary and layer name
  if show:
     self.model.summary(def train(self, batch_size, model_path, epochs):
      train_dataset = MPIIDataGen("../../data/mpii/mpii_annotations.json",
"../../data/mpii/images"
        inres=self.inres, outres=self.outres, is_train=True)
#here MPIIDataGen is a data generator function (not shown here) - it takes
in json file and the images to preapre data for training similar to how we
use image data generator in Chapter6.
        train_gen = train_dataset.generator(batch_size, self.num_stacks,
sigma=1, is_shuffle=True,rot_flag=True, scale_flag=True, flip_flag=True)
csvlogger = CSVLogger(os.path.join(model_path, "csv_train_" +
str(datetime.datetime.now().strftime('%H:%M')) + ".csv"))
modelfile = os.path.join(model_path, 'weights_{epoch:02d}_{loss:.2f}.hdf5')
checkpoint = EvalCallBack(model_path, self.inres, self.outres)
xcallbacks = [csvlogger, checkpoint]
self.model.fit_generator(generatepochs=epochs, callbacks=xcallbacks)
```

The preceding code is a typical example of how you can set up a neural network for training. We covered this in extensive detail in Chapter 6, *Visual Search Using Transfer Learning*. The key features are as follows:

- create_hourglass_network is the main model.
- train_dataset uses MPIIDatagen, which is an external module that's used to input data.
- train_gen inputs the train_dataset and augments the image.
- It contains callbacks and checkpoints so that we can understand the internal state of the model during training.
- model.fit_generator begins the training process.

Creating the hourglass network

The actual implementation of the hourglass model's code will be illustrated here. The code for this is called `create_hourglass_network`. As described previously, the code has the following components.

Front module

The following code describes the front module:

```
def create_front_module(input, num_channels, bottleneck):
    _x = Conv2D(64, kernel_size=(7, 7), strides=(2, 2), padding='same',
activation='relu', name='front_conv_1x1_x1')(input)
    _x = BatchNormalization()(_x)
    _x = bottleneck(_x, num_channels // 2, 'front_residual_x1')
    _x = MaxPool2D(pool_size=(2, 2), strides=(2, 2))(_x)
    _x = bottleneck(_x, num_channels // 2, 'front_residual_x2')
    _x = bottleneck(_x, num_channels, 'front_residual_x3')
    return _x
front_features = create_front_module(input, num_channels, bottleneck)
```

As discussed previously, this consists of a Conv2D block with a total of 64 filters with a filter size of 7 x 7 and a stride of 2. The output of the block is `(None, 32, 32,6)`. The next few lines run through the batch normalization, bottleneck, and max pooling layers. Let's define the bottleneck block.

Left half-block

The code for the left half-block is as follows:

```
def create_left_half_blocks(bottom, bottleneck, hglayer, num_channels):
# create left half blocks for hourglass module
# f1, f2, f4 , f8 : 1, 1/2, 1/4 1/8 resolution
hgname = 'hg' + str(hglayer)
f1 = bottleneck(bottom, num_channels, hgname + '_l1')
_x = MaxPool2D(pool_size=(2, 2), strides=(2, 2))(f1)
f2 = bottleneck(_x, num_channels, hgname + '_l2')
_x = MaxPool2D(pool_size=(2, 2), strides=(2, 2))(f2)
f4 = bottleneck(_x, num_channels, hgname + '_l4')
_x = MaxPool2D(pool_size=(2, 2), strides=(2, 2))(f4)
f8 = bottleneck(_x, num_channels, hgname + '_l8')
return (f1, f2, f4, f8)
```

The preceding code performs two specific actions:

- It defines the filter coefficients `(f1, f2, f4, and f8)` with resolutions of `1, ½, ¼, and 1/8`.
- For each of the filter blocks, it generates the final output by applying max pooling with a filter of 2 and a stride of 2.

Next, the following code iterates through 0 to 2 to create three filter blocks per filter resolution:

```
for i in range(2):
head_next_stage, head_to_loss = create_left_half_blocks (front_features,
num_classes, num_channels, bottleneck, i)
outputs.append(head_to_loss)
```

Connect left to right

If you look at the image provided at the beginning of the *Coding an hourglass model* section, you will notice that the left and right blocks are connected by the `connect_left_to_right` block. The code that's used to connect the left block to the right block is as follows:

```
def connect_left_to_right(left, right, bottleneck, name, num_channels):
'''
:param left: connect left feature to right feature
:param name: layer name
:return:
'''
_xleft = bottleneck(left, num_channels, name + '_connect')
_xright = UpSampling2D()(right)
add = Add()([_xleft, _xright])
out = bottleneck(add, num_channels, name + '_connect_conv')
return out
```

Note that each right block is generated by upsampling and is added to the left block to generate the final output. In the preceding code, `_xleft` shows the left block, `_xright` shows the right block, and the `add` function is adding the two.

Right half-block

The code for the right block is as follows:

```
def create_right_half_blocks(leftfeatures, bottleneck, hglayer,
num_channels):
lf1, lf2, lf4, lf8 = leftfeatures
```

```
rf8 = bottom_layer(lf8, bottleneck, hglayer, num_channels)
rf4 = connect_left_to_right(lf4, rf8, bottleneck, 'hg' + str(hglayer) +
'_rf4', num_channels)
rf2 = connect_left_to_right(lf2, rf4, bottleneck, 'hg' + str(hglayer) +
'_rf2', num_channels)
rf1 = connect_left_to_right(lf1, rf2, bottleneck, 'hg' + str(hglayer) +
'_rf1', num_channels)
return rf1
```

In the preceding code, `lf8, lf4, lf2, and lf1` have left features. The corresponding right block's features – `rf8, rf4, rf2, and rf1` – are generated by applying the left to right bottleneck block to each of the left features. The following code applies this logic by iterating through 0 to 2 for each of the left ranges:

```
for i in range(2):
head_next_stage, head_to_loss = create_right_half_blocks (front_features,
num_classes, num_channels, bottleneck, i)
outputs.append(head_to_loss)
```

Head block

The code for the head block is as follows:

```
def create_heads(prelayerfeatures, rf1, num_classes, hgid, num_channels):
# two head, one head to next stage, one head to intermediate features
head = Conv2D(num_channels, kernel_size=(1, 1), activation='relu',
padding='same', name=str(hgid) + '_conv_1x1_x1')(rf1)
head = BatchNormalization()(head)
# for head as intermediate supervision, use 'linear' as activation.
head_parts = Conv2D(num_classes, kernel_size=(1, 1), activation='linear',
padding='same',name=str(hgid) + '_conv_1x1_parts')(head)
# use linear activation
head = Conv2D(num_channels, kernel_size=(1, 1), activation='linear',
padding='same',name=str(hgid) + '_conv_1x1_x2')(head)
head_m = Conv2D(num_channels, kernel_size=(1, 1), activation='linear',
padding='same',name=str(hgid) + '_conv_1x1_x3')(head_parts)
head_next_stage = Add()([head, head_m, prelayerfeatures])
return head_next_stage, head_parts
```

The head has two main blocks, with each consisting of a 1 x 1 Conv2D filter. It is using the activation layer and padding. As a refresher, please refer to the hourglass architecture diagram shown under the *Human pose estimation–stacked hourglass model* section to understand the connection between the following components:

- Head to next stage
- Head to intermediate features

The following logic applies the head block to each of the ranges from 0 to 2, which correspond to the left and right blocks, respectively:

```
for i in range(2):
    head_next_stage, head_to_loss = create_head_blocks (front_features,
num_classes, num_channels, bottleneck, i)
    outputs.append(head_to_loss)
```

Hourglass training

The hourglass network is trained on a FLIC human pose dataset with 5,000 images (4,000 for training and 1,000 for testing) and a MPII human pose dataset with 40,000 images (28,000 for training and 12,000 for testing).

Note that in this book, we are not using MPII datasets to train the hourglass model. The information that's provided about the MPII dataset is included to explain how the hourglass model was trained for human pose estimation.

The average accuracy of all the joints reaches about 70% in about 20,000 training iterations, with a max accuracy of around 80%.

So far, we have discussed OpenPose and the stacked hourglass methods of pose estimation. In the next section, we will discuss PoseNet.

Human pose estimation – PoseNet

TensorFlow released the PoseNet model, which is used to detect human poses using a browser. It can be used for both single poses and multiple poses.

PoseNet is based on two papers from Google. One uses the top-down approach, while the other uses the bottom-up approach.

Top-down approach

The first paper is titled *Toward Accurate Multi-person Pose Estimation in the Wild* and was written by George Papandreou, Tyler Zhu, Nori Kanazawa, Alexander Toshev, Jonathan Tompson, Chris Bregler, and Kevin Murphy. You can find the paper at `https://arxiv.org/abs/1701.01779`.

This is a two-stage, top-down approach:

- The bounding box coordinates (*x,y,w,h*) are determined using Faster R-CNN with the ResNet-101 network backbone. Faster R-CNN and ResNet were introduced in `Chapter 5`, *Neural Network Architecture and Models*, but using them together in real-world implementations will be introduced in `Chapter 10`, *Object Detection Using R-CNN, SSD, and R-FCN*. This classification has only been done on one category–humans. All the bounding boxes that are returned are adjusted so that they have fixed aspect ratios and are then cropped to 353 x 257 in size.
- 17 key points of the person/people located within each bounding box are estimated using ResNet-101, replacing the last layer with 3 x 17 outputs. A combined classification and regression approach has been used to find an offset vector or distance between each location of the human body and each of the 17 keypoint locations. The probability that the distance is less than a radius is calculated for every 17 key points, resulting in 17 heatmaps. The ResNet-101 model with 17 heatmaps is trained using a Sigmoid activation function.

Bottom-up approach

The second paper is titled *PersonLab: Person Pose Estimation and Instance Segmentation with a Bottom-Up, Part-Based, Geometric Embedding Model*, and was written by many of the same authors of the first paper; namely, George Papandreou, Tyler Zhu, Liang-Chieh Chen, Spyros Gidaris, Jonathan Tompson, and Kevin Murphy. You can find the paper at `https://arxiv.org/abs/1803.08225`.

In this box-free, bottom-up approach, the authors use a convolutional neural network to detect individual key points and their relative displacements to group key points into person pose instances. In addition, a geometric embedding descriptor was designed to determine person segmentations. The model is trained using the ResNet-101 and ResNet-152 architectures.

Like the top-down approach, a radius with a 32-pixel size is defined, corresponding to each of the 17 key points. Then, 17 independent binary classification tasks are defined with a heatmap probability of 1 if the spatial location in the image is within the radius of the key point location; otherwise, it is set to 0. Like in the top-down approach, this distance between image location and the key points is known as a short-range offset vector. Thus, there are 17 such offset vectors. Like in the top-down method, the heatmap and offset vector are grouped together using a two-dimensional Hough score map.

In this method, we have somebody associated with key points, but this doesn't allow us to group key points per person when multiple person instances are present in an image. To solve this, 32 separate mid-range two-dimensional offset fields are developed to connect pairs of key points. In addition to this, a simple semantic segmentation model consisting of a single 1 x 1 Conv2D layer is developed that performs dense logistic regression and computes the probability that each image pixel belongs to at least one person. The details of semantic segmentation were described in `Chapter 8`, *Semantic Segmentation and Neural Style Transfer*.

Refer to the following papers on top-down versus bottom-up for prediction images at: `https://arxiv.org/abs/1701.01779`, and `https://arxiv.org/abs/1803.08225`. Both papers contain plenty of example images.

Predicting a key point is more or less the same between the two approaches, but the top-down methods begin by drawing bounding boxes, whereas the bottom-up approach performs semantic segmentation.

PoseNet implementation

So far, we've discussed the theory behind PoseNet's top-down and bottom-up approaches. In this section, we will use PoseNet to identify these actions. Details of how to implement the PoseNet model can be found at `https://github.com/tensorflow/tfjs-models/tree/master/posenet`. Take a look at this link to understand the documentation of PoseNet.

Next, we will perform a live demo. This live demo, which is completed using a webcam, can be started by typing the following link in your web browser: `https://storage.googleapis.com/tfjs-models/demos/posenet/camera.html`.

Although the top-down and bottom-up approaches use the ResNet-101 model, the PoseNet model uses MobileNetV1 or ResNet-50. The difference between them is illustrated in the following table:

	MobileNet V1	**ResNet 50**
Stride	16	32
Input resolution	Width: 640, height: 480	Width: 257, height: 200

The PoseNet website illustrates how to tune the model parameters. The model parameters can be tuned using the parameter window shown in the following screenshot:

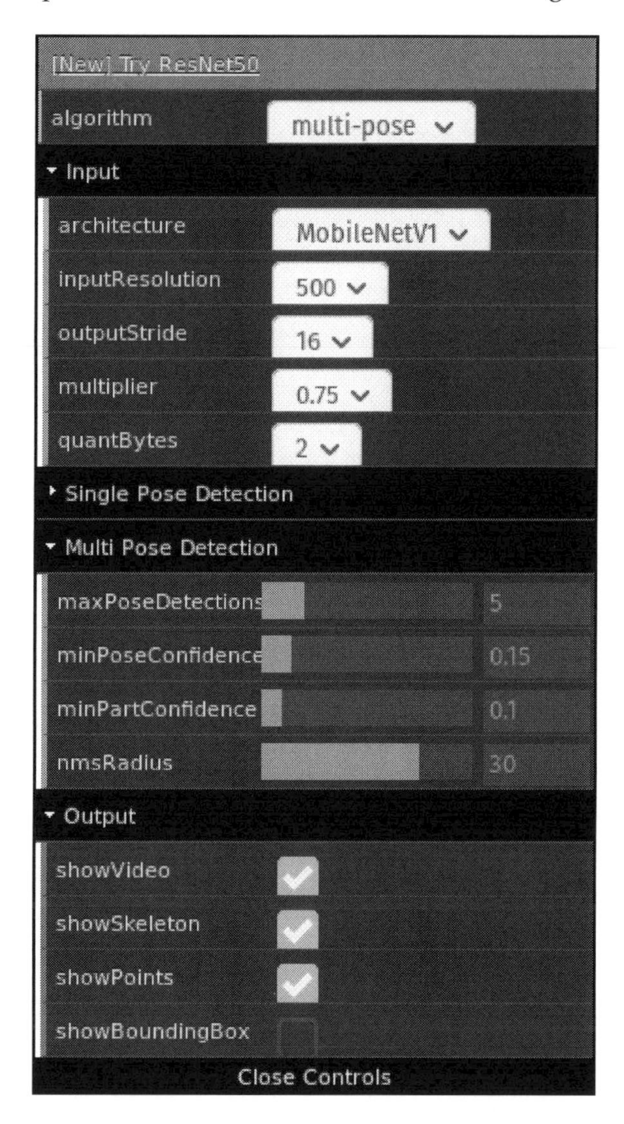

In the preceding screenshot, we can demonstrate both models by changing the input image resolution – this seems to have the best effect.

The following image compares the output of PoseNet for eight different configurations (up and down poses in 200 and 500 resolution for MobileNetV1 and ResNet):

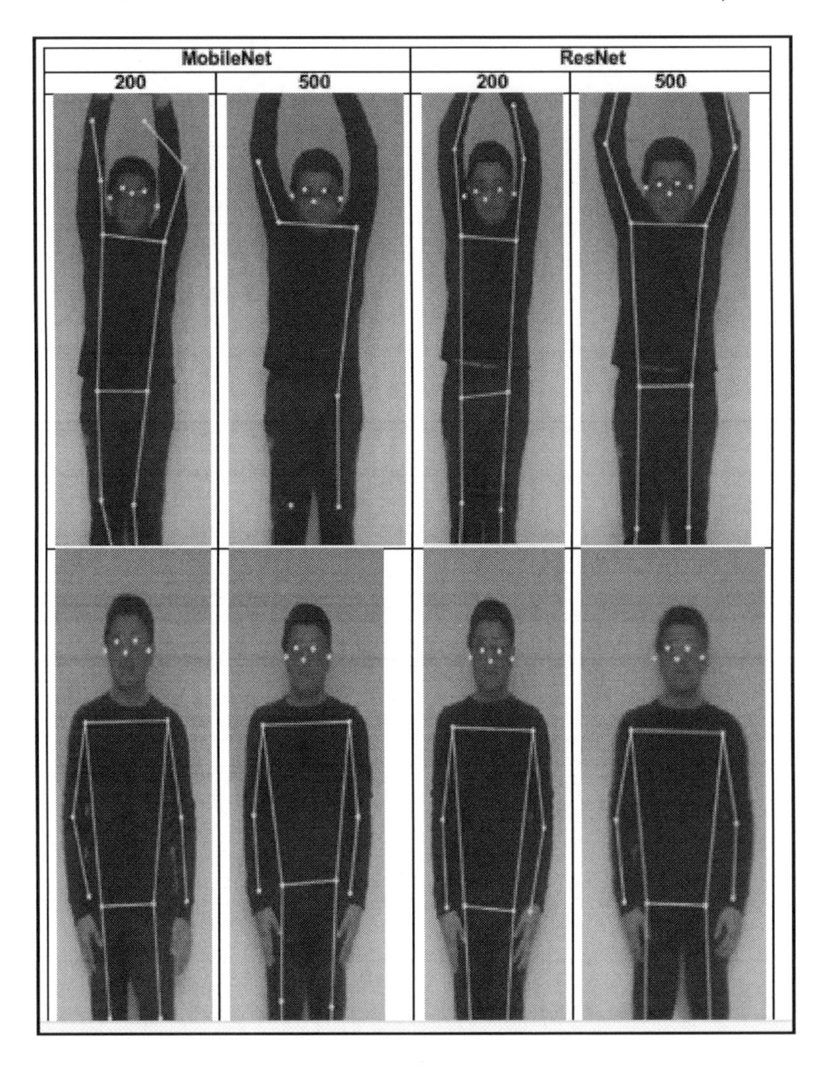

The preceding image illustrates that, on average, ResNet is more accurate than MobileNetV1 when the person's hands are up in the air. When the hand position is down, the performance is more or less the same. Also, the 200 resolution results in better key point prediction compared to 500 resolution. The bounding box option is available but not shown. The following image shows the bounding box for ResNet for additional configurations:

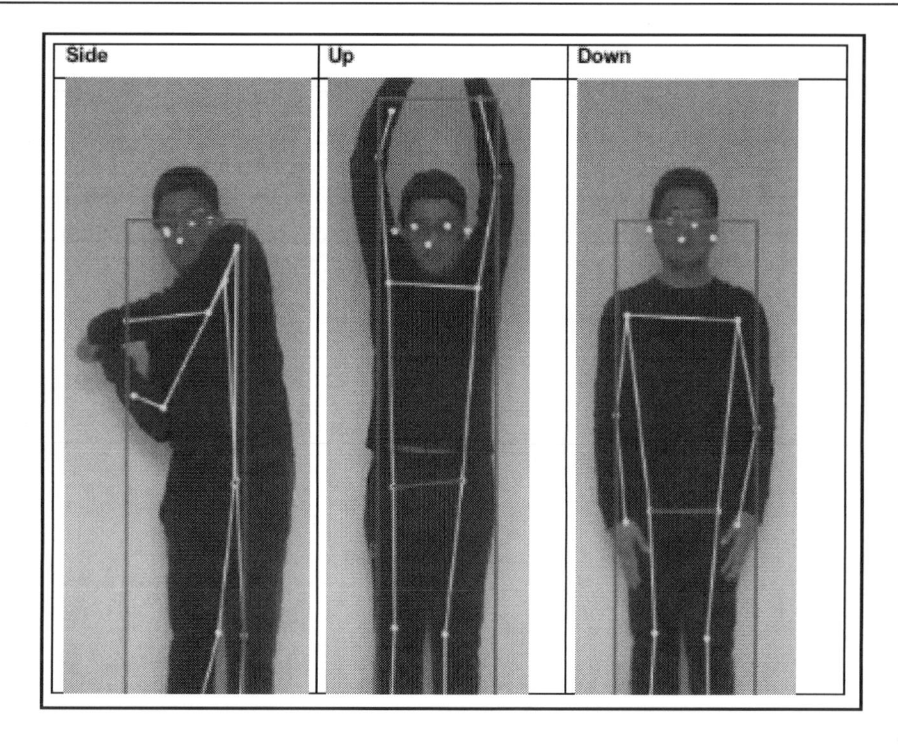

Note how the bounding box's size and position change for different orientations. The key points are stored in a vector. The angle between the key points that are generated can be used to predict actions. The preceding image consists of three distinct actions – side motion, up, and down. The key point angles for these actions do not overlap, so the predictions will be reliable.

Applying human poses for gesture recognition

So far, we've learned how to train with given key points to generate human poses. The process for gesture recognition is similar. Follow these steps to perform hand gesture recognition for hand movement:

1. Collect images of different hand positions – up, down, left, and right.
2. Resize the images.
3. At this point, you can either label the images with key points. If you label the images for key point joints, then each image has to be represented with the corresponding key point joints.
4. Load the image and its corresponding labels into two different arrays.

5. The next step is to perform image classification, similar to what we did in `Chapter 6`, *Visual Search Using Transfer Learning*.
6. The CNN model can be up to three Conv2D layers, one max-pooling layer, and one ReLU layer.
7. For keypoint estimation, instead of classification, we will use the distance between each keyframe gesture position and choose the gesture with the minimum distance.

So far, we have learned how to develop a two-dimensional neural network for training. The network we develop can also be used for production.

Action recognition using various methods

An accelerometer measures the *x*, *y*, and *z* component of accelerations, as shown in the following diagram:

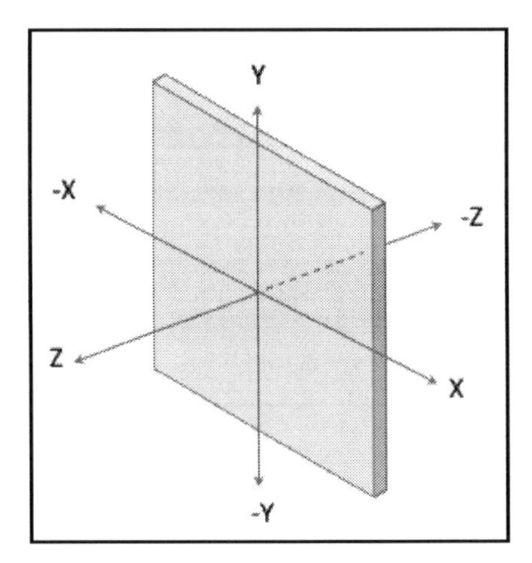

This property of the accelerometer enables it to be placed in a wearable device, such as a cell phone mounted on a person's wrist with a wrist band, smartwatch, or even in a shoe, to measure the XYZ component of acceleration. In this section, we will learn how accelerometer data can be analyzed using neural networks to identify human activity. We will develop a machine learning model with TensorFlow. This is the only section of this book that discusses how to use raw data without an image and how to pass that to a neural network to develop a model and draw inference from it.

Human activity recognition involves classifying different types of activity based on accelerometer data. The challenge here is to correlate accelerometer data generated from the body movements of different types and to differentiate between similar accelerometer traces based on different body movements and activity. For example, left-hand movement and right-hand movement may result in similar accelerometer data when mounted to the waist of a person's body. This alleviates the fact that the accelerometer data should be combined with pose estimation or video image data. In this section, we will discuss two different tools we can use for human activity recognition.

Recognizing actions based on an accelerometer

This method involves the following steps:

1. **Processing the input accelerometer data**: The accelerometer data is sensitive to where it is located. For example, if mounted in the waist region, the hand movements will not see a big change in the accelerometer compared to when mounted in the arm. Also, for a different position, different data needs to be collected and then combined.
2. **Preparing data so that it can be input into TensorFlow**: Load the data using `tf.data.Dataset` to develop a simple, highly efficient data pipeline. The `tensor_slices` command extracts a slice of data from the input.
3. **Developing the CNN model and training it**: One or two dense layers with the flatten and softmax functions at the end.
4. **Check against test data**: Verify the data against the test data.

Refer to the code at the following GitHub page for a code example that follows these steps, at: `https://github.com/PacktPublishing/Mastering-Computer-Vision-with-TensorFlow-2.0/blob/master/Chapter09/Chapter9_TF_Accelerometer_activity.ipynb`.

Two files can be found at the previous link: `Chapter9_TF_Accelerometer_activity.ipynb` and `sample.csv`. Download both files and put them under the same folder.

The `sample.csv` file is a sample CSV file containing accelerometer *(x,y,z)* data for six different actions: Jogging (0), Walking (1), Upstairs (2), Downstairs (3), Sitting (4), and Standing (5), with each actions containing 5,000 data points. In your actual scenario, these data values can be different based on placement location and the type of accelerometer being used. It is better to take the training data with the same accelerometer for inference to avoid inference errors.

Next, the data is split into two parts based on the index file: train and test. Here, we will evaluate two different splits, 18 and 28, which means that in one case, if the index file is less than 18, then data belongs to the train folder; otherwise, it belongs to the test folder. The model is loaded with three dense (fully connected) layers that are 128 in resolution. The final softmax layer is replaced with a Sigmoid function. The following image shows the model's iteration for three different scenarios:

- Softmax with the split at index 18 for train versus test
- Sigmoid function with the split at index 18 for train versus test
- Softmax with the split at index 28 for train versus test:

Softmax, split at 18

```
Train on 12018 steps, validate on 17987 steps
Epoch 1/5
12018/12018 [==============================] - 40s 3ms/step - loss: 0.2205 - acc: 0.9184 - val_loss: 0.8585 - val_acc: 0.8224
Epoch 2/5
12018/12018 [==============================] - 39s 3ms/step - loss: 0.1113 - acc: 0.9631 - val_loss: 1.0003 - val_acc: 0.8382
Epoch 3/5
12018/12018 [==============================] - 39s 3ms/step - loss: 0.0917 - acc: 0.9700 - val_loss: 0.9439 - val_acc: 0.8114
Epoch 4/5
12018/12018 [==============================] - 39s 3ms/step - loss: 0.0815 - acc: 0.9734 - val_loss: 1.0577 - val_acc: 0.7949
Epoch 5/5
12018/12018 [==============================] - 39s 3ms/step - loss: 0.0732 - acc: 0.9768 - val_loss: 0.8594 - val_acc: 0.8380
```

Sigmoid, split at 18

```
Train on 12018 steps, validate on 17987 steps
Epoch 1/5
12018/12018 [==============================] - 41s 3ms/step - loss: 0.2211 - acc: 0.9175 - val_loss: 0.9594 - val_acc: 0.7825
Epoch 2/5
12018/12018 [==============================] - 40s 3ms/step - loss: 0.1068 - acc: 0.9655 - val_loss: 1.1869 - val_acc: 0.7216
Epoch 3/5
12018/12018 [==============================] - 40s 3ms/step - loss: 0.0866 - acc: 0.9726 - val_loss: 1.0440 - val_acc: 0.8428
Epoch 4/5
12018/12018 [==============================] - 40s 3ms/step - loss: 0.0794 - acc: 0.9745 - val_loss: 0.9185 - val_acc: 0.7304
Epoch 5/5
12018/12018 [==============================] - 40s 3ms/step - loss: 0.0770 - acc: 0.9764 - val_loss: 1.0192 - val_acc: 0.8467
```

Softmax, split at 28

```
Train on 19458 steps, validate on 10547 steps
Epoch 1/5
19458/19458 [==============================] - 45s 2ms/step - loss: 0.2492 - acc: 0.9009 - val_loss: 1.5317 - val_acc: 0.6379
Epoch 2/5
19458/19458 [==============================] - 44s 2ms/step - loss: 0.1207 - acc: 0.9558 - val_loss: 1.2396 - val_acc: 0.6741
Epoch 3/5
19458/19458 [==============================] - 44s 2ms/step - loss: 0.1040 - acc: 0.9637 - val_loss: 1.2310 - val_acc: 0.6623
Epoch 4/5
19458/19458 [==============================] - 44s 2ms/step - loss: 0.0888 - acc: 0.9698 - val_loss: 2.0962 - val_acc: 0.6556
Epoch 5/5
19458/19458 [==============================] - 44s 2ms/step - loss: 0.0835 - acc: 0.9708 - val_loss: 1.7320 - val_acc: 0.7360
```

The preceding data shows that each iteration takes about 40 seconds and that the final accuracy is around 0.97. The following plots illustrate this graphically:

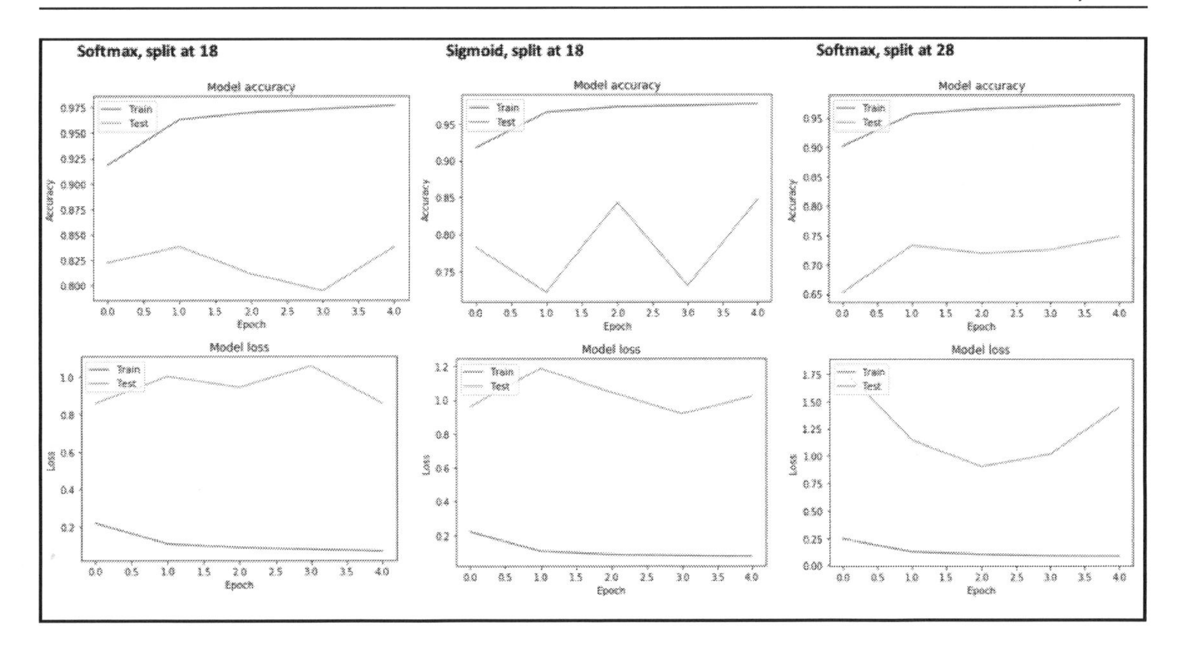

The preceding plots show that train accuracy is more or less the same for the three conditions that were studied. To analyze this further, let's look at the confidence maps shown in the following plots:

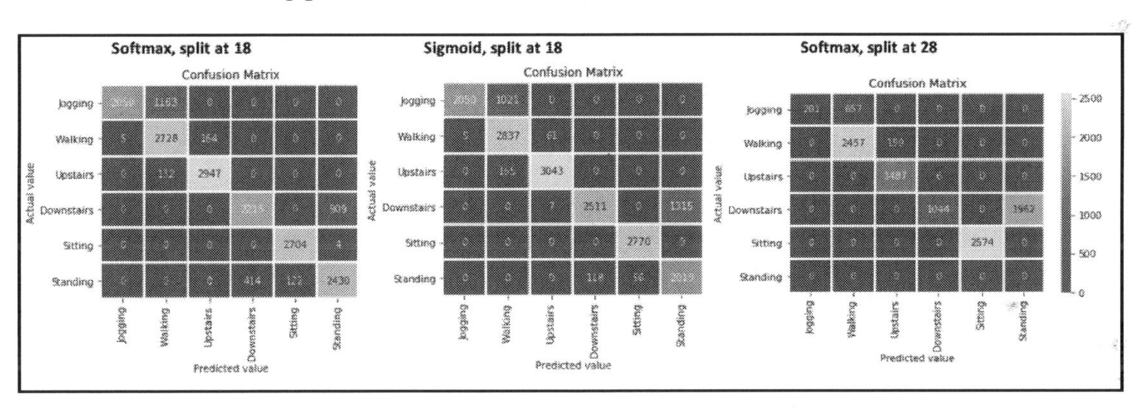

The confusion matrix dictates how well the test data compares with the predicted data. Here, we can see that the Softmax function with a training split at index 18 gives a better result than other standing and walking cases. As expected, the Softmax versus Sigmoid activation functions did not result in any significant difference. Once the model has been developed, the model's predicted function can be used to predict data for real test situations.

Combining video-based actions with pose estimation

Action recognition can be two-dimensional and three-dimensional. The two-dimensional action recognition methods use the joint information of the body, which is represented by key points. These key points are represented in a vector called a feature map. On the other hand, the three-dimensional action recognition methods need not only the feature map but the whole body's skeleton data. This data can be obtained using depth sensors such as Microsoft Kinect or Intel RealSense. In 2018, Diogo C. Luvizon, David Picard, and Hedi Tabia introduced their paper titled *2D/3D Pose Estimation and Action Recognition using Multitask Deep Learning*. The details of this paper can be found at `https://arxiv.org/abs/1802.09232`.

In this paper, the author integrated high-level body joint-based pose information with low-level visual features (from object recognition and feature identification) in a multitask framework. This method is capable of doing both two-dimensional and three-dimensional action recognition. The two-dimensional pose map is extended to a three-dimensional map using volumetric representations.

A combination of these techniques helps make action recognition more robust against similar body joint movements, such as drinking water and making a phone call.

Action recognition using the 4D method

4D action recognition means that the three-dimensional actions of volume representation work as a function of time. Think of this as volume-tracking an action. Quanzeng You and Hao Jiang proposed a novel 4D method titled *Action4D: Online Action Recognition in the Crowd and Clutter*. The details of this paper can be found at `http://openaccess.thecvf.com/content_CVPR_2019/html/You_Action4D_Online_Action_Recognition_in_the_Crowd_and_Clutter_CVPR_2019_paper.html`.

This method tracks humans using 4D representations and recognizes their actions in a cluttered and crowded environment. The concepts of the paper are as follows:

- A three-dimensional point cloud is created for each scene using multiple RGBD images.
- Detection in a crowded scene is supplemented by an innovative tracking proposal that does not use background subtraction, which means it is less prone to errors in crowded spaces.

- The tracking process uses people candidate proposal by training a three-dimensional CNN (with three-dimensional convolution, ReLU, and pooling layers) to classify each candidate volume as people versus nonpeople.
- Actions are recognized using a sequence of three-dimensional volumes that go through a sequence of three-dimensional convolution and pooling layers in what is called Action4D.

Summary

In this chapter, we learned about and implemented three different methods of pose estimation – OpenPose, stacked hourglass, and PostNet. We learned how to predict human key points using OpenCV and TensorFlow. Then, we learned about the detailed theory and TensorFlow implementation of the stacked hourglass method. We showed you how to evaluate human poses in a browser and use a webcam for real time estimation of key points. Human pose estimation was then linked to the action recognition model to demonstrate how the two can be used to improve accuracy. The acceleration-based code showed how TensorFlow 2.0 can be used to load data, train the model, and predict actions.

In the next chapter, we will learn how to implement R-CNN and combine it with other CNN models such as ResNet, Inception, and SSD to improve the prediction, accuracy, and speed of object detection.

10

Object Detection Using R-CNN, SSD, and R-FCN

In `Chapter 7`, *Object Detection Using YOLO*, we learned about YOLO object detection, and then, in the previous two chapters, we learned about action recognition and image in-painting. This chapter marks the beginning of the **end-to-end** (**E2E**) object detection framework by developing a solid foundation of data ingestion and training pipeline followed by model development. Here, we will gain a deep insight into the various object detection models, such as R-CNN, **single-shot detector** (**SSD**), **region-based fully convolutional networks** (**R-FCNs**), and Mask R-CNN, and perform hands-on exercises using Google Cloud and Google Colab notebooks. We will also carry out a detailed exercise on how to train your own custom image to develop an object detection model using a TensorFlow object detection API. We will end the chapter with a deep overview of various object tracking methods and a hands-on exercise using Google Colab notebooks.

The chapter is broken down into eight subsections:

- An overview of SSD
- An overview of R-FCN
- An overview of the TensorFlow object detection API
- Detecting objects using TensorFlow on Google Cloud
- Detecting objects using TensorFlow Hub
- Training a custom object detector using TensorFlow and Google Colab
- An overview of Mask R-CNN and a Google Colab demonstration
- Developing an object tracker model to complement the object detector

An overview of SSD

SSD is a very fast object detector that is well suited to be deployed on mobile and edge devices for real-time prediction. In this chapter, we will learn about how to develop a model using SSD and in the next chapter, we will evaluate its performance when deployed on edge devices. But before getting into the detail of SSD, we will get a quick overview of other object detector models we have learned about in this book so far.

We learned in `Chapter 5`, *Neural Network Architecture and Models*, that Faster R-CNN consists of 21,500 region proposals (60 x 40 sliding windows with 9 anchor boxes), which are warped into 2K fixed layers. These 2K layers are fed to a fully connected layer and bounding box regressors to detect the bounding boxes in an image. The 9 anchor boxes result from 3 scales with a box area of 128^2, 256^2, 512^2, and three aspect ratios—1:1, 1:2, and 2:1.

The 9 anchor boxes are illustrated as follows:
128x128: 1:1; 128x128: 1:2; 128x128: 2:1
256x256: 1:1; 256x256: 1:2; 256x256: 2:1
512x512: 1:1; 512x512: 1:2; 512x512: 2:1

In `Chapter 7`, *Object Detection Using YOLO*, we learned that YOLO uses a single CNN that simultaneously predicts multiple bounding boxes for objects in an entire image. YOLO v3 detection is done in three layers. YOLO v3 uses 9 anchors: (10, 13), (16, 30), (33, 23), (30, 61), (62, 45), (59, 119), (116, 90), (156, 198), (373, 326). In additioin, YOLO v3 uses 9 masks, which are linked to the anchors as explained following:

- **First layer**: mask = 6, 7, 8; corresponding anchors: (116, 90), (156, 198), (373, 326)
- **Second layer**: masks = 3, 4, 5; corresponding anchors: (30, 61), (62, 45), (59, 119)
- **Third layer**: mask = 0, 1, 2; corresponding anchors: (10, 13), (16, 30), (33, 23)

SSD was introduced in 2016 by Wei Liu, Dragomir Anguelov, Dumitru Erhan, Christian Szegedy, Scott Reed, Cheng-Yang Fu, and Alexander C. Berg in a paper titled *SSD: Single Shot MultiBox Detector* (`https://arxiv.org/abs/1512.02325`).

It results in a faster speed than Faster R-CNN while its accuracy compares to YOLO. The improvements come from eliminating region proposals and applying small convolution filters to feature maps to predict multiple layers at different scales.

The key features of the SSD are outlined as follows:

- SSD original paper uses VGG16 as a base network to extract feature layers but other networks, such as Inception and ResNet, can also be considered.

- SSD adds an additional six feature layers on top of the base network, consisting of `conv4_3`, `conv7` (`fc7`), `conv8_2`, `conv9_2`, `conv10_2`, and `conv11_2`, for object detection.
- A set of default boxes is associated with each feature map cell, such that the default box position is fixed relative to the feature map cell. Each default box predicts the score of each of the *c* classes and four offsets relative to the ground truth, resulting in `(c + 4)k` filters. These filters are applied to the feature map (with a `m x n` size), yielding `(c + 4)kmn` outputs. The following table illustrates this. What's unique about SSD is that the default boxes are applied to several feature maps of different resolutions:

Layer name	Detections	Net filter outputs
`Conv4_3`	38 x 38 x 4 = 5776	3 x 3 x 4 x (c+4)
`Conv7`	19 x 19 x 6 = 2166	3 x 3 x 6 x (c+4)
`Conv8_2`	10 x 10 x 6 = 600	3 x 3 x 6 x (c+4)
`Conv9_2`	5 x 5 x 6 = 150	3 x 3 x 6 x (c+4)
`Conv10_2`	3 x 3 x 4 = 36	3 x 3 x 4 x (c+4)
`Conv11_2`	4	
Total	8732	

- The design of the default box is created using the scale factor and the aspect ratio, such that a feature map of a specific size (based on the ground truth prediction) is matched to particular scales of the objects.
- The scale range can linearly vary from `smin(0.2)` to `smax(0.95)`, whereas the aspect ratio (`ar`) can take five values (`1`, `2`, `0.5`, `3.0`, and `0.33`), where *k* varies between `1` to `m`.
- For aspect ratio `1`, an additional default box is added. So, there is a maximum of six default boxes per feature map location.
- The coordinate of the default box center is `((i+0.5)/|fk|, (j+0.5)/|fk|)`, where `|fk|` is the size of the `kth` square feature map and the values of `i` and `j` varies from `0` to `|fk|`. This is repeated for each of the six default boxes.

- SSD makes predictions of various object sizes and shapes by matching the default box of a given scale and aspect ratio to that of the ground truth object and eliminating what doesn't match. The matching of the default box to the ground truth object is done using a Jaccard overlap, also known as **intersection over union** (**IOU**), which was introduced in `Chapter 7`, *Object Detection Using YOLO*. For example, if an image consists of `human` and `bus` and both have different aspect ratios and scales, SSD is clearly able to identify the two. The problem comes when two classes are near one another with an identical aspect ratio, as we will see later.
- With R-CNN, the region proposal network performs a screening to limit the number of samples being considered as 2K. SSD, on the other hand, does not have region proposals, so it generates a much greater number of bounding boxes (8,732, as we learned previously) and many of them are negative examples. SSD rejects the extra negative example, using hard negative mining to keep a balance between negative and positive at, at most, 3:1. Hard negative mining is a technique used to sort using confidence loss so that the highest values are kept.
- SSD uses non-maximum suppression to select a single bounding box with the highest confidence for a given class. The concept of non-max suppression was introduced in `Chapter 7`, *Object Detection Using YOLO*. A non-max suppression algorithm picks the object class with the highest probability and discards any bounding boxes with IOU greater than `0.5`.
- SSD also uses hard negative mining by getting the false-negative images as input during training. SSD keeps a 3:1 ratio of negatives to positives.
- For training, the following parameters are used: either a `300x300` or `512x512` image size, a learning rate of 10^{-3} for 40,000 iterations and 10^{-4} to 10^{-5} for the subsequent 10,000 iterations, a decay rate of `0.0005`, and a momentum of `0.9`.

An overview of R-FCN

R-FCN is more similar to R-CNN than SSD. R-FCN was developed in 2016 by a team, mainly from Microsoft Research, consisting of Jifeng Dai, Yi Li, Kaiming He, and Jian Sun in a paper titled *R-FCN: Object Detection via Region-Based Fully Convolutional Networks*. You can find the link for the paper at `https://arxiv.org/abs/1605.06409`.

R-FCN is also based on region proposal. The key difference from R-CNN is instead of starting with 2K region proposal network, R-FCN waits until the last layer and then applies selective pooling to extract features for prediction. We will train our custom model using R-FCN, in this chapter, and we will compare the final results with other models. The architecture of R-FCN is described in the following diagram:

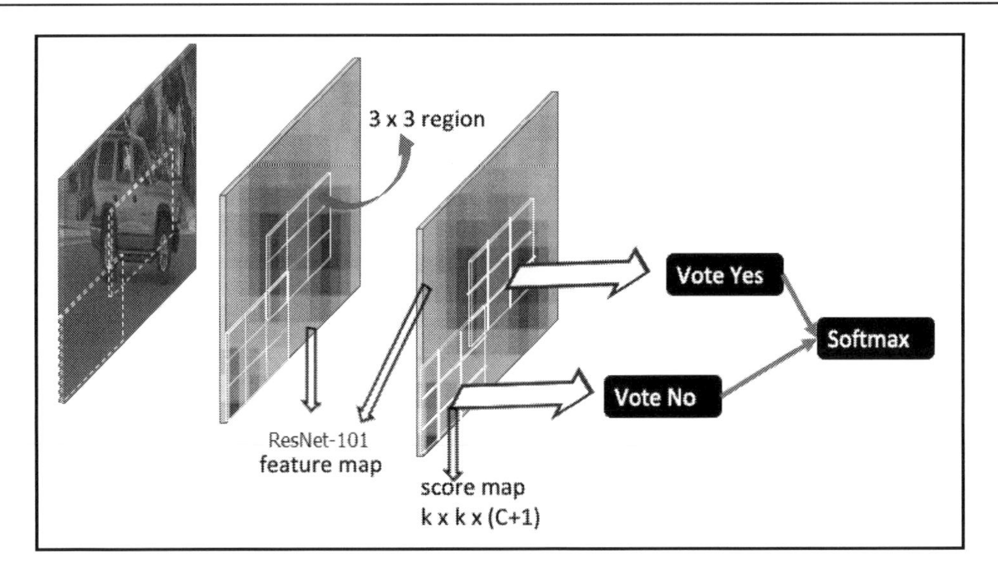

In the preceding figure, an image of a car is passed through ResNet-101, which generates a feature map. Note that we learned in `Chapter 4`, *Using Deep Learning on Images*, how to visualize intermediate layers of a **convolutional neural network** (**CNN**) and its feature map. This technique is essentially the same. Then, we take a `k x k` kernel inside the feature map (in this image, k = 3) and slide it across the image to create a $k^2(C+1)$ score map. If the score map contains an object, we vote `yes`, and if not, we vote `no`. The vote across different regions is flattened to create a softmax layer, which is mapped to object classes for detection.

The key features of R-FCN are described in more details as follows:

- A fully convolutional **region proposal network** (**RPN**) is computed on the entire image, similar to R-CNN.
- Instead of sending the 2K warped region to a fully connected layer as R-CNN does, R-FCN uses the last convolutional layer of features prior to prediction.
- ResNet-101, minus the average pooling layer and the fully connected layer, is used for feature extraction. So, only the convolutional layers are used to compute feature maps. The last convolutional block in ResNet-101 has 2,048 dimensions, which are passed to a 1,024-dimensional 1 × 1 convolutional layer for dimensional reduction.
- The 1,024 convolutional layer produces a k^2 score map, which corresponds to $k^2(C + 1)$ channel outputs, with `C` object categories plus the background.
- Selective pooling is applied to extract responses from only a score map out of the k^2 score map.

- This approach of extracting features from the last layer minimizes the amount of computation and so R-FCN is even faster than Faster R-CNN.
- For bounding box regression, average pooling is used on a `4k`^{2} convolution layer, resulting in a `4k`^{2} dimension vector for each region-of-interest layer. The `4k`^{2} vector from each of the `k`^{2} layers is aggregated into four-dimensional vector, which characterizes the bounding box location and geometry as *x*, *y*, width, and height.
- For training, the following parameters are used—the decay rate is `0.0005`, the momentum is `0.9`, the image is resized to `600` pixels in height, the learning rate is `0.001` for 20,000 batches, and `0.0001` for 10,000 batches.

An overview of the TensorFlow object detection API

The TensorFlow object detection API can be found at `https://github.com/tensorflow/models/tree/master/research/object_detection`. At the time of writing this book, the TensorFlow object detection API is available only for TensorFlow version 1.x. When you download TensorFlow 1.x in the terminal, it installs the `models/research/object detection` directory to your PC. If you have TensorFlow 2.0 on your PC, then you can download the research directory from GitHub at `https://github.com/tensorflow/models/tree/master/research`.

The TensorFlow object detection API has pre-trained models that you can detect using your webcam (`https://tensorflow-object-detection-api-tutorial.readthedocs.io/en/latest/camera.html`) as well as example training on a custom image (`https://tensorflow-object-detection-api-tutorial.readthedocs.io/en/latest/training.html`). Go through the previous two links and try it yourself and then come back to the next section.

In this chapter, we will use the TensorFlow object detector to perform the following tasks:

- Object detection using Google Cloud with a pre-trained model on the Coco dataset
- Object detection using TensorFlow Hub with a pre-trained model on the Coco dataset
- Train a custom object detector in Google Colab using transfer learning

In all of these examples, we will use the burger and french fries dataset to detect and predict.

Detecting objects using TensorFlow on Google Cloud

The following instruction describes how to use the TensorFlow object detection API on Google Cloud to detect an object. In order to do that, you must have a Gmail and Google Cloud account. Depending on the region, Google Cloud can give free access for a limited time once you submit your credit card information. The exercise listed here should be covered in this free access. Follow the following steps to create a **virtual machine (VM)** instance in Google Cloud Console. A VM is needed to run the TensorFlow object detection API and make an inference with it:

1. Log in to your Gmail account and go to `https://cloud.google.com/solutions/creating-object-detection-application-tensorflow`.
2. Create a project as shown in the screenshot below. Here, `R-CNN-trainingpack` is the name of my project. Your project name will likely be different.
3. Follow the 10 instructions under **Launch a VM instance**—this is also illustrated in the screenshot that follows *Step 12*.
4. In Google Cloud Console, navigate to the **VM Instances** page.
5. Click **Create instance** at the top. It should take you to another page where you have to enter the instance name.
6. Enter the name of the instance in small letters. Note the instance name is different than project name.
7. Click on **Machine type** and select **n1-standard-8 (8vCPU, 30 GB memory).**
8. Click on **Custom** and adjust the horizontal bars to set **Machine type** to **8 vCPUs** and **Memory** to **8GB**, as shown in the following screenshot.
9. Select **Allow HTTP traffic** under **Firewall**.
10. Just under **Firewall**, you will see the **Management, Security, Disks, Networking, Sole tenancy** link, as shown in the screenshot that illustrates the steps for the VM instance creation. Click that and then click the **Networking** tab.
11. Within the Networking tab select **Network interfaces** section. Next, within the **Network interfaces** section, we will assign a static IP address by assigning aa new IP address in the **External IP** drop-down list. Give it a name (say, `staticip`) and click **Reserve**.
12. After all of these steps are done, check to make sure you have filled everything per the instructions and then click **Create**, as in the following screenshot, to create a VM instance.

The following screenshot shows the creation of a project called `R-CNN-trainingpack` in Google cloud platform:

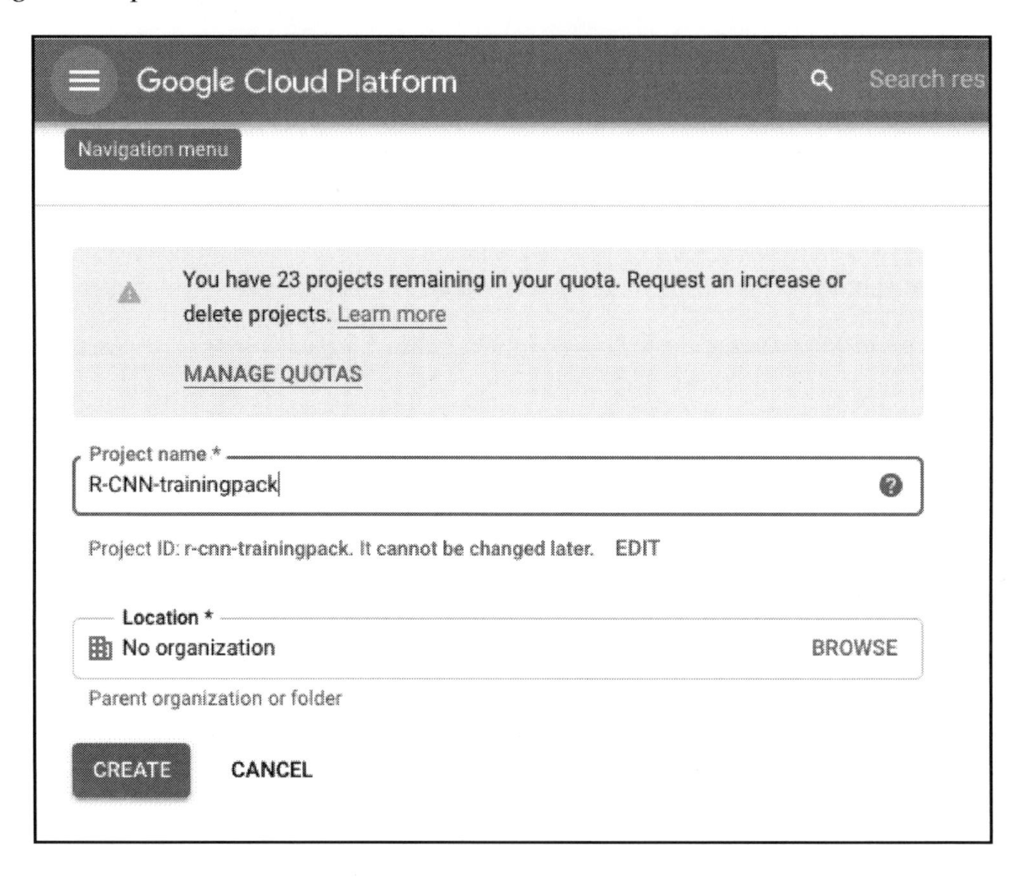

The project creation is the first step and then we will create an instance within a project, as shown in the next screenshot. This screenshot illustrates the steps for the VM instance creation that we have just described:

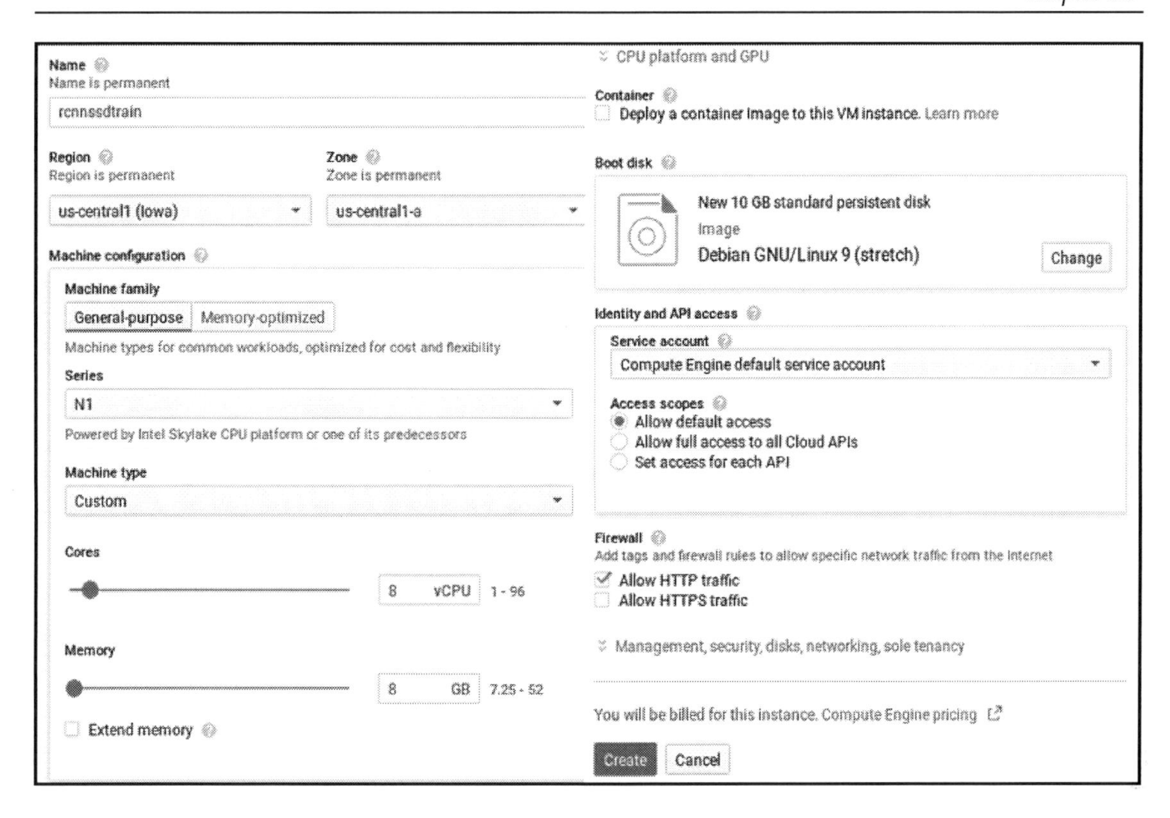

Then, follow these instructions to create an object detection inference on a test image:

- Next, we will use **Secure Socket Shell** (**SSH**) client to securely access the instance over the internet. You will be required to enter a username and password. Set the username to `username` and the password to `passw0rd`; remember, it is not `o` but `0`, as in zero.
- Install the **TensorFlow object detection API** library and the prerequisite packages using the instructions described at `https://cloud.google.com/solutions/creating-object-detection-application-tensorflow`.

After you have correctly followed the preceding instructions and uploaded an image, you will get an output as shown:

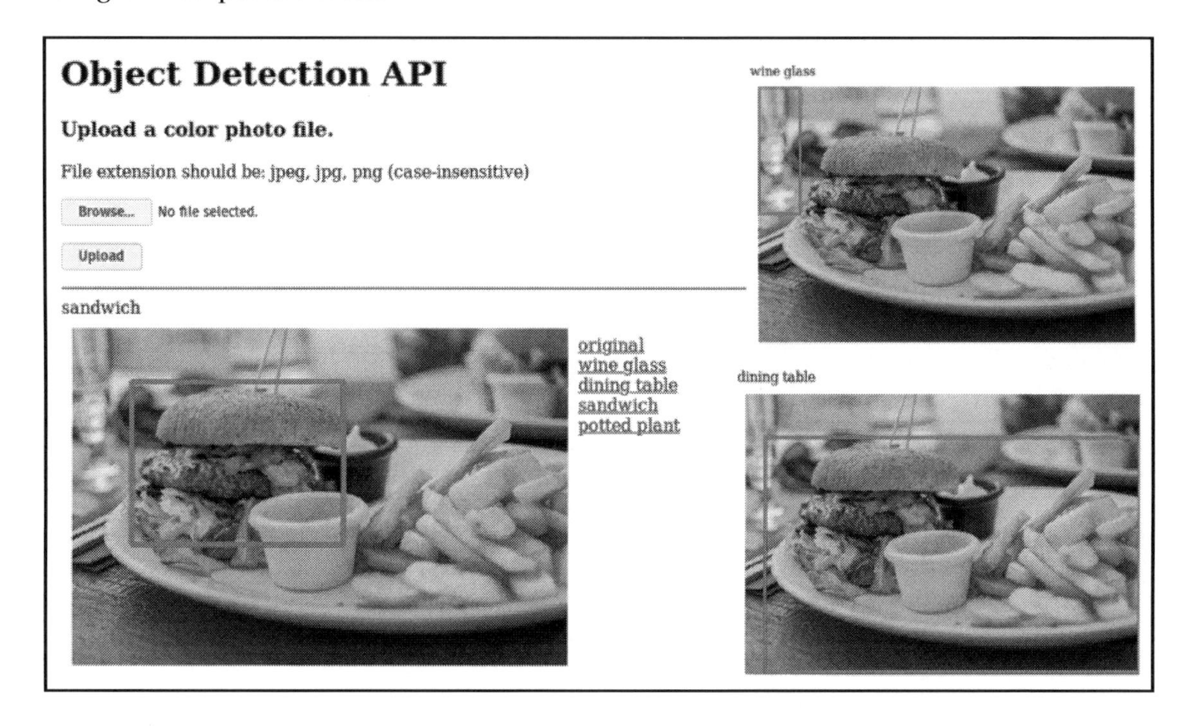

In this screenshot, the burger, wine glass, and table are detected but the french fries are not detected. We will see, in the next section, why that is the case and then we will train our own neural network to detect both.

Detecting objects using TensorFlow Hub

In this example, we will import the TensorFlow library from `tfhub` and use it to detect objects. TensorFlow Hub (`https://www.tensorflow.org/hub`) is a library where code is available and ready to use for computer vision applications. The code is extracted from TensorFlow Hub (`https://github.com/tensorflow/hub/blob/master/examples/colab/object_detection.ipynb`), except the image is inserted locally, rather than extracted for the cloud.

The modified code used for this exercise can be found at `https://github.com/PacktPublishing/Mastering-Computer-Vision-with-TensorFlow-2.0/blob/master/Chapter10/Chapter10_Tensorflow_Object_detection_API.ipynb`.

Here, we install the TensorFlow libraries by importing `tensorflow_hub` and `six.moves`. `six.moves` is a Python module used to provide a common package between Python 2 and Python 3. It displays an image and draws a bounding box on the image. Before running through the detector, the image is converted into an array. The detector is a module loaded directly from the hub that does all the neural network processing in the background. The following shows the output when running the sample image on `tfhub` on two different models:

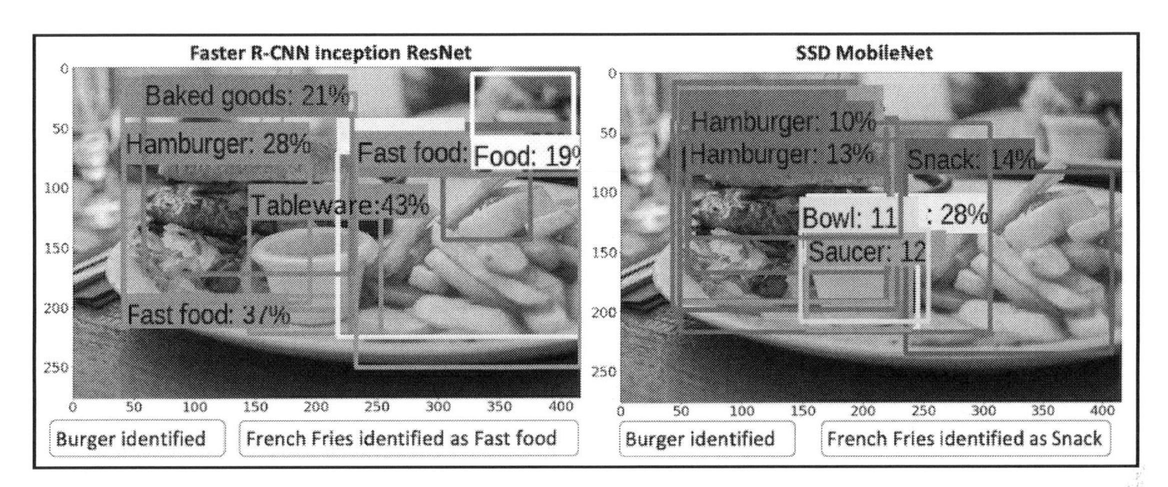

As you can see, R-CNN with Inception and ResNet as a feature extractor correctly predicts both the burger and french fries, and also a number of other objects. SSD with the MobileNet model detects the burger but is unable to detect the french fries—it classifies it in the `snacks` category. We will learn more about this in the next section when we train our own object detector and develop our own model and make inferences based on that.

Training a custom object detector using TensorFlow and Google Colab

In this exercise, we will use the TensorFlow object detection API to train a custom object detector using four different models. **Google Colab** is a VM that runs on the Google server, so all of the packages for TensorFlow are maintained and updated properly:

#	Model	Feature Extractor
1	Faster R-CNN	Inception
2	SSD	MobileNet

3	SSD	Inception
4	R-FCN	ResNet-101

Note that at the time of writing this book, the TensorFlow object detection API has not been migrated to TensorFlow 2.x, so run this example on the Google Colab default version, which is TensorFlow 1.x. You can install TensorFlow 2.x in Google Colab by typing `%tensorflow_version 2.x`—but then, the object detection API will result in an error. The demo exercise has TenorFlow version 1.14 and numpy version 1.16 installed.

We will use transfer learning for this exercise, which starts with pre-trained models trained on the Coco datasets, and then build on the top of that by training with our own dataset. TensorFlow already has pre-trained models stored in the ModelZoo GitHub site, which is available at `https://github.com/tensorflow/models/blob/master/research/object_detection/g3doc/detection_model_zoo.md`. These models are mainly R-CNN, SSD, and R-FCN with different feature extractors. The corresponding configuration files can be found at `https://github.com/tensorflow/models/tree/master/research/object_detection/samples/configs`.

The Coco dataset (`http://cocodataset.org`) has the following categories:

```
Person, bicycle, car, motorcycle, airplane, bus, train, truck, boat,
traffic light, fire hydrant, stop sign, parking meter, bench, bird, cat,
dog, horse, sheep, cow, elephant, bear, zebra, giraffe, backpack, umbrella,
handbag, tie, suitcase, frisbee, skis, snowboard, sports, ball, kite,
baseball, bat, baseball, glove, skateboard, surfboard, tennis, racket,
bottle, wine, glass, cup, fork, knife, spoon, bowl, banana, apple,
sandwich, orange, broccoli, carrot, hot dog, pizza, donut, cake, chair,
couch, potted plant, bed, dining table, toilet, tv, laptop, mouse, remote,
keyboard, cell phone, microwave oven, toaster, sink, refrigerator, book,
clock, vase, scissors, teddy bear, hair drier, toothbrush
```

As you can see, the Coco dataset does not have `burger` or `French fries` as a category. Items close to these in shape are `sandwich`, `donut`, and `carrot`. So, we will get the model weights and use transfer learning on our own datasets to develop a detector. The Jupyter notebook on the GitHub site has the Python code that performs an E2E training job.

The training work uses the TensorFlow object detection API, which calls various Python `.py` files during execution. Our finding, after carrying out numerous exercises, is that it is better to run this job from a Google Colab notebook, rather than from your own PC. This is because many of the libraries are written in the TensorFlow 1.x version and need to be converted to be able to work in TensorFlow 2.0. Some examples of errors that occurred when the job was run using Anaconda on a local PC are shown here:

```
module 'keras.backend' has no attribute 'image_dim_ordering'
self.dim_ordering = K.common.image_dim_ordering()
module 'tensorflow_core._api.v2.image' has no attribute 'resize_images'

rs = tf.image.resize(img[:, y:y+h, x:x+w, :], (self.pool_size,
self.pool_size))
 61     outputs.append(rs)
 62
 AttributeError: module 'tensorflow_core._api.v2.image' has no attribute
'resize_images'
```

When the job is run in TensorFlow on Colab, the dependencies between modules are well configured. So, many of the simple errors that take a lot of time to resolve do not arise and you can spend your time on training developments, rather than fixing errors to begin training.

In the following section, step-by-step guidelines are provided to set up the training portfolio. Details of the code can be found at `https://github.com/PacktPublishing/Mastering-Computer-Vision-with-TensorFlow-2.0/blob/master/Chapter10/Chapter10_Tensorflow_Training_a_Object_Detector_GoogleColab.ipynb`.

Collecting and formatting images as .jpg files

This section describes how to process the image so that it has a common format and size. The steps are listed here:

1. Understand how many classes you are going to work with and ensure your images have an equal distribution of classes. This means that, for example, if we have two classes to work with (`burger` and `french fries`), the images should consist of approximately a third of the spread as burgers, a third as french fries, and a third that is a mix of two. It is not okay just to have an image of a burger and an image of french fries without including an image of a combination.
2. Make sure the image includes different orientations. For an image that has even shapes, such as circular shapes for burgers, or uneven shapes, such as for french fries, the image orientation does not matter, but for specific shapes, such as a car, pen, and boat, getting images from different orientations is critical.

3. Convert all images to `.jpg` format.
4. Resize all images for the neural network to process quickly. In this example, a `416x416` image size is considered. In Linux, you can use ImageMagick to batch resize images .
5. Convert `file.jpg`—resize it to a `416x416` image size `file.jpg`.
6. Rename the images to `classname_00x.jpg` format.

For example, `dec2f2eedda8e9.jpg` should be converted to `burger_001.jpg`. Keep all images in one folder. Since our images consist of a burger, french fries, and a combination, and our total number of files is 100, for the image file name, create three classes as `burger_001 ...burger_030.jpg`, `fries_031 ...fries_060.jpg`, and `comb_061 ...comb_100.jpg`.

Annotating images to create a .xml file

In this section, we will describe how to create an annotation file. There is one annotation file that corresponds to each image file. The annotation file is typically in `.xml` format. The steps to create the annotation file are described here:

1. In this step, use `labelImg` to create an annotation file. This step has already been discussed in `Chapter 7`, *Object Detection Using YOLO*, but is repeated here again. Download `labelImg` using the terminal command `pip install labelImg`.
2. After downloading it, just type `labelImg` in the terminal to open.
3. Define your source (the `.jpg` file) and your destination (the `.xml` file) directory.
4. Select each image and draw a rectangle around it. Define the class name and save it.
5. If there are multiple classes in a given image, draw a rectangle around each and assign relevant class names to it.

Often, people make the mistake of just drawing a rectangle around one class and skipping the other. This will result in only one class being detected during inference.

This screenshot shows how we label two classes in one image:

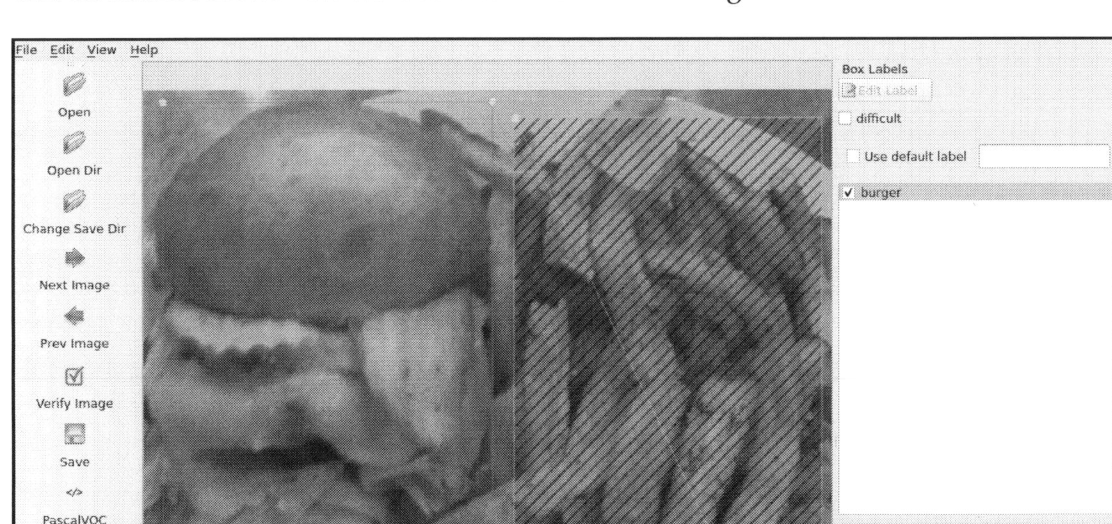

This shows two classes—`burger` and `fries`—and how `labelImg` is used to draw a bounding box around them. The output of `labelImg` is the `.xml` file, which is stored in a separate folder.

Every `.xml` file has the corresponding `.jpg` file written within it. So, if you manually change the `.jpg` file name later on, then the filesystem will not work and you have to rerun `labelImg` again. Similarly, if you resize the image after the `labelImg` operation, the annotation file location will change and you will have to rerun `labelImg`.

Separating the file by train and test folders

In this section, we will divide our dataset into `train` and `test` folders. This is needed as the `train` model uses the `train` dataset to generate the model and `test` dataset to validate. Note that sometimes the `test` and `val` names can be used interchangeably to mean the same thing. But in general, we need a third folder to also check our final model against some unknown images that the model has not seen before. The folder containing those images is called `val`—it will be discussed later.

Follow the steps listed here to separate images into `train` and `test` folders. Note that these tasks will be done on Google Colab:

1. If you follow the preceding steps, you have two folders—one for the image and one for annotation. Next, we create two separate folders—`train` and `test`.
2. Copy all of the `.jpg` and `.xml` files into any folder. So, now the folder will consist of back-to-back `.jpg` and `.xml` files.
3. Copy 70% of the files (the `.jpg` and the corresponding `.xml` file) from the filename class into the `train` folder. So, after this exercise, you will have about 140 files in the `train` folder (70 `.jpg` files and 70 `.xml` files).
4. Copy the remaining 30% of files to the `test` folder.
5. Upload both the `train` and `test` folders to Google Drive under `data`.
6. Create a validation folder titled `val` and insert some images into it from all classes.

Note that in this example, a 70/30 split between the `train` and `test` folders is used but in general, numbers can vary from 90/10 to 70/30.

7. Under **My Drive** (shown in the following screenshot), create a folder called `Chapter10_R-CNN` and then within it, create a folder called `data`:

8. After creating the `data` folder, create two new folders inside it in Google Drive called `annotations` and `images`, as shown. The next task will be to populate these directories.

This screenshot shows the directory structure within `Chapter10_R-CNN` and the naming conventions:

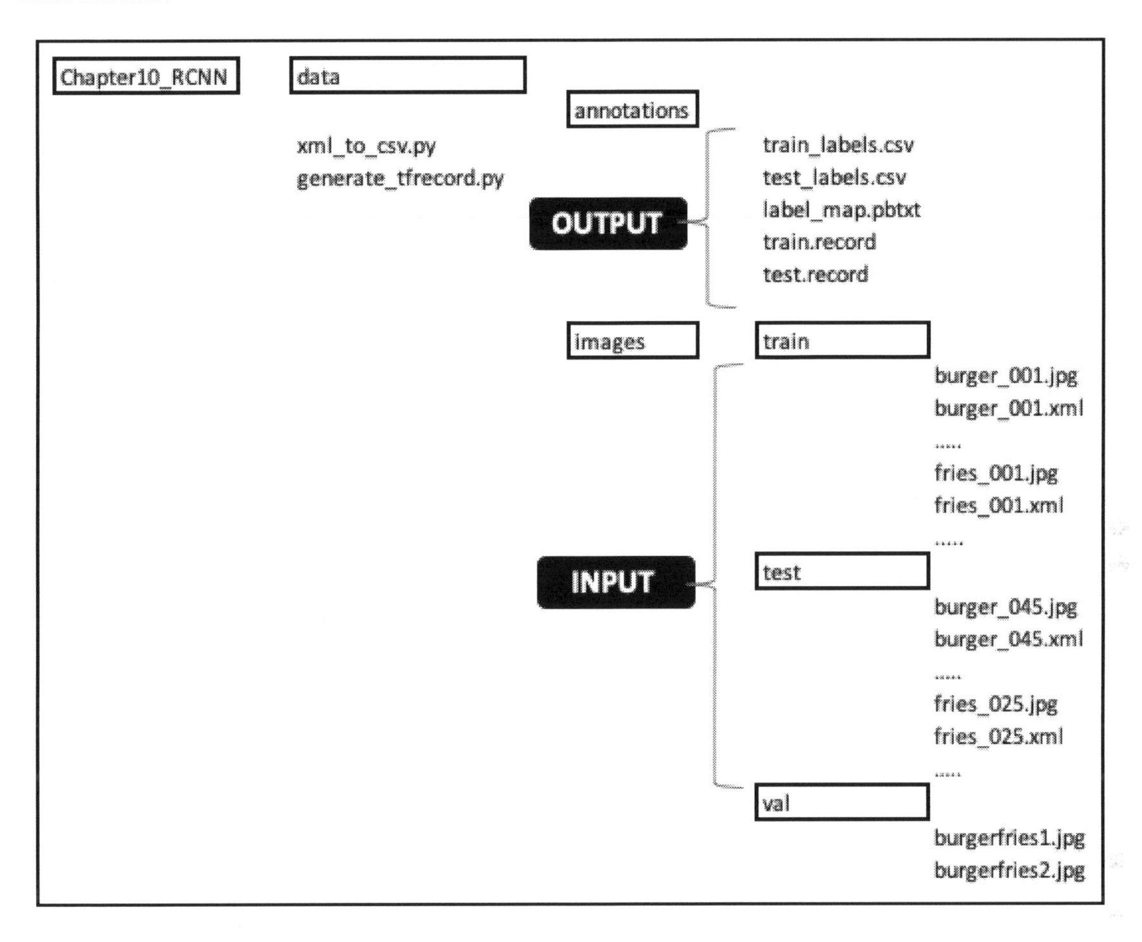

The directory structure as shown in the preceding diagram should be established in Google Drive. Follow the format described here to get started:

- **INPUT** represents the `images` folder and all the image data needs to be supplied. Remember to follow the naming conventions, outlined in the earlier diagram, and upload the `.jpg` file as well as the `.xml` file to the appropriate directory, shown in the preceding diagram.

We could not upload our image data to the GitHub site because of size limitations. So, images used in this section can be downloaded from Kaggle food images (for the burger and french fries sample) at `https://www.kaggle.com/kmader/food41` or you can take pictures with your phone and upload them.

- `annotations` is the output folder, which should be empty and will be filled in the next section. Do not confuse the `annotations` folder with annotating images to create the `.xml` file. All of the `.xml` files go in the `images` folder.

Configuring parameters and installing the required packages

Now that our image preparation work is complete, we will start coding in the Google Colab notebook. The first step is parameter configuration and getting required packages for the training work—this involves the type of model, the parameters for training, and so on. Follow these steps to execute this:

1. Before proceeding to the next step, save the `Chapter10_Tensorflow-Training_a_Object_Detector_GoogleColab.ipynb` Python file to Google Drive and open it as a Colab notebook.
2. Run the cell `Configure` parameters and then install the required packages by pressing the *Shift* + *Enter* buttons.
3. If everything goes correctly, you should see the output showing model configuration selection, shown in the following code block. The following output creates test models from `config` parameters and is a prerequisite before we start building data and preparing for testing:

```
Running tests under Python 3.6.9: /usr/bin/python3
 [ RUN ] ModelBuilderTest.test_create_experimental_model
 [ OK ] ModelBuilderTest.test_create_experimental_model
 [ RUN ] ModelBuilderTest.test_create_faster_R-
CNN_model_from_config_with_example_miner
 [ OK ] ModelBuilderTest.test_create_faster_R-
CNN_model_from_config_with_example_miner
 [ RUN ] ModelBuilderTest.test_create_faster_R-
CNN_models_from_config_faster_R-CNN_with_matmul
 [ OK ] ModelBuilderTest.test_create_faster_R-
CNN_models_from_config_faster_R-CNN_with_matmul
 [ RUN ] ModelBuilderTest.test_create_faster_R-
CNN_models_from_config_faster_R-CNN_without_matmul
```

```
 [ OK ] ModelBuilderTest.test_create_faster_R-
CNN_models_from_config_faster_R-CNN_without_matmul
 [ RUN ] ModelBuilderTest.test_create_faster_R-
CNN_models_from_config_mask_R-CNN_with_matmul
 [ OK ] ModelBuilderTest.test_create_faster_R-
CNN_models_from_config_mask_R-CNN_with_matmul
 [ RUN ] ModelBuilderTest.test_create_faster_R-
CNN_models_from_config_mask_R-CNN_without_matmul
 [ OK ] ModelBuilderTest.test_create_faster_R-
CNN_models_from_config_mask_R-CNN_without_matmul
 [ RUN ] ModelBuilderTest.test_create_rfcn_model_from_config
 [ OK ] ModelBuilderTest.test_create_rfcn_model_from_config
 [ RUN ] ModelBuilderTest.test_create_ssd_fpn_model_from_config
 [ OK ] ModelBuilderTest.test_create_ssd_fpn_model_from_config
 [ RUN ] ModelBuilderTest.test_create_ssd_models_from_config
 [ OK ] ModelBuilderTest.test_create_ssd_models_from_config
 [ RUN ] ModelBuilderTest.test_invalid_faster_R-
CNN_batchnorm_update
 [ OK ] ModelBuilderTest.test_invalid_faster_R-CNN_batchnorm_update
 [ RUN ]
ModelBuilderTest.test_invalid_first_stage_nms_iou_threshold
 [ OK ] ModelBuilderTest.test_invalid_first_stage_nms_iou_threshold
 [ RUN ] ModelBuilderTest.test_invalid_model_config_proto
 [ OK ] ModelBuilderTest.test_invalid_model_config_proto
 [ RUN ] ModelBuilderTest.test_invalid_second_stage_batch_size
 [ OK ] ModelBuilderTest.test_invalid_second_stage_batch_size
 [ RUN ] ModelBuilderTest.test_session
 [ SKIPPED ] ModelBuilderTest.test_session
 [ RUN ] ModelBuilderTest.test_unknown_faster_R-
CNN_feature_extractor
 [ OK ] ModelBuilderTest.test_unknown_faster_R-
CNN_feature_extractor
 [ RUN ] ModelBuilderTest.test_unknown_meta_architecture
 [ OK ] ModelBuilderTest.test_unknown_meta_architecture
 [ RUN ] ModelBuilderTest.test_unknown_ssd_feature_extractor
 [ OK ] ModelBuilderTest.test_unknown_ssd_feature_extractor
 -------------------------------------------------------------------
----
 Ran 17 tests in 0.157s
 OK (skipped=1)
```

Creating TensorFlow records

This is a very important step and many of us struggle with it. Follow these steps to create your `tfRecord` file. You must install all the required packages in the previous step before proceeding to this step:

1. In the preceding figure, under the `Chapter10_R-CNN` folder, there are two files just under `data` called `xml_to_csv.py` and generate `tfrecord.py`. These files should be copied from your local drive to Google Drive.
2. When you install TensorFlow using `pip install TensorFlow` or `pip install tensorflow-gpu`, it creates a `models-master` directory under your `home` directory. Within this, navigate to the `research` folder and then to the `object_detection` folder and you will find `xml_to_csv.py` and generate `tfrecord.py`. Copy these and insert them in Google Drive, as described previously. You can also run the following steps locally, but I have noticed errors when run locally using TensorFlow 2.0, so for this exercise, we will run it in Google Colab.
3. Next, we will link the `Chapter10_R-CNN` folder in Google Drive to your Colab notebook. This is done by using the following command:

```
from google.colab import drive
drive.mount('/content/drive')
```

4. After completing the preceding step, you will be prompted to enter the Google Drive key, and then once that's entered, Google Drive is mounted to the Colab notebook.
5. Next, we go to the Google Drive `Chapter10_R-CNN` directory from the Colab notebook using this command:

```
%cd /content/drive/My Drive/Chapter10_R-CNN
```

6. Now, you can execute the steps to generate the `tfRecord` file.
7. Enter the commands exactly as shown. This command converts all the `.xml` files from the `train` data into the `train_labels.csv` file in the `data/annotations` folder:

```
!python xml_to_csv.py -i data/images/train -o
data/annotations/train_labels.csv -l data/annotations
```

8. This command converts all the `.xml` files from the `test` data into the `test_labels.csv` file in the `data/annotations` folder:

```
!python xml_to_csv.py -i data/images/test -o
data/annotations/test_labels.csv
```

9. This command generates the `train.record` file from `train_labels.csv` and the image `jpg` file from the `train` folder. It also generates the `lable_map.pbtxt` file:

```
!python generate_tfrecord.py --
csv_input=data/annotations/train_labels.csv --
output_path=data/annotations/train.record --
img_path=data/images/train --label_map
data/annotations/label_map.pbtxt
```

10. This command generates the `test.record` file from `test_labels.csv` and the image `jpg` file from the `test` folder. It also generates the `lable_map.pbtxt` file:

```
!python generate_tfrecord.py --
csv_input=data/annotations/test_labels.csv --
output_path=data/annotations/test.record --
img_path=data/images/test --label_map
data/annotations/label_map.pbtx
```

11. If everything goes well, then the preceding lines of code will generate the following output. This signifies the successful generation of the training and test `tfRecord` file. Note that the extension can be either `tfRecord` or `record`:

```
/content/drive/My Drive/Chapter10_R-CNN
 Successfully converted xml to csv.
 Generate `data/annotations/label_map.pbtxt`
 Successfully converted xml to csv.
 WARNING:tensorflow:From generate_tfrecord.py:134: The name
tf.app.run is deprecated. Please use tf.compat.v1.app.run instead.
 WARNING:tensorflow:From generate_tfrecord.py:107: The name
tf.python_io.TFRecordWriter is deprecated. Please use
tf.io.TFRecordWriter instead.
 W0104 13:36:52.637130 139700938962816 module_wrapper.py:139] From
generate_tfrecord.py:107: The name tf.python_io.TFRecordWriter is
deprecated. Please use tf.io.TFRecordWriter instead.
 WARNING:tensorflow:From
/content/models/research/object_detection/utils/label_map_util.py:1
38: The name tf.gfile.GFile is deprecated. Please use
tf.io.gfile.GFile instead.
 W0104 13:36:52.647315 139700938962816 module_wrapper.py:139] From
/content/models/research/object_detection/utils/label_map_util.py:1
```

```
38: The name tf.gfile.GFile is deprecated. Please use
tf.io.gfile.GFile instead.
 Successfully created the TFRecords: /content/drive/My
Drive/Chapter10_R-CNN/data/annotations/train.record
 WARNING:tensorflow:From generate_tfrecord.py:134: The name
tf.app.run is deprecated. Please use tf.compat.v1.app.run instead.
 WARNING:tensorflow:From generate_tfrecord.py:107: The name
tf.python_io.TFRecordWriter is deprecated. Please use
tf.io.TFRecordWriter instead.
 W0104 13:36:55.923784 140224824006528 module_wrapper.py:139] From
generate_tfrecord.py:107: The name tf.python_io.TFRecordWriter is
deprecated. Please use tf.io.TFRecordWriter instead.
 WARNING:tensorflow:From
/content/models/research/object_detection/utils/label_map_util.py:1
38: The name tf.gfile.GFile is deprecated. Please use
tf.io.gfile.GFile instead.
 W0104 13:36:55.933046 140224824006528 module_wrapper.py:139] From
/content/models/research/object_detection/utils/label_map_util.py:1
38: The name tf.gfile.GFile is deprecated. Please use
tf.io.gfile.GFile instead.
 Successfully created the TFRecords: /content/drive/My
Drive/Chapter10_R-CNN/data/annotations/test.reco
```

Preparing the model and configuring the training pipeline

Next, the base model is downloaded and unzipped using the following command. During the configuring parameters steps in the *Configuring parameters and installing required packages* section, the model and the corresponding configuration parameter has been selected. There is a choice of four different models (two variants of SSD, Faster R-CNN, and R-FCN) corresponding to the configuration parameters and the batch size. You can start with the batch size indicated and adjust as needed during model optimization:

```
MODEL_FILE = MODEL + '.tar.gz'
DOWNLOAD_BASE = 'http://download.tensorflow.org/models/object_detection/'
DEST_DIR = '/content/models/research/pretrained_model'
```

Here, the destination directory is the Google Colab notebook itself and the `content/models/research` directory is there—so, no need to create one yourself. This is done when you install the required package section.

This step will also download a number of classes automatically from your `label_map.pbtxt` file and adjust the size, scale, and aspect ratio and convolution hyperparameters ready for the training job.

Monitoring training progress using TensorBoard

TensorBoard is a tool used to monitor and visualize training progress in real time. It plots training loss and accuracy, so there is no need to manually plot it. TensorBoard lets you visualize the model graph and has many other functions. Visit `https://www.tensorflow.org/tensorboard` to learn more about TensorBoard's capabilities.

TensorBoard running on a local machine

TensorBoard can be added to your model training by adding the following lines of code. Check the code supplied on the GitHub page for the exact location:

```
tensorboard_callback = tf.keras.callbacks.TensorBoard(log_dir=log_dir,
histogram_freq=1)
history = model.fit(x=x_train, y=y_train, epochs=25,
validation_data=(x_test, y_test), callbacks=[tensorboard_callback])
```

Then, TensorBoard graphs can be visualized after training has started by typing the following in the terminal:

```
%tensorboard --logdir logs/fit
```

TensorBoard running on Google Colab

This section describes how to run TensorBoard on Google Colab. This involves the following steps:

1. In order to run TensorBoard on Google Colab, the TensorBoard page has to be accessed from your local PC. This is done through a service called **ngrok**, which links your local PC to TensorBoard. **Ngrok** is downloaded and extracted to your PC by using the following two lines of code:

   ```
   !wget
   https://bin.equinox.io/c/4VmDzA7iaHb/ngrok-stable-linux-amd64.zip
   !unzip ngrok-stable-linux-amd64.zip
   ```

2. Next, TensorBoard is opened using this code:

   ```
   LOG_DIR = model_dir
   get_ipython().system_raw(
    'tensorboard --logdir {} --host 0.0.0.0 --port 6006 &'
    .format(LOG_DIR))
   ```

3. After this, `ngrok` is called to start TensorBoard using port `6006`, which is a transmission communication protocol to communicate and exchange data:

```
get_ipython().system_raw('./ngrok http 6006 &')
```

4. The last step is to set up a public URL to access Google Colab TensorBoard using this command:

```
! curl -s http://localhost:4040/api/tunnels | python3 -c \
 "import sys, json;
print(json.load(sys.stdin)['tunnels'][0]['public_url'])"
```

Training the model

After all of the preceding steps are complete, we are ready for the most important step—training our custom neural network.

Training the model is performed using the following five steps, also outlined in the code:

1. Specify the configuration file.
2. Specify the output model directory.
3. Specify where to send the `STDERR` file.
4. Specify the number of training steps.
5. Specify the number of validation steps:

```
!python /content/models/research/object_detection/model_main.py \
 --pipeline_config_path={pipeline_fname} \
 --model_dir={model_dir} \
 --alsologtostderr \
 --num_train_steps={num_steps} \
 --num_eval_steps={num_eval_steps}
```

The explanation for this code is as follows:

- The pipeline configuration path is defined by `pipeline_fname`, which is the model and configuration file.
- `Model_dir` is the `training` directory. Note that `TensorBoard LOG_DIR` is also mapped to `model_dir`, so TensorBoard gets the data during training.
- The number of training and evaluation steps are defined up front during the configuration setting and can be adjusted as required.

Once training starts successfully, you will start to see messages in your Jupyter notebook. After some of the warnings on some packages are deprecated, you will start seeing comments on the training steps and will have successfully opened a dynamic library:

```
INFO:tensorflow:Maybe overwriting train_steps: 1000

 Successfully opened dynamic library libcudnn.so.7
 Successfully opened dynamic library libcublas.so.10
 INFO:tensorflow:loss = 2.5942094, step = 0
 loss = 2.5942094, step = 0
 INFO:tensorflow:global_step/sec: 0.722117
 global_step/sec: 0.722117
 INFO:tensorflow:loss = 0.4186823, step = 100 (138.482 sec)
 loss = 0.4186823, step = 100 (138.482 sec)
 INFO:tensorflow:global_step/sec: 0.734027
 global_step/sec: 0.734027
 INFO:tensorflow:loss = 0.3267398, step = 200 (136.235 sec)
 loss = 0.3267398, step = 200 (136.235 sec)
 INFO:tensorflow:global_step/sec: 0.721528
 global_step/sec: 0.721528
 INFO:tensorflow:loss = 0.21641359, step = 300 (138.595 sec)
 loss = 0.21641359, step = 300 (138.595 sec)
 INFO:tensorflow:global_step/sec: 0.723918
 global_step/sec: 0.723918
 INFO:tensorflow:loss = 0.16113645, step = 400 (138.137 sec)
 loss = 0.16113645, step = 400 (138.137 sec)
 INFO:tensorflow:Saving checkpoints for 419 into training/model.ckpt.
 model.ckpt-419
 INFO:tensorflow:global_step/sec: 0.618595
 global_step/sec: 0.618595
 INFO:tensorflow:loss = 0.07212131, step = 500 (161.657 sec)
 loss = 0.07212131, step = 500 (161.657 sec)
 INFO:tensorflow:global_step/sec: 0.722247
 ] global_step/sec: 0.722247
 INFO:tensorflow:loss = 0.11067433, step = 600 (138.457 sec)
 loss = 0.11067433, step = 600 (138.457 sec)
 INFO:tensorflow:global_step/sec: 0.72064
 global_step/sec: 0.72064
 INFO:tensorflow:loss = 0.07734648, step = 700 (138.765 sec)
 loss = 0.07734648, step = 700 (138.765 sec)
 INFO:tensorflow:global_step/sec: 0.722494
 global_step/sec: 0.722494
 INFO:tensorflow:loss = 0.088129714, step = 800 (138.410 sec)
 loss = 0.088129714, step = 800 (138.410 sec)
 INFO:tensorflow:Saving checkpoints for 836 into training/model.ckpt.
 I0107 15:44:16.116585 14036592158
 INFO:tensorflow:global_step/sec: 0.630514
 global_step/sec: 0.630514
```

```
 INFO:tensorflow:loss = 0.08999817, step = 900 (158.601 sec)
 loss = 0.08999817, step = 900 (158.601 sec)
 INFO:tensorflow:Saving checkpoints for 1000 into training/model.ckpt.
 Saving checkpoints for 1000 into training/model.ckpt.
 INFO:tensorflow:Skip the current checkpoint eval due to throttle secs (600
secs).

 Average Precision (AP) @[ IoU=0.50:0.95 | area= all | maxDets=100 ] =
0.505
 Average Precision (AP) @[ IoU=0.50 | area= all | maxDets=100 ] = 0.915
 Average Precision (AP) @[ IoU=0.75 | area= all | maxDets=100 ] = 0.493
 Average Precision (AP) @[ IoU=0.50:0.95 | area= small | maxDets=100 ] =
-1.000
 Average Precision (AP) @[ IoU=0.50:0.95 | area=medium | maxDets=100 ] =
0.200
 Average Precision (AP) @[ IoU=0.50:0.95 | area= large | maxDets=100 ] =
0.509
 Average Recall (AR) @[ IoU=0.50:0.95 | area= all | maxDets= 1 ] = 0.552
 Average Recall (AR) @[ IoU=0.50:0.95 | area= all | maxDets= 10 ] = 0.602
 Average Recall (AR) @[ IoU=0.50:0.95 | area= all | maxDets=100 ] = 0.611
 Average Recall (AR) @[ IoU=0.50:0.95 | area= small | maxDets=100 ] =
-1.000
 Average Recall (AR) @[ IoU=0.50:0.95 | area=medium | maxDets=100 ] = 0.600
 Average Recall (AR) @[ IoU=0.50:0.95 | area= large | maxDets=100 ] = 0.611

 SavedModel written to: training/export/Servo/temp-
b'1578412123'/saved_model.pb
 INFO:tensorflow:Loss for final step: 0.06650969.
 Loss for final step: 0.06650969.
```

Pay attention to the preceding output as it is displayed. Depending on your CPU/GPU capability, it will take different times to execute this step. The most important thing to note in the preceding training output is the accuracy and recall values during training.

Running an inference test

This step involves exporting trained inference graphs and running inference tests. The inference is done using the following Python command:

```
!python /content/models/research/object_detection/export_inference_graph.py
\
 --input_type=image_tensor \
 --pipeline_config_path={pipeline_fname} \
 --output_directory={output_directory} \
 --trained_checkpoint_prefix={last_model_path}
```

Here, `last_model_path` is `model_dir`, where model checkpoints are stored during training, and `pipeline_fname` is the model path and config file. Checkpoints cover the value of parameters used by the model during training. The following image shows the output of the four different models developed during training. These run one by one by executing the preceding procedure and by only selecting the different model types:

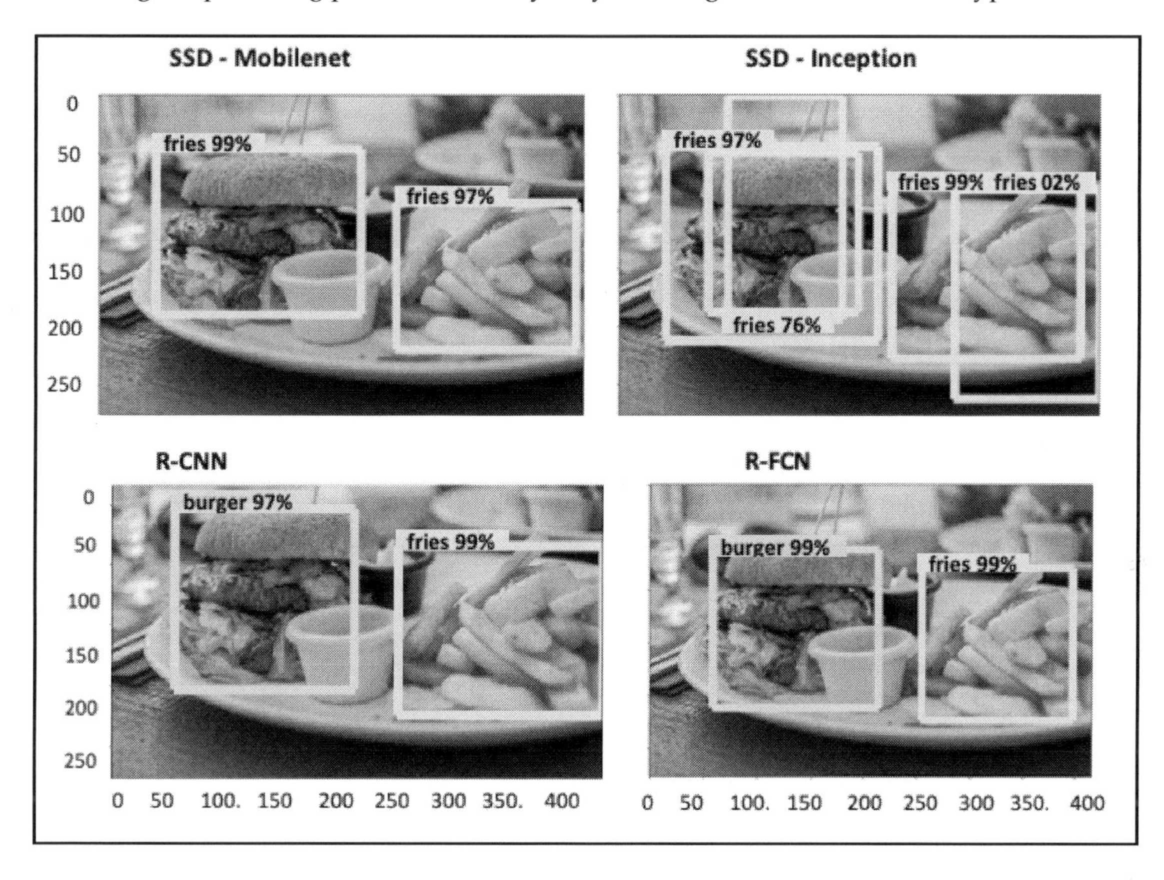

Note that the preceding model with the code block is run for four different models, as outlined earlier. Before running the next model, click on **Runtime** at the top of the Google Colab page and select **Factory reset runtime**, so you start fresh for the new model. Note that the SSD model is still not able to detect the objects correctly, whereas R-CNN and R-FCN are able to correctly detect the burger and french fries. This is probably due to the fact that the size of the burger and french fries are pretty much the same and we learned from the SSD overview that SSD is better at detecting images of different scales.

Once TensorBoard is set up, the output can be visualized in TensorBoard.

TensorBoard has three tabs—scalars, images, and graphs. Scalars include mAP (precision), recall, and loss values, images include the preceding visual image, and graphs include the TensorFlow graph `frozen_inference_graph.pb` file. Note that the difference between precision and recall is defined as follows:

- Precision = True positive/(True positive + false positive)
- Recall = True positive/(True positive + false negative)

Caution when using the neural network model

Note that we only used 68 images to train our neural network and it gave us very good predictions. This brings up four questions:

1. Does the model that we developed predict correctly in all situations? The answer is no. The model has only two classes—`burger` and `fries`—so it may detect other objects that are similar, for example, to the shape of a burger, such as a donut. To fix this issue, we need to load images similar to `burger` and classify them as not `burger`, then train the model with those additional image sets.
2. Why do we hear that we need thousands of images to train a neural network? If you are training a neural network from scratch, or even using transfer learning to get weights from another model, such as Inception or ResNet, but the model has not seen your new images before, then you will need at least 1,000 images. 1,000 comes from ImageNet datasets that have 1,000 images for each class.
3. If we need thousands of images to train, then why did it work in our case? In our case, we used transfer learning and downloaded the weights of ImageNet datasets. The ImageNet datasets already have `cheeseburger` as one class, so transfer learning on less than 100 images worked well.
4. In situations where the model was developed using less than 1,000 images, when will it not detect any objects at all? In situations where the object is very different from any object in the ImageNet classes, for example when detecting a scratch on a car body, infrared images, and so on.

An overview of Mask R-CNN and a Google Colab demonstration

Mask R-CNN (`https://arxiv.org/abs/1703.06870`) was proposed by Kaiming He, Georgia Gkioxari, Piotr Dollar, and Ross Girshick at **CVPR** 2017. Mask R-CNN efficiently detects objects in an image using R-CNN, while simultaneously object segmentation tasks for each region of interest. So, the segmentation task works in parallel with classification and bounding box regression. The Mask R-CNN's high-level architecture is as follows:

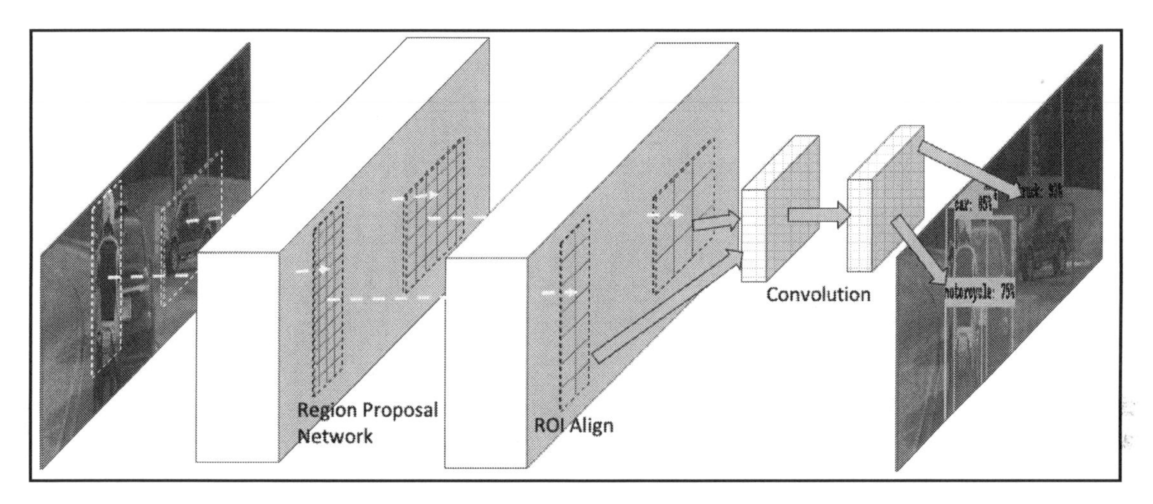

The details of the Mask R-CNN implementation is as follows:

- Mask R-CNN follows the general two-stage principle of Faster R-CNN but with a modification—the first stage, **RPN**, remains the same as Faster R-CNN. The second stage, Fast R-CNN, which starts with feature extraction from **Region of Interest (RoI)**, classification, and bounding-box regression, also outputs a binary mask for each RoI.
- A mask represents a spatial shape of the input object. Mask R-CNN predicts an (*M* x *N*) mask for each RoI using the fully convolutional network for semantic segmentation.
- RoI Align is applied at the output of the region proposal network after dividing the feature map into an *M* x *N* grid and then applying a 2 x 2 bin and four sampling points in each bin, chosen using bilinear interpolation. RoI Align is used to align the extracted feature with the input.

- The backbone neural network uses ResNet-50 or -101 by extracting the final convolution layer of the fourth stage.
- The training image is rescaled such that the shorter edge is 800 pixels. Each mini-batch has two images per GPU with a 1:3 ratio of positive to negative samples. Training continues for 160,000 iterations, with a learning rate of `0.02` up to 120,000 iterations, and thenit drops to `0.002`. Weight decays of `0.0001` and a momentum of `0.9` are used.

The Mask R-CNN image segmentation demonstration is written in Google Colab and is found at `https://github.com/PacktPublishing/Mastering-Computer-Vision-with-TensorFlow-2.0/blob/master/Chapter10/Chapter10_Mask_R_CNN_Image_Segmentation_Demo.ipynb`.

The notebook loads a sample image and creates the TensorFlow session by activating the TPU. It then loads a pre-trained model mask R-CNN and then performs instance segmentation and prediction. The notebook is taken from the Google Colab site with only one modification—the image load function. The following image shows the output of Mask R-CNN:

Mask R-CNN is trained on the Coco dataset outlined earlier. So, `human`, `car`, and `traffic light` are already predetermined classes for this. Each human, car, and traffic light is detected with bounding boxes and the shape is drawn using segmentation.

Developing an object tracker model to complement the object detector

Object tracking initiates with object detection, assigns a unique set of IDs for each detection, and maintains that ID as the object moves around. In this section, different types of object tracking models are described in detail.

Centroid-based tracking

As the name suggests, centroid-based tracking involves tracking the centroid of the image cluster developed using thresholding. At initialization, IDs are assigned to the bounding box centroid. In the next frame, the IDs are assigned by looking at the relative distance between two frames. This method works when objects are far apart but does not work when objects are very close to each other.

SORT tracking

SORT was introduced by Alex Bewley, Zongyuan Ge, Lionel Ott, Fabio Ramos, and Ben Upcroft in their paper titled *Simple Online and Realtime Tracking* (`https://arxiv.org/abs/1602.00763`). This paper uses Faster R-CNN for detection, while the Kalman filter and the Hungarian algorithm were used for **Multiple Object Tracking (MOT)** in real time. Details of the tracking implementations can be found at `https://github.com/abewley/sort`.

DeepSORT tracking

At CVPR 2017, Nicolai Wojke, Alex Bewley, and Dietrich Paulus came up with DeepSORT tracking in their paper titled *Simple Online and Real-Time Tracking with a Deep Association Metric*. The details of the paper can be found at `https://arxiv.org/abs/1703.07402`.

DeepSORT is an extension of SORT and integrates appearance information within the bounding box using a CNN trained to discriminate pedestrians. Details of the tracking implementation can be found at `https://github.com/nwojke/deep_sort`.

The details of the architecture are outlined as follows:

- The tracking scenario is defined on an eight-dimensional state space $(u, v, \gamma, h, x, y, \gamma, h)$, where (u, v) is the bounding box center location, γ is the aspect ratio, and h is the height.

- A Kalman filter predicts the future state based on the current location and speed information. In DeepSORT, a Kalman filter based on location and velocity is used to find the next tracking position.
- For each track, *k*, the number of frames is counted and incremented during Kalman filter prediction and reset to `0` during object detection. Tracks exceeding a threshold value or not associated with detection within the first three frames are deleted.
- The association between the predicted Kalman state and newly arrived measurement is solved by a combination of the Mahalanobis distance between the two states (predicted and new measurement) and the cosine similarity between the appearance descriptors.
- A matching cascade is introduced that gives priority to more frequently seen objects.
- The IoU association is calculated to account for sudden disappearances from the scene.
- A wide ResNet neural network, which has reduced depth and increased width, has been used for improved performance over a thin residual network. The wide ResNet layer has two convolutional layers and six residual blocks.
- DeepSort uses a model trained on 1.1 million human images of 1,251 pedestrians and extracts a 128 dim vector for each bounding box for feature extraction.

The OpenCV tracking method

OpenCV has a number of built-in tracking methods:

- **A BOOSTING tracker**: An old tracker based on Haar cascades.
- **A MIL tracker**: Has better accuracy than the BOOSTING tracker.
- **A Kernelized Correlation Filters (KCF) tracker**: This is faster than the BOOSTING and MIL trackers.
- **A CSRT tracker**: This is more accurate than KCF but the tracking can be slower.
- **The MedianFlow tracker**: This tracker works when the object has a regular movement and is visible for the entire sequence.
- **The TLD tracker**: Do not use it.
- **The MOSSE tracker**: A very fast tracker but not as accurate as CSRT or KCF.
- **The GOTURN tracker**: A deep learning-based object tracker.

The implementation of the preceding methods in OpenCV is as follows:

```
tracker = cv2.TrackerBoosting_create()
tracker = cv2.TrackerCSRT_create()
tracker = cv2.TrackerKCF_create()
tracker = cv2.TrackerMedianFlow_create()
tracker = cv2.TrackerMIL_create()
tracker = cv2.TrackerMOSSE_create()
tracker = cv2.TrackerTLD_create()
```

Siamese network-based tracking

Siamese network-based object tracking was proposed in 2016 by Luca Bertinetto, Jack Valmadre, Joao F. Henriques, Andrea Vedaldi, and Philip H. S. Torr in their landmark paper *Fully-Convolutional Siamese Networks for Object Tracking*. The details of the paper can be found at `https://arxiv.org/abs/1606.09549`.

In this paper, the authors trained a deep convolution network to develop a similarity function offline and then applied this to real-time object tracking. The similarity function is a Siamese CNN that compares a test bounding box to a training bounding box (ground truth) and returns a high score. If the two bounding boxes contain the same object and a low score, then the objects are different.

A Siamese network passes two images through an identical neural network. It calculates the feature vector by removing the last fully connected layer, which is described in `Chapter 6`, *Visual Search Using Transfer Learning*. It then compares the two feature vectors for similarity. The Siamese network used does not have any fully connected layers. So, only convolutional filters are used, so the network is fully convolutional with respect to an input image. The advantage of the fully convolutional network is that it is size-independent; so, any input size can be used for the `test` and `train` images. The following diagram explains the architecture of the Siamese network:

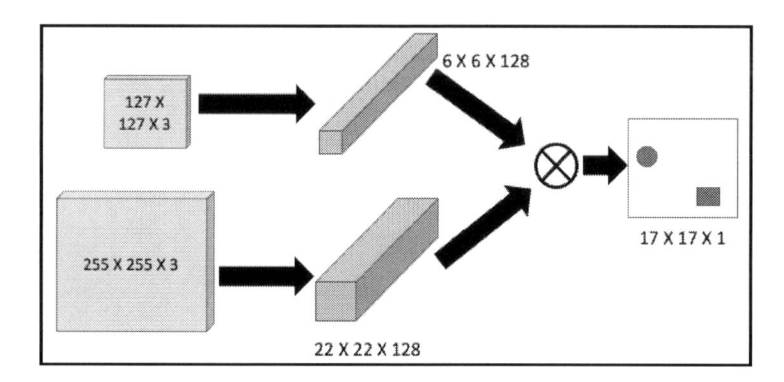

In the diagram, the output of the network is a feature map. The process is repeated twice through the CNN (f_θ), once each for the test (x) and train (z) images, resulting in two feature maps, which are cross-correlated, as shown:

$$g_\theta(z, x) = f_\theta(z) * f_\theta(x)$$

The tracking starts as follows:

- Initial image location = Previous target location
- Displacement = Stride multiplied by the location of the maximum score relative to the center
- New location = Initial location + displacement

So, a rectangular bounding box is used to initialize the target. At each subsequent frame, its position is estimated using tracking.

SiamMask-based tracking

At CVPR 2019, Qiang Wang, Li Zhang, Luca Bertinetto, Weiming Hu, and Phillip H.S.Torr came up with SiamMask in their paper *Fast Online Object Tracking and Segmentation: A Unifying Approach*. More details about the paper can be found at `https://arxiv.org/abs/1812.05050`.

SiamMask uses a single bounding box initialization and tracks object bounding boxes at 55 frames per second.

Here, the simple cross-correlation of the Siamese network is replaced by a depth-wise correlation to produce a multi-channel response map:

- A w x h binary mask (one for each feature map) is designed using a simple two-layer 1 x 1 convolutional neural network, *hf*. The first layer has 256 channels and the second layer has 63 x 63 channels.
- ResNet-50 is used for the CNN until the end of the third stage, ending with a 1 x 1 convolution layer. Note that ResNet-50 has four stages, but only the top three stages are considered and the modification of a convolution of stride 1 used to reduce the output stride to 8 is made.
- Dilated (atrous) convolution is used in DeepLab (described in detail in `Chapter 8`, *Semantic Segmentation and Neural Style Transfer*) to increase the receptive field. The final output of ResNet's third stage is appended with a 1 x 1 convolution with 256 outputs.

Details of the SiamMask implementations as well as training can be found at `https://github.com/foolwood/SiamMask`.

SiamMask can also be run on a YouTube video file using Google Colab at `https://colab.research.google.com/github/tugstugi/dl-colab-notebooks/blob/master/notebooks/SiamMask.ipynb`.

Note that in order for it to run successfully, the video file must start with a human image.

Summary

In this chapter, you got a deep overview of various object detector methods and practical methods of training an object detector using your own custom image from start to finish. Some of the key concepts learned are how to work with Google Cloud to evaluate an object detector, how to use `labelImg` to create an annotation file, how to link Google Drive to a Google Colab notebook to read files, how to generate a TensorFlow `tfRecord` file from `.xml` and `.jpg` files, how to start a training process and monitor readings during training, how to create TensorBoard to observe training accuracy, how to save a model after training, and how to perform inference with the saved model. Using this methodology, you can select your object class and create an object detection model for inference. You also learned various techniques for object tracking, such as Kalman filtering and neural network-based trackings, such as DeepSORT and Siamese network-based object tracking methods. As a next step, you can connect an object detection model to a tracking method to track a detected object.

In the next chapter, we will learn about computer vision in the edge by optimizing and deploying neural network models in edge devices, such as cell phones. We will also learn about using Raspberry Pi for real-time object detection.

4
Section 4: TensorFlow Implementation at the Edge and on the Cloud

In this section, you will use all your knowledge of computer vision and CNN acquired so far to package, optimize, and deploy a model in edge devices to solve real-life computer vision problems. Training large datasets in local machines takes time, so you will learn how to package your data and upload to containers in the cloud and then initiate training. You'll also see how to overcome some common bugs to complete your training and generate models successfully.

By the end of this section, you will be able to do the following:

- Understand how edge devices use various hardware acceleration and software optimization techniques to make inferences based on a neural network model with minimum delay (chapter 11)
- Understand the theory of the MobileNet model, as this is often deployed in edge devices due to its speed (chapter 11)
- Deploy a neural network model in a RaspBerry Pi for object detection using the Intel OpenVINO toolkit and TensorFlow Lite (chapter 11)
- Perform object detection on an Android phone and iPhone by deploying a model using TensorFlow Lite in Android Studio and Xcode (chapter 11)
- Use Create ML to train a custom object detector and deploy it on the iPhone using Xcode and Swift (chapter 11)
- Develop a general understanding of the infrastructure of the various cloud platforms – **Google Cloud Platform (GCP)**, **Amazon Web Services (AWS)**, and **Microsoft Azure cloud platform** (chapter 12)

- Develop an end-to-end machine learning platform for custom object detection using GCP, AWS, and Azure (chapter 12)
- Understand how to use TensorFlow to train and package at scale (chapter 12)
- Perform visual searches using GCP, AWS, and Azure (chapter 12)

This section comprises the following chapters:

- `Chapter 11`, *Deep Learning on Edge Devices with CPU/GPU Optimization*
- `Chapter 12`, *Cloud Computing Platform for Computer Vision*

11

Deep Learning on Edge Devices with CPU/GPU Optimization

So far, we have learned how to develop deep learning models by preprocessing data, training models, and generating inferences using a Python PC environment.

In this chapter, we will learn how to take the generated model and deploy it on edge devices and production systems. This will result in a complete end-to-end TensorFlow object detection model implementation. A number of edge devices and their nominal performance and acceleration techniques will be discussed in this chapter.

In particular, TensorFlow models have been developed, converted, and optimized using the **TensorFlow Lite** and **Intel Open Visual Inference and Neural Network Optimization** (**OpenVINO**) architectures and deployed to Raspberry Pi, Android, and iPhone. Although this chapter focuses mainly on object detection on Raspberry Pi, Android, and iPhone, the approach we will describe can be extended to image classification, style transfer, and action recognition for any edge devices under consideration.

This chapter is broken down into the following sections:

- Overview of deep learning on edge devices
- Techniques used for GPU/CPU optimization
- Overview of MobileNet
- Image processing with Raspberry Pi
- Model conversion and inference using OpenVINO
- Application of TensorFlow Lite
- Object detection on Android using TensorFlow Lite

- Object detection on Raspberry Pi using TensorFlow Lite
- Object detection on iPhone using TensorFlow Lite and Create ML
- A summary of various annotation methods

Overview of deep learning on edge devices

In terms of computers, the edge is the very end device that sees things and measures parameters. Deep learning on edge devices implies injecting AI into the edge device so that along with seeing, it can also analyze an image and report its content. An example of an edge device for computer vision is a camera. Edge computing makes image recognition on-premises quick and efficient. The AI component inside a camera consists of a powerful yet tiny processor that has deep learning capabilities.

This AI on the edge can perform a mix of three separate functions, depending on the choice of hardware and software platforms you use:

- Hardware acceleration to make the device run faster
- Software optimization to reduce the model size and remove unnecessary components
- Interacting with the cloud to batch process image and tensors

The benefit of this is increased speed, reduced bandwidth, increased data privacy, and network scalability. This is done by embedding a controller inside the camera to give the camera the processing power it needs to work.

Edge computing means the workload is transferred from the cloud to the device. This requires highly efficient edge devices, optimized software to perform detection without significant lag, and an efficient data transfer protocol to send select data to the cloud for processing and then feed the output back to the edge device for real time decision making. Selecting the correct edge device depends on your application requirements and how it interfaces with the rest of the subsystem. Some examples of edge devices are as follows:

- NVIDIA Jetson Nano
- Raspberry Pi + Intel neural network stick
- Coral Dev board + Coral USB accelerator
- Orange Pi + Intel neural network stick
- ORDOID C2
- Android phone
- iOS phone

The following table summarizes the performance specifications of the various edge devices listed previously. You can use this table to determine your selection process:

Devices	GPU	CPU	Memory	Accelerator
NVIDIA Jetson Nano 69 mm x 45 mm	128 core NVIDIA Maxwell	Quad-core ARM Cortex A57	4 GB RAM, 16 GB storage	Parallel processor
Raspberry Pi 4 85 mm x 56 mm		ARM Cortex A72 @ 1.5 GHz	4 GB RAM, 32 GB storage	
Coral Dev Board 48 mm x 40 mm	Integrated GC7000 Lite Graphics	Quad-core Cortex-A53, plus Cortex-M4F	1 GB LPDDR4	Google Edge TPU ML accelerator coprocessor
Orange Pi 85 mm x 55 mm	ARM Mali-400 MP2 GPU @600MHz	4x Cortex-A7 @ 1.6 GHz	1 GB DDR3 SDRAM	
ORDOID C2 85 mm x 56 mm	Mali450MP3	ARM Cortex-A53 Quad-core @ 1.5 GHz	2 GB DDR3 SDRAM	
Intel Neural network stick	Intel Movidius Myriad X **Vision Processing Unit** (**VPU**) with 16 processing cores and a network hardware accelerator	Intel OpenVINO toolkit		
Coral USB accelerator	Google Edge TPU ML accelerator coprocessor, AUTOML Vision Edge support	TensorFlow Lite model support		
Android Pixel XL 155 mm x 76 mm	Ardeno 530	2 x 2.15 GHz Kryo and 2 x 1.6 GHz Kryo	4 GB RAM	
iPhone XR 155 mm x 76 mm	A12 Bionic chip	A12 Bionic chip	3 GB RAM	

Techniques used for GPU/CPU optimization

Central processing units (**CPUs**) mainly perform serial processing, whereas a **graphical processing unit** (**GPU**) runs processes in parallel and can perform a large number of operations at once, resulting in faster processing. The data in a GPU is called a thread. GPUs are programmed using the **Compute Unified Device Architecture** (**CUDA**) and **Open Computing Language** (**OpenCL**). A CPU performs a lot of different types of calculations, whereas a GPU specializes in a given calculation, such as image processing. For edge devices to provide results without lag, they must be accompanied by accelerators, GPUs, and software optimization.

The following are some methods that are commonly used for GPU/CPU optimization:

- Model optimization methods such as image size, batch normalization, gradient descent, and so on.
- Magnitude-based weight pruning makes the model sparse by zeroing out the model weights, which makes it easier to compress. Refer to the following link for pruning techniques: `https://www.tensorflow.org/model_optimization/guide/pruning/`
- A GPU memory partition such as NVIDIA Jetson Nano.
- Heterogeneous computing across CPU, GPU, and FPGA using a common API for Intel neural network sticks.
- SWAP space to allocate disk space for RAM memory.
- Using **tensor processing units (TPUs)** in combination with a CPU or a GPU. A CPU performs the arithmetic operation in sequence, while a GPU performs multiple arithmetic operations at once. TPUs were developed by Google to accelerate neural network processing. In a TPU, the arithmetic operations are directly connected to each other, without using any memory.
- Quantization, that is, converting weights from 32-bit into 8-bit.
- iOS phones use different metals to access the GPU for faster image processing. For more details, please refer to `https://developer.apple.com/metal/`.
- For Android phones, please refer to the VR performance benchmark to understand the available GPU/CPU optimization methods: `https://developers.google.com/vr/develop/best-practices/perf-best-practices`.

Overview of MobileNet

MobileNet was introduced by a team of Google engineers in CVPR 2017 in their paper titled *MobileNets: Efficient Convolutional Neural Networks for Mobile Vision Applications*. You can find this MobileNet paper at `https://arxiv.org/abs/1704.04861`.

MobileNet proposes a depthwise separable convolution architecture that shrinks the neural network model so that it can work on the resource restriction issues of edge devices. MobileNet architecture consists of two main parts:

- Depthwise separable convolution
- Pointwise 1 x 1 convolution

Note that we described the importance of 1 x 1 convolution in `Chapter 4`, *Deep Learning on Images*, and `Chapter 5`, *Neural Network Architecture and Models*. You may want to revisit those chapters as a refresher.

The following diagram shows how depthwise convolution works:

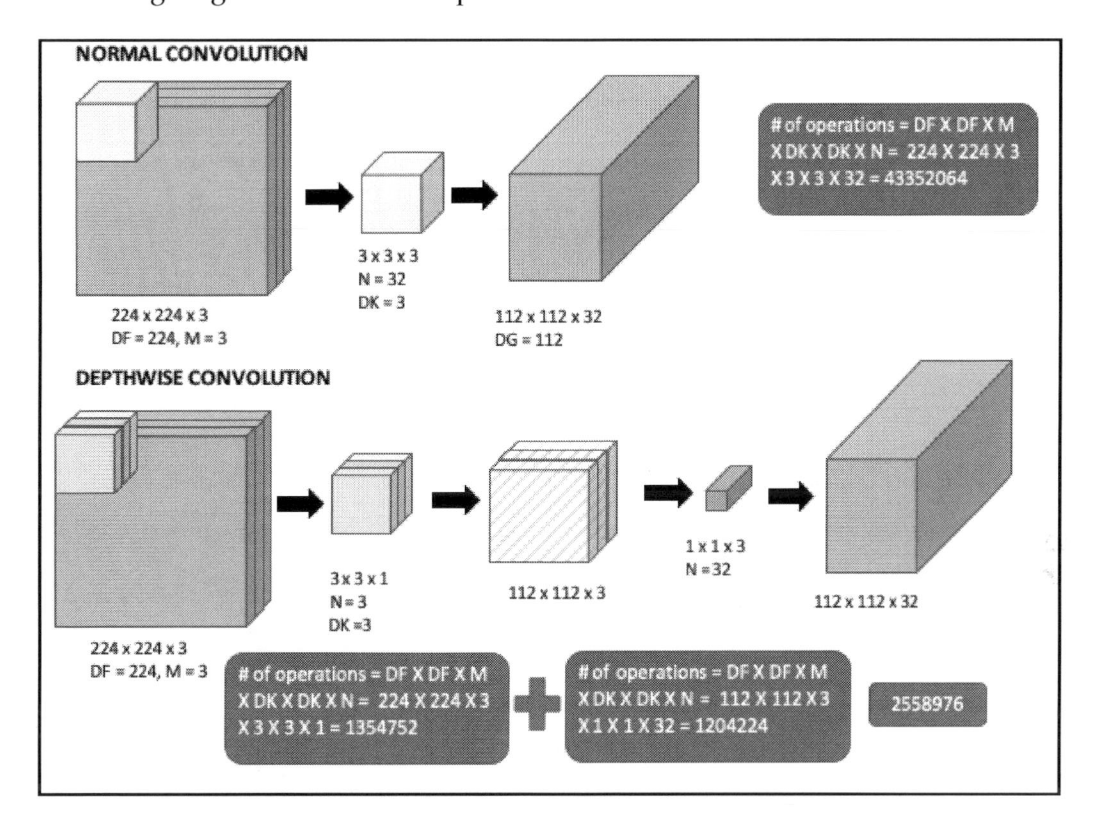

In the preceding diagram, we can see the following:

- We get a reduction in the number of operations compared to normal convolutions.
- In MobileNet, the convolution layers are followed by batch normalization and ReLU nonlinearity, except for the final layer, which is connected to a softmax layer for classification.
- The MobileNet architecture can be reduced through depth multiplication and resolution multiplication.

Image processing with a Raspberry Pi

Raspberry Pi is a single-board tiny computer without a GPU that can be connected to an external camera and other sensor modules and can be programmed in Python to perform computer vision work such as object detection. Raspberry Pis have built-in Wi-Fi, so they can be connected to the internet seamlessly to receive and transfer data. Because of its tiny shape and powerful computing, the Raspberry Pi is a perfect example of an edge device for IoT and computer vision work. Detailed information on Raspberry Pi can be found at `https://www.raspberrypi.org/products/`. The following photo shows the complete setup for a Raspberry Pi:

The detailed hardware setup for the Raspberry Pi will be described in the following subsections.

Note that this image will be listed in the following setup section several times.

Raspberry Pi hardware setup

The following are some important points to consider before starting your Raspberry Pi setup work:

- Order the latest version Raspberry Pi 4 – you can get it from Raspberry Pi directly or from any online store.
- Get the Raspberry Pi with 4 GB RAM and a 32 GB MicroSD card. Most of the time, the Raspberry Pi comes with the MicroSD card programmed with NOOBS. Check this before ordering one.
- If your Raspberry Pi does not come with a programmed MicroSD card, then purchase a 32 GB MicroSD card and then install NOOBS on it by going to `https://www.raspberrypi.org/downloads/noobs/`. To do that, you have to install the MicroSD card in a MicroSD adapter for PCs and then download NOOBS onto the card using your regular PC. Once programmed, remove the MicroSD card from the adapter and insert it into the Raspberry Pi MicroSD slot, which is located underneath the Raspberry Pi in the diagonally opposite location of the USB slots and near the power button. See the photo shown in the previous section for more information.
- Most Raspberry Pis don't come with the camera module, so order it separately. The camera module port is located next to the HDMI port, which has a black plastic clip on it. The camera comes with a white ribbon cable. You can open the black plastic clip in the camera module by pulling it up and then inserting the white ribbon cable into it all the way so that the shiny surface is facing the HDMI port next to it. After inserting the ribbon cable, close the plastic clip by pushing it down all the way so that the ribbon is firmly attached to the camera module port. See the photo in the previous section for more information.
- Connect a mouse cable, a keyboard cable, and the HDMI cable to an external monitor. Note that this is optional as you can connect Raspberry Pi using a PC over a Wi-Fi connection.
- Purchase an Intel Neural Network Stick 2 and insert it into one of the USB ports. Note that the Intel Neural network stick takes up extra width, so you have to be creative with all three USB ports (neural network stick, USB for keyboard, and USB for mouse).
- Once all the connections are complete, connect the power supply. The red light in the Raspberry Pi will light up, and the green light next to it will flash occasionally, indicating that the microSD card is powered on. This indicates everything is functioning properly. The next section will discuss how to set up the camera.

Raspberry Pi camera software setup

In this section, we will look at the various code segments in Python that we need in order to set up our Raspberry Pi for computer vision.

We can set the camera up as video player. Use the following commands, one by one, in the Raspberry Pi Terminal. These commands make the necessary package updates and boot the new Raspbian installation:

```
$sudo apt update
$sudo apt full-upgrade
$sudo raspi-config
```

After entering the last command, some dialog will appear in the Raspberry Pi. Select the necessary interfacing options, select a camera, and click **yes** for the question, "Would you like the camera interface to be enabled?" Then, reboot the Raspberry Pi and enter the following command in the Terminal after it boots up:

```
$raspivid -o video.h264 -t 10000
```

You will notice that video is recorded for 10 seconds and saved in `video.h264` format. The first time you do this, you'll notice the camera is out of focus. Adjust the round cap on the camera (after taking the cover off) until it is in focus.

This concludes how to set up the camera software. If you want to learn more about this process, please refer to `https://www.raspberrypi.org/documentation/usage/camera/raspicam/raspivid.md`.

OpenCV installation in Raspberry Pi

For detailed instructions, please go to `https://software.intel.com/en-us/articles/raspberry-pi-4-and-intel-neural-compute-stick-2-setup`.

During installation, I found that I had to navigate between several pages to get everything right. Here are the step-by-step instructions that worked for me. You are welcome to use the official site or the instructions given here to get everything working:

Each of the following lines is a separate instruction. This means that to enter one command, hit *Enter* and wait for it to be displayed in your console, indicating it's completed, before entering the next command.

1. Enter the following commands in the Terminal to install the necessary components for OpenCV:

```
$sudo su
$apt update && apt upgrade -y
$apt install build-essential
```

2. Install CMake to manage the build process:

```
$wget
https://github.com/Kitware/CMake/releases/download/v3.14.4/cmake-3.
14.4.tar.gz
$tar xvzf cmake-3.14.4.tar.gz
$cd ~/cmake-3.14.4
```

3. Install any additional dependencies, such as `bootstrap`:

```
$./bootstrap
$make -j4
$make install
```

4. Install OpenCV from the source in the Raspberry Pi drive:

```
$git clone https://github.com/opencv/opencv.git
$cd opencv && mkdir build && cd build
$cmake -DCMAKE_BUILD_TYPE=Release -DCMAKE_INSTALL_PREFIX=/usr/local
..
$make -j4
$make install
```

The preceding command will install OpenCV.

5. To verify the installation process, open another Terminal while keeping the current one open, and enter the following command:

```
$python3
>>> import cv2
>>> cv2.__version__
```

This should display the latest OpenCV version that's installed on your system.

OpenVINO installation in Raspberry Pi

OpenVINO is an Intel trademark and stands for Open Visual Inference and Neural Network Optimization toolkit. It provides developers with a deep learning acceleration toolkit on Intel hardware such as CPUs (Intel Core and Xeon processors), GPUs (Intel Iris Pro graphics and HD graphics), VPUs (Intel Movidius neural computing stick), and FPGAs (Intel Arria 10GX).

To download OpenVINO on your desktop, go to `https://software.intel.com/en-us/openvino-toolkit/choose-download`.

After downloading OpenVINO, you will have to enter your name and email. Then, you will be able to download OpenVINO. Follow the instructions to unzip the file and install the dependencies. Note that this process will not work for Raspberry Pi. So, for Raspberry Pi, use the following commands:

```
$cd ~/dldt/inference-engine
$mkdir build && cd build
$cmake -DCMAKE_BUILD_TYPE=Release \
-DCMAKE_CXX_FLAGS='-march=armv7-a' \
-DENABLE_MKL_DNN=OFF \
-DENABLE_CLDNN=OFF \
-DENABLE_GNA=OFF \
-DENABLE_SSE42=OFF \
-DTHREADING=SEQ \
..
$make
```

The preceding commands will return a series of displays in the Terminal.

Installing the OpenVINO toolkit components

To install the OpenVINO toolkit components, go to `https://docs.openvinotoolkit.org/latest/_docs_install_guides_installing_openvino_raspbian.html`.

The following steps have been listed as a reference:

1. Open a new Terminal window, type in `sudo su`, and press *Enter*.
2. Click on the following link and download `R3 l_openvino_toolkit_runtime_raspbian_p_2019.3.334.tgz`. Note that the numbers after `p_` and `before.tgz` can change in future versions: `https://download.01.org/opencv/2019/openvinotoolkit/R3/`.

3. Create an installation folder:

```
$sudo mkdir -p /opt/intel/openvino
```

4. Unzip the downloaded file:

```
$sudo tar -xf l_openvino_toolkit_runtime_raspbian_p_2019.3.334.tgz
--
$strip 1 -C /opt/intel/openvino
```

5. Next, install CMake, if it isn't already installed:

```
sudo apt install cmake
```

By setting up the environmental variable, OpenVINO will be initialized every time you start the Terminal. This keeps you from having to remember your command prompt every time.

Setting up the environmental variable

You can either set the environmental variable locally or set it globally with the help of the following steps:

1. To set it locally, run the following command in the Terminal:

```
$source /opt/intel/openvino/bin/setupvars.sh
```

2. To set it globally, run the following command in the Terminal:

```
$echo "source /opt/intel/openvino/bin/setupvars.sh" >> ~/.bashrc
```

3. To test the changes you've made, open a new Terminal. You will see the following output:

```
[setupvars.sh] OpenVINO environment initialized
Pi$raspberripi: $
Type sudo su and you should get
root@raspberripi:
```

Adding a USB rule

USB rules are required to perform inference on the Intel Movidius Neural Computing Stick. Follow these steps:

1. The following command will help you to add any current Linux users to the group:

```
$sudo usermod -a -G users "$(whoami)"
```

2. Now, reboot the Raspberry Pi and log in again:

```
sh
/opt/intel/openvino/install_dependencies/install_NCS_udev_rules.sh
```

Running inference using Python code

Once you've completed all the installation procedures, the next task is to perform inference using the Intel Movidius Neural Computing stick that's attached to the Raspberry Pi with a camera module. The camera module here is the edge device, while the Raspberry Pi with the Intel Movidius Neural Computing stick is the processor unit.

Note the Raspberry Pi itself cannot perform inference with the neural network as processing will be very slow. With an Intel OpenVINO neural computing stick, you will see a very little delay. As a comparison, refer to the *Object detection on Raspberry Pi using TensorFlow Lite*, where a TensorFlow model will be deployed to a Raspberry Pi using tflite without a neural network stick. You will notice that in that case, the delay is significant.

Let's take a look at the following command:

```
$mkdir build && cd build
$cmake -DCMAKE_BUILD_TYPE=Release -DCMAKE_CXX_FLAGS="-march=armv7-a"
/opt/intel/openvino/deployment_tools/inference_engine/samples
$make -j2 object_detection_sample_ssd
$wget --no-check-certificate
https://download.01.org/opencv/2019/open_model_zoo/R1/models_bin/face-detec
tion-adas-0001/FP16/face-detection-adas-0001.bin
$wget --no-check-certificate
https://download.01.org/opencv/2019/open_model_zoo/R1/models_bin/face-detec
tion-adas-0001/FP16/face-detection-adas-0001.xml
```

Run the sample code provided in the `openvino_fd_myriad.py` file, as follows:

```
python3 openvino_fd_myriad.py
```

Refer to the following GitHub page for the complete code: `https://github.com/PacktPublishing/Mastering-Computer-Vision-with-TensorFlow-2.0/blob/master/Chapter11/Chapter%2011_openvino_fd_myriad.py`. Also, take a look at the `out.png` file to look at the bounding box drawn on the image.

Advanced inference

So far, we have just performed face detection with the OpenVINO toolkit. In this section, we will learn how to perform a variety of computer vision tasks using an Intel Movidius Neural Network Stick connected to a Raspberry Pi such as pedestrian detection, vehicle and bike detection, license plate detection, age and gender recognition, facial landmark recognition, emotion recognition, pose estimation, action recognition, gaze recognition, and many others.

A list of all the `bin` and `xml` files we'll be using is provided by the Intel Open Source Technology Center at `https://download.01.org/opencv/2019/open_model_zoo/`.

Note that when you click on the preceding link, you will see four folders labeled `R1, R2, R3, and R4`. Click on the one with the latest date, which in this case is R1. This can be seen in the following screenshot:

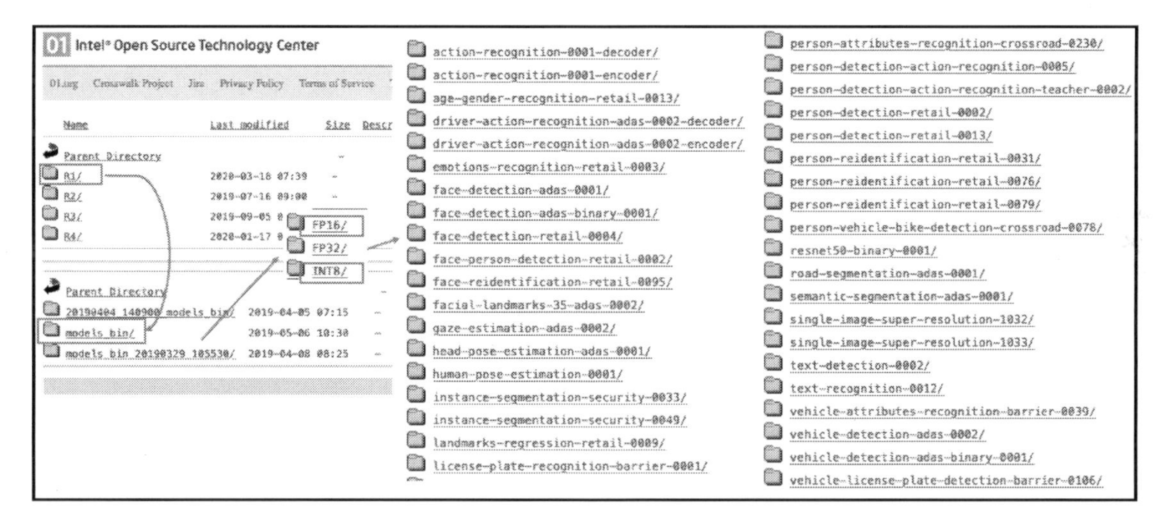

Then, click on the latest folder, which in this case is `models_bin`. This will open up a dialogue box showing either FP16, FP32, or INT8. For some models, INT8 is not present.

Now, let's try to understand what these parameters mean so that we can make an informed decision about which one to select for our specific application. FP16 uses 16 bits instead of 32 bits for FP32, thus reducing the training and inference time. INT8, on the other hand, uses 8-bit integers for neural network training for weight, gradients, and activations. So, out of all three methods, INT8 should be the fastest one, and Intel claims it still maintains accuracy.

If you want to understand more about the 8-bit training method used by Intel, please refer to the paper titled *Scalable Methods for 8-bit Training of Neural Networks*, published at `https://arxiv.org/abs/1805.11046`. For faster processing on edge devices such as Raspberry Pis, the recommended method is to use FP16 or INT8, if available.

The Open Model Zoo described previously has various pre-built models such as models for face detection, person detection, bike detection, and more. These models have already been trained, so we will use those models just for inference purposes in this chapter. If you want to know how to train, then you can follow the steps of gathering your own data, training, and building a model described in `Chapter 10`, *Object Detection Using R-CNN, SSD, and R-FCN.*

Next, we'll look at some tables that group the models into four types.

Face detection, pedestrian detection, and vehicle detection

The following table describes various face detection, person detection, and vehicle and bike detection models. Carefully note the input and output for each model listed in the table as this will need to be entered in the Python code for inference:

Model	Category	Input	Output	Note on output class
face-detection-adas-0001	face detection	image: [1xCxHxW]-shape [1x3x384x672]	blob [1, 1, N, 7]	[image_id, label, conf, x_min, y_min, x_max, y_max]
face-detection-adas-binary-0001	face detection	image: [1xCxHxW]-shape [1x3x384x672]	blob [1, 1, N, 7]	[image_id, label, conf, x_min, y_min, x_max, y_max]
face-detection-retail-0004	face detection	image: [1xCxHxW]-shape [1x3x300x300]	blob [1, 1, N, 7]	[image_id, label, conf, x_min, y_min, x_max, y_max]
face-detection-retail-0005	face detection	image: [1xCxHxW]-shape [1x3x300x300]	blob [1, 1, N, 7]	[image_id, label, conf, x_min, y_min, x_max, y_max]
person-detection-retail-0013	person & car detection	image: [1xCxHxW]-shape [1x3x320x544]	blob [1, 1, N, 7]	[image_id, label, conf, x_min, y_min, x_max, y_max]
pedestrian-detection-adas-0002	person & car detection	image: [1xCxHxW]-shape [1x3x384x672]	blob [1, 1, N, 7]	[image_id, label, conf, x_min, y_min, x_max, y_max]
pedestrian-detection-adas-binary-0001	person & car detection	image: [1xCxHxW]-shape [1x3x384x672]	blob [1, 1, N, 7]	[image_id, label, conf, x_min, y_min, x_max, y_max]
pedestrian-and-vehicle-detector-adas-0001	person & car detection	image: [1xCxHxW]-shape [1x3x384x672]	blob [1, 1, N, 7]	[image_id, label, conf, x_min, y_min, x_max, y_max]
vehicle-detection-adas-0002	person & car detection	image: [1xCxHxW]-shape [1x3x384x672]	blob [1, 1, N, 7]	[image_id, label, conf, x_min, y_min, x_max, y_max]
vehicle-detection-adas-binary-0001	person & car detection	image: [1xCxHxW]-shape [1x3x384x672]	blob [1, 1, N, 7]	[image_id, label, conf, x_min, y_min, x_max, y_max]
person-vehicle-bike-detection-crossroad-0078	person & car detection	image: [1xCxHxW]-shape [1x3x1024x1024]	blob [1, 1, N, 7]	[image_id, label, conf, x_min, y_min, x_max, y_max]
person-vehicle-bike-detection-crossroad-1016	person & car detection	image: [1xCxHxW]-shape [1x3x512x512]	blob [1, 1, N, 7]	[image_id, label, conf, x_min, y_min, x_max, y_max]
vehicle-license-plate-detection-barrier-0106	license plate	image: [1xCxHxW]-shape [1x3x300x300]	blob [1, 1, N, 7]	[image_id, label, conf, x_min, y_min, x_max, y_max]

As we can see, although the model type are different, the input is essentially the same. The only difference is the dimensions of the input image. The output is also the same – all of them generate a rectangular bounding box.

Landmark models

The following table describes models for age-gender and emotion recognition, facial landmark recognition, vehicle color and type recognition, and person attributes such as shirts, hats, and backpacks being worn. Note the input and output for each model listed in the table as this will need to be entered in the Python code for inference:

Model	Category	Input	Output	Note on output class
age-gender-recognition-retail-0013	attribute	image: [1xCxHxW]- shape [1x3x60x60]	"age_conv3", prob	age = age_conv3 *100
vehicle-attributes-recognition-barrier-0039	attribute	image: [1xCxHxW]- shape [1x3x72x72]	color, type	color classes [white, gray, yellow, red, green, blue, black], type classes [car, bus, truck, van]
emotion-recognition-retail-0003	attribute	image: [1xCxHxW]- shape [1x3x64x64]	prob	five emotions ('neutral', 'happy', 'sad', 'surprise', 'anger').
landmarks-regression-retail-0009	landmark	image: [1xCxHxW]- shape [1x3x48x48]	blob of shape [1,10]	5 landmarks normalized coordinates in the form (x0, y0, x1, y1, ..., x4, y4). Actual x value = normalized value* bounding box width, Actual y value = normalized value* bounding box height
facial-landmarks-35-adas-0002	landmark	image: [1xCxHxW]- shape [1x3x60x60]	blob of shape [1,70]	35 landmarks normalized coordinates in the form (x0, y0, x1, y1, ..., x34, y34). Actual x value = normalized value* bounding box width, Actual y value = normalized value* bounding box height
person-attributes-recognition-crossroad-0230	attribute	image: [1xCxHxW]- shape [1x3x160x80]	blob 453, blob 456, blob 459	blob 453 has 8 attributes: [is_male, has_bag, has_backpack, has_hat, has_longsleeves, has_longpants, has_longhair, has_coat_jacket], blob 456 - top color, blob 459 bottom color

Here, the input is the same: there are different dimensions for different models, but the outputs are different. For landmarks, the output can be either 5 points or 35 points of contour in the face. For a person attribute, the output can be a binary result for each of the eight attributes. Vehicle attributes can be color or type, whereas emotion attributes will result in a probability for each of the five classes.

Models for action recognition

The following table describes models for pose estimation and action recognition. Note the input and output for each model listed in the table as this will need to be entered in the Python code for inference:

Model	Category	Input	Output	Note on output class
head-pose-estimation-adas-0001	pose estimation	image: [1xCxHxW]- shape [1x3x60x60]	angle_y_fc, angle_p_fc, angle_r_fc	yw, pitch, roll
person-detection-action-recognition-0005	action recognition	image: [1xCxHxW]- shape [1x3x400x680]	box coordinates in SSD format, detection confidence, prior box in SSD format, action confidence (anchor 1, 2, 3, 4)	
person-detection-action-recognition-0006	action recognition	image: [1xCxHxW]- shape [1x400x680x3]	box coordinates in SSD format, detection confidence, action confidence (anchor 1, 2, 3, 4, 5)	
person-detection-action-recognition-teacher-0002	action recognition	image: [1xCxHxW]- shape [1x3x400x680]	box coordinates in SSD format, detection confidence, prior box in SSD format, action confidence (anchor 1, 2, 3, 4)	
person-detection-raisinghand-recognition-0001	action recognition	image: [1xCxHxW]- shape [1x3x400x680]	box coordinates in SSD format, detection confidence, prior box in SSD format, action confidence (anchor 1, 2, 3, 4)	

The preceding table shows that the input structure remains the same for all models, with just a change in image shape. The output for pose recognition shows three angles: yaw, roll, and pitch.

License plate, gaze, and person detection

Lastly, the following table shows multi-input blobs for a license plate, gaze estimation, and person detection:

Model	Category	Input	Output	Note on output class
license-plate-recognition-barrier-0001	license plate - 2 input	image: [1xCxHxW]- shape [1x3x24x94]; seq_ind - set this to [0, ,1, ,1 .. 1] 88 values	"decode", shape: [1, 88, 1, 1]	
person-detection-retail-0002	person detection 2 input	Two inputs: 1) image: [1xCxHxW]- shape [1x3x544x992] 2) image_info shape [1,6] [544, 992, 992/frame_width, 544/frame_height, 992/frame_width, 544/frame_height]	blob [1, 1, N, 7]	[image_id, label, conf, x_min, y_min, x_max, y_max]
gaze-estimation-adas-0002	gaze estimation 3 input	three input blobs: 1) left eye image - [1xCxHxW] shape [1,3,60,60], 2) right eye image - [1xCxHxW] shape [1,3,60,60] 3) head pose angle - [BXC] shape [1,3]	gaze direction vector	output not normalized

The following code outlines the principal components of the first two tables; that is, for the face detection, people detection, car detection, and landmark detection. Let's take a look:

1. Refer to the following GitHub link to extract the code: `https://github.com/PacktPublishing/Mastering-Computer-Vision-with-TensorFlow-2.0/blob/master/Chapter11/Chapetr11_openvino_fd_video.py`.

2. After importing OpenCV and the video capture, the model can be loaded using the following command. It will load the face detection model:

```
cvNet = cv2.dnn.readNet('face-detection-adas-0001.xml', 'face-
detection-adas-0001.bin')
cvNet.setPreferableTarget(cv2.dnn.DNN_TARGET_MYRIAD)
```

3. The following command can be used to load the landmark detection model. Any of the other models listed can be opened with this command. The only important thing to remember is that the models should reside in the same directory where you are executing the Python code from:

```
cvLmk = cv2.dnn.readNet('facial-landmarks-35-
adas-0002.xml','facial-landmarks-35-adas-0002.bin')
cvLmk.setPreferableTarget(cv2.dnn.DNN_TARGET_MYRIAD)
```

4. Next, we read the video frame using the following command and define the rows and columns of the frame:

```
  ret, frame = cam.read()
 rows = frame.shape[0]
  cols = frame.shape[1]
```

5. Next, we use OpenCV's `blobFromImage` function to extract a four-dimensional blob from the frame of the given size and depth. Note that the size of the blob should be equal to the input size specified in the corresponding model listed in the preceding table. For face detection, the blob input size is (672, 384), so the blob expression is written as follows:

```
  cvNet.setInput(cv2.dnn.blobFromImage(frame, size=(672, 384),
ddepth=cv2.CV_8U))
  cvOut = cvNet.forward()
```

For landmark detection, the blob input size is (60, 60), so the blob expression can be expressed as follows:

```
  cvLmk.setInput(cv2.dnn.blobFromImage(frame, size=(60, 60),
ddepth=cv2.CV_8U))
  lmkOut = cvLmk.forward()
```

Once the preceding steps have been completed, we can move on and draw the output for visualization. This is executed by two `for` statements with a nested loop:

- The first `for` statement finds the rectangular bounding box coordinate using `xmin, ymin, xmax, and ymax` and creates a rectangle using `cv2.rectangle` if `confidence > 0.5`.
- The second `for` statement draws 35 circles within the face bounding box, whose `x` and `y` coordinates are as follows:

```
x = xmin + landmark output (i) * (xmax-xmin)
y = ymin + landmark output (i) * (ymax-ymin)
```

Now, we can draw the circle using `cv2.circle`. This principle has been summarized in the following code, where we draw a facial landmark. Notice the two `for` statements that we discussed previously:

```
    # Draw detected faces on the frame.
  for detection in cvOut.reshape(-1,7):
      confidence = float(detection[2])
     xmin = int(detection[3] * cols)
      ymin = int(detection[4] * rows)
      xmax = int(detection[5] * cols)
      ymax = int(detection[6] * rows)
      if confidence > 0.5 :
        frame = cv2.rectangle(frame, (xmin, ymin), (xmax, ymax), color=(255,
255, 255),thickness = 4)
    for i in range(0, lmkOut.shape[1], 2):
      x, y = int(xmin+lmkOut[0][i]*(xmax-xmin)),
ymin+int(lmkOut[0][i+1]*(ymax-ymin))
      # Draw Facial key points
      cv2.circle(frame, (x, y), 1, color=(255,255,255),thickness = 4)
```

Although the code described here discusses facial landmark and face detection, the same Python code can be updated so that we can perform any of the other types of detection, such as license plate, human, bike, and so on. All you need to do is change the input by changing the set input and then adjust the `for` statement value. This example of face key point detection is a complicated example that involves both face and landmark detection – that is why two `for` loop statements are used. For example, in license plate detection, you just need to use one `for` loop statement.

Now, let's learn about inference using OpenVINO.

Model conversion and inference using OpenVINO

This section discusses how to use a pre-trained model or a custom trained model to make inference using OpenVINO. Inference is the process of using a model to perform object detection or classification and is divided into three steps:

1. Running inference using a pre-trained model from ncappzoo.
2. Converting the custom model into IR format for inference.
3. Summary of all the steps involved in a flowchart.

These steps will be discussed in detail in the following subsections.

Running inference in a Terminal using ncappzoo

As we mentioned previously, OpenVINO's toolkit installation for Raspberry Pi is different to how it's done on a regular PC. The installation for Raspberry Pi does not include the Model Optimizer. **Neural Compute Application Zoo (ncpappzoo)** is an open source repository. Let's take a look at how to use ncappzoo:

1. To use ncappzoo, clone the open source version of OpenVINO and the **Deep Learning Development Toolkit** (**DLDT**) and change the PYTHONPATH. By doing this, the model optimizer will be installed in the Raspberry Pi. The steps are shown in the following code block:

```
$cd ~
$git clone https://github.com/opencv/dldt.git
$ dldt/model-optimizer
$pip3 install -r requirements_tf.txt
$pip3 install -r requirements_caffe.txt
$export PATH=~/dldt/model-optimizer:$PATH
$export PYTHONPATH=~/dldt/model-optmizer:$PYTHONPATH
```

2. Now, clone the `repo` with the following command:

```
$git clone https://github.com/movidius/ncappzoo.git
```

3. Go to `/ncappzoo/apps/`, find the relevant `app` folder directory, and execute the following command:

```
$make run
```

This will open up a window where we can display inference on the image.

Converting the pre-trained model for inference

This section describes the steps involved in converting a custom TensorFlow model created using the TensorFlow Keras object classification model we developed in `Chapter 6`, *Visual Search Using Transfer Learning*, or using a model created using the TensorFlow Object Detection API, as we did in the previous chapter. The steps described in the previous section will work if you already plan on using a pre-trained optimized model from Intel Open Source Technology Center. In the next section, we'll describe how to perform conversion using two types of TensorFlow models.

Converting from a TensorFlow model developed using Keras

This section describes how to convert a TensorFlow model into OpenVINO IR format. For more information, please refer to the following link: `https://docs.openvinotoolkit.org/latest/_docs_MO_DG_prepare_model_convert_model_Convert_Model_From_TensorFlow.html`.

The steps can be summarized as follows:

1. **Configure the model optimizer**. As described at the very beginning of this chapter, any model that's being deployed for edge devices must be optimized, which involves removing any unnecessary components without sacrificing accuracy. The following code performs this task globally:

```
<INSTALL_DIR>/deployment_tools/model_optimizer/install_prerequisite
s directory and run: $install_prerequisites.sh
```

2. **Convert into a frozen model.** Note that the models we developed in `Chapter 6`, *Visual Search Using Transfer Learning*, were not frozen.
3. **Convert the frozen TensorFlow model into IR form**. The **intermediate representation** (**IR**) of the model is read by the inference engine. The IR is a OpenVINO-specific graph representation. The output of the IR representation is an `xml` file and a `bin` file, which we are already familiar with. The conversion is done by the `mo.py` tool, as shown in the following code:

```
Go to the <INSTALL_DIR>/deployment_tools/model_optimizer
directoryin the Terminal and execute
$python3 mo_tf.py --input_model <INPUT_MODEL>.pb
```

It is important that you specify the following parameters during frozen model development and understand them well, as the `mo.py` tool can sometimes produce an error if it can't find it in the frozen model:

- `input_model`: The name of the pre-trained model being used
- `input_shape`: For example, [1, 300,300,3]

Converting a TensorFlow model developed using the TensorFlow Object Detection API

This section describes how to convert a frozen graph created using the TensorFlow Object Detection API. If the model is developed using the TensorFlow Object Detection API, then the detailed process is different to what we covered in the previous section. More information can be found at `https://docs.openvinotoolkit.org/latest/_docs_MO_DG_prepare_model_convert_model_tf_specific_Convert_Object_Detection_API_Models.html`.

The model that we obtained in `Chapter 10`, *Object Detection Using R-CNN, SSD, and R-FCN*, using the TensorFlow Object Detection API is already frozen. Follow these steps to convert it:

1. Before converting, refer to the following link to configure the model optimizer: `https://docs.openvinotoolkit.org/latest/_docs_MO_DG_prepare_model_Config_Model_Optimizer.html`.
2. Now, we are ready for conversion. Prepare three files, as follows:
    - The frozen inference graph for the model: This is a file with a `.pb` extension that's generated by training the model (R-CNN, SSD, or R-FCN) with your custom image. In this example, it is `frozen_inference_graph_fasterRCNN.pb`.
    - The configuration `json` file: This is the corresponding `json` file that describes the custom attributes, nodes, ports, endpoints, and starting points of your frozen TensorFlow graph.
    - The config file used to generate the model: This is the same file that you used to generate the model using the TensorFlow Object Detection API in `Chapter 10`, *Object Detection Using R-CNN, SSD, and R-FCN*. For example, for R-CNN, we used `faster_rcnn_inception_v2_pets.config`.

After you've completed the previous steps, execute the following code in the Terminal:

```
$python3 mo_tf.py --input_model frozen_inference_graph_fasterRCNN.pb --
transformations_config faster_rcnn_support_api_v1.14.json --
tensorflow_object_detection_api_pipeline_config
faster_rcnn_inception_v2_pets.config
```

Here, you need to replace the file with `.pb` extension with your specific model file name with `.pb` extension. The result of the conversion will be an `xml` and a `bin` file.

Once we have the `xml` and `bin` files, we can test the model using the Python file and the instructions described in the *Advanced inference* section.

If you have issue during tarining you can use OpenVINO forum shown in linbke below to see answers for similar issues or can post your questions `https://software.intel.com/en-us/forums/intel-distribution-of-openvino-toolkit`

Summary of the OpenVINO Model inference process

The entire model inference process described previously can be represented with a flow chart:

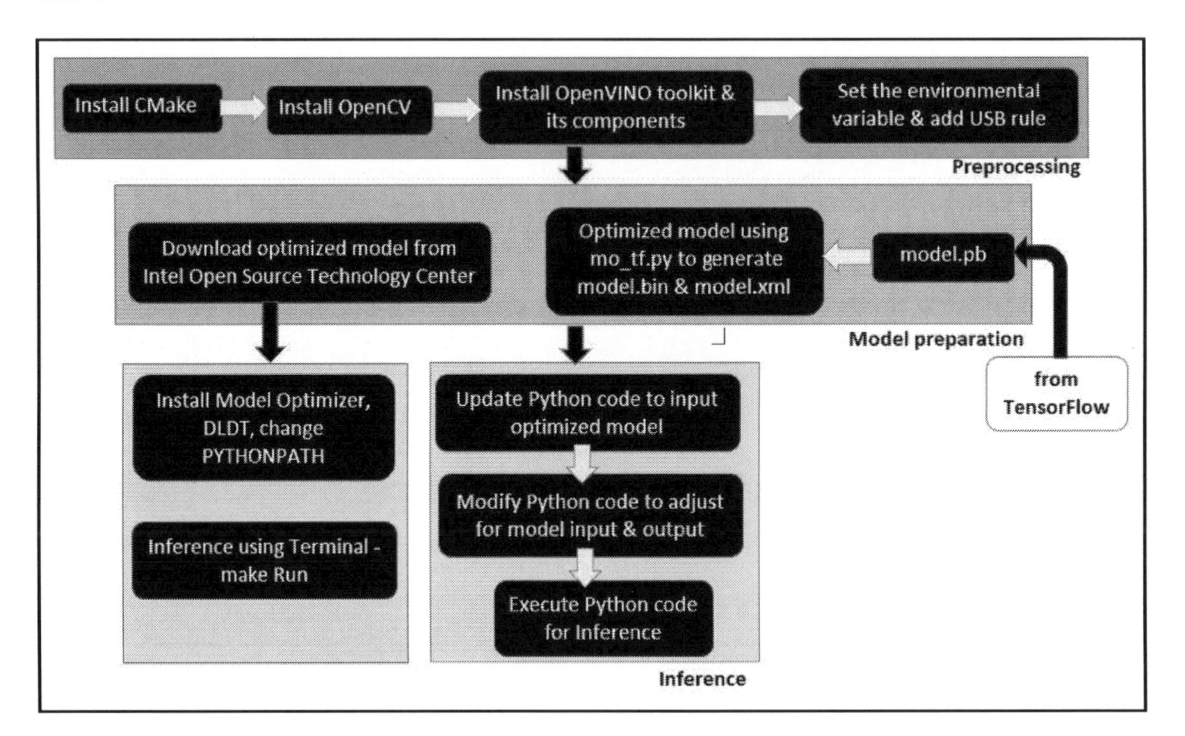

The preceding diagram indicates that the process can be divided into three key segments:

1. **Preprocessing step**: Here, we install OpenCV and set the environmental variable.
2. **Model preparation**: Here, we convert the model into the optimized model format.

3. **Inference**: This can be divided into two independent methods – by performing inference over the Terminal by going to the appropriate director and executing `make run` or performing inference using the Python code. I found that on an Intel PC, all these steps are easy to execute. However, in a Raspberry Pi environment, working in the Terminal using the `make Run` command causes different types of errors; for example, sometimes, it cannot find the `.bin` or `.xml` file. Other times, the environmental variable isn't initialized or the `CMakeLists.txt` file couldn't be found. Executing the Python code provided does not create any of those issues in Raspberry Pi. This also gives us a better understanding of the computer vision environment as all we are doing is getting the model, understanding the input and output, and then generating some code so that we can display our results.

Before proceeding to the next section let's summarize the model optimization techniques we learned so far:
1) Batch Normalization operation fused with convolution operations - OpenVINO uses this
2) Move convolution with stride greater than 1 with filter size 1 to upper convolution layers. Add pooling layer to align input shape - OpenVINO uses this
3) Replace large filter by two small filters, example replace 3 x 3 x 3 with #32 with 3 x 3 x 1 with #3 and 1 x 1 x 3 with #32 - MobileNet uses this.

Application of TensorFlow Lite

TensorFlow Lite is the TensorFlow deep learning framework for inference on edge devices. Similar to OpenVINO, TensorFlow Lite has built-in pre-trained deep learning modules. Alternatively, an existing model can be converted into TensorFlow Lite format for on-device inference. Currently, TensorFlow Lite provides inference support for PCs with a built-in or external camera, Android devices, iOS devices, Raspberry Pis, and tiny microcontrollers. Visit `https://www.tensorflow.org/lite` for details on TensorFlow Lite.

The TensorFlow Lite converter takes a TensorFlow model and generates a `FlatBuffer tflite` file. A `FlatBuffer` file is an efficient cross-platform library that can be used to access binary serialized data without the need for parsing. Serialized data is usually a text string. Binary serialized data is binary data written in string format. For details on FlatBuffer, please refer to the following link: `https://google.github.io/flatbuffers/`.

The TensorFlow output model can be of these types:

- **SavedModel format**: A saved model is executed by `tf.saved_model` and the output is `saved_model.pb`. It is a complete TensorFlow format that includes learned weights and a graph structure.
- **tf.keras models format**: The `tf.kears` models are `tf.keras.model.compile` files, which we introduced in `Chapter 4`, *Deep Learning on Images*, and `Chapter 6`, *Visual Search Using Transfer Learning*.
- **Concrete functions**: A TensorFlow graph with a single input and output.

Converting a TensorFlow model into tflite format

This section will describe how to convert a TensorFlow model into a `tflite` format. If we don't do this, the model we've developed can be used for inference in your local PC, but can't be deployed to edge devices for real-time inference. Three methods will be described regarding this conversion:

- The Python API, which is used in local PCs for `tflite` conversion
- Google Colab using `tflite` conversion
- Google Colab using `toco`

Since this is an object detection conversion, where our model was developed based on the TensorFlow object detection API, we will use the `toco` method in Google Colab.

Python API

The Python API makes it easy for us to use the TensorFlow Lite converter. In this section, we will describe the Python API that uses the tflite converter. For more information, please refer to the following link: `https://www.tensorflow.org/lite/convert/python_api`.

Three methods are suggested, depending on the type of converter you have – a saved model, a Keras model, or concrete functions. The following code shows how to call `tf.lite.TFLiteConverter` from the Python API to convert each of the three models (saved model, Keras model, or concrete functions):

```
$import tensorflow as tf
$converter = tf.lite.TFLiteConverter.from_saved_model(export_dir)
$converter = tf.lite.TFLiteConverter.from_keras_model(model)
$converter =
tf.lite.TFLiteConverter.from_concrete_functions([concrete_func])
tflite_model = converter.convert()
```

Next, we will learn how to convert the trained model we developed in `Chapter 10`, *Object Detection Using R-CNN, SSD, and R-FCN*, using the TensorFlow Object Detection API in Google Colab using two different methods – `tflite_convert` and `toco`.

TensorFlow Object Detection API – tflite_convert

In the following code, we are defining the location of the frozen model `.pb` file and the corresponding `tflite` file. Then, we're resizing the input color image to (300,300) in shape for each of the three RGB axes and converting the image into a normalized tensor, which then becomes the input array for the conversion. There are four output arrays, all of which are defined as follows:

- `TFLite_Detection_PostProcess`—detection boxes
- `TFLite_Detection_PostProcess:1`—detection classes
- `TFLite_Detection_PostProcess:2`—detection scores
- `TFLite_Detection_PostProcess:3`—number of detections

```
!tflite_convert \
--graph_def_file=/content/models/research/fine_tuned_model/tflite_graph.pb
\
--output_file=/content/models/research/fine_tuned_model/burgerfries.tflite
\
--output_format=TFLITE \
--input_shapes=1,300,300,3 \
--input_arrays=normalized_input_image_tensor \
--output_arrays=
'TFLite_Detection_PostProcess','TFLite_Detection_PostProcess:1','TFLite_Det
ection_PostProcess:2','TFLite_Detection_PostProcess:3' \
--change_concat_input_ranges=false \
--allow_custom_ops
```

TensorFlow Object Detection API – toco

TOCO stands for TensorFlow Optimized Converter. For a detailed understanding of toco, please visit the following GitHub page: `https://github.com/tensorflow/tensorflow/tree/master/tensorflow/lite/toco`.

The following code describes how to convert a TensorFlow model using toco. The first part of the code is the same as what we did previously, except we're using `toco` instead of `tflite`. The later part uses a quantized inference type. Quantization is a process that's used to reduce model size while improving hardware acceleration latency. There are different methods of quantization, as described at `https://www.tensorflow.org/lite/performance/post_training_quantization`.

In this case, we are using full integer quantization. No dequantization is being used, but the mean value and standard deviation value are used to determine the fixed-point multiplier in the inference code:

```
"!toco \\\n",
 "--
graph_def_file=\"/content/models/research/fine_tuned_model/tflite_graph.pb\
" \\\n",
 "--
output_file=\"/content/models/research/fine_tuned_model/burgerfries_toco.tf
lite\" \\\n",
 "--input_shapes=1,300,300,3 \\\n",
 "--input_arrays=normalized_input_image_tensor \\\n",
 "--
output_arrays='TFLite_Detection_PostProcess','TFLite_Detection_PostProcess:
1','TFLite_Detection_PostProcess:2','TFLite_Detection_PostProcess:3' \\\n",
 "--inference_type=QUANTIZED_UINT8 \\\n",
 "--mean_values=128 \\\n",
 "--std_dev_values=128 \\\n",
 "--change_concat_input_ranges=false \\\n",
 "--allow_custom_ops"
```

Details of the Google Colab notebook for training and conversion can be found at the following GitHub link: `https://github.com/PacktPublishing/Mastering-Computer-Vision-with-TensorFlow-2.0/blob/master/Chapter11/Chapter11_Tensorflow_Training_a_Object_Detector_GoogleColab_tflite_toco.ipynb`.

Note that, between the two models, we have used toco. The reason for this is that the converted model, when using tflite, results in no bounding box detection on Android phones.

TensorFlow models can be represented as saved models or Keras models. The following code shows how to save the model as a saved model or a Keras model:

- **Saved model**: A saved model includes the TensorFlow weights and checkpoints. It is initiated by the `model.save` function:

```
tf.saved_model.save(pretrained_model, "/tmp/mobilenet/1/")
tf.saved_model.save(obj, export_dir, signatures=None, options=None)
```

- **Keras model**: The following code describes how to compile a Keras model and prepare it for training using the `history.fit` command. Note that we performed coding exercises with this in `Chapter 4`, *Deep Learning on Images*, and `Chapter 6`, *Visual Search Using Transfer Learning*:

```
model.compile(loss='sparse_categorical_crossentropy',
optimizer=keras.optimizers.RMSprop())
history = model.fit(x_train, y_train, batch_size=64, epochs=20)
model.save('path_to_my_model.h5')
```

Model optimization

Model optimization, also known as quantization, can be performed with post-training quantization to improve CPU/GPU performance, without sacrificing accuracy. The optimization process can be performed using the following:

- Floating point to 8-bit precision (optimize for size)
- Full integer quantization using integer input and output for a microcontroller
- A bit of both – dynamically quantize with 8 bits but any outputs are stored in floating point form
- Pruning is another dynamic optimization method to eliminate the low value weights from the neural network during training. It can be initiated by following lines of code:

```
from tensorflow_model_optimization.sparsity import keras as
sparsity
pruning_params = {
    'pruning_schedule':
sparsity.PolynomialDecay(initial_sparsity=0.50,
                                final_sparsity=0.90,
                                begin_step=end_step/2,
                                end_step=end_step,
                                frequency=100)
}

l = tf.keras.layers
sparsity.prune_low_magnitude(l.Conv2D(64, (3, 3),
activation='relu'),**pruning_params
```

Please refer to the TensorFlow site for details: `https://www.tensorflow.org/lite/performance/post_training_quantization`.

Note that model optimization using Google Colab for object detection models using toco was discussed in the previous section.

In the following code, we are optimizing the saved model for size, which reduces the final output model to 1/3rd or 1/4th of its original size:

```
import tensorflow as tf
converter =
tf.lite.TFLiteConverter.from_saved_model(saved_model_dir)converter.optimiza
tions = [tf.lite.Optimize.OPTIMIZE_FOR_SIZE]
tflite_quant_model = converter.convert()
```

The following code describes full integer quantization, as well as optimization for size:

```
import tensorflow as tf
converter = tf.lite.TFLiteConverter.from_saved_model(saved_model_dir)
converter.target_spec.supported_ops = [tf.lite.OpsSet.TFLITE_BUILTINS_INT8]
converter.inference_input_type = tf.uint8
converter.inference_output_type = tf.uint8

converter.optimizations = [tf.lite.Optimize.OPTIMIZE_FOR_SIZE]
tflite_quant_model = converter.convert()
```

Object detection on Android phones using TensorFlow Lite

The steps required to deploy the TensorFlow lite converted model will be described in this section. Alternatively, you can follow the instructions at `https://github.com/tensorflow/examples/tree/master/lite/examples/image_classification/android` to build a sample app. A detailed flow chart regarding object detection on Android phones is as follows:

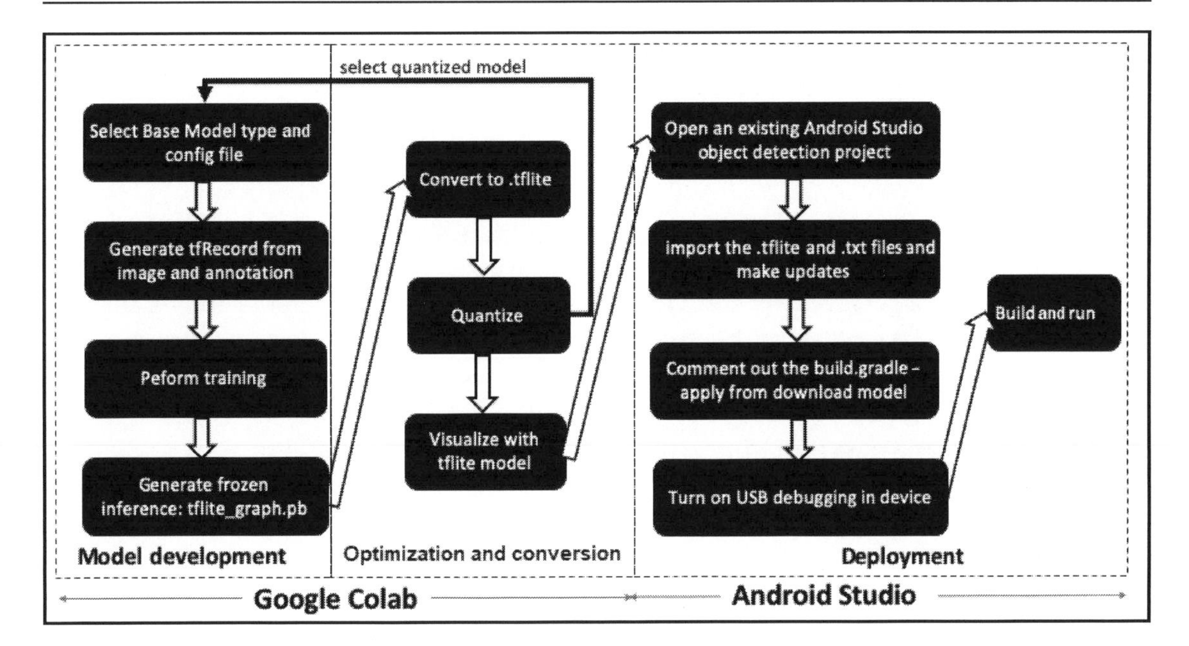

We need two files:

- The TensorFlow Lite converted file in `.tflite` form
- An updated labelmap `.txt` file showing the class

The `.tflite` file comes directly from Google Colab if we export it, as explained in the *TensorFlow Object Detection API – toco* section. The `lablemap.txt` file comes from the `label_map.pbtxt` file by listing only the names of the class.

The sample files can be found at the following GitHub page: `https://github.com/PacktPublishing/Mastering-Computer-Vision-with-TensorFlow-2.0/blob/master/burgerfries_toco.tflite`.

The steps for taking a `tflite` model and generating inference in an Android phone are as follows:

1. In the burger and fries example, the `.txt` file will have one column and two rows, as follows:

```
burger
fries
```

2. Place both of those files in your PC in the same directory. Open Android Studio. If you have never used Android Studio before, you will have to download it from `https://developer.android.com/studio`. Follow the download instructions given at the site.
3. After downloading it, on Mac or Windows, double-click to open it. For Linux, you'll have to go to a Terminal and navigate to the `android-studio/bin` directory and type `./studio.h`.
4. Download some sample examples by typing the following in the Terminal: `git clone https://github.com/tensorflow/examples`.
5. Open Android Studio and open an existing project, setting the folder to `examples/lite/examples/object_detection/android`.
6. Within the Android Studio project, go to the app and then go to **assets**, as shown in the following screenshot:

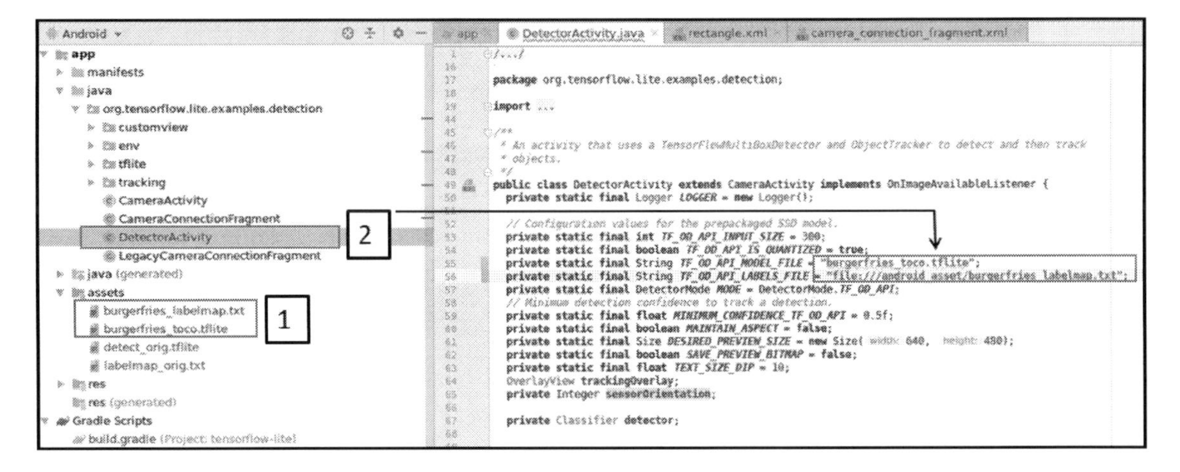

7. Right-click on **assets** and select **Show in Files** from the menu list. Drag and drop the `.tflite` and `.txt` files we created in the very first step into the **assets** directory. Close the folder and go back to **Android Studio**.
8. Double-click on the `.txt` file to open it and add a new line at the top. Fill it with `???`. So, the `.txt` file will have three lines for the two classes:

```
???
Burger
fries
```

9. Select **Java**, then **Tracking**, and double-click on **DetectorActivity**. Change the names of the `.tflite` and `.txt` files to their actual names, as shown in the following screenshot. Then, click on **build gradle**:

Note that for the `.txt` file, keep the path, that is, `file:///android_asset/burgerfries_labelmap.txt`. Later, we will mention that if the `.tflite` file is not generated using `toco`, then keeping the previous path will cause the app to crash. To prevent a crash, you can just keep the filename (for example, `burgerfries_labelmap.txt`). However, note that this doesn't create a bounding box for the detected image.

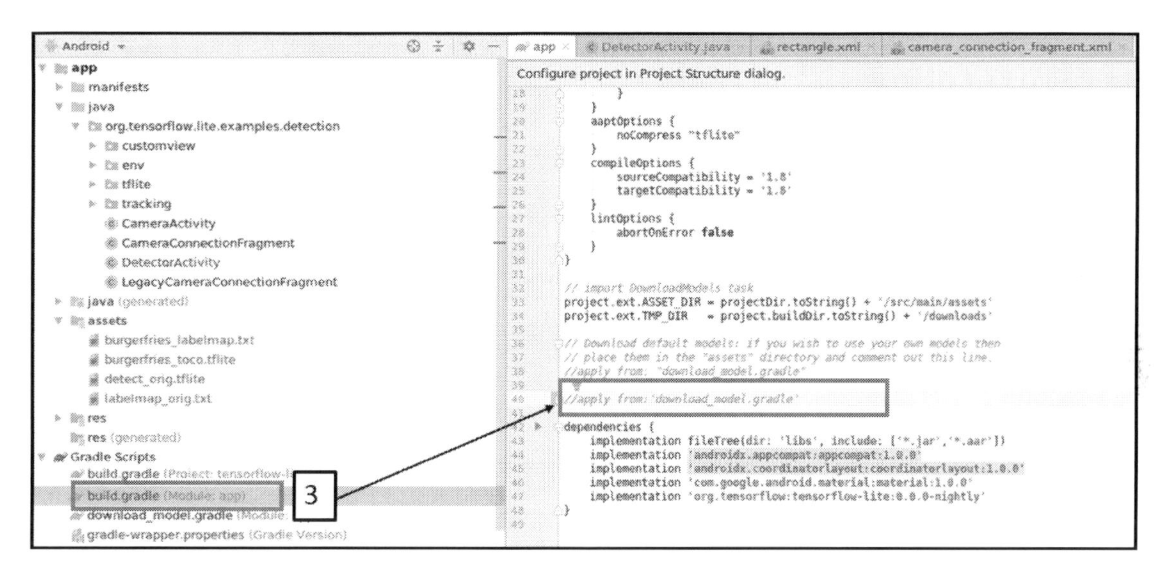

10. Comment out `///apply from download_model.gradle`. Verify that the dependencies appear, as shown in the preceding screenshot.
11. Now, connect your Android device to your PC using a USB cable. Go to your device and, under settings, click on **Developer options** to make sure it is on. Then, turn on USB debugging. For many Android phones, this option comes up by itself.

12. Click on **Build** at the top and then **Make Project**. After Android Studio has finished compiling (look at the bottom of the screen to see if all activities have been completed), click on **Run** and then **Run app**. The app will be downloaded to your device. An option box will appear on your device; select `ok` to be able to run the app. The following is an image of the app working:

As we can see, the phone is able to clearly detect a real picture of both burgers and fries with very high accuracy. This concludes the Android app deployment exercise.

Object detection on Raspberry Pi using TensorFlow Lite

The Python `quickstart` package listed under TensorFlow Lite (`https://www.tensorflow.org/lite/guide/python`) describes how to install the TensorFlow Lite package for Raspberry Pi. However, there are several notable exceptions. Due to this, we have listed the entire process here:

1. First and foremost, install the TensorFlow Lite interpreter. Raspberry Pi has ARM7 and Python3.7 installed, so run the following two commands in the Terminal:

```
$sudo su
$pip3 install tflite_runtime-1.14.0-cp37-cp37m-linux_armv7l.whl
```

2. As per the official TensorFlow Lite documentation, some changes need to be made in the `label_image.py` file (`https://github.com/tensorflow/tensorflow/tree/master/tensorflow/lite/examples/python`):

```
$import tflite_runtime.interpreter as tflite,
$interpreter = tf.lite.Interpreter(model_path=args.model_file)
```

Note that when those changes are made in Raspberry Pi 4 and the code is executed in the Terminal by typing `python3 label_image.py`, an error will occur, stating that Python couldn't find the TensorFlow Lite interpreter, even though it has been installed. The preceding steps were repeated for Raspberry Pi 3 and no errors occurred.

3. Next, follow the steps provided at the following link to install the TensorFlow Lite directory and files: `https://github.com/tensorflow/examples.git`.
4. If everything goes well, you should have a directory in the Raspberry Pi called `pi/examples/lite/examples`. Within this folder, you should have directories such as `image_classification`, `object_detection`, `image_segmentation`, `posenet`, `style_transfer`, and so on.
5. Next, we will perform two examples on Raspberry Pi – one for image classification and another for object detection.

Image classification

Now let's perform the following steps for image classification:

1. Go to the `image_classification` directory, that is, `pi/examples/lite/examples/image_classification/raspberry_pi`, using the File Manager. You will see a file named `classify_picamera.py`. Now, go to `https://www.tensorflow.org/lite/guide/hosted_models` and download the object detection models and `label` files folder named `mobilenet_v2_1.0_224.tflite` and the `labels_mobilenet_v2_1.0_224.txt` file. Copy those files into `pi/examples/lite/examples/image_classification/raspberry_pi`.

2. Next, go to the directory using the Terminal using `pi/examples/lite/examples/image_classification/raspberry_pi` and execute the following command:

   ```
   $Python3 classify_picamera.py –model mobilenet_v2_1.0_224.tflite
   –labels labels_ mobilenet_v2_1.0_224.txt
   ```

3. You should see the Raspberry Pi camera module light up and start classifying images.

Object detection

After you've installed TensorFlow lite on Raspberry Pi, we can now perform object detection. Follow these steps:

1. Go to the object detection directory, that is, `pi/examples/lite/examples/object_detection/raspberry_pi`, using the File Manager. You will see a file called `detect_picamera.py`.
2. Now, go to `https://www.tensorflow.org/lite/guide/hosted_models` and download the object detection models and label files folder named as `coco_ssd_mobilenet_v1_1.0_quant_2018_06_29`. Within this folder, you will see two files: `detect.tflite` and `labelmap.txt`.
3. Copy those files into `pi/examples/lite/examples/object_detection/raspberry_pi`.
4. Next, go to the object detection directory using a Terminal using `pi/examples/lite/examples/object_detection/raspberry_pi` and execute the following command:

   ```
   $Python3 detect_picamera.py –model detect.tflite –labels
   labelmap.txt
   ```

   Now, you should see the Raspberry Pi camera module light up and start showing bounding boxes around the images.

5. Next, copy the `burgerfries.tflite` and `labelmap` files into the folder. Then, change the Python path shown in the preceding command line to reflect your new filename and execute it. The following image is the image being used for `object_detection`:

There are several things to note here:

- I used a wide-angle camera in the Raspberry Pi and was unable to detect the food items correctly.
- I transferred to a regular Raspberry Pi camera and was able to detect what can be seen in the preceding image.
- The detection shown here is not as good as it is when using a cell phone and there is a lag.

This example clearly shows how the same model behaves differently on different devices.

In the TensorFlow Development Summit 2020, TensorFlow engineers announced they would make a significant improvement to latency – 55 ms to 37 ms for floating point CPU execution, 36 ms to 13 ms for quantized fixed-point CPU execution, 20 ms to 5 ms for OpenCL Float 16 GPU execution, and 2 ms for quantized fixed point Edge TPU execution. A test with a Raspberry Pi that just has CPU was performed before this change was made. So, due to the preceding changes, you should see an improvement in performance on Raspberry Pi. TF Lite 2.3 will result in further improvements.

Object detection on iPhone using TensorFlow Lite and Create ML

So far, we have learned how to convert a TensorFlow model into tflite format and performed inference on an Android phone and Raspberry Pi. In this section, we will use the tflite model and perform inference on an iPhone. Object detection on iPhone or iPad can follow two different paths, as discussed in the following subsections.

TensorFlow Lite conversion model for iPhone

In this section, we will describe how to use a tflite model on iPhone for object detection. For details, please refer to the steps outlined on the following GitHub page: `https://github.com/tensorflow/examples/tree/master/lite/examples/image_classification/ios`.

Essentially, the procedure can be broken down into the following steps:

1. This process should be completed on macOS with the latest version of Xcode installed. You should also have an Apple Developer certificate.
2. In the Terminal, run Xcode's command-line tools (`run xcode-select --install`). Note that you need to complete this step, even if you have Xcode installed already.
3. Type `git clone https://github.com/tensorflow/examples.git` into the Terminal.
4. Install `cocoapods` by typing `$sudo gem install cocoapods` into the Terminal.
5. Call the final directory where the TensorFlow examples will be installed `examples-master` or `examples`. Change the following folder address accordingly.
6. In the Terminal, type the following command:

```
$cd examples-master/lite/examples/object_detection/ios
$pod install
```

7. The preceding process will perform three main tasks:
    - Install TensorFlow Lite in Xcode
    - Create a file called `ObjectDetection.xcworkspace` in your folder
    - Launch Xcode automatically and open the `ObjectDetection` file

The following screenshot shows the comments that you'll see in your Terminal during the pod installation process:

```
$ cd examples-master/lite/examples/object_detection/ios
$ pod install
Analyzing dependencies
Adding spec repo `trunk` with CDN `https://cdn.cocoapods.org/`

CocoaPods 1.9.0.beta.2 is available.
To update use: `sudo gem install cocoapods --pre`
[!] This is a test version we'd love you to try.

For more information, see https://blog.cocoapods.org and the CHANGELOG for this version at https:
//github.com/CocoaPods/CocoaPods/releases/tag/1.9.0.beta.2

Downloading dependencies
Installing TensorFlowLiteC (2.1.0)
Installing TensorFlowLiteSwift (2.1.0)
Generating Pods project
Integrating client project

[!] Please close any current Xcode sessions and use `ObjectDetection.xcworkspace` for this projec
t from now on.
Pod installation complete! There is 1 dependency from the Podfile and 2 total pods installed.
```

8. In the signing section of Xcode, select your development team.
9. Make the following changes to the app:

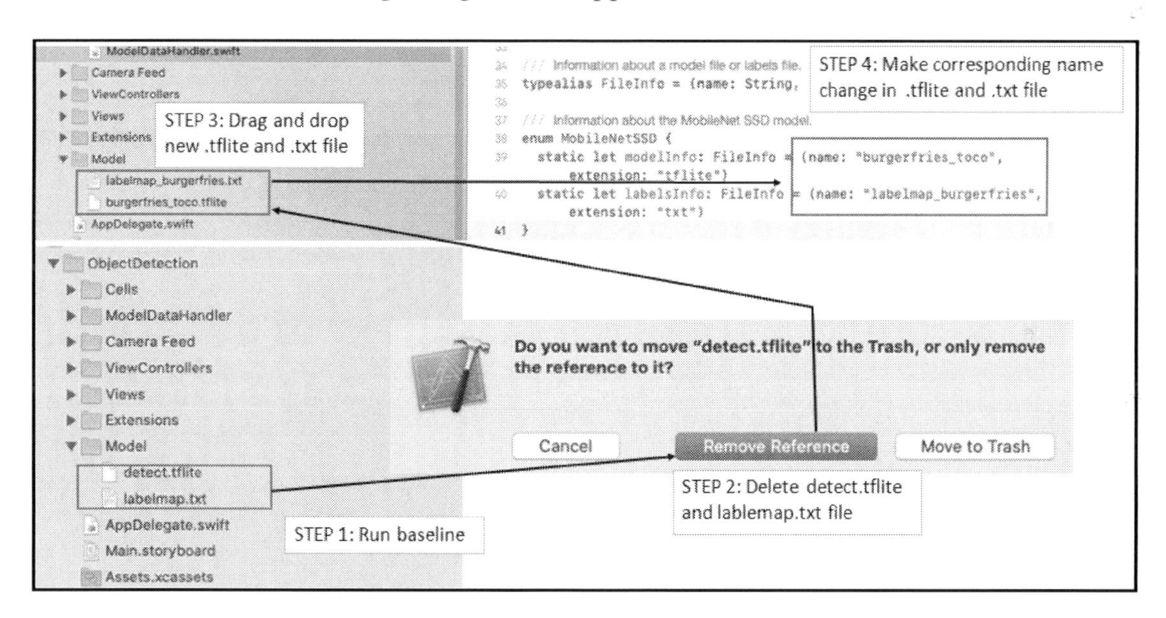

The changes described in the preceding screenshot explain how to replace the baseline `detect.tflite` and `labelmap.txt` files with your changes. Note that if you do not make any changes and run Xcode by connecting your phone to macOS, then it will show a general detector, as shown in the following image:

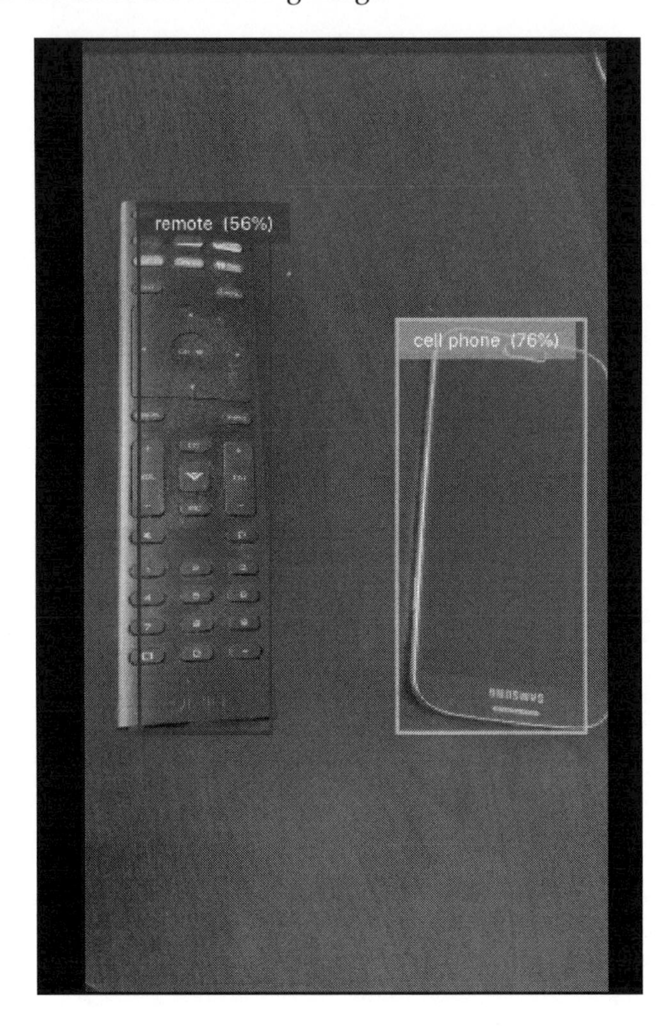

To make your specific model change, delete the old model by right-clicking it and then install the new model by dragging and dropping. Make the necessary changes to the filename inside the code, as shown in *Step 4*. The following screenshot shows the output you will see:

The preceding screenshot clearly shows very good detection, even though the image has been rotated.

Core ML

Core ML is Apple's machine learning framework, which integrates neural network models from various sources such as TensorFlow, converts them if necessary, and then optimizes the GPU/CPU performance for on-device training and inference, all while minimizing app size and power usage. Core ML 3, which was introduced in WWDC 2019, updates the neural network model for specific user data on the device, thus eliminating device-to-cloud interaction and maximizing user privacy. For more information, visit `https://developer.apple.com/machine-learning/core-ml`. Core ML itself builds on top of low-level primitives such as Accelerate and BNNS, as well as Metal Performance Shaders. All of the Core ML models have an `.mlmodel` extension.

The core part of Core ML is Create ML, which is an Apple machine learning framework for image classification and object detection. The system is similar to TensorFlow but far easier to use to generate a model with zero coding. On macOS, open Xcode and bring in `.mlmodel`, as shown in the following screenshot:

```
ViewController.swift
VisionObjectRec...Controller.swift    M
Main.storyboard
Assets.xcassets
LaunchScreen.storyboard
burger_fries_detector.mlmodel         A

20  func setupVision() -> NSError? {
21      // Setup Vision parts
22      let error: NSError! = nil
23
24      guard let modelURL = Bundle.main.url(forResource: "burger_fries_detector",
            withExtension: "mlmodelc") else {
25          return NSError(domain: "VisionObjectRecognitionViewController", code: -1,
                userInfo: [NSLocalizedDescriptionKey: "Model file is missing"])
```

Now, the whole model development process in Create ML involves just three steps:

1. Preparing the data – that is, the input file
2. Dragging the data into Core ML and clicking **train**
3. Saving the model (note that I couldn't find a way to save to desktop, so I emailed it to myself and saved the file) and analyzing the data

The following screenshot shows the training process in Create ML:

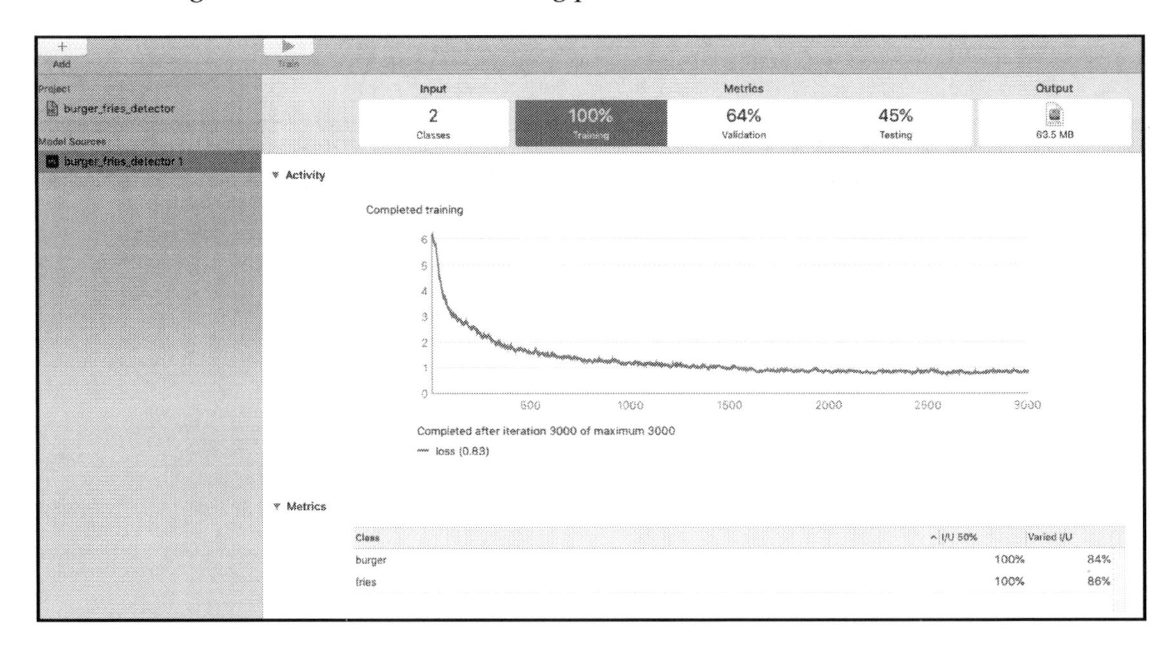

Some key points to note regarding the preceding screenshot are as follows:

- The final training loss is 0.83, which indicates very good results – any value below 1 should indicate good detection. Note that this was obtained using only 68 images, indicating that we don't need a lot of images to develop a good neural network model.
- Note how easy it is to develop a model using Create ML compared to TensorFlow – absolutely zero coding, no conversion needed, and no need to go to a separate site to see the graph. Everything is compact and easy to use.

Once you've developed the model, port it to the following vision framework written in Swift. It will detect an object with bounding boxes: `https://developer.apple.com/documentation/vision/recognizing_objects_in_live_capture`.

The following are some items to note regarding the app development:

- You must have an Apple developer account and team to sign in to Xcode.
- You need to delete the existing model and drag the latest model into Xcode, as shown on the left of the following screenshot:

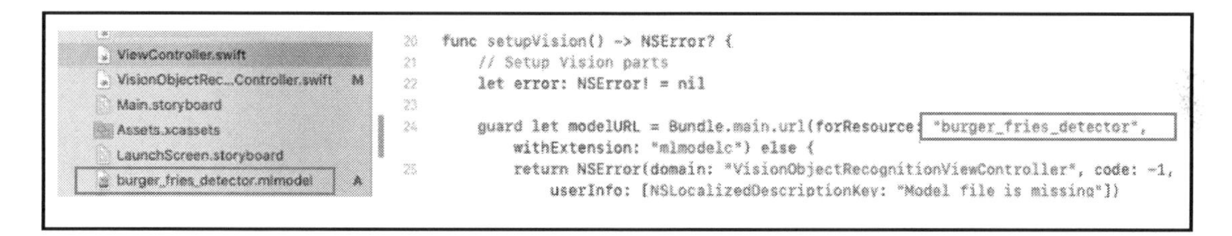

- After doing this, go to `ViewController.swift` and rename the default model name to your model name, as shown on the right of the preceding image. Finally, build the model and run it on your iPhone.

The following screenshot shows the model output. It shows a comparison of the detection provided by the model we developed using Create ML versus the one we developed using TensorFlow and converted into `.tflite` form:

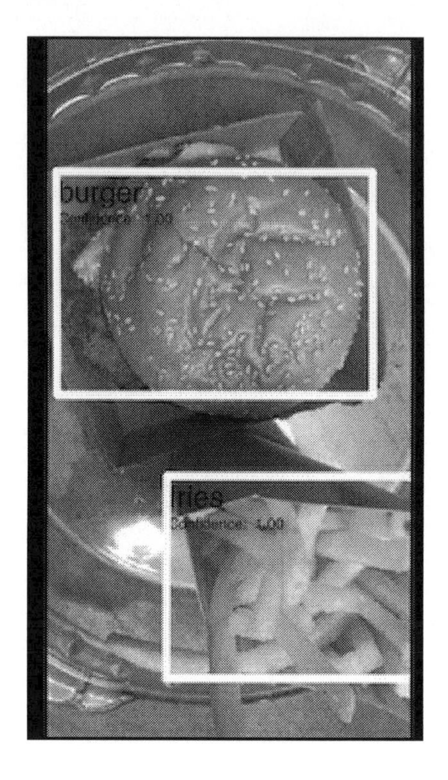

Converting a TensorFlow model into Core ML format

The converter only converts part of the TensorFlow model. The full MobileNet-SSD TF model contains four subgraphs: `Preprocessor`, `FeatureExtractor`, `MultipleGridAnchorGenerator`, and `Postprocessor`. The Core ML tool only converts the`FeatureExtractor` subgraph from the model; the other tasks have to be converted by the developer on their own.

A summary of various annotation methods

Image annotation is a core part of object detection or segmentation. This part is the most tedious in terms of manual work in neural network development. Previously, we described three tools that are used for annotation: `LebelImg`, `VGG Image Annotator` and `RectLabel`. However, there are many other tools available, such as Supervisely, and Labelbox. Some of these tools perform semi-automatic annotations. The biggest challenge is creating 100,000 annotations and doing so correctly within a pixel level accuracy. If the annotation is incorrect, then the model that's developed will not be correct, and finding an incorrect annotation in 100,000 images is like finding a needle in a haystack. For large-scale project work, the annotation workflow can be divided into two categories:

- Outsource labeling work to a third party
- Automated or semi-automated labeling

In the next section, we will discuss both approaches.

Outsource labeling work to a third party

Many businesses perform labeling work as one of their core business model. Each of the cloud service providers collaborates with human labelers to perform accurate image labeling services for neural network development work. The following is some information regarding where to find third-party data labeling services. Please note that this list is not comprehensive, so please do your own research outside this list to find a data labeling service that suits your needs:

- Google Cloud – data labeling. For details, please go to `https://cloud.google.com/ai-platform/data-labeling/docs`.
- Amazon Sagemaker Ground Truth – data labeling using Amazon Mechanical Turk. For details, please go to `https://aws.amazon.com/sagemaker/groundtruth`.
- Hive AI data labeling service. For details, please go to `https://thehive.ai`.
- Cloud Factory data labeling service. For details, please go to `https://www.cloudfactory.com`.

The cost of data labeling services can get expensive.

Automated or semi-automated labeling

In this section, we will discuss a completely free automated annotation tool that should reduce the degree of human labeling. This is Intel's **Computer Vision Annotation Tool (CVAT)** tool, which is very promising and performs complete automatic annotation as a starting point just by loading a model. You can find out more about the tool at `https://software.intel.com/en-us/articles/computer-vision-annotation-tool-a-universal-approach-to-data-annotation`.

The tool has the capability to create annotations for bounding boxes and polygon and semantic segmentation, and can also perform automatic annotation. The tool can output annotations as VOC XML, JSON TXT, or TFRecord files. This means that if you use the tool, then there is no need to convert images into TFRecord form – you can go straight to training the neural network. Follow these steps to learn how to use the tool:

1. Perform the necessary installation. All the instructions are carried out in a Terminal and involve installing Docker, building a Docker image, and cloning the CVAT source code. More information can be found at `https://github.com/opencv/cvat/blob/master/cvat/apps/documentation/installation.md`.
2. Install the Faster R-CNN ResNet Inception Atrous model that's been trained on coco datasets by going to `https://github.com/opencv/cvat/blob/master/components/tf_annotation/README.md`.
3. Install the OpenVINO model. If you're using TensorFlow, then you don't need to install the OpenVINO model – just go straight to *Step 4*. However, if you want to use models from Intel Open Model Zoo or your own custom model, follow the instructions at this link: `https://github.com/opencv/cvat/blob/master/cvat/apps/auto_annotation/README.md`.
4. Open Google Chrome and type in `localhost:8080`. This will open CVAT. Note that CVAT only works on the Google Chrome browser currently.
5. Select your model from the drop-down list, as shown in the following screenshot:

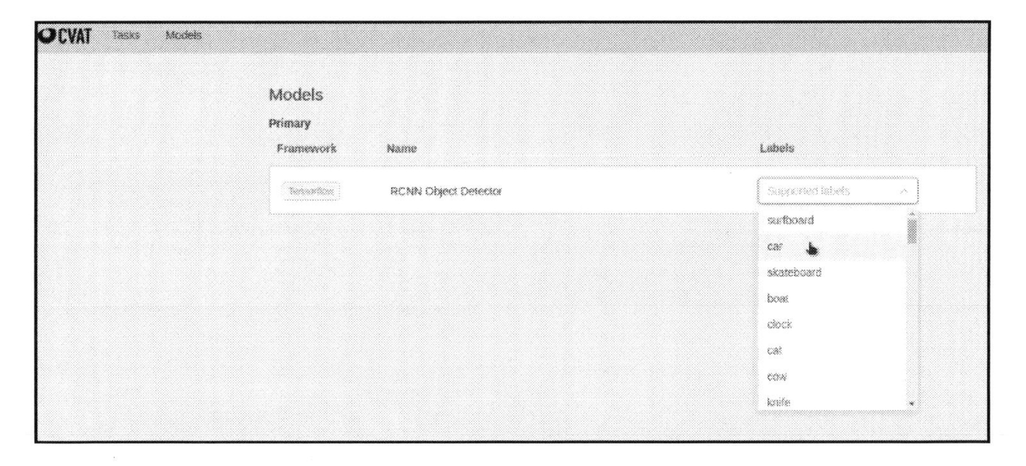

For TensorFlow, there is only one model to choose from. However, you still need to select the class from the drop-down list, as shown in the preceding screenshot. Note that you can select multiple classes, but it doesn't display selected classes.

6. Create a task by giving it a name. Then, name all the classes and add all the images, as shown in the following screenshot:

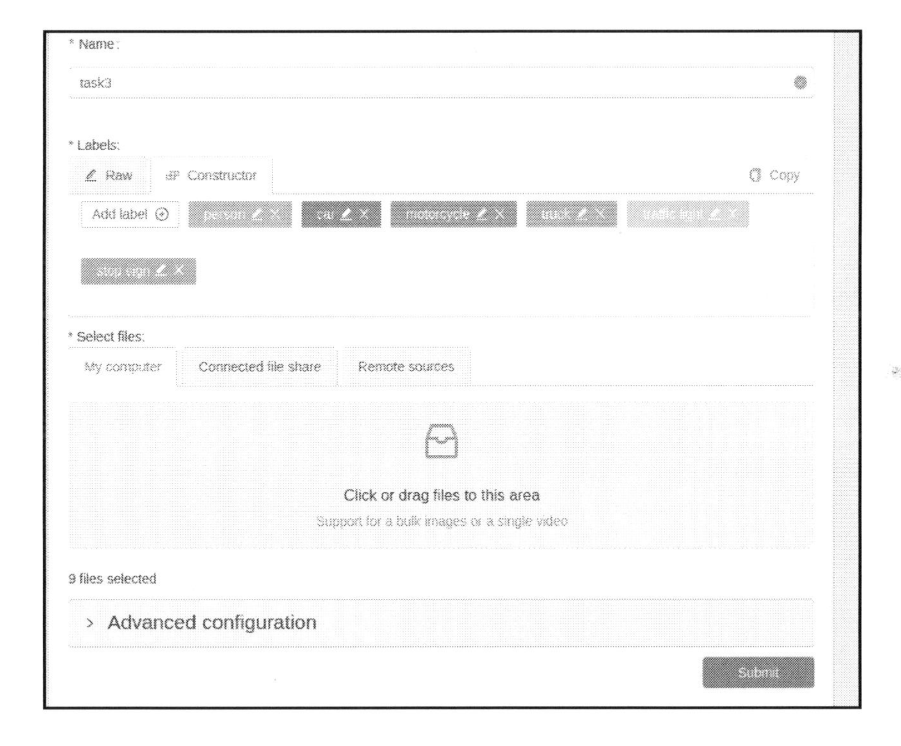

As shown in the preceding screenshot, nine images have been uploaded. Then, hit the **Submit** button, which will create the task. You can assign different people to different tasks.

7. Under **Task**, left-click on the new menu bar, next to the action, and select automatic annotation. You will see a menu bar, showing its progress.
8. After it's finished automatic annotation, click on **Job** # – you will notice that there are annotations for all your images. The following screenshot shows the automatic annotation report for all nine images that were uploaded:

In the preceding example, we batch loaded all nine images at once to demonstrate the automation process' effectiveness. It detected all the objects (car, person, truck, and motorcycle) correctly. The model didn't draw the traffic light and stop sign in some cases. So, in this example, only the traffic light and stop sign need to be manually annotated; we can rely on the tool for all the other objects. Next, we took the output of the tool in VOC XML form and loaded the image, along with the `.xml` file, into the `labelImg` tool for the labeling bounding box. The following screenshot shows the result. Notice that this is the bottom-left picture in the preceding screenshot:

The data shows very accurate labeling work. This tool is constantly getting updated. Like any other tool, if you run into any issues that haven't been covered here, submit a work ticket.

I found one issue regarding the tool: its inconsistent output means that for some images, it will draw bounding box annotations while for other images, it won't. I resolved this issue by moving to a different Linux PC and doing a fresh install of CVAT. To fix this issue on your current PC, you can uninstall Docker in your current directory of CVAT, delete the CVAT folder, and make sure port `8080` is not being called by another program. Then, you can reinstall CVAT.

Summary

In this chapter, you learned how to develop and optimize a convolutional neural network model on the farthest edge of the network. At its core, a neural network requires lots of data to train, but in the end, it comes out with a model that is able to complete a task without human intervention. In the previous chapters, we learned about the necessary theory and implemented models, but we never did any practical exercises. In practice, a camera can be used for surveillance, to monitor machine performance, or to evaluate a surgical procedure. In each of these cases, embedded vision is used for real time on-device data processing, which requires a smaller and more efficient model to be deployed on edge devices.

In this chapter, you learned about the performance of various single-board computers and accelerators, thus enabling you to make an informed decision regarding what device you choose for your specific application. Then, we learned how to set up a Raspberry Pi and deploy a neural network on it through the use of the OpenVINO toolkit and TensorFlow Lite. We did this to make an on-device inference. After that, we learned how to convert the TensorFlow model into a TensorFlow Lite model and deployed it on Android and iOS devices. We also learned about Apple's Core ML platform and used Create ML to train a neural network in order to develop an object detector model. Then, we compared that with the TensorFlow Lite object detector model. We concluded this chapter with an overview of image annotation and automatic annotation methods.

In the next chapter, we will learn how to use cloud processing to train a neural network and then deploy it on devices.

12
Cloud Computing Platform for Computer Vision

Cloud computing uses the internet to access data universally from remote hardware. Such data storage is done using a cloud platform. For computer vision, the data is mostly images, annotation files, and resultant models. The cloud platform not only stores data, but it also performs training, deployment, and analysis. Cloud computing differs from edge computing, which we learned about in `Chapter 11`, *Deep Learning on Edge Devices with CPU/GPU Optimization*, in terms of there being no investment in infrastructure and the almost instantaneous speed of analysis.

In this chapter, you will learn how to package your application for training and deployment in **Google Cloud Platform** (**GCP**), **Amazon Web Services** (**AWS**), and the **Microsoft Azure cloud platform**. You will learn how to prepare your data, upload to cloud data storage, and monitor training. You will also learn how to send an image or an image vector to the cloud platform for analysis and get a JSON response back. This chapter discusses a single application as well as running distributed TensorFlow on the compute engine. After training is complete, this chapter will discuss how to evaluate your model and integrate it into your application to operate at scale.

This chapter is split into the following sections:

- Training an object detector in GCP
- Training an object detector in the AWS SageMaker cloud platform
- Training an object detector in the Microsoft Azure cloud platform
- Training at scale and packaging
- The general idea behind cloud-based visual search
- Analyzing images and search mechanisms in various cloud platforms

Training an object detector in GCP

In the last two chapters, we learned how to set up Google Colab to train a custom object detector using SSD, R-CNN, and R-FCN with Inception and MobileNet as backbone pre-trained networks. Our network was used to detect burgers and French fries. In this section, we will learn how to do the same task using GCP. A detailed description of the work can also be found at `https://medium.com/tensorflow/training-and-serving-a-realtime-mobile-object-detector-in-30-minutes-with-cloud-tpus-b78971cf1193`.

I started with the preceding article but found many sections have to be streamlined and additional details need to be added to get it working on my Ubuntu PC. The following subsections provide the step-by-step process for training an object detector using the GCP.

Note that this section involves many large steps that connect your local terminal to GCP and the flow of information can get confusing at times.It is recommended that you review the flowchart provided at the very end of this section, just before the beginning of the section, Training an object detector in the AWS Sagemaker cloud platform, to understand the general flow of information.

Creating a project in GCP

In this section, a project will be created in GCP. A project consists of billing, data storage, APIs, authentication, and team member information to get your training job started. GCP is Google's machine learning platform for storing, building, training, and deploying a model. Log in to the GCP console by going to `https://console.cloud.google.com`.

First, log in with your Gmail ID and password and you will see the following console:

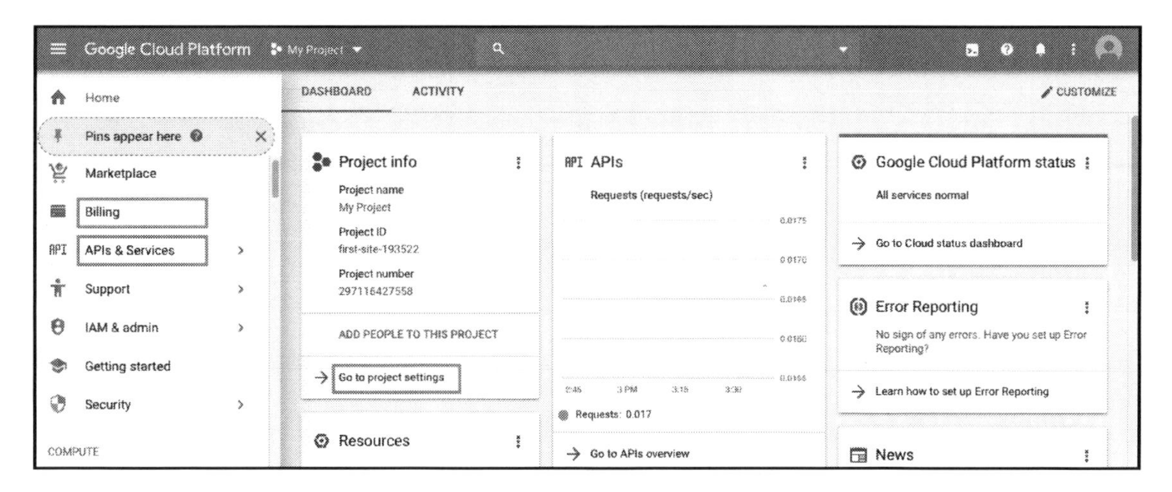

Once you are in the console, take some time to get familiar with the various options. In particular, you have to fill in information for billing, APIs, and project settings. Detailed instructions are outlined in the following subsection.

The GCP setup

Go to `https://console.cloud.google.com` to set up GCP and log in with your Gmail account. In the screenshot in the preceding section, there are three rectangular boxes—those are the three main sections that you need to set up. The steps are outlined as follows:

1. First, click on **Go to project settings**, give the project a name, and assign team members (if multiple people will be working on the project).
2. Then, click on **Billing** on the left and provide your credit card information. At the time of writing, Google is providing a free trial with $300 of credit, but you still need to provide your credit card information.
3. Once this is done, click on **API & Services**, then click on **Enable API & Services** and select **AI Platform Training & Prediction API** under **Machine Learning**.

4. Click on **Enable** and the API will be enabled. The following screenshot shows the **AI Platform Training & Prediction API** after it is enabled:

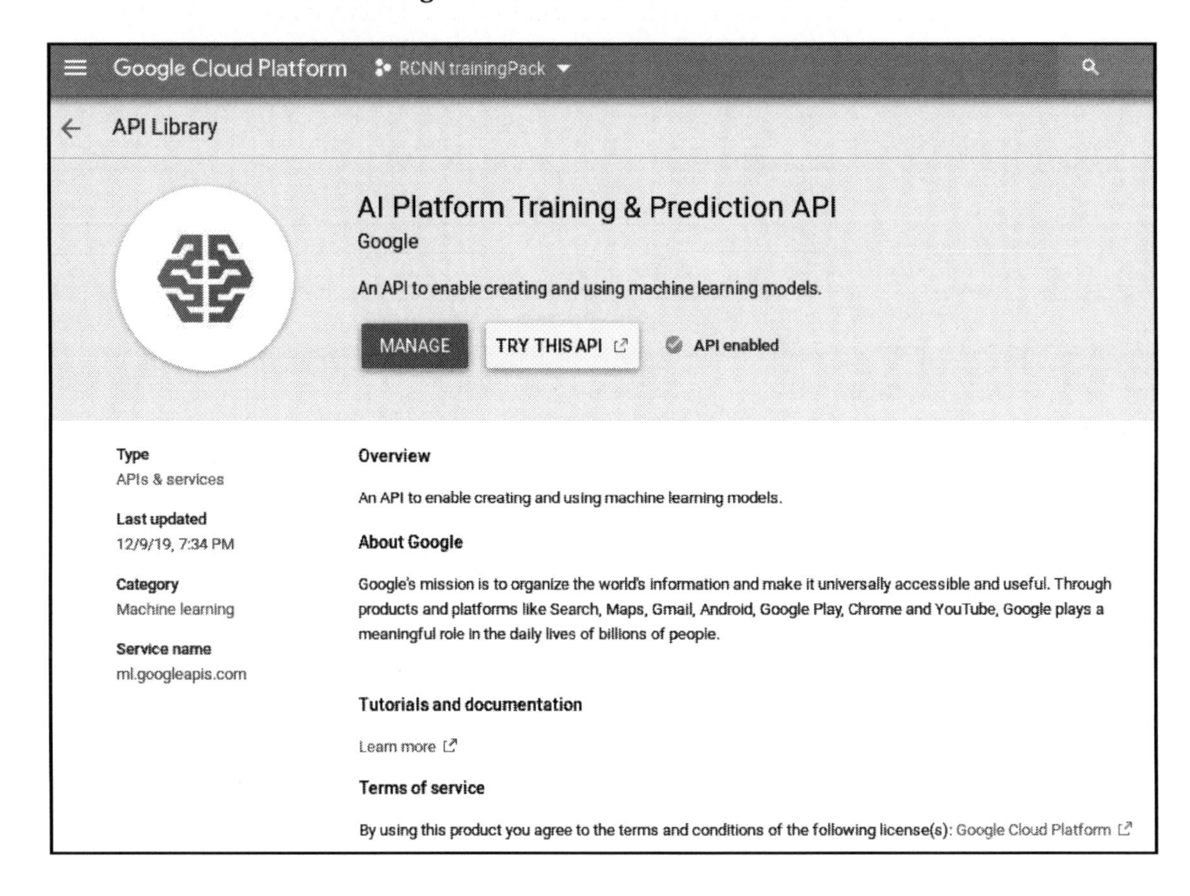

The Google Cloud Storage bucket setup

Storage buckets are containers that hold data. All cloud service providers have storage buckets. Buckets have the same format as the directory structure of your PC. Buckets can contain images (`.jpg` files), annotations, TFRecord, a checkpoint file, and model outputs. In this section, we will learn how to install a **Google Cloud Storage** (**GCS**) bucket to store the training and testing data.

Setting up a bucket using the GCP API

To set up a bucket using the GCP API, follow these steps:

1. After you sign up for billing, scroll down the left-hand menu, click on **Storage**, then **CREATE BUCKET**, and give it a name:

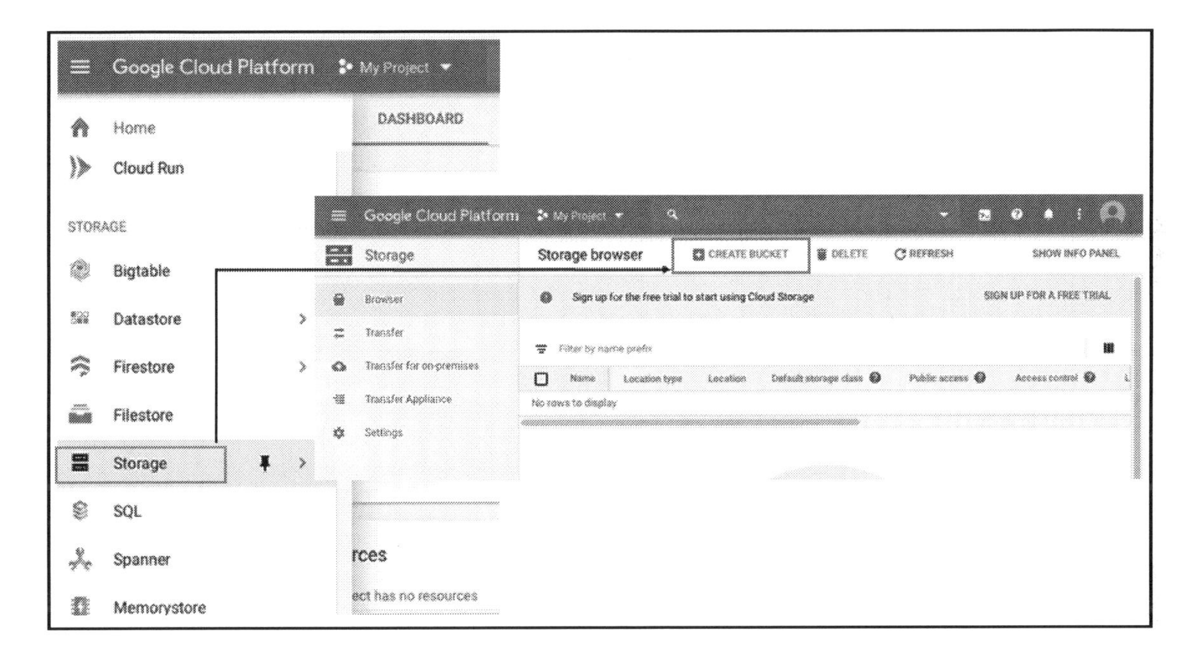

2. After the bucket is created, the next task will be to create a folder called `data` in the bucket and then upload files to it. Take a look at the following screenshot to see how to do that:

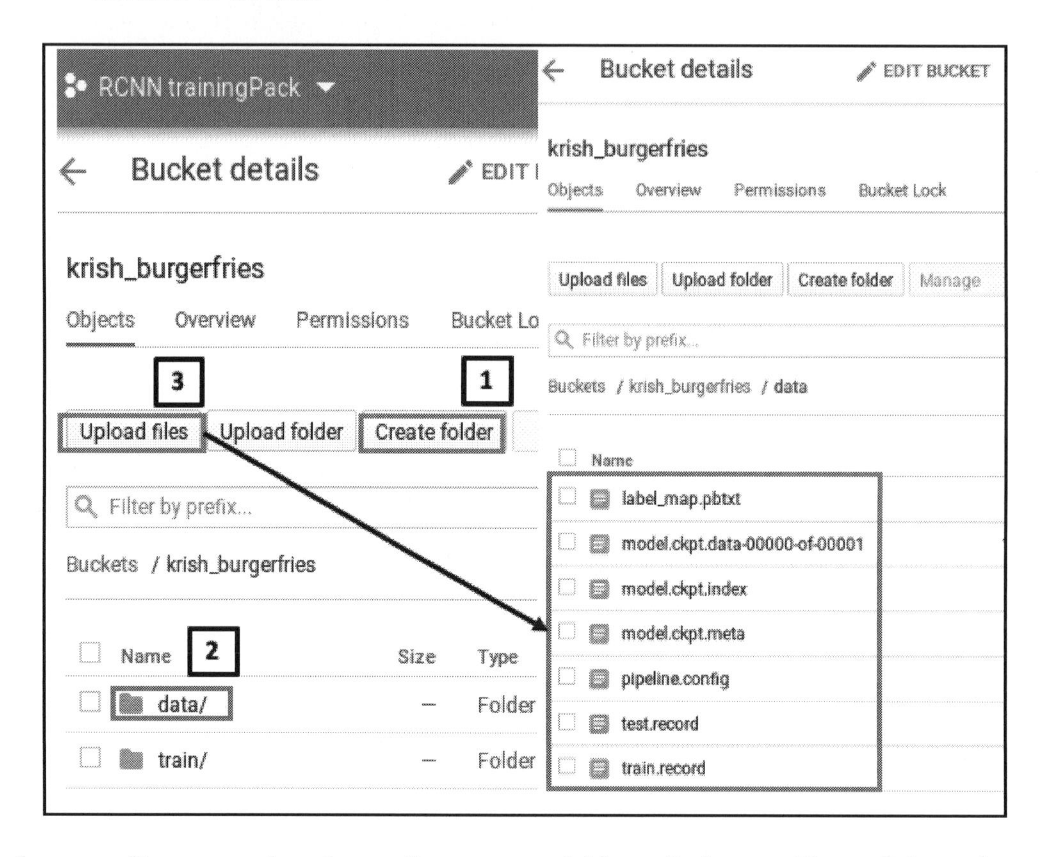

As the preceding screenshot shows, first create a folder called `data`. Then, click on **data**, click on **Upload files**, and upload `test.record`, `train.record`, `label_map.pbtxt`, `pipeline.config`, and `model.ckpt*` (three files). We will describe how to get those files in the next section.

Setting up a bucket using Ubuntu Terminal

This process involves setting up the Google Cloud SDK and then linking the Google Cloud project and bucket to your terminal so that you can upload files there. Remember, training will be initiated by the terminal command, so even if you set it up using the preceding API, you still need to execute the steps shown in the following sections (starting with the *Setting up the Google Cloud SDK* section) to link the terminal to GCP.

Setting up the Google Cloud SDK

The Google Cloud SDK is a set of command-line tools that enables your PC to interact with Google Cloud. Since, in this section, we will be using Ubuntu Terminal to interact with Google Cloud, we need to set up the SDK first. Enter the following commands in Terminal:

```
$ echo "deb [signed-by=/usr/share/keyrings/cloud.google.gpg]
http://packages.cloud.google.com/apt cloud-sdk main" | sudo tee -a
/etc/apt/sources.list.d/google-cloud-sdk.list
$ curl https://packages.cloud.google.com/apt/doc/apt-key.gpg | sudo apt-key
--keyring /usr/share/keyrings/cloud.google.gpg add -
$ sudo apt-get update && sudo apt-get install google-cloud-sdk
$ gcloud init
```

In the first three lines of the preceding code, we get a list of SDKs, then use `apt-key` to authenticate the package, and then install the SDK. In the fourth line, we will use `gcloud.init` to set up `gcloud` configurations.

Again, as mentioned previously, if you face any difficulty in following this section, you can review the flowchart provided at the very end of this section to understand the general flow of information.

Next, we will link your local PC to the Google Cloud project.

Linking your terminal to the Google Cloud project and bucket

In the steps in the preceding section, we set up the Google Cloud SDK. Now, we need to carry out the most important step, which is linking Ubuntu Terminal to the Google Cloud project and the bucket you created previously.

Why do you need to link Ubuntu Terminal to the Google Cloud project? The answer is we initiate the training command using Terminal in the local PC, but our data is stored in the storage bucket in GCP and the model will be generated in the GCP. So, we need to link our PC Terminal to GCP to accomplish the training task.

Enter the following steps in sequential order in Terminal:

1. Set up the project—in this case, it is `rcnn-trainingpack`:

```
$ gcloud config set project rcnn-trainingpack
```

2. To open the storage bucket, enter the `gsutil` Python command, as shown:

```
$ gsutil mb gs://krish_burgerfries
```

3. Next, we set up the environmental variable to define the storage bucket and the project that the file belongs to:

```
$ export PROJECT="rcnn-trainingpack"
$ export YOUR_GCS_BUCKET="krish_burgerfries"
```

4. Add a TPU-specific service account by entering the following command:

Tensor Processing Unit (TPU) is an AI accelerator developed by Google to process lots of data quickly to train a neural network.

```
$ curl -H "Authorization: Bearer $(gcloud auth print-access-token)"
https://ml.googleapis.com/v1/projects/${PROJECT}:getConfig
```

The preceding commands will return the following output to your Terminal window. Note that the service name and project name will be different for your application:

```
{"serviceAccount": "service-444444444444@cloud-
ml.google.com.iam.gserviceaccount.com",
"serviceAccountProject": "111111111111",
 "config": {"tpuServiceAccount": "service-111111111111@cloud-
tpu.iam.gserviceaccount.com" }}

{"serviceAccount": "service-444444444444@cloud-
ml.google.com.iam.gserviceaccount.com",
"serviceAccountProject": "111111111111",
"config": {
"tpuServiceAccount": "service-111111111111@cloud-
tpu.iam.gserviceaccount.com" }}
```

5. Export the TPU account as an environmental variable by typing the entire `tpuServiceAccount` path, as shown:

```
$ export TPU_ACCOUNT="service-111111111111@cloud-
tpu.iam.gserviceaccount.com"
```

6. Grant the `ml.serviceAgent` role to the TPU account:

```
$ gcloud projects add-iam-policy-binding $PROJECT      --member
serviceAccount:$TPU_ACCOUNT --role roles/ml.serviceAgent
```

This should result in a series of comments in Terminal, starting with `Updated IAM policy for the project [rcnn-trainingpack].`

Installing the TensorFlow object detection API

Now that we have linked Terminal to the storage bucket and Google Cloud project, the next step will be to link it to the TensorFlow object detection API. Follow the set of instructions provided at `https://github.com/tensorflow/models/blob/master/research/object_detection/g3doc/installation.md`.

The preceding installation link has many lines of codes that are not listed here. You will be able to execute most of the code correctly. The last two lines of codes in this procedure are described as follows:

```
# From tensorflow/models/research/
export PYTHONPATH=$PYTHONPATH:'pwd':'pwd'/slim
python object_detection/builders/model_builder_test.py
```

The instruction says that the preceding step is critical for installation to be successful; however, if you have TensorFlow 2.0 installed on your PC, you are likely to get the following error:

```
AttributeError: module 'tensorflow' has no attribute 'contrib'
```

Even if this error is fixed, it will result in another error related to TensorFlow 2.0's incompatibility with the TensorFlow object detection API. So, we will describe an alternative path instead. The other alternative is to use `https://github.com/tensorflow/models/tree/v1.13.0`, which is similar to running it in Google Colab using TensorFlow 1.15, as we did in `Chapter 10`, *Object Detection Using R-CNN, SSD, and R-FCN*, and `Chapter 11`, *Deep Learning on Edge Devices with CPU/GPU Optimization*.

Preparing the dataset

As outlined in the *Setting up a bucket using the GCP API* section, we will need to populate the following `bucket: test.record`, `train.record`, `label_map.pbtxt`, `pipeline.config`, and `model.ckpt*` (three files). We will explain, in the following subsection, how to populate each of these.

TFRecord and labeling map data

TFRecord files are efficient TensorFlow file formats for storing image and annotation files in a single binary format for super-fast reading by the TensorFlow model. TFRecord was already introduced in `Chapter 10`, *Object Detection Using R-CNN, SSD, and R-FCN*. In this section, we will describe how to prepare the data and then upload it.

Data preparation

First, copy the TFRecord files—that is, `train.record` and `test.record`—from the Google Colab project from `Chapter 10`, *Object Detection Using R-CNN, SSD, and R-FCN*, and `Chapter 11`, *Deep Learning on Edge Devices with CPU/GPU Optimization*, into a directory on your PC. Also, copy `label_map.pbtxt` in the `pbtxt` file in the same directory.

Data upload

Here, we will look at the data upload method using Terminal:

1. With the help of the following command, we will upload `train.record` to GCP. This uses the `gsutil` Python command to copy the file from your local directory to the GCS bucket. Make sure that you also include the subdirectory. For example, in this case, `YOUR_GCS_BUCKET` will be the name of your bucket; if it is `burgerfries`, then the command will be `$burgerfries/data`, where `data` is the subdirectory under `burgerfries`, where the files are stored:

```
$ gsutil -m cp -r
/Documents/chapter12_cloud_computing/burgerfries/annotation/train.r
ecord gs://${YOUR_GCS_BUCKET}/data/
Copying
file:///Documents/chapter12_cloud_computing/burgerfries/annotation/
train.record [Content-Type=application/octet-stream]...
\ [1/1 files][  2.6 MiB/  2.6 MiB] 100% Done
```

2. Next, the following command will be used to upload `test.record` to GCP:

```
$ gsutil -m cp -r
/Documents/chapter12_cloud_computing/burgerfries/annotation/test.re
cord gs://${YOUR_GCS_BUCKET}/data/
Copying
file:///Documents/chapter12_cloud_computing/burgerfries/annotation/
test.record [Content-Type=application/octet-stream]...
\ [1/1 files][  1.1 MiB/  1.1 MiB] 100% Done
Operation completed over 1 objects/1.1 MiB.
```

3. The following command will help us upload `label_map.pbtxt` to GCP:

```
$ gsutil -m cp -r
/Documents/chapter12_cloud_computing/burgerfries/annotation/label_m
ap.pbtxt gs://${YOUR_GCS_BUCKET}/data/
Copying
file:///Documents/chapter12_cloud_computing/burgerfries/annotation/
label_map.pbtxt [Content-Type=application/octet-stream]...
/ [1/1 files][   75.0 B/   75.0 B] 100% Done
Operation completed over 1 objects/75.0 B.
```

If you are not using Terminal, just use **Upload command** in the Google Cloud bucket to upload files, shown in the screenshot in the *Using the GCP API* section.

The model.ckpt files

In this section, we will learn how to download the checkpoint file of the pre-trained model. Checkpoints are the weights of the model. These weights will be uploaded to the GCS bucket to initiate training using transfer learning:

1. Go to the TensorFlow Model Zoo GitHub page and download the appropriate `model.tar` file:

```
https://github.com/tensorflow/models/blob/master/research/object_
detection/g3doc/detection_model_zoo.md
```

2. The following is the unzipped version of the appropriate file that we downloaded:

```
ssd_mobilenet_v1_0.75_depth_300x300_coco14_sync_2018_07_03.tar.gz
```

Checkpoints capture the exact value of all parameters used by the model. When you unzip the file, you will notice that there are the following types of files:

- `model.ckpt.data-00000-of-00001`: A binary data file containing a value for the training variable weights, gradients, and so on
- `model.ckpt.index`: A binary file describing the index value for each checkpoint
- `model.ckpt.meta`: Describes the saved graph structure; it is a protocol buffer
- `Checkpoint`: Keeps a record of the latest checkpoint file

The model config file

The model `config` file is a text file that defines the following important characteristics of the model:

- The model name
- The number of classes
- The image minimum/maximum dimensions
- The model parameters
- The location of the checkpoint, TFRecord, and `map.pbtxt`

During training, the model uses the `config` file to input and set parameters. You can find the list of `config` files in the TensorFlow directory under the following path:

```
models-master/research/object-detection/samples/configs
```

Note that at the time of writing, the preceding directory is available only in TensorFlow 1.x and not in 2.x. So, if you have TensorFlow 2.0 installed on your PC, use the alternative step discussed below to get the `config` file.

Alternatively, you can go to `https://github.com/tensorflow/models/tree/master/research/object_detection/samples/configs` and copy the `config` file in your text editor. Download the corresponding `.config` file from the preceding link, too.

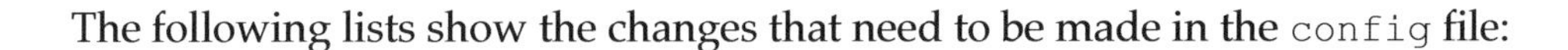

The following lists show the changes that need to be made in the `config` file:

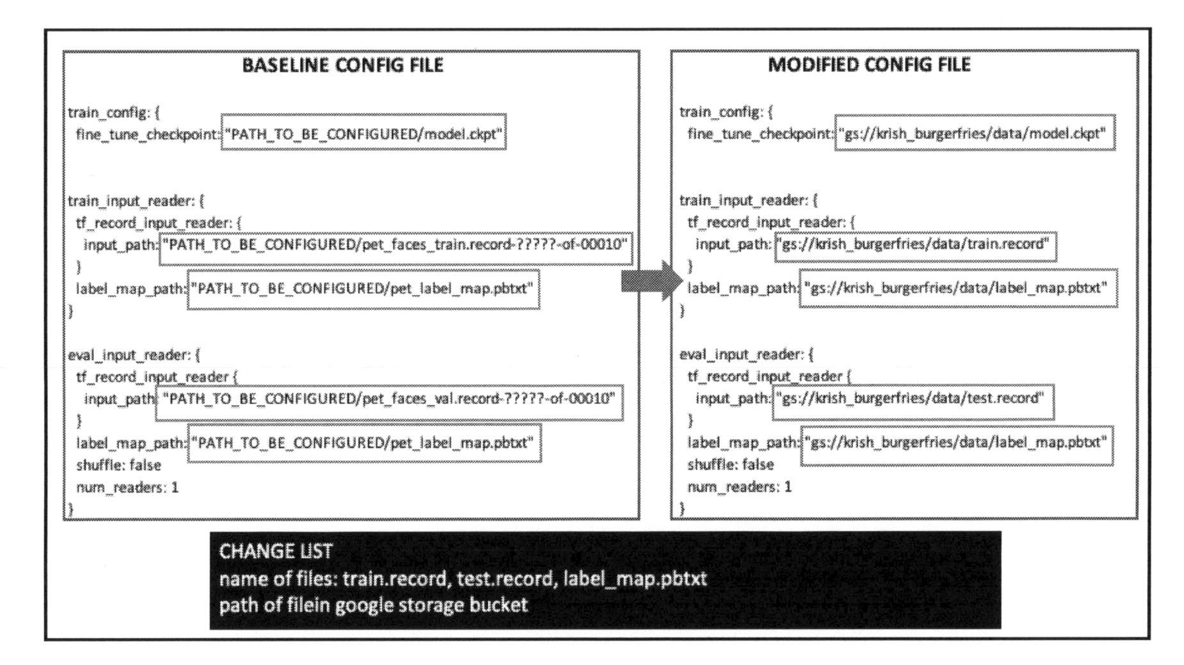

In the preceding lists, all changes are marked with a rectangle. The left-side list shows the original `config` file and the right-side list shows the changed `config` file. Here, it is assumed that the `TFRecord` filenames are `train.record` and `test.record`, the `pbtxt` filename is `label_map.pbtxt`, and the path in the Google storage drive is `krish_burgerfries/data`. If your filename or path is different, you can change it accordingly.

Now, go to the TensorFlow `research` directory by typing the following command in the Terminal:

```
$cd models-master/research
```

Refer to the following command for the package object detection API, `pycocotools`, and `tf-slim`:

```
models-master/research$ bash
object_detection/dataset_tools/create_pycocotools_package.sh
/tmp/pycocotools
models-master/research$ python setup.py sdist
models-master/research$ (cd slim && python setup.py sdist)
```

Training in the cloud

After all the preceding steps have been completed, we will be ready for training. As described previously, training is initiated in the terminal by executing the following command:

1. The command is long, but copy it to a text editor and only change `{YOUR_GCS_BUCKET}` to `burgerfries` (in your case, if the name is different, then change it to that name). Once completed, paste it in the terminal and hit *Enter*:

```
$ gcloud ml-engine jobs submit training
`whoami`_object_detection_`date +%s` --job-
dir=gs://${YOUR_GCS_BUCKET}/train --packages
dist/object_detection-0.1.tar.gz,slim/dist/slim-0.1.tar.gz,/tmp/pyc
ocotools/pycocotools-2.0.tar.gz --module-name
object_detection.model_tpu_main --runtime-version 1.15 --scale-tier
BASIC_TPU --region us-central1 -- --
model_dir=gs://${YOUR_GCS_BUCKET}/train --tpu_zone us-central1 --
pipeline_config_path=gs://${YOUR_GCS_BUCKET}/data/pipeline.config
```

2. Just like the training, execute the validation with the help of the following command. The command is long again, but copy it to a text editor and only change `{YOUR_GCS_BUCKET}` to `burgerfries` (in your case, if the name is different, then change it to that name). Once you have done that, paste it in the terminal and hit *Enter* on your keyboard:

```
$ gcloud ml-engine jobs submit training
`whoami`_object_detection_eval_validation_`date +%s` --job-
dir=gs://${YOUR_GCS_BUCKET}/train --packages
dist/object_detection-0.1.tar.gz,slim/dist/slim-0.1.tar.gz,/tmp/pyc
ocotools/pycocotools-2.0.tar.gz --module-name
object_detection.model_main --runtime-version 1.15 --scale-tier
BASIC_GPU --region us-central1 -- --
model_dir=gs://${YOUR_GCS_BUCKET}/train --
pipeline_config_path=gs://${YOUR_GCS_BUCKET}/data/pipeline.config -
-checkpoint_dir=gs://${YOUR_GCS_BUCKET}/train
```

3. Once the training begins, you can evaluate the training job by executing the following command:

```
$ gcloud ai-platform jobs describe
krishkar_object_detection_1111111111
```

Here, the number at the end will be different for your application and will be printed in the terminal for you. After typing the preceding command, you can check the training job at `https://console.cloud.google.com/mlengine/jobs/xxxxx_eval_validation_1111111111?project=rcnn-trainingpack`.

Note that the `xxxxx` and `1111111111` parts of the URL are just examples; your value will be different and printed in the terminal for you.

Viewing the model output in TensorBoard

In `Chapter 10`, *Object Detection Using R-CNN, SSD, and R-FCN*, we learned how to view the TensorFlow model output results in TensorBoard using Google Colab. In this section, we will show you how to start TensorBoard from the cloud platform by executing a command in the terminal:

1. Let's start by entering the following command in your terminal:

```
tensorboard --logdir=gs://${YOUR_GCS_BUCKET}/train
```

After running the preceding command, if you come across an error, such as `ValueError: Duplicate plugins for name projector`, then copy `diagnose_tensorboard.py` as a text file from `https://raw.githubusercontent.com/tensorflow/tensorboard/master/tensorboard/tools/diagnose_tensorboard.py` and save it to your directory.

2. In the Terminal, go to the directory where `diagnose_tensorboard.py` is installed and execute the following command:

```
$ python diagnose_tensorboard.py
```

It will run and provide suggestions for possible fixes. In my case, it asked for the following fix:

```
### Suggestion: Fix conflicting installations

 "Conflicting package installations found. Depending on the order
of installations and uninstallations, behavior may be undefined.
Please uninstall ALL versions of TensorFlow and TensorBoard, then
reinstall ONLY the desired version of TensorFlow, which will
transitively pull
 in the proper version of TensorBoard. (If you use TensorBoard
without TensorFlow, just reinstall the appropriate version of
```

```
TensorBoard directly.)

 Namely:

 pip uninstall tb-nightly tensorboard tensorflow-estimator
tensorflow-estimator-2.0-preview tensorflow-gpu tf-nightly-gpu-2.0-
preview

 pip install tensorflow # or `tensorflow-gpu`, or `tf-nightly`,
..."
```

3. Execute the commands as per the suggestion and TensorBoard will work.
4. Navigate to `localhost:6006` to view the TensorBoard results.

In TensorBoard, you will see a graph of the neural network used, as well as images displaying the bounding box on the test images. Note that in TensorFlow, we did not upload the image, but it gets the image from the `TFRecord` files. TensorBoard also displays accuracy and precision data, as shown:

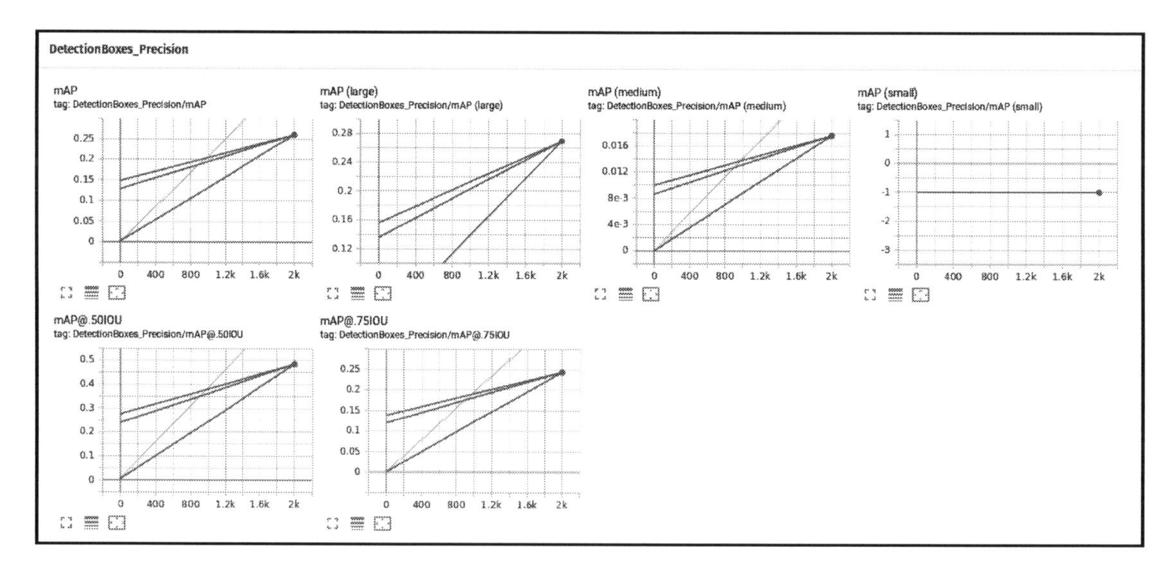

The precision data is modest but can be improved with more images—in our sample example, we only used 68 images to do the training.

Now that we have created the model and observed its output, in the next section, we will describe how to package the model so that you can deploy it on an edge device, such as a cell phone, for real-time display. Packaging a model here implies freezing the model, which implies the model cannot be trained anymore.

The model output and conversion into a frozen graph

So far, we have learned how to upload images in TFRecord format to GCP and then used the SSD MobileNet model to train our custom model for burgers and fries. In this section, we will review the components of the model output and learn how to freeze the model. Freezing the model involves saving the TensorFlow graph and weights in a format that you can use for inference later on. The model output is stored in `train` folders and contains the following files:

- `graph.pbtxt`: This is a text file describing the value, list, and shape of every node on the TensorFlow graph
- `model.ckpt-xxxx.data-00000-of-00001`: This is a binary file indicating the values of all the variable files
- `model.ckpt-xxxx.index`: This is a binary file representing a table, where each key is the name of a tensor, and its value
- `model.ckpt-xxxx.meta`: This describes the saved graph structure
- `train_pipeline.config`: This text file describes the model parameters—it is also illustrated in the two preceding sections under the model config file

Note that I have used `xxxx` in the preceding steps just as an example. Your value will be different. Enter that information instead of `xxxx`.

Grab the latest data file (right-click and download)—so, in this example, grab the file containing `-2000`.

The next task will be to convert the checkpoint output into a frozen inference graph. There are three methods explained in the following section:

1. Execute `freeze_graph.py` from TensorFlow Core:

```
$ python freeze_graph.py --input_graph=train_graph.pbtxt --
input_checkpoint=train_model.ckpt-2000 --
output_graph=frozen_graph.pb --output_node_name=softmax
```

2. Execute `freeze_graph` from the TensorFlow Python tools:

```
    import tensorflow as tf
    from tensorflow.python.tools import freeze_graph
    checkpoint_path = './'+'train_model'+'.ckpt-2000'
    freeze_graph.freeze_graph('train_graph.pbtxt', "", False,
checkpoint_path,    "output/softmax", "save/restore_all",
"save/Const:0",'frozentensorflowModel.pb', True, "")
```

For both of the preceding methods, we get two types of error:

```
  IndexError: tuple index out of range
  AttributeError: module 'tensorflow_core.python.pywrap_tensorflow'
has no    attribute    'NewCheckpointReader'
```

3. Execute an `export` function on `tflite graph.py` from the terminal and then download the relevant files:

```
    $export CONFIG_FILE=gs://${YOUR_GCS_BUCKET}/data/pipeline.config
    $export
CHECKPOINT_PATH=gs://${YOUR_GCS_BUCKET}/train/model.ckpt-2000
    $export OUTPUT_DIR=/tmp/tflite
```

4. Then, execute the following command in the terminal from the Docker file, as described at `https://github.com/tensorflow/models/tree/master/research/object_detection/dockerfiles/android`.

   A Docker is a virtual machine that enables developers to package an application with all of its components. For TensorFlow, the advantage of using a Docker is the isolation of the TensorFlow installation from your PC operating system. This isolation eliminates many of the TensorFlow-related errors that we have previously observed:

```
$python object_detection/export_tflite_ssd_graph.py \
--pipeline_config_path=$CONFIG_FILE \
--trained_checkpoint_prefix=$CHECKPOINT_PATH \
--output_directory=$OUTPUT_DIR \
--add_postprocessing_op=true
```

In the following section, we will describe the `tflite` conversion process mentioned in `Chapter 11`, *Deep Learning on Edge Devices with CPU/GPU Optimization*.

Executing export tflite graph.py from Google Colab

In `Chapter 10`, *Object Detection Using R-CNN, SSD, and R-FCN*, and `Chapter 11`, *Deep Learning on Edge Devices with CPU/GPU Optimization*, we used Google Colab to convert the checkpoint into a frozen graph. We will use the same method here, except we will import the configuration, checkpoint, and output directory as shown:

```
CONFIG_FILE = '/content/sample_data/train_pipeline.config'
CHECKPOINT_PATH = '/content/sample_data/train_model.ckpt-2000'
OUTPUT_DIR = '/content/sample_data'
```

Upload the files to Google Drive and then drag them into a folder in Google Colab called `sample_data`. You can create a different name instead of `sample_data`. After that, execute the following code:

Note that if you do not bring the files by dragging them into Google Colab and instead link the Google Colab to Google Drive where your file is residing, it may generate an error as it won't be able to find the file at the time of execution.

```
import re
import numpy as np
!python
/content/models/research/object_detection/export_tflite_ssd_graph.py \
    --input_type=image_tensor \
    --pipeline_config_path={CONFIG_FILE} \
    --output_directory={OUTPUT_DIR} \
    --trained_checkpoint_prefix={CHECKPOINT_PATH} \
    --add_postprocessing_op=true
```

The code for this conversion can be found in the following GitHub link:

`https://github.com/PacktPublishing/Mastering-Computer-Vision-with-TensorFlow-2.0/blob/master/Chapter12/Chapter12_Gcloud_Tensorflow_TrainedModelConvert.ipynb`

So, in summary, the following diagram represents the flowchart for training a custom object detector on GCP:

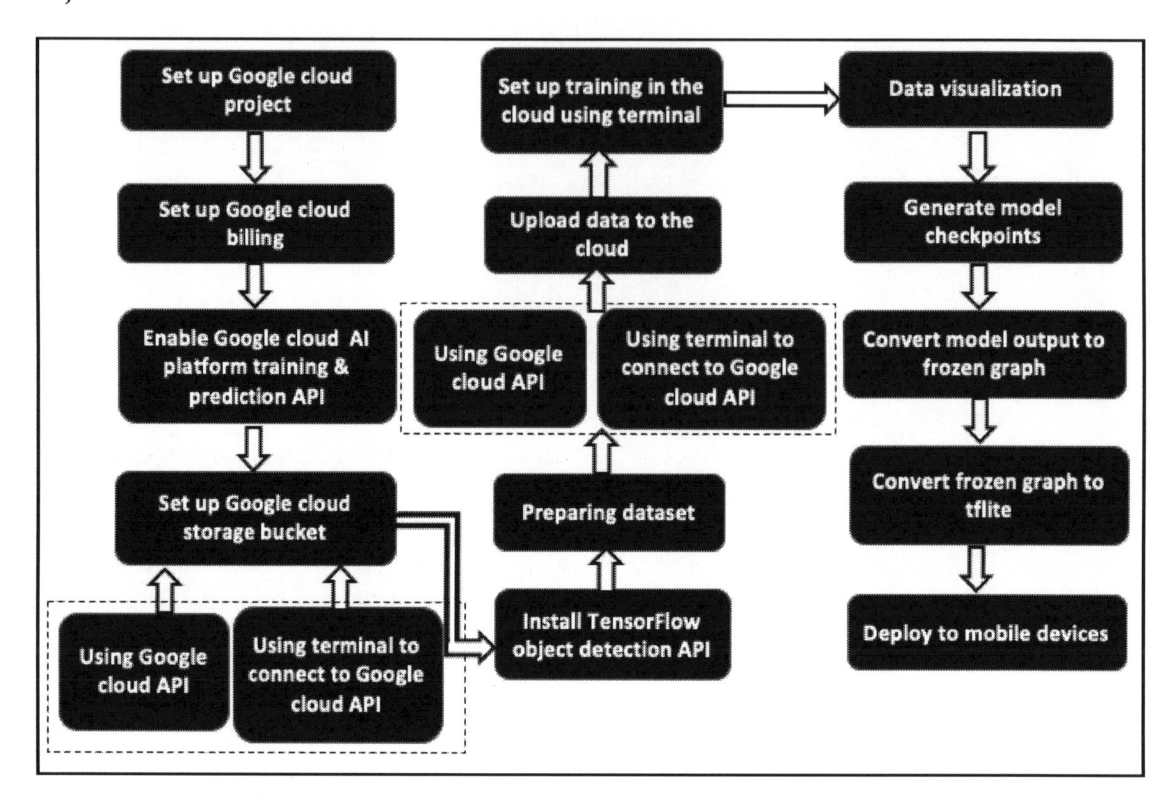

It starts by creating a project, followed by creating the billing, setting up the API and storage bucket, preparing the TensorFlow object detection API, preparing and uploading datasets, and then beginning training. The two rounded rectangles within the dotted rectangle indicate two different methods of completing the same task. Once training is complete, the steps involved are generating a frozen graph, converting the `tflite` form, and deploying to mobile devices. The deployment procedure to mobile devices follow the same method as in `Chapter 11`, *Deep Learning on Edge Devices with CPU/GPU Optimization*, so it is not described here.

Training an object detector in the AWS SageMaker cloud platform

AWS (`https://aws.amazon.com`) is the Amazon cloud platform used to perform a wide variety of tasks in the cloud. AWS SageMaker is the machine learning platform used to train and deploy models using the AWS interactive platform. AWS SageMaker interacts with AWS S3 buckets to store and retrieve data. The step-by-step process of training an object detector is described in the following section.

Setting up an AWS account, billing, and limits

Increase the service limit to `ml.p3.2xlarge` or something similar by contacting AWS Support. Note that it may take up to two business days for the instance type to get approved, so plan accordingly. If this is not done, then you will get the following error:

```
ResourceLimitExceeded
```

The account-level service limit, `ml.p3.2xlarge`, for training job usage is zero instances, with a current utilization of zero instances and a request delta of one instance. Please contact AWS Support to request an increase in this limit.

Converting a .xml file to JSON format

AWS SageMaker annotation data uses a JSON format instead of `.xml`, which we used before. Convert `.xml` files to COCO JSON format with the help of the following steps:

1. Download or clone the repository from `https://github.com/yukkyo/voc2coco`.
2. Once you clone the repository and download it, go the directory where the `voc2coco.py` Python file resides in the terminal.
3. Create a directory called `trainxml`, which contains all the `.xml` files. This directory should reside in the same main directory as `voc2coco.py`.
4. In the same main directory, create a file called `trainlist.txt`, which should list all of the `.xml` file names. You can copy this in the terminal and copy and paste all the `.xml` files into a text file to create such a file.

5. Next, create a `classname.txt` file, which should list all the classes in the `training` folder. In this example, it will have two lines—`burger` and `fries`.
6. Then, run the Python code, as follows, from the terminal under the main directory:

```
$ python voc2coco.py  --ann_dir trainxml  --ann_ids trainlist.txt
--labels classname.txt  --output train_cocoformat.json
```

   The final output is the `cocoformat.JSON` file, which is one combined JSON file for all of the `.xml` files.

7. Convert the `COCO JSON` file into individual JSON files.
8. Then, convert the `COCO JSON` file into individual JSON files using the `Chapter12_cocojson_AWSJSON_train.ipynb` Jupyter Notebook. This file can be found on the `https://github.com/PacktPublishing/Mastering-Computer-Vision-with-TensorFlow-2.0/blob/master/Chapter12/Chapter12_cocojson_AWSJSON_train.ipynb`. This is a modification of the object detection code provided by Amazon. This code, instead of getting a `COCO JSON` file from GitHub page, will take the `cocoformat.JSON` file created in the previous step from your local drive and then convert it into multiple `.JSON` files in the generated folder.

Uploading data to the S3 bucket

The S3 bucket is the cloud storage container to store data in AWS. This section describes how to upload data from our PC to the S3 bucket:

1. Create a main folder to indicate the project data.
2. Within that folder, upload four files and an output folder, as follows:
    - `train_channel`: The `train` image `.jpg` file
    - `train_annotation_channel`: The `train` annotation `.JSON` file. Each file corresponds to each `train` image.
    - `validation_channel`: The `validation` image `.jpg` file
    - `validation_annotation_channel`: The `validation` annotation `.JSON` file. Each file corresponds to each `validation` image.
3. Create an output folder to store the checkpoint and output model files.

Creating a notebook instance and beginning training

Let's follow these steps:

1. Select the instance type (select an instance for accelerated computing, such as `ml.p2.nxlarge`, where *n* can be 1, 2, 8, and so on). Note that if the instance type is standard, such as `ml.m5.nxlarge`, or compute-optimized, such as `ml.c5.nxlarge`, then the training will fail. So, request a service limit increase, as we described previously.
2. Select a maximum run time—start with 1 hour and increase it for very large jobs.
3. Assign a path to the S3 bucket for each of the four channels described previously so that the algorithm knows where to pull data from.
4. Assign the path to the output folder mentioned previously. An example of an output path is shown in the preceding code block. In this case, `sample1` is the S3 bucket name, `DEMO` is a folder with `sample1` in it, and within this, there are six folders—two data folders that are consisted of `.jpg` images, two annotations folders that are consisted of `.json` files, an output, and checkpoint files. Note that the path needs to be correct; otherwise, it will likely generate errors:

```
s3://sample1/DEMO/s3_train_data/
s3:// sample1/DEMO/s3_train_annotation/
s3:// sample1/DEMO/s3_validation_data/
s3:// sample1/DEMO/s3_validation_annotation/
s3:// sample1/DEMO/s3_checkpoint/
s3:// sample1/DEMO/s3_output_location/
```

5. Set up training either through the Python notebook (`https://console.aws.amazon.com/sagemaker/home?region=us-east-1#/notebook-instances`) or through the training API (`https://console.aws.amazon.com/sagemaker/home?region=us-east-1#/jobs/create`).
6. Once training finishes, the output will be stored in `s3_output_location`, defined in the previous code, as a `model.tar.gz` file. The checkpoints will be stored in the `s3_checkpoint` location, defined in the preceding code.
7. The next step will be to set the model up for inference. AWS has detailed step-by-step instructions for inference, which can be found at `https://console.aws.amazon.com/sagemaker/home?region=us-east-1#/models/create`.

Fixing some common failures during training

Here are some reasons for failure during training, along with their fixes:

- **Failure 1 - s3 bucket related issue**: No S3 objects are found at the `s3://DEMO-ObjectDetection/s3_train_data/` S3 URL given in the input data source. Please ensure that the bucket exists in the selected region (`us-east-1`), the objects exist under that S3 prefix, and the `arn:aws:iam::11111111:role/service-role/AmazonSageMaker-ExecutionRole-xxxxxxx` role has `s3:ListBucket` permissions on the `DEMO-ObjectDetection` bucket. Or, the `The specified bucket does not exist` error message from S3. **Solution**: Change the S3 bucket path, described previously. Repeat one each for the `train`, `validation`, `annotation`, and `image` data files.

- **Failure 2 - Batch size issue**: `ClientError`: The `validation` set does not have enough files with annotations. Please make sure the number of files with valid annotations is greater than `mini_batch_size` and the number of GPUs in the instance. **Solution**: The important thing to remember is the batch size needs to be smaller than the number of `validation` files. So, if the number of `validation` files is 32 and the batch size was 32, then change the mini-batch size from 32 to 12 to fix this error.
- **Failure 3 - Content type issue**: `ClientError`: Unable to initialize the algorithm. `ContentType` for the `train_annotation` channel is empty. Please set a content type for the `train_annotation` channel (caused by `KeyError`). Caused by `u'train_annotation'`. **Solution**: Make sure the content type is not blank. Change the content type to `application/x-image`.

- **Failure 4 - Channel naming issue**: `ClientError`: Unable to initialize the algorithm. Failed to validate input data configuration (caused by `ValidationError`). Caused by `u'train'` is a required property. Failed validating `u'required'` in schema: `{u'$schema': u'http://json-schema.org/draft-04/schema#', u'additionalProperties': False,u'definitions': {u'data_channel': {u'properties': {u'ContentType': {u'type': u'string'},u'RecordWrapperType': {u'enum': [u'None', u'RecordIO'], u'type': u'string'}, u'S3DistributionType': {u'enum': [u'FullyReplicated', u'ShardedByS3Key'], u'type': u'string'}`. **Solution**: AWS expects the channel name to be `train_validation`, `train_annotation`, and `validation_annotation`. In you have `_channel` appended to it (`train_channel`, `validation_channel`, `train_annotation_channel`, and `validation_annotation_channel`), then it will result in an error. So, to fix it, remove `_channel` from the filename.

If, during the process, you run into issues, contact an AWS Support person by creating a ticket. After we fix all the errors, successful training will have the following parameters:

- `base_network` is `resnet-50`
- `early_stopping` is `false`
- `early_stopping_min_epochs` is `10`
- `early_stopping_patience` is `5`
- `early_stopping_tolerance` is `0.0`
- `epochs` is `30`
- `freeze_layer_pattern` is `false`
- `image_shape` is `300`
- `label_width` is `350`
- `learning_rate` is `0.001`
- `lr_scheduler_factor` is `0.1`
- `mini_batch_size` is `12`
- `momentum` is `0.9`
- `nms_threshold` is `0.45`
- `num_classes` is `2`

- `num_training_samples` is `68`
- `optimizer` is `sgd`
- `overlap_threshold` is `0.5`
- `use_pretrained_model` is `1`
- `weight_decay` is `0.0005`

Note that the output of the training will be saved in the S3 output location, along with the checkpoint.

After doing the preceding exercises, you will be familiar with training a neural network model in GCP and AWS. Next, we will perform training using the Microsoft Azure cloud platform.

Training an object detector in the Microsoft Azure cloud platform

In this section, we will use Azure Custom Vision to train an object detector. A detailed description of training an object detector using the Microsoft Azure cloud platform can be found at `https://docs.microsoft.com/en-us/azure/cognitive-services/custom-vision-service/get-started-build-detector`.

A step-by-step description of the various processes in training the object detector is described in the following section.

Creating an Azure account and setting up Custom Vision

In this section, we will set up an Azure account and set up the Azure Custom Vision platform. The steps following will help you to configure an Azure account and sign up for the Custom Vision platform. As described for GCP, the process is the same for any cloud platform—set up the billing information and set up a project—which is shown in the following screenshot:

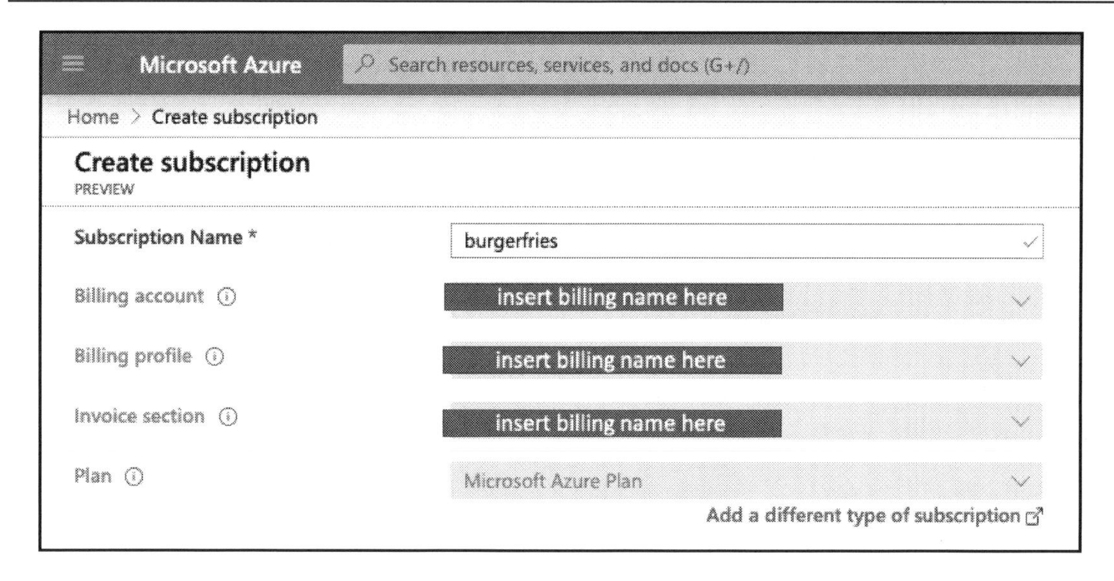

The specific steps for setting up the training is as follows:

1. Sign up to a Microsoft account and set up the billing information. At the time of writing, Microsoft is giving $200 credit for free for first-time users in the US region (check this for your region).
2. Set up a subscription. In the **Subscription** tab, click on **Add**, then give your subscription a name and set up the billing information.
3. Set up the project, then select and create the project, and give it a name.
4. Set up the resources, then select the **Resource group** from the menu.
5. Select **Object detection**, then after all of this, create object detection using Custom Vision.

Setting the account settings is a very important part and if not done correctly, it will take a considerably longer time. Once the account is set up, the next steps will actually move very quickly.

Uploading training images and tagging them

In this section, we will upload training images to the Azure Custom Vision platform. Follow these steps:

1. Click on **Add images** and add all your `train` and `validation` images.
2. Once you add them, your images will show up in the **untagged** section.

3. Note that you will not have anywhere to upload your annotation `.xml` or `.JSON` files that you created in the previous projects to, but don't worry—Azure makes it very simple to tag your images.
4. To start off, annotate about 10% (or about 20) of your images. You will notice, even before that, the bounding box automatically goes to the object of interest and all you have to do is resize it. If it does not find an object, add a bounding box and write the corresponding class. The following screenshot shows the smart label option:

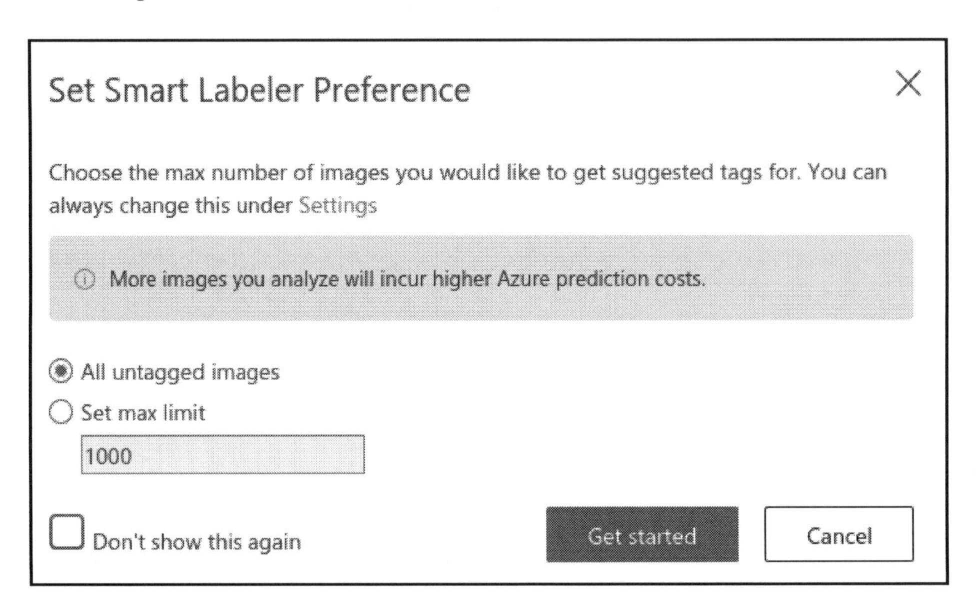

5. Once you tag the images, they will move to the tagged section. After you have 10% (or about 20) of the images tagged, initiate quick training with those images. After the training is complete, go back to **untagged images** and the **smart labeler** option to tag all the untagged images.
6. After you perform the previous step, you will notice that many of the images will be automatically tagged. Just accept the change if you think the label is correct and adjust the size and location of the bounding box. If the image has multiple classes and the smart label only captures a few of them, manually label the others. Once you annotate about 100 images this way, start your training (either quick training if you have more images or advanced training if 100 is the maximum number of images) and use the newly generated model to train the other images.

7. Continue the preceding process until all the images are tagged. Then, start training and use the **advanced training** option. Set up the time in hours (start with 1 hour) and increase it if needed later on. The training in the cloud is very fast—about 100 images are trained in less than 10 minutes.

   After the training is complete, you will be able to see the performance metrics. Note that you will be able to see this after the quick training described previously. The following screenshot shows the performance parameters, in terms of **Precision, Recall**, and **mAP**, for the newly trained model:

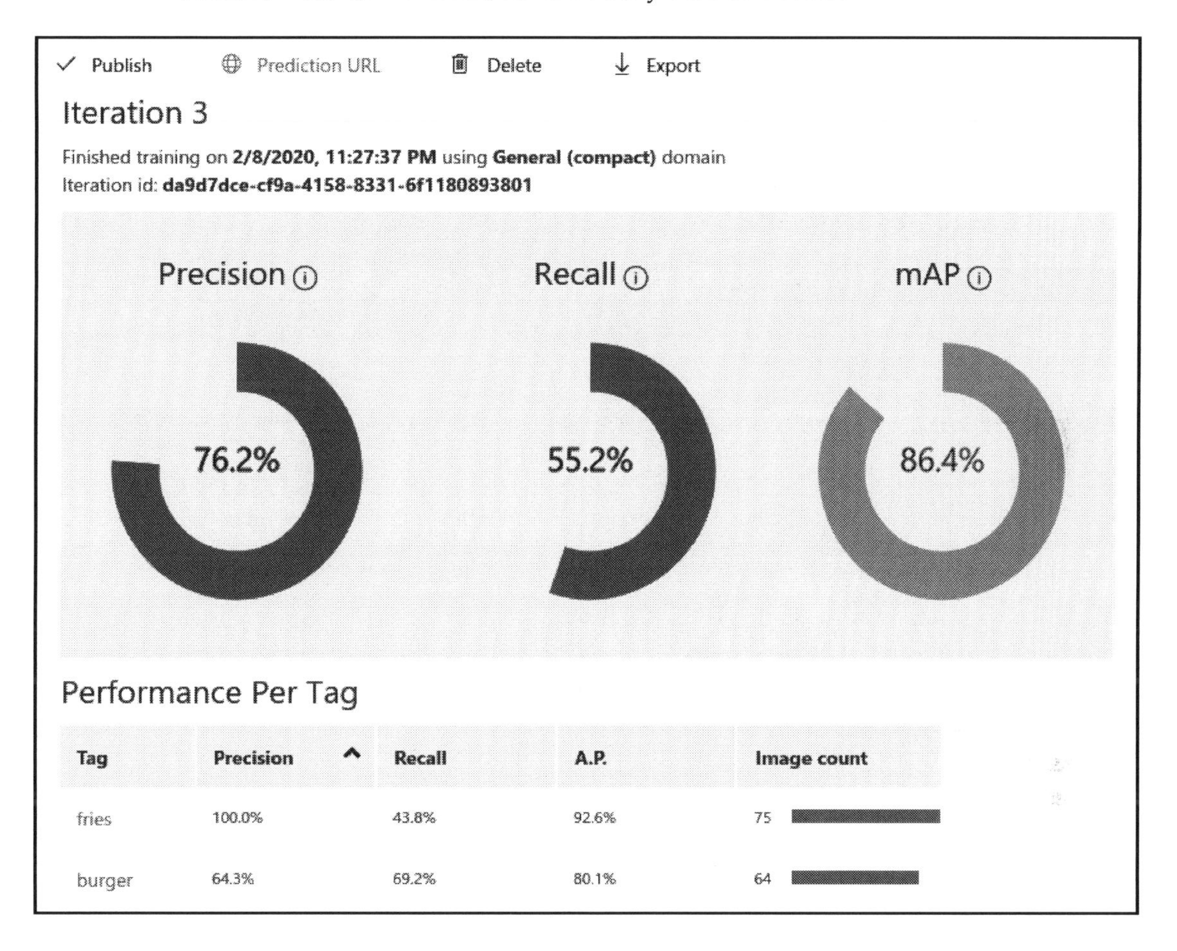

Note that the **Precision** number shown in the previous screenshot will likely decrease as the model sees more and more images. So, a model developed on 20 images will have higher precision than a model developed on 100 images. This is because the model developed on 20 images has fewer training errors but will have higher testing errors (in the `test` image, the burger is not recognized—only fries are recognized). The **mAP** number is the mean average precision over 11 equally spaced recall levels (0, 0.1, ... 1). The **mAP** value is unaffected by the addition of images. The **Performance** parameter shows the values for both `burger` and `fries`.

8. Now, let's bring back our old `validation` image and see the result. To do that, click on **Predictions** at the top and insert the `validation` image. It will draw a bounding box around the classes, as shown:

9. The prediction is correct, as shown. Next, we will export the model. To do that click on **Export**, as in the following screenshot. Note that if you click on **TF**, you will have the option to export as TensorFlow Lite or as TensorFlow. Similarly, if you click on **iOS**, you will have the option to export as **CoreML**:

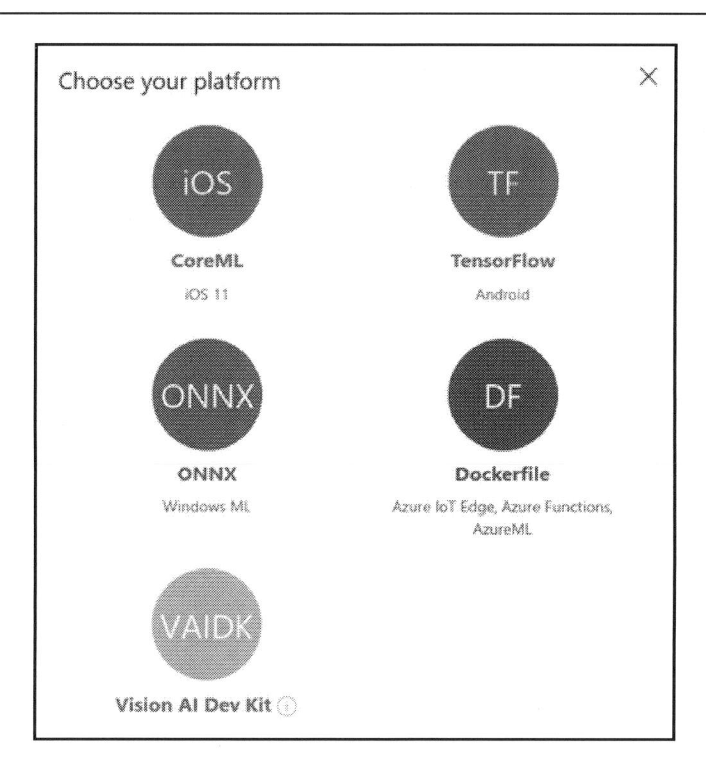

The preceding screenshot shows the various export options available in TensorFlow Lite.

Training at scale and packaging

TensorFlow has an API called `tf.distribute.Strategy` to distribute training across multiple GPUs. Training at scale for Google Cloud is described in detail at `https://cloud.google.com/ai-platform/training/docs/training-at-scale`.

Distributed training using TensorFlow is covered using the `tf.distribute.Strategy` API. Using this API, TensorFlow training can be distributed using multiple GPUs or TPUs. For a detailed overview of distributed training, including examples, go to `https://www.tensorflow.org/guide/distributed_training`.

Distributed training can also be set up in a cloud compute engine. In order to turn this functionality on, enable Cloud Shell in GCP. In the TensorFlow cluster, set up a virtual machine instance of a master and several workers and execute training jobs in each of these machines. For detailed information, you can go to `https://cloud.google.com/solutions/running-distributed-tensorflow-on-compute-engine`.

Application packaging

Application packaging involves uploading code, the `TFRecord` file, and the model `.config` file to GCP, which the model can access during training. In the *Training an object detector in GCP* section, we executed training in GCP by using `gcloud` to package our application, as follows:

```
$ gcloud ml-engine jobs submit training `whoami`_object_detection_`date
+%s` --job-dir=gs://${YOUR_GCS_BUCKET}/train --packages
dist/object_detection-0.1.tar.gz,slim/dist/slim-0.1.tar.gz,/tmp/pycocotools
/pycocotools-2.0.tar.gz --module-name object_detection.model_tpu_main --
runtime-version 1.15 --scale-tier BASIC_TPU --region us-central1 -- --
model_dir=gs://${YOUR_GCS_BUCKET}/train --tpu_zone us-central1 --
pipeline_config_path=gs://${YOUR_GCS_BUCKET}/data/pipeline.config
```

Note that in the preceding training, we used `gcloud ml-engine`, which lets you manage the AI platform job and training models. There is another platform, called `gcloud ai-platform`, that can also be used to package your application, as follows:

```
gcloud ai-platform jobs submit training $JOB_NAME \
    --staging-bucket $PACKAGE_STAGING_PATH \
    --job-dir $JOB_DIR  \
    --package-path $TRAINER_PACKAGE_PATH \
    --module-name $MAIN_TRAINER_MODULE \
    --region $REGION \
    -- \

    --user_first_arg=first_arg_value \
    --user_second_arg=second_arg_value
```

An explanation of the preceding code is as follows:

- `--staging-bucket`: This is the cloud storage path to stage the `training` package
- `--job-dir`: This is the cloud storage path for the output file location
- `--package-path`: This specifies the local path to the directory of your application
- `--module-name`: This specifies the name of the application module
- `--job-dir` flag: This is the job directory

The general idea behind cloud-based visual search

In `Chapter 6`, *Visual Search Using Transfer Learning*, we learned how to do a visual search on your local PC. The method uses passing an image through a neural network, such as VGG16 or ResNet, and converting it into an image vector by removing the last fully connected layer and then comparing the image with other images of known classes in the database to find the nearest neighbor match and then displaying the results.

We started with 200 images in our example, but if the number of images goes to 1 million and the results have to be accessed from a web page, storing the images locally will not make sense. In these cases, cloud storage is optimal. In that case, instead of storing the images in the cloud, we can store the image vector, and then when the user uploads an image, convert the image into a vector and send it to the cloud for processing. In the cloud, we perform a k-nearest neighbor search to find and display the closest match. The image vector is uploaded to the cloud using the REST API or the **Message Queuing Telemetry Transport** (**MQTT**) service. Each of the services has its own authentication for security.

Here, we will discuss basic coding infrastructure to send the image to the cloud service and to receive it as a JSON message:

- **Client-side request infrastructure**: The following code describes how to send an image URL as a POST request to an external web server. Here, `api_host` is the webserver address. The `headers` file is the operating parameters—in this case, the image. `image_url` is the actual image location:

```
api_host = 'https://.../'
headers = {'Content-Type' : 'image/jpeg'}
image_url = 'http://image.url.com/sample.jpeg'
img_file = urllib2.urlopen(image_url)
response = requests.post(api_host, data=img_file.read(),
headers=headers, verify=False)
print(json.loads(response.text))
```

- **Server-side request infrastructure**: The following code describes the typical server-side code. The server on the database side will request the image (picture) using the `request.files.get` method and `picture.save` is used to save the image:

```
@app.route('/', methods=['POST'])
def index():
 picture = request.files.get('file')
 picture.save('path/to/save')
 return 'ok', 200
```

The preceding code architecture shows the basis of the REST API method to send and receive the image from the cloud. GCP, AWS, and Azure have APIs in place to perform the visual search, facial recognition, and many other tasks. In the following section, this is described in detail. Each of the cloud platforms has its own way of sending image data to the cloud, which may be different from each other, but the basic principle is the same as the previous one. The cloud web page will have image information with visual search result in a JSON format that can be accessed from the local PC by using the cloud server URL and authentication method.

Analyzing images and search mechanisms in various cloud platforms

In this section, we will discuss the visual search task using three different cloud platforms—GCP, AWS, and Azure. We have already covered a visual search in `Chapter 6`, *Visual Search Using Transfer Learning*, where we learned how to compare an image vector to a large number of images in your PC directory to find the closest match based on the Euclidean distance. In this section, you will learn how to upload an image to the cloud using the REST API from your PC and the cloud search engine will search for the closest image and display it. So, all the heavy lifting will be done by the cloud engine.

Note that in this section, the basic idea of visual search is introduced. The content can go much deeper, where you can get the cloud API from GCP, AWS, or Azure and insert it in your application program written in Python, C++, or JavaScript to call the cloud engine and perform the search.

Visual search using GCP

GCP has a vision API to perform cloud-based image information, including facial detection and image content analysis. For more details, visit `https://cloud.google.com/vision`. See the example results that were uploaded for a sofa in the following screenshot; detection was carried out along with several examples of visually similar images:

As we learned in `Chapter 6`, *Visual Search Using Transfer Learning*, for visually similar images it is essential to search within the image class. If the image is not from the web, it is likely to detect similar visual images of a different class, as you can see in the sofa examples here. However, if the image is taken from the web, the matching is exact or very close.

In the last section, we learned how to train using the GCP. AutoML Vision is another way of getting this accomplished easily. For detailed, step-by-step instructions, go to `https://cloud.google.com/vision/automl/docs/quickstart`.

For visual search, go to `https://cloud.google.com/vision/product-search/docs/quickstart`.

When you try an API from your Python script, you will need the following:

- A Google Cloud account to set up the project and enable billing.
- Enable the Cloud Vision product search API.
- A Google application credential—a key file.
- Select a service account and create it so that a key is downloaded to your PC.
- Set up the environmental variable in your terminal by exporting the following three items:
    - `GOOGLE_APPLICATION_CREDENTIAL`: The key path in your PC
    - `PROJECT_ID`
    - `LOCATION_ID`
- Create `request.json` and then you will receive a `response.json` file.

Visual search using AWS

AWS has many tools for computer vision. Among those, two primary tools are Amazon Rekognition (`https://aws.amazon.com/rekognition`) and AWS SageMaker (`https://aws.amazon.com/sagemaker`). Visit the AWS website for more tools for your needs. AWS Rekognition is a cloud-based **Software as a Service (SaaS)** platform for image and video analysis. It has many features, such as face detection and analysis, face search and verification, and celebrity recognition. Just like the Google Cloud Vision API, you can upload an image and it can provide the details of the image information, as shown:

In the preceding screenshot, the sofa is correctly detected, along with different categories and the corresponding JSON for the bounding box and image information. You can also upload face images and it can provide detailed information on the facial expression, age, and gender, as well as whether two faces from very different angles belong to the same person, as shown:

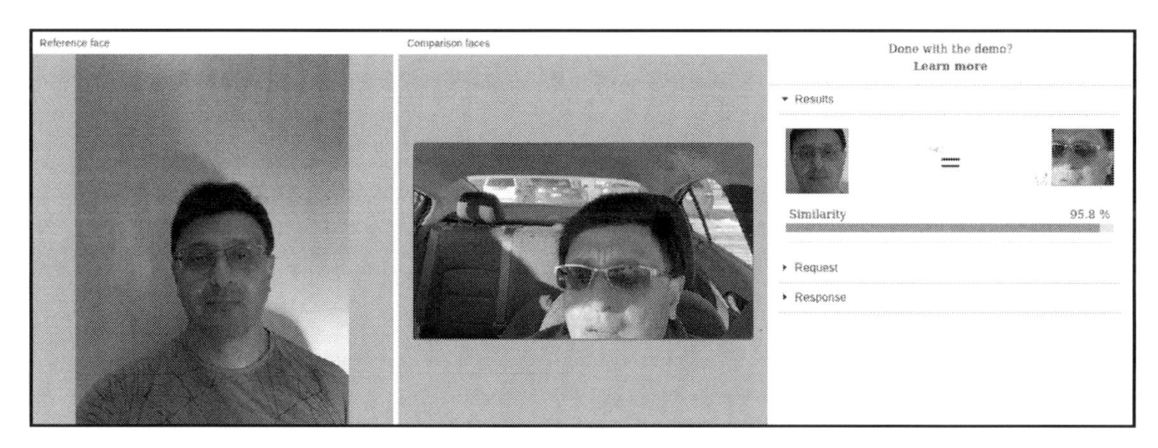

Note that the facial recognition system is able to detect two faces belonging to the same person, each taken from different angles with and without sunglasses.

AWS Rekognition can also analyze an image on your local PC using `boto`, as described at `https://docs.aws.amazon.com/rekognition/latest/dg/images-bytes.html`.

AWS SageMaker was introduced during training. It can also be used to perform a visual search by converting the image into a vector. For a detailed exercise, refer to the Python notebook described at `https://github.com/awslabs/visual-search/blob/master/notebooks/visual-search-feature-generation.ipynb`.

Note that the best way to execute this will be to run this from the AWS SageMaker notebook instance. Upload this file (listed in the preceding link) to the Jupyter Notebook and then select the MXNet Python package. Reference your S3 bucket and execute the cells. Analyze the code and compare it to what we learned in `Chapter 6`, *Visual Search Using Transfer Learning*. You will see that the basic principle is the same, except the analysis is done on a cloud platform, so it will have several levels of authentication that we did not have to deal with in `Chapter 6`, *Visual Search Using Transfer Learning*.

Visual search using Azure

Azure is Microsoft's cloud machine learning platform that's used to build, manage, and deploy an application. Like GCP and AWS, Azure has many features, but the ones we will be interested in for our computer vision work is Azure AI and Azure Machine Learning (`https://azure.microsoft.com/en-us/services/`). In AI and Machine Learning, the applications related to computer vision are Azure Bot Service, Azure Cognitive Search, Bing Image Search, Bing Visual Search, and Computer Vision. For example, if you want to perform a visual search, then go to `https://docs.microsoft.com/en-us/azure/cognitive-services/bing-visual-search/visual-search-sdk-python`.

The basic steps for a visual search in the Azure cloud platform are as follows:

1. Get an Azure account and select the pricing information.
2. Get your subscription key.
3. Select the path for `test` images on your PC.
4. Send the search request as `request.post`:

```
response = requests.post(BASE_URI, headers=HEADERS, files=file)
response.raise_for_status()
```

In the preceding code, the `raise_for_status` method implies raising an exception if the request is unsuccessful, such as `404 Client Error: NOT FOUND`.

Caution—cloud platform usage can get expensive as you have to give your credit card details for billing. The critical thing to note is even if you complete your training job and shut down your PC, you will continue to incur charges unless you shut down your project in the cloud platform completely.

Summary

In this chapter, you learned how to send image data to the cloud platform for analysis. In previous chapters, we learned how to perform training on a local PC, but in this chapter, you have learned how to perform the same task using a cloud platform and also, how to trigger training in multiple instances, using Google Cloud Shell for distributed training.

This chapter has included many examples and links and you will gain more knowledge by reviewing those links and performing the exercises. We then learned how to send images to a cloud platform for instance analysis. The image content analysis was extended to perform a visual search in the cloud platform. We also learned how to use all three cloud platforms—GCP, AWS, and Azure. Remember to make sure to shut down your project when you have completed your task, even though you are not training, to stop incurring unnecessary charges.

Other Books You May Enjoy

If you enjoyed this book, you may be interested in these other books by Packt:

Hands-On Computer Vision with TensorFlow 2
Benjamin Planche, Eliot Andres

ISBN: 978-1-78883-064-5

Learn how to clean your data and ready it for analysis

- Create your own neural networks from scratch
- Classify images with modern architectures including Inception and ResNet
- Detect and segment objects in images with YOLO, Mask R-CNN, and U-Net
- Tackle problems faced when developing self-driving cars and facial emotion recognition systems
- Boost your application's performance with transfer learning, GANs, and domain adaptation
- Use recurrent neural networks (RNNs) for video analysis
- Optimize and deploy your networks on mobile devices and in the browser

Deep Learning for Computer Vision
Rajalingappa Shanmugamani

ISBN: 978-1-78829-562-8

- Set up an environment for deep learning with Python, Tensorflow, and Keras
- Define and train a model for image and video classification
- Use features from a pre-trained Convolutional Neural Network model for image retrieval
- Understand and implement object detection using the real-world Pedestrian Detection scenario
- Learn about various problems in image captioning and how to overcome them by training images and text together
- Implement similarity matching and train a model for face recognition
- Understand the concept of generative models and use them for image generation
- Deploy your deep learning models and optimize them for high performance

Leave a review - let other readers know what you think

Please share your thoughts on this book with others by leaving a review on the site that you bought it from. If you purchased the book from Amazon, please leave us an honest review on this book's Amazon page. This is vital so that other potential readers can see and use your unbiased opinion to make purchasing decisions, we can understand what our customers think about our products, and our authors can see your feedback on the title that they have worked with Packt to create. It will only take a few minutes of your time, but is valuable to other potential customers, our authors, and Packt. Thank you!

Index

D

E

F

G

L

M

N

O

P

R

S

T

Printed in Great Britain
by Amazon

49267501R00244